JACQUES PEPIN

NEW COMPLETE TECHNIQUES

PHOTOGRAPHS BY
Léon Perer AND Tom Hopkins

BLACK DOG
& LEVENTHAL
PUBLISHERS
NEW YORK

Cover design by Red Herring Design
Cover photograph: Tom Hopkins

Black Dog & Leventhal Publishers
Hachette Book Group
1290 Avenue of the Americas
New York, NY 10104

www.hachettebookgroup.com
www.blackdogandleventhal.com

Revised First Edition: November 2012

Black Dog & Leventhal Publishers is an imprint of Hachette Books, a division of Hachette Book Group. The Black Dog & Leventhal Publishers name and logo are trademarks of Hachette Book Group, Inc.

The publisher is not responsible for websites (or their content) that are not owned by the publisher.

The Hachette Speakers Bureau provides a wide range of authors for speaking events. To find out more, go to www.HachetteSpeakersBureau.com or call (866) 376-6591.

Print book interior design by Red Herring Design

ISBN: 978-1-57912-911-8

Printed in China

IM

10 9 8 7 6 5 4 3

CONTENTS

> "This is a seminal work, and like no other. Jacques Pépin is not only a renowned chef, a foremost authority on French cuisine, and a great teacher; also, as all of us know who have seen him in action, he is truly a master technician. For us to have all this information in our hands, fully illustrated and explained, is indeed a treasure."
>
> **—JULIA CHILD**

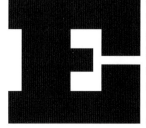

Even though I wrote *La Technique* and *La Méthode* thirty-five years ago, I am happy to say that, with some minor changes, the culinary techniques demonstrated in the books are as current and useful today as they were at that time. A good cook still beats egg whites, bones a chicken, and makes a caramel cage in the same way. Just as in 1974, the greatest hindrance to good performance in the kitchen is an inadequate knowledge of basic techniques.

Along with the hundreds of techniques collected in the original two volumes, *La Technique* and *La Méthode*, we have incorporated color photography and additional techniques from my two-volume set, *The Art of Cooking*, which was published in the 1980s. Furthermore, we have underlined the text in recipe captions that specifically describes what is shown in that picture. In my opinion, both improvements to the current edition will help cooks more readily comprehend what's being demonstrated.

Jacques Pépin's *New Complete Techniques* uses step-by-step pictures and detailed, descriptive text to acquaint cooks of every level with the basic procedures that make up the core, the center, and the heart of the profession. Do you want to learn how things really work in the kitchen? It is the goal of this book to teach you, and in the process, to help you understand and hone the basic manual skills that are almost impossible to explain solely in words. This book, quite simply, will teach you how to cook in a way a conventional cookbook could never do.

Don't be discouraged if you can't master some of these techniques instantly. Some, like the fluting of a mushroom, take practice and patience. Others, like peeling garlic, are quite simple. Remember that as your mastery grows, you will become better able to tackle even difficult recipes with ease and proficiency. In time, you will open your favorite cookbooks and experience them in a new light!

When professionals work with ease and rapidity, it is a result of long years of practice and discipline. There are no secrets or tricks, only feats of skill (*tours de main*) acquired with prolonged effort. Through endless repetition, these techniques will become so much a part of you that you'll never forget them. People often tell me that what surprises them most is watching me cook and talk at the same time. This is because my hands are trained to the point where I do not have to think about the processes I use as I make a recipe—it's automatic. Instead of fighting the mechanics of cooking, I can concentrate on thinking about the combination of ingredients, about taste, and about texture. You may be very creative and imaginative in the kitchen, but you cannot take advantage of those qualities if you don't know the basics. A solid background must precede inventiveness. An artistic mind might create a stunning decoration for a cold salmon, but the dish will be triumphant only if the salmon is first properly cleaned and poached, and the aspic rich and crystal-clear—and this requires knowledge of the proper techniques.

For many years I have dabbled in painting, and although I have occasionally come up with what I think is a great idea for a picture, my hands are rarely good enough to express what I have in my head. This is because my knowledge of painting techniques is weak; I haven't repeated them day after day after day for hours, so my hands very often are not skilled enough to realize my ideas. In cooking, however, after so many years of practice, I can eliminate a great many potential problems or obstacles along the way as I think about a recipe, and then my hands can do the rest. I can usually come pretty close to my vision on the first try.

In this book, I do not pretend to have explicated the whole spectrum of cooking skills; I haven't

touched on Asian cooking, for example, concentrating more on the general cooking techniques that I have used all my life. I may have taken for granted very ordinary chores, such as peeling a potato or melting butter. And even with the help of the step-by-step photos, some of the techniques, like making a butter flower, still require a fair amount of patience and perseverance to achieve. Others, like peeling and seeding a tomato or making a rabbit out of an olive, can be mastered instantly. You will discover that there is great satisfaction in conquering dishes that may have frustrated you in the kitchen before. Knowledge of the basics is so rewarding, in that it allows you to try out new ideas, to remedy potentially catastrophic miscalculations, and to tackle any kind of recipe because you will comprehend the mechanics behind it.

Start with simple techniques and work gradually toward the more involved and complicated ones. And have fun! Remember, you are not learning new recipes, you are acquiring a whole new way of cooking, and with this book, you begin your apprenticeship.

Happy cooking!

Jacques Pépin

June 2012

Today's cooking equipment comes in all types, shapes, prices, and materials. The enormous interest in food, heightened by cooking schools, cookbooks, newspapers, magazine articles, the Internet, etc., has spurred the manufacturers into bringing many different types of paraphernalia onto the market, and a lot of it is good. However, it is often hard for people to differentiate. What pots should one buy? Should they be copper? Stainless steel? Heavy aluminum? No-stick? Black cast iron? Enameled cast iron? It is difficult to choose because ultimately there is no ideal pot. Every material has its good and bad points. The thick, heavy, hand-hammered copper is the best to conduct, diffuse, and retain heat. While attractive, it is very heavy, very expensive, and needs constant polishing. Pots should not be lined with tin, as used to be done, but with stainless steel, which is cleaner and more durable.

Heavy aluminum pans, customarily used in professional kitchens, are much lighter and easier to handle. Heavy aluminum is the best heat conductor after copper and it's tough. However it tends to discolor food, especially when acidic ingredients such as wine, vinegar, and tomatoes are used. (When using a whisk for an emulsion, such as hollandaise, you will often have a brownish dirty color mixed with your sauce.) At home, the discoloration happens regularly just from boiling water. The pan is not used often enough and moisture in the air will cause darkening. The same heavy aluminum pot used in a restaurant kitchen may not discolor since it is used over and over again and is washed between each use, preventing any buildup. The best are heavy aluminum pans lined with stainless steel.

The no-stick lined pans are very good, especially the permanent no-stick, which have a tougher, more durable, finish than the ones made years ago.

Stainless steel cleans easily, keeps shiny, does not discolor food but, unfortunately, does develop "hot spots" or patches of burn. The transfer of heat is fast but stainless steel does not retain heat well. Fortunately, stainless steel pans are now made with thick bottoms, and aluminum or copper "sandwiched" between layers of stainless steel.

The dark cast iron skillet and kettle are good, sturdy, and practically indestructible. They are inexpensive, easy to care for and hold the heat fairly well. However, they are heavy and if not used often will get rusty, stain, and discolor food. The enameled cast iron is attractive, cleans well, and will chip if dropped. Eventually, the inside will darken and discolor.

Earthenware is attractive, good for prolonged oven cooking, and can be used as service pieces. Since they are fragile, and extreme temperatures may cause cracking, don't use them for stove-top cooking.

For baking, flat, heavy, not too shiny, aluminum cookie sheets are the best. The iron or steel cookie sheets will warp and the heat conductivity is too rapid. Silicone liners, as well as no-stick aluminum foil, are an inexpensive and vast improvement for preventing dough from sticking. All kinds of plastic and silicone shaped containers are good when working with chocolate. Microplanes are terrific to grate the skin of citrus fruits, as well as garlic, onions, etc.

Should you have a plastic or wooden chopping block? My preference is wood—it is attractive, with just enough bounce, and it does not dull the knife's blade. Both types should be thick, heavy, and wide. Your chopping block won't perform properly if you do not have a high, sturdy table, which does not bounce when you use a meat pounder or a cleaver. However, I do not use my block for rolling out dough. I prefer rolling it directly on a marble, granite, or formica counter. It is clean and non-porous, with no taste attached to it.

What kind of electrical appliances should you get? A food processor (the stronger the better) is a must, as well as an electric mixer. Should you cook with gas, electricity or microwaves? Cooking is harder to control on electric tops, although the electric oven is excellent. Microwaves are efficient for melting chocolate or cooking bacon. But gas is my favorite. Professional stoves are a good investment. They are strong, have great capacity and never go out of style. We enjoy seeing the flames, and control is there at all times. Ultimately, the best heat is wood (hard wood). For barbecuing, it is a must. Never briquettes. Briquettes are a derivative of petroleum and they are not good for your health. A steak well charred on a dirty grill over briquettes has more tar than several packs of cigarettes.

Good whisks with thick, heavy threads are a must, as well as "piano-wire" whips (very thin, flexible, and tightly woven). Both are necessary—the whisk for thick sauces and the whip to whip egg whites and heavy cream. Rubber and wooden spatulas, as well as a series of stainless steel and ceramic bowls, wire racks, strainers, metal spoons, skimmers, vegetable peelers, etc., are all necessary implements.

Then there are the knives, an extension of your fingers. There is always a controversy about knives. The current trend is toward high carbon steel and ceramic knives. They do not discolor or oxidize when used for cutting lemons, tomatoes, or onions. Stainless steel is a very hard metal and difficult to sharpen, although it keeps a good edge once sharpened. The knives should be very sharp to perform correctly. You should have a minimum of three knives. A very large (10- to 12-inch/25- to 30-centimeter blade) chopping knife, a thinner, 8-inch (20-centimeter) all-purpose knife, and a small paring knife. Several paring knives would be even better. Have a good sharpener. A steel or ceramic sharpener (good for stainless steel) is necessary but

both sharpen only the tiny cutting edge of the knives. After a year or so, depending on how often you use your knives, this tiny amount of metal will be worn away. The carbon knife must then be sent out to be sharpened professionally unless you have the know-how, and possess a large stone with which to grind the metal. Send dull knives out to a person who sharpens lawn mowers, scissors, or electric saws. Then the knives can again be utilized for one year, using the steel sharpener periodically. Ceramic knives must go back to the manufacturer to be sharpened.

You will notice that expensive, good equipment is usually well-designed and pleasant to look at. Visit pot and pan shops. Many specialize in gadgetry and gimmicks. Some have an enormous, confusing potpourri of paraphernalia, among which, if you have the proper lore, you will discern the good from the bad. There are a few good shops that specialize in good equipment only. When you have chosen a good shop, follow the judgment of the salesperson; once you get to know a place, the people will give you good advice. Have a tag sale and get rid of your bad tools. Buy pieces one by one if you can't afford to spend a lot. Some people will spend a small fortune in a good restaurant without blinking an eye, but won't spend the same amount for a few pieces of equipment. It is worth the investment, since they will go on working for you, your children, and, maybe, your grandchildren.

Have your pots, molds, strainers, etc., hung from the wall or the ceiling, as is done in a professional kitchen. They will be easy to get to and you will use them more often.

Even though you may have the best ingredients to start with, nothing is more frustrating when preparing a meal than when your oven does not keep a constant heat, your pan is discolored, your knife is dull, your pots dented, etc. It won't work! Finally, cook, cook, cook, cook, and cook again! I know people who have great kitchens with all the latest and best equipment. It is only there for show. The more you cook, the easier it becomes. The more the equipment is used, the better it performs and you will get attached to certain tools. ■

THE BASICS

How to Sharpen Knives

(Aiguisage des Couteaux)

A knife is useless if it is not sharp. You can tell if your knife is sharp if it can cut a soft, ripe tomato into thin slices with ease. If the knife is dull, it will just crush the tomato. If you looked at the cutting edge of a knife through a magnifying glass, you'd see that it is made up of hundreds of tiny teeth—like a saw. Through repeated use, these teeth get twisted and bent out of alignment. This is what makes a knife dull; a sharpener gets these little teeth back into alignment.

The harder the metal the knife is made of, the harder it will be to sharpen, but the longer it will hold its edge. A sharpener has to be made of a material that's a shade harder than the metal it is to abrade. (The hardness of metals is measured on the Rockwell Scale.)

Steels are metal sharpeners. They have a fine grain and give a super finish to an already sharp knife. Butchers and professional cooks use a steel constantly, giving the knife a few strokes before each use. A ceramic sharpener is better than a steel for sharpening hard metals such as stainless steel. (Ceramic is harder than the hardest metal on the Rockwell Scale.)

Eventually, repeated sharpening wears away the little teeth of the cutting edge. At this point the knife needs to be ground to thin the blade into a new cutting edge. This is done with an abrasive stone.

THE BASICS

USING A CERAMIC SHARPENER

1. Start with the heel of the blade at the tip of the sharpener and <u>slide the knife down the length of the sharpener so the cutting edge abrades against it</u>. Apply steady and strong pressure. Keep the knife at the same angle constantly.

2. <u>End with the point of the blade near the base of the steel sharpener</u>. This is one steady stroke, one hand moving toward the other, every inch of the cutting edge making contact with the sharpener. Repeat on the other side of the sharpener to sharpen the other side of the knife.

USING A STEEL SHARPENER

3. This photograph is an alternative way of sharpening. In this photo, we are using a steel sharpener with a high-carbon-steel knife. <u>Start with the heel of the blade at the base of the steel and pull the hands away from one another</u>, finishing with the tip of the sharpener at the tip of the blade. Repeat on the other side. Make sure that the whole blade gets worked against the sharpener. Keep the angle about 25 degrees and the pressure the same.

USING A GRINDING STONE

4. Once a year, twice a year, once every two years—depending on the kind of beating your knives get—you will need to grind them down to form a new cutting edge. You can send your knives out and have them ground by a professional or you can do it yourself if you have a sand wheel or a <u>large stone like the one pictured here</u>. This stone is held in place by suction so that you can apply a lot of pressure without having it slide around the way smaller stones do. It has three sides, each of a different coarseness. You begin with the coarsest side and finish with the finest.

5. Rub mineral oil on the stone to keep stone grindings loose so they can be wiped off and don't seal and glaze the surface of the stone, which would prevent abrasion. <u>Start at the tip of the knife and apply strong pressure down and forward so that the whole side of the blade is in contact with the stone</u>. Move back and forth, applying pressure. Keep the angle constant. Repeat on the other side. As the knife gets sharper and thinner at the end, go to a finer stone. When you are through, clean your knife. Keep it sharp with a steel sharpener.

Holding the Knife to Chop Vegetables

(Position du Couteau)

An apprentice chef cannot "graduate to the stove" until he has mastered the basic techniques for correctly chopping, dicing, mincing, and slicing vegetables, fruits, or meat. Perfectly prepared vegetables not only have an attractive texture, but add a good "bite" and taste to the finished dish. Practice, obviously, is of the very essence, and good knives are just as important. Knives should be sharpened professionally at least once every year or two. In the interim, keep a good edge with either a steel or carborundum sharpener.

1. Handling your knife properly is your first concern. Hold the item to be cut with fingertips tucked under, so the blade "rests" and <u>slides directly against the middle section of your fingers</u> or against your index finger, if it is more comfortable. The knife follows, in fact, "glued" to the fingers and slides up and down the fingers at the same rate all the time. The speed at which the fingers move back determines the thickness of the slices. See steps 6 and 7 for more illustration of this technique.

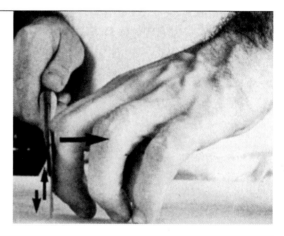

2. To mince an onion, cut off the root and the stem end on opposite ends. Some onions have extremely thin skins which are hard to remove. Some are quite thick. In either case, <u>remove one layer of onion, or several if necessary, so there is no yellow or dry skin visible.</u>

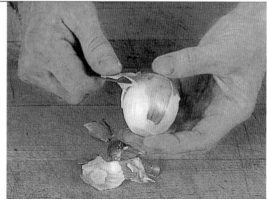

3. Cut into halves through the root. <u>Place one of the halves flat side down and, holding your fingers and knife properly,</u>

4. <u>cut vertical slices from one end to the other, up to, but not through, the root end</u>. The knife does not go in a straight down motion while cutting, but rather in a down and back motion at the same time.

5. Holding the knife flat, <u>cut 3 or 4 horizontal slices from top to bottom, up to the root end.</u>

6. <u>Finally, cut across the onion, again up to the root end.</u> (If the dice is not fine enough, chop some more with a large knife.)

7. To slice a potato, place it on its flattest side so that it does not roll under your fingers. If the potato is not stable, cut a slice off so the potato can sit firmly on the cut end. Slice to desired thickness by controlling the progress of the fingers that hold the potato in place.

8. To chop parsley, use a bigger knife. Place the blade perpendicular to the chopping block and gather the washed parsley top into a tight ball. Slice the bunch across.

9. Slice, going down and forward, or down and backward, sliding the knife along the fingers.

10. Holding the handle firmly in one hand, the other hand relaxed on top of the blade (this hand does not apply much pressure on the blade, but rather directs it), bring the front of the blade down first, then the back. Repeat in a staccato and rapid up and down motion until the parsley is finely chopped. Draw the pieces together in a heap as you go along.

11. To dice an eggplant, hold the eggplant firmly with the tips of your fingers and cut lengthwise in equal slices.

12. Stack 2 or 3 slices on top of each other. Using the same technique, cut into square sticks.

13. Cut the sticks across to form little cubes. Very small cubes or dices of vegetables are called *brunoise*.

How to Julienne

(Julienne)

To cut into julienne is to cut into very thin strips. A julienne is aesthetically very pleasing and very nice as a garnish for soups, fish, meat, etc. A vegetable julienne (such as carrots, leeks, and celery) is usually blanched and finished by being cooked a few minutes with fish, veal, or whatever it will be served with. Being cut so thin, it cooks very fast.

JULIENNE OF CARROTS (Julienne de Carottes)

1. To peel: Trim both ends of the carrot to form a flat end to start from. <u>Working toward you, peel a whole strip of carrot in one stroke, from end to end</u>. Rotate the carrot and proceed all the way around. Use long, regular, slow strokes. Your speed will improve with practice. Short nervous strokes (or peeling one half of the carrot then turning the carrot around and peeling the other half) take twice the time.

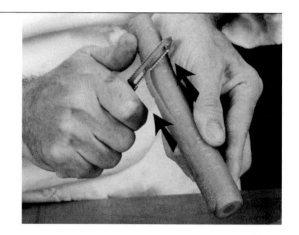

2. <u>Slice the carrot into very thin lengthwise slices</u>. If you do not have a *mandoline* or a similar type of vegetable slicer, and if you're not proficient enough with a knife, use a good vegetable peeler. Apply as much pressure as you can so the slices are not too thin.

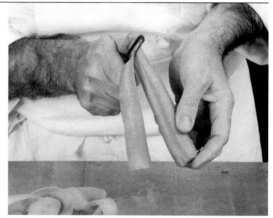

3. Stack 3 or 4 of the thin slices on top of one another, fold and then <u>slice into a fine julienne</u>.

JULIENNE OF LEEKS (Julienne de Poireaux)

4. For the julienne of leeks, only the white and the very light green part of the leek is used. Remove the dark green part and the root, keeping the green part in the refrigerator for soups or stocks or to put in a stew. <u>Split the trimmed leek in half.</u>

5. <u>Separate all of the layers of the leek</u>. (Note that in our leek the center is woody. This happens when the leek is old and grows a tough central core. Remove and discard.)

6. <u>Fold a few of the leaves at a time</u>, so that the inside of the leaves shows on the outside.

7. <u>Cut into very thin strips</u>. Wash and then drain.

JULIENNE OF CELERY (Julienne de Céleri)

8. Separate the stalks. <u>Use a vegetable peeler to remove the top layer of fiber from the large outer stalks if necessary.</u> (By scratching the celery, you can find out if it is fibrous or not.)

9. Cut each stalk into 4- to 5-inch (10- to 13-centimeter) pieces. <u>Flatten each piece with the palm of your hand.</u> (It will probably crush in the center.)

10. <u>Using the flat of your knife held horizontally to the table, cut the celery into 2 or 3 thin slices.</u>

11. <u>Pile all the slices on top of one another and cut into thin strips.</u> A julienne of celery is never as thin as a julienne of leeks or carrots, but it is used in the same way.

Garlic

(Ail)

*There are many types of garlic readily available, the best of which is the "red garlic,"
so-called because of the reddish color of the skin. Garlic affects food in different ways
depending on how it is cut and used. You can roast a chicken with three full heads (about
40 unpeeled cloves) of garlic and serve them with the chicken. Guests can pick up the
cloves and suck the tender insides out of the peel. Prepared this way, it is astounding how
mild and sweet garlic is. The scent and taste are barely noticeable. However, the smell
of one clove of garlic, peeled, crushed, chopped fine, and added at the last minute to
sautéed potatoes or string beans, or to a salad, can permeate a whole room and remain
on your breath for hours. The same crushed, chopped garlic—when cooked slowly for
a long time, as in a stew—loses most of its pungency and harmonizes, quite modestly,
with the other herbs and ingredients. Crushing the garlic releases more essential oil and
gives more flavor than slicing it or leaving it whole. Raw garlic, chopped to a purée, is the
most powerful. Mixed with olive oil, it becomes the garlic-loaded mayonnaise of Provence
(aïoli or ailloli), known as* beurre de Provence *(the butter of Provence).*

*One important point: When making scampi, escargots, sautéed potatoes, zucchini, or
any dish where the garlic is added at the end and slightly cooked, be careful not to burn
it. Burned garlic hopelessly ruins a dish.*

1. Holding the "head" on a bias, <u>crush with the heel of your
hand</u> to separate the cloves.

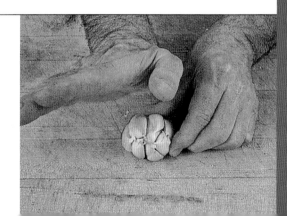

2. First, cut off the root end of the clove. Then, using the flat side of a heavy knife, smack the clove just enough to crack the shell open. <u>Remove the clove from the shell</u>.

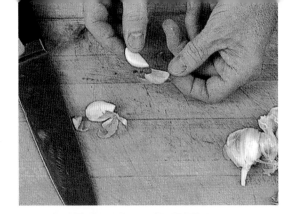

3. <u>Place the blade flat on the clove and smack it down and forward</u> to crush the clove to a pulp.

4. <u>Chop to a purée</u>, by rocking the knife back and forth.

Leeks

(Poireaux)

Leeks are called the "asparagus of the poor" in France. This hardy winter vegetable is unbeatable for soups. Leeks are great cooked in water and served with a vinaigrette sauce and excellent in stews and quiches.

1. Leeks have to be cleaned properly because the centers are usually full of sand. <u>Trim off the greener part of the leaves</u> and wash them. Keep these leaves for stock or clarifying consommé.

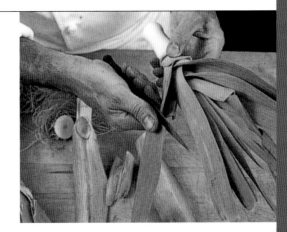

2. Remove the roots. Remove the dried and yellowish skin around the leek, if any. Holding the leek, leafy side down, <u>insert your knife through the white part approximately 2 inches (5 centimeters) down from the root</u>, and cut through the entire length of the leek.

3. <u>Repeat 2 or 3 times to split the leek open</u>. Wash thoroughly under cold water. Use as needed.

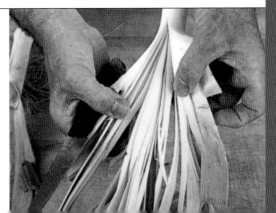

Duxelle of Mushrooms

(Duxelle de Champignons)

A duxelle of mushrooms is a mixture of mushrooms chopped very, very fine and cooked, sometimes with shallots, sometimes without, and seasoned with salt and pepper. Duxelle is one of the staples of classic French cooking and is used in many dishes—as a coating, as a stuffing, as a seasoning. With the addition of cream or milk, it becomes a purée of mushrooms and is served as a vegetable.

¾ **pound (340 grams) mushrooms, finely chopped**
2 shallots, peeled and very finely chopped (½ cup/75 grams)
1 tablespoon (14 grams) unsalted butter
Salt to taste
Freshly ground black pepper to taste

1. One of the best ways to chop mushrooms is in a food processor. However, don't put them into the processor whole. <u>Cut them into coarse slices or chunks first.</u>

2. Place a large handful of mushrooms in the processor. Pulse several times. If the machine is left on for the whole duration, half the mushrooms fly around the blade—not getting properly chopped—while the other half turns into a purée. The on-and-off technique allows the mushrooms to fall back on the blade so that they all get uniformly chopped. (Use this method whenever you chop in a food processor.) Melt the butter in a skillet, add the shallots and cook on medium heat for about ½ minute. <u>Add the chopped</u>

mushrooms, a dash of salt, and a dash of pepper and cook, mixing occasionally with a wooden spoon, for about 10 minutes. The mushrooms will render some liquid, and will be ready when the liquid has evaporated and the mixture is dry and starts to sizzle. Transfer to a bowl, cover with waxed paper, and set aside.

3. If you used mushrooms that were open, large and black inside, older mushrooms (which are often used for duxelle since they are hard to use for anything else), <u>press them in a cloth towel</u> to extrude some of the dark juices after they have been chopped.

4. <u>As you can see, pressing the mushrooms in a towel does get rid of the extra juices</u>. From this point, proceed as explained in step 2. If the mushrooms are plump, firm and white, there is no reason to press the juices out.

Tomatoes

(Tomates)

Peeled and seeded tomatoes are a requisite ingredient in many recipes. They are used to make tomato balls—a perfect garnish for roasts, chicken and the like— and fondue de tomates, *which is a fresh tomato sauce that's both easy to make and very good.*

PEELING AND SEEDING TOMATOES
(Tomates Emondés)

1. Remove the stem from the tomato using the point of a knife. <u>Dip the tomatoes in boiling water—they should be fully immersed—and let sit for approximately 20 seconds if well ripened.</u> If the tomatoes are not ripe, it will take a little longer for the skin to come loose.

2. When cold enough to handle, <u>remove and peel. The skin should slip off easily.</u> An alternative method is to impale the tomato on a fork and, holding it by the fork handle, roll it over an open flame. "Roast" it for 15 to 20 seconds; the skin should slide off easily.

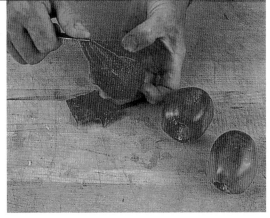

3. <u>Cut the tomato into halves widthwise</u>—not through the stem.

4. <u>Press gently to extrude all the seeds</u>. You now have pure tomato flesh or pulp. The seeds, skin, and juice can be used in a stock or long-simmered sauce.

TOMATO BALLS FOR GARNISH
(Boules de Tomates)

1. Peel and seed the tomato. <u>Cut each half in two</u>.

2. <u>Place a tomato quarter in a strong kitchen towel</u>, the outside against the towel.

3. <u>Squeeze the tomato flesh</u>

4. to form a nice, small, fleshy ball. Sprinkle with salt and a dash of ground pepper. Moisten with melted butter and heat in a hot oven for a few minutes before serving.

TOMATO SAUCE (Fondue de Tomates)

1. Peel and seed the tomatoes and cut coarsely into 1-inch (2.5-centimeter) cubes. Prepare 3 cups (450 grams) of cubed tomatoes and proceed with the recipe below.

1 tablespoon good olive oil
3 tablespoons chopped onion
3 cups (450 grams) cubed tomatoes
Salt and freshly ground black pepper
1 clove garlic, crushed and chopped very fine
1 tablespoon tomato paste, optional

Heat the oil in a saucepan. When it is hot, add the chopped onion and sauté for 1 minute. Add the tomatoes and the salt and pepper to taste. Cook on a high heat for 5 to 6 minutes to evaporate some of the liquid. Add the garlic, and the tomato paste if the tomatoes are too watery or too pale in color. Cook 3 to 4 minutes and taste for seasoning. Add more salt and pepper, if necessary.

Brown Stock (Classic and Fast), Half-Glaze, and Meat Glaze

(Fond Brun [Classique et Rapide], Demi-Glace, et Glace de Viande)

Cooks often get confused when they hear names such as brown stock (fond brun), demi-glace (half-glaze), brown sauce, glace de viande (meat glaze), sauce espagnole, fond lié (thickened stock), jus, broth, bouillon, and so forth. It is confusing. However, it is an area that is too important to French cooking to bypass.

Let's start with the most basic—stock. (We will use the word "stock" instead of broth, bouillon, or jus.) What is a stock? It is a liquid obtained by boiling bones with water. There are two basic stocks: one white, one brown. The white stock is bones and water boiled together with seasoning. The brown stock is made from bones that were browned in the oven or on top of the stove. The browned bones give the stock a darker color and a nuttier taste. A brown stock reduced by half becomes syrupy and is called a demi-glace *(half-glaze). Reduced to its extreme, to the consistency of jam, it becomes a* glace, *or glaze.*

A stock must cook a certain amount of time, which varies depending on how large the bones are and what type of bone is used. With small pieces of bones, or with thin bones like the bones of a chicken, three hours of cooking is sufficient, whereas larger veal or beef bones require up to 10 to 12 hours. Time is essential to extract all the nutrients and taste from the bones. Water is added to the bones, but not a fixed amount. Throughout, the cooking water evaporates and more is added regularly to replenish the stock. When the stock is cooked, it is strained and reduced to its proper consistency.

We make our brown stock with veal, beef, and chicken bones mixed together. The chicken bones, besides being readily available and inexpensive, add a pleasant nutty and sweet taste to the stock. In fact, if we are low on other bones, we'll make up the difference with more chicken bones. It is, of course, better to use fresh bones; however, in a home kitchen you rarely have enough fresh bones on hand. So when you order a roast of beef or veal from your butcher, ask him for a few bones and then freeze them. A few times a year, empty the freezer, make large amounts of stock and freeze it in small containers. It should last you for a few months and

be very inexpensive. Make great quantities of stock if you have pots and pans large enough. Three pounds (1.4 kilograms) of bones take as much cooking as 20 pounds (9 kilograms).

Brown stock is a carrier—a vehicle—which permits you to make sauces. It is not a sauce in itself, but is used to "wet" (*mouiller* as we say in France) a stew or deglaze a pan, or add to other bones (game, lamb, etc.) to produce a more concentrated and differently flavored stock. Though it is gelatinous when cooked and holds together, a stock is not concentrated enough to be called a sauce. However, 3 quarts (3 scant liters) of brown stock reduced by half will yield 1½ quarts (1.4 liters) of a slightly syrupy and darker liquid which is concentrated enough to become a "sauce" and which has a name of its own—*demi-glace* (half-glaze). Furthermore, if that quart and a half of *demi-glace* is reduced to its extreme, it will yield about 2 to 2½ cups (473 to 591 milliliters) of what is called *glace de viande* (meat glaze). The *glace de viande* is not a sauce any longer. It has transcended the condition of a sauce and is now a strengthening and flavoring agent. The *glace de viande* hardens enough when cooled to be unmolded and cut into cubes. In the freezer, it will keep almost indefinitely if the reduction is correct. These cubes of *glace de viande* are added to sauces to make them stronger and richer. Thus a basic stock, taken to different stages of concentration and volume, changes its name as well as its function.

Stocks should be started with cold water and cooked, uncovered, at a slow, gentle boil. This way, the albumin in the bones and meat will harden and come to the surface of the liquid in the form of a gray foam which can be removed with a skimmer. The fat will also rise to the surface. However, if the stock is covered and boiling too fast, the albumin won't separate and the fat will emulsify back into the liquid (see the discussion of emulsion in the techniques for hollandaise) instead of rising to the top. The stock will then be cloudy, less digestible, and more caloric.

The classic brown stock is usually seasoned with carrots, onions, thyme, bay leaf, peppercorns, etc., but not salt because if salt is added at the beginning and the stock is then reduced to a glaze, the concentration of salt will be overpowering. A stock, purified by slow cooking and properly skimmed, will be high in proteins, clear, meaty, and practically tasteless. This may seem paradoxical but it's not. The stock has been too lightly seasoned to have much of an identifying taste of its own. And it shouldn't have one if it is to become a *demi-glace* transformed (as we will a little later) into a red wine sauce for beef, a chicken and mushroom sauce, or sauce for a sautéed piece of veal. In each of these cases, the *demi-glace* must take on the identity of that particular dish. It is the "hidden and modest" friend which enables a cook to produce a well-finished, long-simmered sauce in minutes. It is what we call in English a basic brown sauce. It doesn't have a specific name or identity of its own yet. With the addition of wine it becomes a sauce *Bordelaise*, with Madeira and truffles a sauce *Périgueux*, with vinegar and shallots a sauce *Bercy*, etc. The progression is from a stock to a *demi-glace* or basic brown sauce to a specific sauce.

What is the proper degree of reduction? The key word is "balance." To achieve a delicate combination of seasoning and correct concentration takes practice, knowledge, and talent.

Making sauces from reduced stocks is particularly well suited for restaurant cooking because it works well with diversified sauces and dishes made one portion at a time. However, it is time-consuming and expensive to make and some cooks do not feel that reductions alone produce a satisfactory result. Besides the question of time and expense, they object to the richness and concentrated taste of the reduction. A truffle sauce for a filet of beef requires a strong reduction but a small delicate quail is overpowered by too potent a sauce.

On occasion, a stock will reduce and intensify in flavor but will lack the gelatinous element to thicken to the right consistency. If you feel your sauce has reached the right taste but it is too thin in texture, thicken it lightly with arrowroot or potato starch. At one time a brown sauce used to be heavily thickened with flour. The classic sauce *Espagnole*, made with a stock, brown *roux*, and tomato paste, though rarely made nowadays, is an example. Carème explains that the *roux*, the binding agent, separates after long, slow cooking, and the fat and the scum from the cooking of the *roux* rise to the top and should be skimmed off. The sauce clarifies and purifies through the long cooking until only the "binding elements" of the flour (the glutinous part) remain to hold the sauce together. Although this sauce works with practice and care, it is more logical and faster to use a starch such as arrowroot—which is like a purified flour (binding element only) and has no taste, cooks instantly, and doesn't "dirty" the sauce. Cornstarch can be used, too, but tends to make the sauce a little more glue-y and gelantinous than either arrowroot or potato starch.

Must one use *demi-glace* to cook well? Some types of cooking require it, some do not. Home cooking and some of the best country cooking is often done without brown stock. In our family, and at friends' where we have had some of our most memorable meals, brown stocks are practically never used. Often good cooks modify the principles behind the brown stock and use leftover juices from a roast chicken or a pot roast the way a professional uses *glace de viande*. Roasting and braising give natural strong juices, the equivalent of a strong reduction, which can be used in the same manner.

Following the Classic Brown Stock and the Fast Brown Stock are recipes using these stocks.

CLASSIC BROWN STOCK, HALF-GLAZE, AND GLAZE

(Fond Brun Classique, Demi-Glace, et Glace de Viande)

YIELD: 3 quarts (3 scant liters) of stock or 1½ quarts (1.4 liters)
demi-glace or about 2 cups (473 milliliters) of *glace de viande*

10 pounds (4.5 kilograms) bones (one-third veal, one-third chicken, one-third beef), cut into 2-inch (5-centimeter) pieces

1 pound (454 grams) carrots, washed and unpeeled, cut into 1-inch (2.5-centimeter) chunks (about 4 to 6 carrots depending on size)

1½ pounds (681 grams) unpeeled onions, cut into 1-inch (2.5-centimeter) pieces (about 4 to 8 onions depending on size)

3 large ripe tomatoes, coarsely chopped (1½ pounds/681 grams)

1 large leek, cut in half

3 celery ribs, cut in pieces

2 bay leaves

½ teaspoon thyme leaves

½ teaspoon black peppercorns

1. Place the pieces of bone in a large roasting pan and brown in the oven at 425 degrees (218°C) for 1½ hours, turning the bones once, halfway through the browning process. Add carrots and onions to the bones and continue cooking in the oven another ½ hour.

2. Remove the bones and vegetables from the oven and transfer to a large stock pot, using a slotted spoon so the drippings of fat are left in the roasting pan. Pour out and discard the fat accumulated in the roasting pan. (The solidified juices left in the pan are in fact a *glace de viande*.)

3. Pour water into the roasting pan, place on top of the stove, bring to a boil and, <u>using a wood spatula, rub the bottom of the pan to melt all the solidified juices.</u> This is called deglazing.

4. Add this liquid to the kettle and then fill it with water. Bring to a boil slowly, turn the heat down and simmer for 1 hour, removing the scum. After 1 hour, add the remaining vegetables and seasonings. Bring to a boil again, then <u>simmer slowly for about 5 to 6 hours.</u> During the cooking process, water will evaporate; replace periodically to keep the same level. The stock can also simmer very gently overnight.

5. <u>Strain the liquid through a fine strainer.</u> (It is better to end up with more yield rather than less. When a lot of liquid is left, the bones get "well washed" and the strained liquid contains all the nutrients of the stock. If the liquid is over-reduced with the bones, when you strain it, a lot of the *glace* and taste will stick to the bones and be lost.) Return to a clean pot and boil down until it reduces to 3 quarts (3 scant liters) of liquid. Remove as much fat as possible from the surface.

6. Let the stock cool overnight, and then remove the solidified fat on the top. <u>Notice that the stock is fat free and gelatinous.</u> Make *demi-glace* or divide among containers and freeze.

7. To make *demi-glace*, reduce the stock by half (again) and cool. <u>Divide into large chunks of about 1 cup</u> (237 milliliters) <u>each</u>. Wrap in plastic wrap and freeze. Stock, which is gelatinous but not quite as solid as the *demi-glace*, should be poured into plastic containers, covered and frozen.

8. To make a *glace de viande*, strain the *demi-glace* again and reduce to its maximum. As it reduces, transfer the liquid to a smaller, sturdy saucepan. The last hour of reduction is delicate and should be done on very low heat because the mixture has a tendency to burn as it gets thicker. <u>The glace will become dark</u> <u>brown and form bubbles on top</u> (like large caramel bubbles) during the last 15 to 20 minutes of cooking. As they break, no steam will escape. If there is any fat left in the mixture, it will separate from the glaze and should be removed with a spoon. At that point, the reduction is completed and essentially there is no more moisture in the mixture.

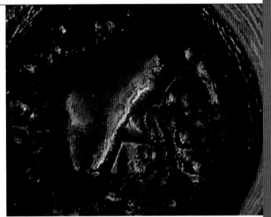

9. <u>Note that the *glace de viande* has the thickness of a caramel.</u> Remember also that it is unsalted. Place the spoon and spatula into the saucepan, cover with water, and bring to a boil. The leftover, sticky *glace* around the pan and utensils should be remelted to be used as a stock. (The bones that have already cooked for hours are often recooked, instead of being discarded, also to make a *glace de viande*. It is not as rich as the one made only through the reduction of stock but it's a bonus. To make it, fill the pot the cooked bones with cold water, bring to a boil and simmer for another 6 hours or cook gently overnight. Strain and reduce to a *glace de viande* as described above in step 8.)

10. <u>When the *glace de viande* is cold, unmold and cut</u> <u>into cubes.</u> They will be hard, rubbery and dark. Keep in an uncovered jar in the refrigerator or freezer. They will become very hard and keep almost indefinitely. Use as a seasoning when needed.

FAST BROWN STOCK (Fond Brun Rapide)

This is a good, classic way of making a stock and yet it is fast. However, you can only make small amounts of it at a time because the bones get browned in a saucepan on top of the stove, and a saucepan can only accommodate so many bones. The bones are cut into small pieces so they brown rapidly and the nutrients and flavors are extracted faster during cooking. In a classic stock, the bones are roasted in the oven, which is a slower way, yet the only way to brown a large quantity of bones.

YIELD: 1 quart or stock or ½ quart (473 milliliters) *demi-glace*

1 pound (450 grams) veal bones

2 pounds (900 grams) chicken bones
   (gizzards, legs, necks, wings), cut into
   1- to 2-inch (2.5- to 5-centimeter)
   pieces

1 carrot, unpeeled, chopped coarsely
   (½ cup/75 grams)

1 large onion, unpeeled, chopped coarsely
   (¾ cups/70 grams)

1 small leek, chopped coarsely (1 cup/
   135 grams)

½ cup (75 grams) celery stems and leaves

1 large tomato, cut in pieces

½ teaspoon thyme leaves

1 bay leaf

½ teaspoon black peppercorns

4 to 5 cloves garlic, unpeeled

⅓ cup (80 grams) parsley stems

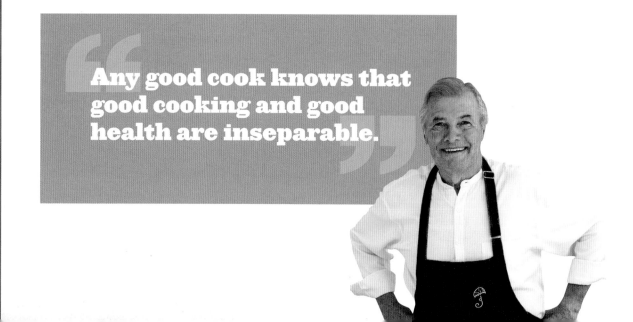

Any good cook knows that good cooking and good health are inseparable.

1. <u>Cut the bones into 1- to 2-inch (2.5- to 5-centimeter)</u> <u>pieces</u> and place in a saucepan large enough to accommodate the bones in one layer. Place on the stove for 5 minutes on high heat. When they start sizzling, reduce to medium and continue cooking for 25 minutes, stirring occasionally with a wooden spoon.

2. <u>The pieces should be well browned all around and the</u> <u>juices solidified in the bottom of the pan.</u> Be careful not to burn the *glace* or solidified juices, or the stock will taste bitter.

3. After the bones have cooked for 30 minutes, <u>use the cover</u> <u>to hold the bones in and invert the saucepan to pour out all</u> <u>the liquid fat.</u> Add the carrots and onions to the bones and keep browning for another 10 minutes on medium to low heat. Add the rest of the ingredients and fill the saucepan with water. Bring to a boil slowly and cook uncovered on medium heat for 3 to 4 hours, replacing the water as it evaporates. Remove the scum every 10 to 15 minutes.

4. <u>Strain through a fine *chinois*</u> or fine sieve. Let cool overnight in the refrigerator and remove the fat. Reduce to 2 cups (473 milliliters) for a *demi-glace*.

STEAK "MARCHAND DE VIN" WITH MARROW (Steak Marchand de Vin à la Moëlle)

YIELD: 3 to 4 servings

1 large shell steak (about 1½ pounds/
   681 grams, trimmed, see page 349)
¼ teaspoon salt
¼ teaspoon freshly ground pepper
1 tablespoon (14 grams) unsalted butter
1 tablespoon chopped shallots
1 small clove garlic, chopped
¼ teaspoon thyme
1 cup (237 milliliters) good dry red wine
2 anchovy fillets
¾ cup (178 milliliters) *demi-glace*

Sprinkle the steak with salt and pepper. Panfry steak in butter over medium heat for about 10 minutes, turning the steak every 4 to 5 minutes. Place the steak on a platter and keep warm in a 160 degree (70°C) oven. Add the shallots to the pan drippings and sauté for 10 to 15 seconds. Add garlic, thyme, and red wine. Reduce to ½ cup (118 milliliters). Chop anchovy fillets or crush with the blade of a knife to a purée and add to the wine mixture with the *demi-glace*. Reduce for 1 to 2 minutes. Taste for seasonings, add salt and pepper if needed, and strain the sauce on top of the steak or slice the steak and serve with the sauce around.

FILET OF BEEF WITH TRUFFLE SAUCE (Filet de Boeuf Périgueux)

YIELD: 6 servings

1¾-pound (795-gram) piece of filet of beef
   (completely trimmed, see page 352), from the
   center, seasoned with
   ½ teaspoon salt
   ¼ teaspoon ground black
      peppercorns
3 tablespoons (42 grams) unsalted butter
1½ cups (355 milliliters) *demi-glace*
1 tablespoon chopped black truffles, preferably
   fresh or canned *Tuber Melanosporum*
½ cup (118 milliliters) good, dry Madeira wine
Salt and pepper to taste

Preheat the oven to 425 degrees (218°C). Brown the meat on all sides in 2 tablespoons (28 grams) butter in a sturdy skillet or saucepan (about 5 minutes). Place the skillet in the oven for 18 minutes. Remove, set the meat on a platter and let rest or settle in a warm place (150 degrees/66°C) for at least 10 to 15 minutes before carving. Place the pan with the drippings on top of the stove and cook on medium heat until the fat is entirely separated from the juices, which should solidify on the bottom of the saucepan. This technique is called "pincer." Set the skillet on the table for 4 to 5 minutes, inclining the skillet so the fat comes to one corner. Pour fat out and add *demi-glace*. Place on the stove on low heat and, with a spatula, loosen all the solidified juices as the sauce boils gently.

   Place the truffles in a clean saucepan with the Madeira wine. Bring to a boil and reduce by half. Strain the *demi-glace* from the skillet directly on top of the Madeira-truffle mixture. Reduce the sauce until it reaches proper consistency and coats the spoon. You should have about 1½ cups (355 milliliters) of sauce left. Season with salt and pepper if needed and finally swirl in the remaining butter, cut into small pieces. Slice the meat thinly and serve 2 to 3 slices per person with the sauce around the meat and partially covering the slices. The plates should be very warm.

HUNTER CHICKEN (Poulet Chasseur)

YIELD: 4 servings

1 tablespoon (14 grams) butter

1 tablespoon olive oil

1 (2¾-pound/1.25-kilogram) chicken, skinned, and quartered (see page 274), keep the carcass bones for stock

2 tablespoons chopped onion

1 clove garlic, peeled, crushed and chopped fine

½ cup (118 milliliters) dry white wine

1 tomato, peeled, seeded and coarsely chopped (1 cup/225 grams)

1 teaspoon tomato paste

1 bay leaf

¼ teaspoon dried thyme

6 to 8 mushrooms, sliced (1¼ cups/144 grams, loosely packed)

½ cup (118 milliliters) *demi-glace*

1 teaspoon salt

¼ teaspoon freshly ground pepper

½ tablespoon finely chopped Italian parsley

½ tablespoon fresh tarragon

Melt the butter in a heavy saucepan, add the olive oil, and brown the chicken over medium heat for 8 to 10 minutes, turning the chicken after 5 to 6 minutes of browning. Add the chopped onion and sauté for 15 to 20 seconds. Add the garlic, white wine, tomato, tomato paste, bay leaf, and thyme. Cover and bring to a boil. Turn the heat down and simmer for 10 minutes. Add the mushrooms. Cover and simmer another 5 minutes. Using a spoon, transfer the chicken and solids to a dish. Add *demi-glace* to the drippings, bring to a boil and reduce to 1 cup (237 milliliters). Season, add parsley and tarragon, pour on top of the chicken, and serve at once.

SAUTÉED VEAL WITH SPINACH (Veau Sauté aux Epinards)

YIELD: 4 servings

⅓ stick (38 grams) butter, plus 2 tablespoons (28 grams)

2 10-ounce (567 grams) packages leaf spinach

Salt and freshly ground pepper to taste

About 12 veal scaloppine, 2 to 3 per person, 2 ounces (57 grams) each, completely trimmed (see page 333)

¾ cup (178 milliliters) *demi-glace*

Put 3 tablespoons (42 grams) of butter in a large saucepan and cook it to a dark stage to obtain a nutty taste. Add the spinach, mix well, and season with ¼ teaspoon of salt and pepper to taste.

Arrange your spinach on individual serving plates. Melt the remaining butter in one or two large saucepans and sauté the scaloppini in foaming butter for approximately 40 seconds on each side, seasoning with salt and pepper. Arrange the veal on top of the spinach. Deglaze the drippings in your saucepan with the *demi-glace*. Stir to melt all the juices and reduce to about 1 cup (237 milliliters). Season with salt and pepper, if needed, and pour about 2 tablespoons of the sauce on the scaloppini and around the spinach on each plate. Serve immediately.

White Stock

(Fond Blanc)

White stocks (whether they be beef, chicken, fish, etc.) are cooked in the same way as brown stock, but the bones are not browned first. The stock may be reduced or thickened with a roux or beurre manié, with excellent results. When the stocks are thickened with a roux they are called veloutés *(mother sauces). With the addition of cream, a velouté becomes a cream sauce and the cream sauce, in turn, takes on different names depending on the garnish. For example, a fish stock becomes a velouté of fish after it is thickened with a roux, then a cream sauce with the addition of cream, then a sauce Dugléré with the addition of sliced mushrooms and tomatoes.*

In a first-class restaurant, where portions are cooked individually, the white stocks are often reduced to a glace, cream is added and the mixture boiled down until it reaches the proper consistency without the addition of flour. It makes a richer and more expensive sauce than a sauce made from a velouté. However, for economy as well as health, home cooks, except on special occasions, do not adhere to the criteria of a starred restaurant and a velouté is more the norm than the exception. A sauce should be light and, if it looks and tastes like glue, the culprit is the cook, not the flour.

YIELD: 3 quarts (3 scant liters)

10 pounds (4.5 kilograms) beef bones (knuckles, shin, and marrow bones are good), or chicken bones or half beef, half chicken

2 large onions

2 to 3 cloves

2 stalks celery

2 leeks, washed

4 carrots, peeled

4 to 5 cloves garlic, unpeeled

2 bay leaves

½ teaspoon thyme

½ teaspoon peppercorns

½ bunch parsley (1 cup/27 grams loose)

Cover the bones with cold water. Bring slowly to a boil and skim the solidified blood and albumin that rises to the surface of the water. Boil for 2 hours, skimming regularly. Most of the scum will rise to the top during these first 2 hours.

1. <u>Stick one of the onions with the cloves</u>. Add to the pot along with the celery, leeks, carrots, garlic, seasoning, and herbs.

2. If desired, to give an amber golden color to the stock (if a *consommé* or aspic is to be made from the stock), <u>cut an unpeeled onion in half and brown in a skillet on medium heat on top of the stove until the cut side turns quite dark</u>. Add to the stock. Boil slowly for another 4 hours, or 2 hours if you use only chicken bones. Evaporation will reduce the liquid. Add water periodically to compensate. Strain and reduce to 3 quarts (3 scant liters). Refrigerate overnight, then discard the fat, which will have solidified on top of the stock. Pack in small containers and freeze.

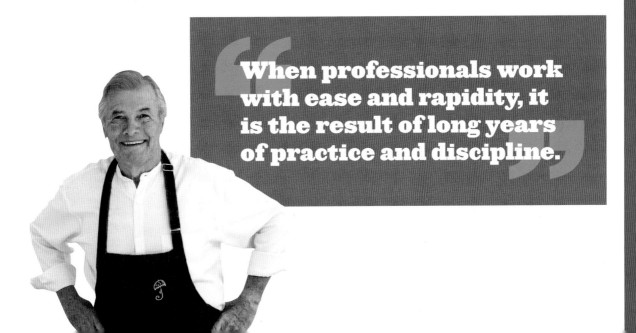

When professionals work with ease and rapidity, it is the result of long years of practice and discipline.

Fish Stock

(Fond de Poisson)

In our discussion of stocks, we have explained that long cooking and reductions enrich and intensify taste. The function of a stock, moreover, is to emphasize and enhance the food it is served with, not conceal it. Paradoxically, the same dish which will improve in taste through long cooking may be destroyed in texture by that same cooking. The way to reconcile these facts is to handle each component of the dish in a different manner. Take a fish for example: The head and bones will be separated from the fillets and cooked into a stock, then reduced to obtain an essence of strong reduction. On the other hand, the fillets will be barely cooked and, when combined with a sauce made from the reduced stock, you will have achieved the perfect balance.

It works the same way with meat. Take a salmis of pheasant: The bird will be roasted briefly at high temperature and the still-pink meat of the breast and thighs set aside, since it is the best and most tender part of the bird. The rest of the pheasant is browned further, seasoned, deglazed with wine and stock, reduced, degreased, and reduced again to intensify the taste and obtain a shiny concentrated sauce. This sauce finally gets served with the juicy, lightly cooked meat. The cycle is completed and each part of the pheasant has been utilized to the utmost and to obtain the best possible results.

Contrary to other types of stocks, fish stocks cook fast—35 to 40 minutes will be sufficient to get the nutrients and taste from the bones. A fish-court bouillon is usually made with fish bones, vegetables, and water. A fumet de poisson *consists of the bones stewed in butter or oil first. With the addition of vegetables, white wine, water, and seasoning, it becomes the base of* veloutés *and sauces.*

YIELD: Approximately 1½ quarts (1.4 liters) of stock

2 tablespoons (28 grams) unsalted butter

2½ pounds (1 kilogram) fish bones (use preferably the bones of flat fish such as sole, flounder, fluke, etc.). If fish heads are used, be sure to remove the gills and wash the bones carefully under cold water or the fish stock will be bitter.

1 medium onion, peeled and sliced

2 to 3 stalks celery, coarsely chopped

¼ cup (9 grams) parsley stems

1 leek, cleaned and sliced (1½ cup/ 100 grams)

2 bay leaves

¼ teaspoon thyme

½ teaspoon black peppercorns, crushed (*mignonette*) (see technique for Pepper Steak on page 351)

1 teaspoon salt

1½ cups (355 milliliters) dry white wine

3 quarts (3 scant liters) water

1. <u>Put the butter in a large skillet or kettle</u> and when it melts, add the fish bones. Steam on medium to high heat for 3 to 4 minutes, stirring with a wooden spatula.

2. When the bones begin to fall apart, <u>add the onion, celery, parsley stems, and leek, and mix well</u>. Steam for another 3 to 4 minutes, stirring. Add all the other ingredients and bring to a boil. Boil on high heat for 35 to 40 minutes.

3. <u>Strain through a fine *chinois*</u> or sieve. You can freeze the fish stock and use it for soups, thicken it with a *roux* so it becomes a *velouté*, or reduce it to a glaze and finish it with cream and butter.

Skimming Technique

(Technique de Dégraissage)

1. With the stock boiling gently, <u>remove the scum with a</u> <u>tight, "net-like" skimmer</u>.

2. For an alternative method, use a ladle. "Push" the fat to one side of the pot by sliding the round back of the ladle on top of the liquid. <u>Then, using the front of the ladle,</u> <u>scoop the fat off</u>. A third alternative is to let the stock cool refrigerated overnight and then remove the fat, which will have solidified on top of the liquid.

Skimming Fat

(Dégraissage des Sauces)

When sauces are cooking, the fat or scum comes up to the surface of the liquid and has to be skimmed off.

1. With the sauce simmering gently, <u>push the top layer of fat or scum to one side of the pan</u>.

2. <u>With the spoon flat, scoop the fat from the side when it is accumulated</u>.

3. <u>Be sure to scoop only the fat</u>. Repeat every 10 or 15 minutes, as needed, while the sauce is simmering.

How to Strain Sauces

(Passage des Sauces au Chinois)

There are two ways to strain stocks or sauces. If it is a clear stock or demi-glace or any of its derivatives, care should be taken to not crush the solids into the liquid or it will make it cloudy.

If you are straining a thickened sauce such as a velouté, béchamel, or hollandaise, you don't have to worry about "dirtying" the mixture and can rub as much through the mesh as possible. In the photographs that follow, we are straining through a fine-meshed chinois (strainer) that is the equivalent of a double layer of cheesecloth or kitchen towel.

To strain a stock very finely, you should put it through a colander with larger holes first to remove the larger solids and then, when the volume is reduced, work it through a finer-meshed chinois. It is particularly important to put demi-glace through a fine strainer to get the glossiness that's possible only when all the impurities have been removed.

If you are buying a chinois, be sure to get one with a guard to protect the mesh from getting dented or crushed.

Any sauce that has to do with eggs and has a tendency to curdle—from a hollandaise to a crème anglaise—can be strained through this type of fine mesh to conceal or minimize a problem.

1. To remove solids from a sauce or stock, when it's important to keep the liquid clear, bang the side of the strainer either with the palm of your hand or a wooden spatula to encourage the clear stock to strain through. If you crush the solids into the strained liquid, the stock or sauce will become cloudy.

2. For thickened sauces, where clarity is not an issue, use the ladle in a plungerlike, push-lift-push motion, forcing the liquid through the mesh.

Strong, Clarified Stock

(Consommé)

Consommé is the beef or chicken concoction that, when perfectly made, is a beautifully clear and sparkling soup. It can be eaten as is or used as a base for other soups, for sauces, or for aspic. It has all the proteins of meat and none of the fat. There are two steps in making consommé. The first is to make the stock and the second is to clarify it. Clarification is the simple process that gives consommé its crystal-clear appearance. If the stock is very strong and concentrated, there is no need to add ground meat to the clarification. Fifteen minutes of cooking is enough to clarify the stock in this case.

A very strong consommé (consommé double) is made by adding meat to the clarification and cooking it for 1 hour, thus concentrating flavor in the liquid. A cold consommé double should be gelatinous without being too firm. With the addition of tomato, it becomes madrilène consommé.

YIELD: Serves 8

1 cup (237 milliliters) cold water

1 pound (454 grams) very lean ground beef

6 large egg whites

½ cup (25 grams) diced celery leaves

¾ cup (170 grams) diced tomato

2 cups (200 grams) sliced green of leek
(or 1 cup/100 grams green of scallions)

½ cup (20 grams) coarsely cut parsley
and tarragon mixed

¾ cup (110 grams) sliced carrots

½ teaspoon black peppercorns

2 bay leaves

½ teaspoon thyme leaves

Salt, if needed

12 cups (3 scant liters) stock

1. In a large kettle, combine all the ingredients except the stock.

2. Add the stock and bring to a boil over high heat, stirring constantly to avoid sticking. Do not worry if the stock becomes very cloudy and a white foam forms. The albumin in the egg whites and the meat is solidifying, and this is the process that will clarify the stock. When the mixture comes to a strong boil, STOP STIRRING and reduce the heat to a simmer. As the mixture simmers, you will notice that the ingredients form a "crust" on the surface of the liquid with one or two holes, through which the liquid boils slightly.

3. Allow the consommé to simmer gently for 1 hour without disturbing the little "geysers" in any way. Turn off the heat and let the consommé settle for 15 minutes. Tilt the pan on one side to get all the liquid out.

4. Strain the liquid through a sieve lined with paper towels or a cloth soaked in cold water and then wrung out. After the consommé has rested 1 hour, check to see if there is any fat on the surface. If so, remove it by blotting the top with paper towels. The consommé can be served hot or cold. With different garnishes, it takes on different names like *célestine* with shredded crêpes, or *royale* with cubes of meat-flavored custard. The crust is usually discarded, but with the addition of whole eggs, bread crumbs and seasonings, it can be turned into a satisfying meat loaf. Be careful to remove the peppercorns for this use.

White Butter Sauce

(Beurre Blanc)

The beurre blanc *(white butter sauce) is an emulsion of butter with wine and/or vinegar which holds together because it is whipped at a proper temperature. Furthermore, the whipping beats air into the mixture, which makes it light and increases its volume. In cooking, the word "emulsion" refers to a fat and liquid or other ingredient bound together into a creamy mixture. Mayonnaise is an example of a cold emulsion and hollandaise an example of a hot emulsion. Other types of emulsions appear throughout this book—in the brill recipe (see page 222), as well as the asparagus stew (see page 81). In the latter recipe, butter and water are brought to a strong boil and it is the boiling that causes the mixture to bind. This is somewhat confusing as, on the one hand, boiling may be necessary to get some sauces into emulsion while, on the other hand, sauces like hollandaise or* beurre blanc *separate if they're brought near the boil. The explanation for this paradox lies in the proportions of fat to liquid.*

If the proportion of butter and liquid are more or less equal, a strong boil will bind the ingredients together and make a creamy sauce that will hold together for some time depending on temperature. If there's a lot more butter than liquid (as there is in the beurre blanc*) too much heat will make the mixture separate. This is an important point to grasp because, when understood, it allows you to bind liquids into fat or to separate fat from liquid at will. For example, in a roast chicken in aspic, the natural juices are boiled down to evaporate the moisture and reduce the mixture to solidified juices and clear fat. As the moisture boils off, the proportion of fat becomes greater and this is why it breaks down and separates from the solidified juices. Once the fat is separated, it can be easily poured off and the solidified juices dissolved with water, then strained and reduced to proper consistency. To reverse the process, let's say that you don't want to remove the fat from your natural juices but the mixture has over-reduced and already separated. If you want to bind the liquid and fat back together again, you just replace some of the evaporated moisture (water), bring to a strong boil, and it will bind together again. In the case of a* beurre blanc *or hollandaise which, again, is almost all fat, if the sauce starts to separate, remove from the heat, add a bit of cold water, and beat with a whisk to bind together again.*

The beurre blanc *can replace a hollandaise on top of any kind of vegetable and is especially good with shellfish and fish.*

YIELD: About 2 cups

1 cup (237 milliliters) water
⅓ cup (48 grams) finely sliced shallots (3 to 5 according to size)
½ teaspoon freshly ground white pepper
½ teaspoon salt
½ cup (118 milliliters) good white wine vinegar
2 tablespoons heavy cream
2½ to 3 sticks (1¼ cups to 1½ cups/283.5 to 340 grams) unsalted butter at room temperature

1. In a saucepan, preferably stainless steel, combine the water, shallots, pepper, salt, and vinegar. Bring to a boil and simmer slowly for about 20 minutes. If the mixture reduces too much during the cooking, add some water. Push the mixture into a sieve, pushing with a spoon to force the shallots through. You should have approximately ½ cup (118 milliliters) of mixture left. If you have too much, reduce it. If you don't have enough, adjust with a bit of water.

2. Add the cream to the mixture and place on very low heat. The mixture should be lukewarm. Add the butter piece by piece, beating rapidly and strongly with a wire whisk after each addition. Do not worry too much about temperature. Up to one stick (½ cup/113 grams) of butter can be added to the saucepan and the whole mixture boiled without it breaking down. As the quantity of butter increases, reduce the heat to low. Keep adding the butter and beating until all of it is used.

3. You should have a warm, creamy, smooth-textured sauce. Keep lukewarm in a double boiler or on the side of your stove. As long as it doesn't begin to solidify, it can keep. At serving time, place it back on the stove and heat while beating with the whisk until hot. Serve immediately.

Hollandaise Sauce

(Sauce Hollandaise)

Although less often made today, hollandaise sauce is a classic that every chef should know how to make. Generally it is made with eight yolks per pound (454 grams) of butter, but the proportion of eggs to butter can be altered in either direction. If your hollandaise is high in egg yolks, it will be less likely to separate but it may become too yolky in taste. If it is high in butter, it will be very delicate in taste but very fragile.

Though a hollandaise sauce is usually made with clarified butter (see note), we prefer to use unclarified butter. Because unclarified butter is whole—it has not been separated into its oil and liquid components and the liquid component discarded— it is more watery, and therefore it makes a slightly thinner sauce. However, it gives the sauce a creamier taste and the extra moisture permits it to withstand higher heats than the conventional hollandaise.

I make the sauce with a base of water and lemon juice is added at the end.

A hollandaise is a base or mother sauce. With the addition of white wine vinegar, shallots, and tarragon it becomes a béarnaise sauce. If you add tomatoes to the béarnaise it becomes a sauce choron. If you add glace de viande to the béarnaise it becomes a sauce Foyot, etc. Hollandaise sauce can be made with a browned butter, which gives it a very nutty taste (sauce Noisette), or perfumed with orange rind and orange juice to make a sauce Maltaise, which is excellent with broccoli, etc.

(Note: To clarify butter, place butter in a 180-degree (80°C) oven until completely melted. Let it rest a few minutes and it will separate into two layers: a milky residue at the bottom and a transparent oily layer at the top. Clarified butter is the oily part. The milky residue is discarded.)

YIELD: About 2 cups

4 large egg yolks
3 tablespoons water
2 sticks (1 cup/113 grams) unsalted butter
Dash of cayenne
Dash of pepper
Salt to taste
1 tablespoon fresh lemon juice

1. Place the yolks and water in a saucepan, preferably stainless steel or enameled cast iron. (Aluminum will discolor the sauce.) The sabayon, which is the first part of the hollandaise, can be made in a double boiler over lukewarm to hot water to prevent curdling or it can be prepared directly on top of the stove.

2. Start beating the mixture, making sure that you "drive" the whisk into the corners of the saucepan where the eggs will have a tendency to overcook and scramble. Cook over medium heat, alternately moving the pan off the heat while beating and then placing it back on the heat, so the mixture never gets too hot. If it comes too close to a boil, the eggs will scramble. On the other hand, if the mixture does not get hot enough during the beating, it will tend to foam too much, increase in volume, and have too light a consistency to be able to hold and absorb the butter.

3. Beat for approximately 4 minutes. The consistency of the mixture should be that of thick, soft, very smooth butter. Between the streaks of the whisk, you should be able to see the bottom of the pan.

4. Add the butter piece by piece, beating after each addition while moving the hollandaise off and on the heat to keep the temperature hot enough so the butter is absorbed and the hollandaise thickens. Season with salt and cayenne pepper and add lemon juice. Notice that the hollandaise doesn't require much salt.

5. If the hollandaise is exposed to too much heat, it will eventually separate and break down. <u>Notice the broken look and the butter separating from the egg yolk</u>. First, the sauce will start getting oily at the edge when it begins to break down. As that starts to happen, you can smooth it out again by beating in 1 tablespoon of hot water. However, if the sauce is completely separated, as shown in our photograph, reconstitute it as explained below.

6. <u>Strain the mixture through a very fine strainer to separate most of the oily liquid part from the sauce</u>.

7. Place 2 tablespoons of water in a saucepan, bring to a boil, remove from the heat, and <u>add the thick part of the broken sauce 1 tablespoon at a time while beating</u>. You will see the sauce becoming smooth again. Keep adding until you have used all of the thick part of the sauce, which now should be smooth, like the original sabayon. Then, while beating, add the liquid butter as though you were making the hollandaise from scratch, moving the pan on and off the heat to keep the temperature warm. If the sauce is recooked too much or if during the process the eggs scramble lightly, the mixture can be strained through a very fine strainer, a chinois, to alleviate the scrambled appearance.

Butter and White Sauce

(Beurre et Béchamel)

Fresh butter, one of the main ingredients in French cooking, is widely used in the professional kitchen for everything from hors d'oeuvre to desserts. And rightly so, because there is no substitute. Buy unsalted butter, rather than salted, because salt is added often to act as a preservative, and salted butter may not always be fresh. Unsalted butter, on the other hand, gives away its age by turning rancid faster than salted butter.

Clarified butter is nothing more than ordinary butter that has been heated until it melts, and the milky residue (milk solids) has sunk to the bottom of the pan. The clear, yellow liquid that sits on top is clarified butter. Classically, it is used to make hollandaise, béarnaise and choron sauces, among others, and it is often called for in sautéeing because it does not burn as readily as unclarified butter.

Butter is so versatile it often is used for three different purposes in the same sauce: to thicken it with either a "roux" or a beurre manié, to enrich it by adding little "nuts" of butter, and to coat the surface of the sauce to prevent a skin from forming.

A roux is a mixture of butter and flour in equal proportions which is cooked before it is combined with a liquid. A roux blanc (white) should be cooked slowly for 1 minute, stirring. It should not be allowed to brown. A roux brun (brown) is cooked until it turns a rich, nut brown, up to 30 minutes. A beurre manié is a mixture of soft butter and flour in equal proportions that has been kneaded until smooth.

White sauce (béchamel) is one of the mother sauces in French cooking. It is made with a beurre manié. With the addition of cream it becomes a sauce crème.

WHITE SAUCE WITH BEURRE MANIE (Sauce Béchamel)

1. Place soft butter and flour in equal proportions in a bowl. A thin sauce will take approximately 2 teaspoons each of flour and butter per cup (237 milliliters) of milk. A thick, heavy sauce (for soufflés) will take up to 3 tablespoons each of flour and butter.

2. <u>Mix with a spoon or a whisk until smooth.</u> This is a *beurre manié*.

3. Bring milk to a boil. <u>With a wire whisk, scoop the *beurre manié*</u> and whisk into the milk vigorously to avoid any lumps. The kneaded butter should incorporate easily without forming any lumps.

4. Bring the sauce to a boil and cook at low heat for 2 to 3 minutes, <u>mixing with the whisk to avoid scalding.</u> Season to taste with salt, pepper, and nutmeg. Often *béchamel* is made by melting butter in a saucepan and then stirring in the same quantity of flour. Cook for about 30 seconds and add cold or hot milk and bring to a boil, stirring with a wire whisk until thickened. Cook for a couple of minutes.

5. When the sauce is cooked, <u>cut a little bit of butter and put it on top.</u>

6. As the butter melts, <u>smear it onto the whole surface of the sauce with the point of a fork.</u> This will form a coating of fat on the surface of the sauce and will prevent a skin from forming. At serving time, stir in the butter which is on top.

LEMON-PARSLEY BUTTER (Beurre Maître D'Hôtel)

1. The *maître d'hôtel* butter is the most frequently used of the many compound butters. It is sliced and used on broiled steak, chops, liver, or on boiled potatoes, cauliflower, or even poached fish. To 2 sticks (1 cup/227 grams) of softened unsalted butter, add 2 tablespoons lemon juice, 2 tablespoons chopped parsley, 1 teaspoon salt, and 1 teaspoon ground black pepper.

2. Mix thoroughly until all the ingredients are well blended. Spread into a strip on the width of a piece of wax paper.

3. Roll the butter back and forth to make it smooth and equal all over.

4. Close both ends of the butter tube and place in the refrigerator or freezer. Cut into slices as needed. The same method is used to make *béarnaise* butter, *Colbert, anchovy,* and so on. Compound butter also can easily be made in a food processor.

Mayonnaise

(Mayonnaise)

Mayonnaise is a very useful cold dressing. Although most people buy prepared mayonnaise, it is important to know how to make it from scratch.

Mayonnaise is usually served with cold foods such as hard-boiled eggs, cut vegetables, salad, cold fish, shellfish, cold meat, and pâté. (Its sister, hollandaise, made with egg yolk and butter, is served warm with fish, eggs, and vegetables such as asparagus, broccoli and the like.) In French cooking, when the ingredients of a particular salad are bound with mayonnaise, it becomes: mayonnaise de volaille (chicken salad), mayonnaise de homard (lobster salad), and so on. Mayonnaise made in the food processor or blender will keep longer when refrigerated than the handmade counterpart because the elements are more finely bound together.

Mayonnaise can become sauce verte, a green sauce made with mayonnaise, watercress, tarragon, parsley, and spinach; sauce gribiche, mayonnaise with hard-cooked eggs, French sour gherkins, capers, and shallots; sauce tartare, mayonnaise with parsley, chives, chervil, and sour pickles; sauce La Varenne, mayonnaise with a purée of fresh mushrooms; sauce russe, mayonnaise with fresh caviar; and, of course, the well-known aïoli, known as the butter of Provence and made with a very substantial amount of pounded garlic and olive oil. Of course, mayonnaise can be made with olive oil (the best is an extra-virgin oil), or peanut oil, or a mixture of both; it is just a question of personal taste. Buy vinegar of the best possible quality. Use good mustard. The quality of the ingredients is sine qua non to the end result. Be sure that the ingredients are at room temperature. If the oil is too cool, the mayonnaise will definitely break down. If kept refrigerated, the mayonnaise must come to room temperature slowly before it is stirred or it will break down. This recipe yields about 2½ cups (592 milliliters) of mayonnaise. The same recipe can be made without the mustard for a milder taste; however, the mixture will be more delicate and more likely to break down.

3 large egg yolks
1½ teaspoons Dijon mustard
1 tablespoon tarragon or wine vinegar
Dash of salt
Dash of freshly ground white pepper
2 cups (473 milliliters) oil (peanut, olive, walnut, or a mixture)

1. Place all ingredients except the oil in a bowl and stir with a wire whisk. <u>Add the oil slowly, whisking at the same time.</u>

2. <u>Keep mixing</u>, adding the oil a little faster as the mayonnaise starts to take shape.

3. <u>Lift the whisk to check the consistency of the mayonnaise.</u>

4. To serve, <u>scoop the mayonnaise into a clean bowl,</u> being careful not to smear the sides of the bowl. (Place the mayonnaise in the middle of the bowl.)

5. <u>Smooth the top with a spatula</u> by turning the spatula in one direction and the bowl in the other direction.

6. When the top is smooth, <u>move the spatula in the same circular and reverse motion, going up and down</u> to make a design on top of the smooth surface.

7. With your finger, <u>push out the mayonnaise left on the blade of the spatula</u> in the center of the decoration.

8. <u>Mayonnaise ready to serve.</u>

9. When the oil is added too fast, or when the ingredients are too cold, the mixture breaks down. It looks like a broken-down custard. Mayonnaise can be put back together with egg yolk, mustard, vinegar, or a small amount of hot water. Place 1 teaspoon of vinegar, if vinegar is used, in a clean vessel. Add 1 teaspoon of the broken sauce and whisk thoroughly. When smooth, add another teaspoon, then another, and when the mayonnaise starts to hold together, you may add the broken sauce at a faster pace.

10. For another method, pour the vinegar or hot water directly into the broken mayonnaise in one place along the edge of the bowl. Using the tip of your whisk, without getting too deep into the mayonnaise, mix the liquid with the top layer of the broken sauce until you see that it is coming together. Keep mixing, pushing your whisk deeper and deeper into the mayonnaise. Then, whisk larger and larger circles until all of the sauce is back together.

Larding: Strips and Leaves
(Lardons et Bardes)

There are basically two kinds of larding needles: the large grooved needle (lardoire) for pot roast and other large pieces of meat and the small butterflied needle (aiguille à piquer) used for small cuts, such as filet mignon or rack of hare. The process of larding smaller cuts with fat was once common but it is rarely done nowadays. Piquage of meat usually is not necessary. It is shown only as part of a known technique.

Because meat is always cut against the grain, larding is done with the grain of meat. Otherwise, one might cut through whole strips of fat while carving.

Lard leaves (bardes) are used to line terrines and pâtés, or to wrap dry meat or game such as partridge or woodcock, and give moisture and enrich the meat during cooking.

LARDING A SMALL CUT OF MEAT

1. The fat used is fat back (*lard dur*) because it is firm and white and is not inclined to disintegrate as easily as fat from other parts of the pig. It is the layer of fat closest to the skin. Keep the piece refrigerated so it can be easily cut into strips. <u>Flatten the piece with a large cleaver</u>.

2. Turn upside down and, <u>with a long, thin knife, start cutting the rind off</u>.

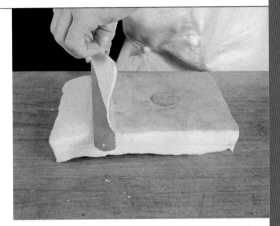

3. <u>With one hand pressing tight on top of the fat back, cut the rind off by keeping your blade flat</u>, moving in a jigsaw fashion.

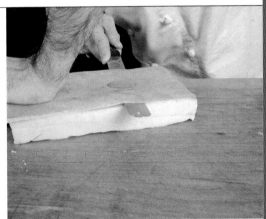

4. Cut the fat in long strips about ½ inch (13 millimeters) wide for the pot roast. <u>Place in iced water to keep the fat firm</u>.

5. Cut in small strips to lard the small cuts. Keep in iced water.

6. Place the fat strips inside the split end of the *aiguille à piquer* as far as it will go.

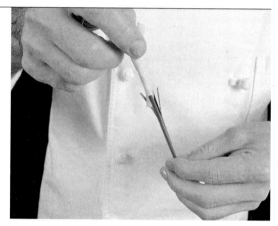

7. With one hand, keep the split end closed on the fat and insert the needle through the meat.

8. Pull with the other hand, leaving a small strip dangling on each side. The meat is larded on a bias in that case.

LARDING A LARGE CUT OF MEAT

1. <u>Cut ½-inch (13-millimeter) slices of fat back</u>.

2. <u>Cut the slices into long strips</u> and keep refrigerated, or in iced water to firm up.

3. <u>This is a plain grooved larding needle</u>. Before placing the fat in it, push the needle through the meat to make an opening. Remove the needle, place the fat in the groove in the larding needle, and insert it into the premade hole, twisting as you push the needle in. Lift the end of the fat, and hold with your finger as you withdraw the needle, or the entire strip may come out.

4. <u>This is another type of larding needle</u>. It is easier to use because of its hinged tip.

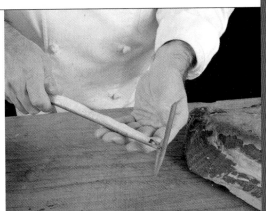

5. <u>With this needle, you place the fat into the groove</u> and close the tip on top of it.

6. <u>Insert the needle, twisting it through the meat</u> (go with the grain of the meat). Lift up the tip and,

7. <u>holding it between your fingers, pull off the removable handle.</u>

8. <u>Holding the end of the fat with your thumb, pull the needle through in the same direction it went in.</u>

9. Repeat until the entire piece of meat is larded <u>every 1½ to 2 inches (4 to 5 centimeters)</u>.

LARD LEAVES FOR TERRINES AND PÂTÉS

1. To make *bardes* or lard leaves, flatten the fat back with a cleaver. Place skin side down on the table. <u>Stick one or two pointed knives through the rind</u> to keep the fat back from sliding during cutting.

2. Using a long, thin knife, <u>cut "leaves" as thin as you can, holding your blade horizontally</u>.

3. <u>Gently lift the leaves of fat from the fat back.</u> This technique requires a certain amount of practice. You could ask your butcher to cut the leaves with his electric ham slicer.

Folding in Ingredients

(Incorporation à la Spatule)

Many recipes, primarily baking recipes, call for folding. The goal is to incorporate something delicate, usually whipped egg whites or cream, into a thicker mixture while retaining the fluffiness and airy quality in the mixture.

1. Use a wooden or rubber spatula, or even a metal one, and <u>slide it gently on top of the mixture</u>.

2. Then, <u>cutting side down, go through the mixture</u> and straighten out the spatula underneath it.

3. <u>Twist the spatula again to come out on the top, cutting side up</u>. While you perform the whole circle with one hand, spin the bowl toward you with the other hand. The motions should be simultaneous. Do not overfold.

Coating a Cookie Sheet

(Plaque Beurrée et Farinée)

There are countless recipes asking the cook to coat a cookie sheet, a soufflé mold, a cake pan, and so on. The reason is primarily to avoid sticking and also to give whatever is cooking a nice golden crust and a buttery taste. In the case of a soufflé, it is even more important; it helps the soufflé slide up during cooking. There are basically three ways to coat a dish. Butter is first rubbed on the surface of the dish; then sugar is added for a sweet dessert, cheese for a cheese soufflé, or flour for an all-purpose coating.

1. Rub soft butter all over the cookie sheet.

2. Add flour to the sheet and shake it thoroughly in all directions so that all the butter is coated with the flour. Pour the flour onto the second pan and repeat the operation. Give a bang to the back of the cookie sheet to get rid of any excess flour. The coating should be light and uniform.

Pastry Bag and Tube

(Poche et Douille)

When a cook wants to give a professional look to his desserts, he uses a pastry bag. It simplifies the work and makes the decoration faster, cleaner, and more uniform. Buy a plastic-lined pastry bag which is easy to use and to wash. A 14- or 16-inch (35- to 40-centimeter) bag is the all-purpose size most commonly used. Buy your pastry bag with a narrow opening at the point. If it is too small for your tube, you can always cut a piece off the tip to enlarge the opening.

1. Fit a pastry bag (preferably made of plastic) with a plain tip. To prevent the batter from running out through the tip as you fill the bag, twist it just above the tip and push the twisted section into the tip. This will hold the batter back until you're ready to begin using the bag.

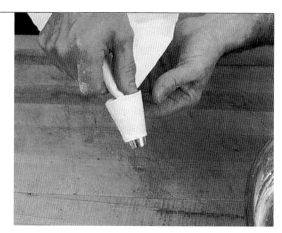

2. Fold the cuff of the pastry bag back on your hand and onto itself to a depth of 1½ to 2 inches (4 to 5 centimeters) so the inside of the bag near the opening is not smeared with the batter. Spoon the batter into the bag.

3. Unfold the edge of the bag and <u>pleat the top</u> like an accordion to close the batter in.

4. To use the bag, <u>hold the pleated end in the hollow between your thumb and finger.</u> If you open your fingers while pressing the mixture out, it will come up instead of going down through the tube.

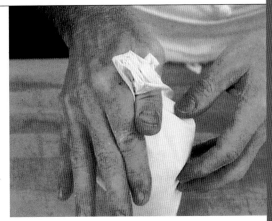

5. Notice the position of your hands when using the bag: <u>The index finger and thumb of one hand hold the bag firmly closed while the lower part of the hand presses on the bag to release the filling. The bag is held near the tip with the other hand to direct the flow from the tip.</u>

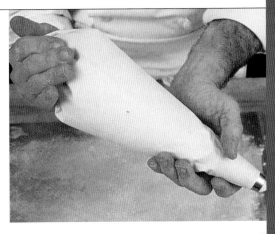

Lining Cake Pans

(Garniture en Papier)

Before baking parchment and wax paper were so widely available, cooks used brown wrapping paper to line cake pans. This served the purpose, but the modern papers which come on rolls are easier to work with. Not all cakes call for lined pans, but when they do, they are essential if the cake is to drop out of its cake pan intact. Nowadays many cooks use no-stick aluminum foil or a silicone pad to prevent sticking.

ROUND

1. Butter half of a square piece of parchment paper. <u>Fold the unbuttered side of the paper onto the buttered side</u> and press together to make a square.

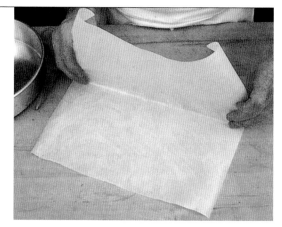

2. <u>Fold the square into smaller and smaller triangles.</u>

3. Holding the paper triangle as shown, measure the radius of a round cake pan 10 to 12 inches (25 to 30 cenimeters) in diameter and cut the paper so it will fit exactly in the pan. Open the triangle and put the paper, buttered-side down, in the pan. As soon as it touches the pan firmly, turn it over so the buttered side is up. The paper is buttered on both sides now and will adhere well to the bottom of the pan and not stick to the batter.

JELLY ROLL PAN

4. To line a jelly roll pan (16 x 12 inches/40 x 30 centimeters) with parchment paper, first cut a rectangular piece of parchment paper a little larger than the pan and butter half of it. Fold the buttered half of the paper onto the unbuttered half.

5. With a knife, make a 1-inch (2.5-centimeter) slit in both of the open corners of the folded paper, open the paper up, and place it buttered-side down in a jelly roll pan, pressing it very lightly (there's just enough butter to grease the pan slightly). Lift the paper and turn it over in the pan. It will adhere well now.

6. The paper will overlap at the corners where it has been cut, making it fit better in the pan.

Paper Casing

(Cuisson en Papillote)

When you see "papillote" on a menu in a French restaurant, you can safely assume that it describes a dish served in an envelope of parchment paper, usually a veal chop or a filleted or whole fish. The paper is cut in the shape of a heart. The meat or fish is partially cooked, placed in the center of the paper, and baked in the oven. When the papillote is folded correctly (it is sealed so that none of the aroma and steam can escape) it browns nicely, inflates, and the dish inside bakes in its own juices. The papillote is served directly on the serving plate and the guest opens it himself.

1. To cook *en papillote*, start by cutting a large rectangular piece of parchment paper. (In the olden times, cooks used brown paper bags.) <u>Fold the rectangle in half.</u>

2. Using scissors or a knife, <u>start cutting from the folded side</u>, following an imaginary line that resembles a question mark.

3. Open the heart shape and place the food on the bottom. The food should be partially cooked and all seasonings and flavorings added. <u>Fold the top paper over the food.</u>

4. Starting at the fold, <u>fold the edge, overlapping the folds as you go along.</u>

5. <u>Fold the tip of the papillote</u> several times to secure the closing.

6. <u>Papillote ready to bake.</u>

Paper Frill

(Papillote)

In addition to the paper receptacle described in the preceding technique, the word papillote *describes a frill—a delicate paper lace rolled into a "hat" and used to adorn the bone of a lamb chop or a ham. Its raison d'être is strictly aesthetic. A papillote is also a Christmas bonbon rolled in a piece of paper decorated with a drawing and a motto, then wrapped in colorful paper with frills at both ends. Another* papillote, *neither aesthetic nor edible, is a little piece of paper used by women to set their hair.*

1. Cut a long rectangle of parchment or wax paper approximately 25 inches (63 centimeters) long by 5 inches (13 centimeters) wide. Fold lengthwise twice. Open the last fold. You now have a rectangle folded in half and scored down the center by the second fold. Using scissors, cut strips ¼ inch (6 millimeters) apart down the length of the paper. (Cut through the folded side to the score line.)

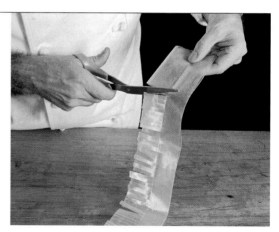

2. Open the rectangle completely and fold in half inside out to give the frills a nice roundness.

3. <u>Secure with staples</u> or plastic tape.

4. <u>Roll the frill on your finger</u>, or on a pencil if you are making small frills for lamb chops.

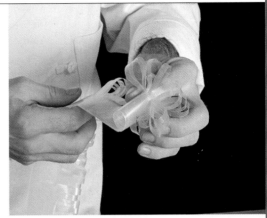

5. <u>Secure the bottom part with a paper clip or a piece of tape.</u>

Paper Cone

(Cornet en Papier)

A paper cone or horn is an invaluable tool for fine and elegant piping. It gives a professional touch to your decoration. Making cornets is not an easy technique to acquire, but it is well worth spending the time to master. They should be made with parchment, sulfurized paper, or the best quality wax paper you can find.

1. Cut a triangle of strong paper with a pair of scissors.

2. Grab both ends with your thumbs and forefingers and twist onto each other to make a cone. Do not worry if the cone is not very pointed.

3. Holding the cone at the seam with both hands (thumbs inside and forefingers outside the cone), move the thumbs down and the fingers up to bring up and tighten the cornet making it needle sharp. Hold the cone tight so that the paper does not unroll.

4. Fold the ends inside the cone to secure it and avoid uncoiling.

5. The cone is ready to be filled. Place some filling in the cone, being careful not to soil the edges. Do not fill more than $1/3$ full.

6. Flatten the cone above the filling and fold one side.

7. Fold the other side.

8. <u>Next fold the center onto itself twice</u> to secure the filling inside.

9. For a plain line, <u>cut off the tip of the cone with a pair of scissors</u>. The smaller the opening, the finer the decoration.

10. To make leaves, <u>cut off a larger piece of the tip on a slant</u>.

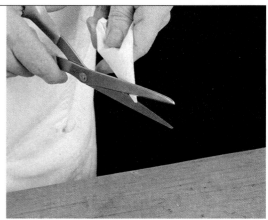

11. <u>Then cut on the other side</u> so that the tip is open on two sides. It is now ready to use.

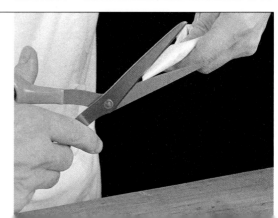

Collar for Soufflé

(Faux Col pour Soufflé)

Frozen soufflés are whipped cream, a liqueur, egg yolks, and sugar mixed together and then frozen. The "rising" of the soufflé is accomplished by the simple device of tying strong parchment paper around the mold and filling the mold up to the "collar." Collars are also used for hot soufflés to keep them from splitting and falling out during baking.

1. Cut a wide piece of strong baking parchment long enough to go completely around the mold and overlap slightly. <u>Then fold the paper two or three times</u>, depending on the width of the paper and on how high you want your soufflé to rise above the mold.

2. <u>Apply your strip of paper to the outside of the mold</u>, pulling the paper together securely and tightly so that the soufflé mixture cannot run down between the paper and the mold.

3. <u>Secure the paper collar with a piece of string</u>, tying it very tightly. For a frozen soufflé, fill the mold up only to its top edge. Place both the filled mold and the remaining mixture in the freezer for 15 minutes. By that time the surplus mixture will have become firmer and will not run. Add the mixture to the mold, filling the collar. Smooth the top surface. Return to the freezer and freeze until firm. At serving time, sprinkle some cocoa over the top to simulate browning in the oven. And don't forget to remove the paper!

VEGETA

BLES

Asparagus

(Asperges)

Asparagus has been commonly cultivated in Europe since the seventeenth century. While the large white, fleshy Argenteuil is less available in the United States, the commonly found varieties are the Italian purple (with almost violet-colored tips) and the green Mary Washington type. There are countless ways of cooking and serving asparagus. The best is the simplest, boiled and served plain with vinaigrette, hollandaise, or melted butter.

1. The white asparagus is on the left. The good green asparagus is in the center. (Notice that the tip is fairly tightly closed, as it should be.) On the right is an "over-the-hill" asparagus spear. The tips are opening like a flower. Fresh asparagus is firm and plump and will snap rather than bend. A soft, wrinkled specimen indicates dehydration and age. Peel the asparagus, starting approximately one-third of the way down the stalk; you can check with your fingernail to see if the skin is fairly fibrous there.

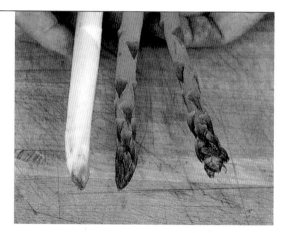

2. To peel, hold the asparagus completely flat on the table, keeping your index finger and thumb on top of it, not underneath, so the asparagus lies flat and can be rolled on the table as it is peeled. Notice that the vegetable peeler is held with the thumb and fingers of the other hand flat and on top, so the blade is perfectly parallel to the stalk. Begin cutting near the tip end of the asparagus one-third of the way down the stalk, pushing the trimmings directly onto your fingers. As you peel, rotate the asparagus by rolling it gently. Peel all around.

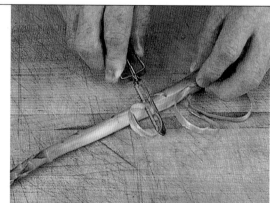

3. When all the asparagus has been peeled, <u>break each piece at the base just above where the peeling stops</u>, removing the trimmings and the base. The asparagus can now be tied in bundles and cooked.

4. Asparagus are often bundled into a portion of about 8 to 10 thin stalks. <u>Grab a handful and align the tips by leveling them on the flat table.</u>

5. <u>Holding the spears firmly in one hand, wrap your middle finger with soft kitchen string.</u>

6. <u>Start bundling the lower part of the bunch.</u> Be sure to make it tight. (This is one reason why you should not use string that is too thin and might cut.)

7. <u>Come across, still holding the bundle tight</u> and

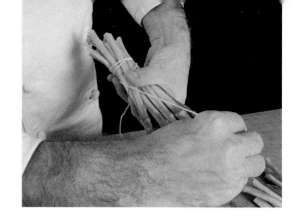

8. <u>tie the front, lower than the tips</u>. Secure with a double knot.

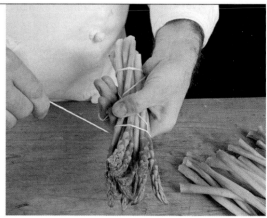

9. <u>Trim the spears at the root end</u>. The asparagus are now the same length. Bring a large pot of salted water to a rolling boil. Lower the asparagus into the water and cover them until it starts boiling again; uncover. If the cover is left on during the whole cooking time, the asparagus will turn yellowish. Boil, depending on size, from 5 to 6 minutes. They should still be crunchy, but cooked enough. Lift the bundle from the boiling water and serve immediately.

10. If cooked ahead or served cold, as soon as the asparagus is done, <u>place the whole kettle under cold water to stop the cooking. To prevent breaking the asparagus, place a spoon across the pot to divert the force of the water so it falls gently on the tender tips.</u> (If only a small amount of asparagus is to be cooked, place ½ inch (13 millimeters) water in a skillet. Spread the asparagus in one layer and cook, covered, for 4 minutes. Lift out the asparagus and let cool on a plate.)

11. Drain the asparagus on paper towels. To serve warm, place a bundle, when needed, in a sieve and lower into boiling water for about 1 minute. Drain and serve immediately. To serve cold, arrange the spears on a large, oblong platter.

12. Garnish the ends with a bunch of curly parsley.

Asparagus Stew

(Ragoût d'Asperges)

This is a very simple, elegant, and delicious dish. It can be served as a first course or as an accompaniment to broiled lamb chops, pan-fried veal steaks, or to any sauceless meat.

YIELD: 4 servings

2 dozen (24) green asparagus spears or a mixture of green
 and white asparagus

⅓ cup (79 milliliters) water

½ teaspoon salt

½ stick (¼ cup/57 grams) unsalted butter, cut into pieces

¼ cup (10 grams) finely chopped parsley

1. Peel the asparagus, then <u>cut on the diagonal into 1-inch (2.5-centimeter) lengths</u>.

2. Place the asparagus in a skillet with the water and salt, cover and bring to a strong boil. Boil for 1½ minutes, <u>uncover and add the butter</u> and the parsley.

3. <u>Return to a strong boil, shaking the pan to bind the ingredients together</u>. Boil for 20 to 30 seconds until the sauce binds and becomes foamy. The mixture will rise like milk ready to boil over.

4. As soon as it foams, remove from the heat (further cooking will reduce the amount of moisture in the sauce and make the butter and water separate). <u>Pour into a serving dish</u> and serve immediately.

Corn Crêpes

(Crêpes de Maïs)

Whole ears of corn are excellent poached (not boiled) in salted water, or cooked in aluminum foil on top of the barbecue. A purée of the pulp is very elegant served with veal or lamb. (Melt sweet butter in a saucepan, add the pulp or fresh polenta, salt and pepper and simmer a few minutes, just enough for the starch to tighten and the purée to thicken into a creamy mixture.) With the pulp, one can also make excellent crêpes.

YIELD: 20 Crêpes

6 medium-sized ears of corn
½ cup (75 grams) all-purpose organic flour
4 large eggs
1 teaspoon salt
¼ teaspoon freshly ground black pepper
½ cup (118 milliliters) milk
½ stick (¼ cup/57 grams) melted unsalted butter

1. Hold the cleaned ear of corn in one hand and, <u>using a sharp knife, cut through the middle of each row of kernels.</u> The object is to open each kernel so the pulp can be "pushed" out.

2. Stand the ear straight up. <u>Using the back (dull side) of the knife, scrape the pulp out of the opened kernels, turning the ear as you go along.</u> You should have approximately 1½ cups (355 milliliters) of pulp. Mix all ingredients thoroughly, starting with the pulp and the flour and then adding the rest. Make the crêpes using a non-stick pan if possible. Brown on one side only and roll up. The crêpes will be very delicate and fragile to handle. Serve as soon as possible as a vegetable or as a garnish for your favorite meat.

Corn Fritters

(Beignet de Maïs)

YIELD: 24 fritters

1¼ cups all-purpose organic flour (about 6-7 ounces/170 to 200 grams)
2 teaspoon double-acting baking powder
1 large egg
¼ teaspoon salt
1 cup (237 milliliters) ice-cold water
2 cups (300 grams) corn kernels (cut from about 2 or 3 ears)
About ½ cup (118 milliliters) corn oil

1. Place the flour, baking powder, egg, salt, and water in the food processor and combine just until smooth. Add corn kernels and process for 5 to 6 seconds, just enough to break the kernels partially. Remove to a bowl. Heat up 2 large saucepans and add ¼ cup (59 milliliters) oil to each pan. When the oil is very hot, drop full tablespoons of the fritter batter (about 7 per skillet) into each skillet. The mixture will spread a little.

2. Cook over high about 2 minutes at the most on each side. Lift out and set on a tray and continue making the rest of the fritters until all the batter is used up.

Artichokes and Artichoke Hearts

(Artichauts et Fonds d'Artichauts)

Cooked artichokes can be served cold as a first course, lukewarm with hollandaise or melted butter as a vegetable, or hot stuffed with meat or other vegetables. The small young artichokes, especially the Provence or the Tuscany violet, are eaten raw with salt and butter or with a vinaigrette. When artichokes get older and turn slightly yellowish, they are used for artichoke hearts or bottoms.

WHOLE

1. A good-sized artichoke weighs about 8 ounces (227 grams). Cut the stem off with a knife, or <u>break it at the base</u> (this helps pull out of the heart the stringy fibers that develop in overmatured artichokes).

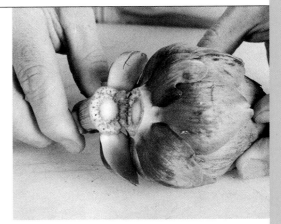

2. <u>Cut off at least 1½ inches (4 centimeters) of the top.</u>

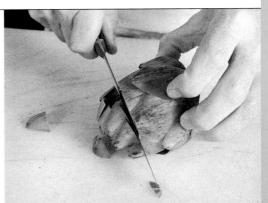

3. <u>Cut off about one-third of the top of each leaf.</u> The ends are tough, bitter and thorny. The reason is also aesthetic.

4. To prevent discoloration (artichokes turn dark very fast), <u>tie a slice of lemon to the bottom of the artichoke where the stem is cut.</u> Restaurants that cook artichokes a day ahead use this technique to keep the bottom white until serving time. The technique is optional.

5. Place the artichoke in a large amount of boiling, salted water. Place a wet paper towel directly on top of the artichoke to keep it wet and immersed during cooking. Boil as fast as possible for 40 to 50 minutes, depending on the size. Do not cover. To test for doneness, pull out a leaf: if done, it pulls out easily. Place under cold water to cool.

6. Serve not too cold. To serve lukewarm, rewarm in hot water for 2 minutes. Drain. <u>Spread the outside leaves at the top wide enough to slide your fingers inside and around the center leaves.</u>

7. <u>Pull out the central leaves</u>; they should come out in one piece like a small funnel or cone. Now, the "choke" is exposed.

8. Using your fingers, or a teaspoon, <u>remove the hairy choke from the cavity</u>.

9. <u>Replace the central leaves upside down on the opened top of the artichoke</u> and garnish with curly parsley. Serve on a tulip napkin or directly on a plate.

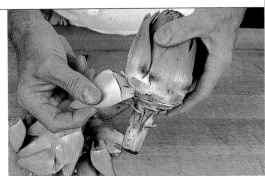

HEARTS

1. The goal is to retrieve as much of the "meat" from the leaves and bottoms as possible. This is a delicate technique and takes practice. For someone not familiar with making artichoke bottoms, start with this technique. <u>Break off each leaf high enough so that the meat remains attached to the body of the artichoke</u>.

2. If you pull the leaf off instead of breaking it off, <u>the lower white part of the leaf with the meat attached will come off as shown in the photograph</u>. Be sure to fold the leaf down and pull down to break it off, leaving the meat attached to the heart.

3. When all of the heart is exposed, <u>cut the stem, which can be peeled and cooked with the heart, and cut the center leaves of the artichoke at the level of the choke</u>.

4. <u>Using a vegetable peeler or a small, sharp knife, trim the remaining green from the heart.</u> Rub with lemon juice to prevent discoloration.

5. Here is another peeling method that is often used by professionals but requires training and practice. It is shown in photographs 5 to 8. The outside leaves are trimmed off the heart with a knife at greater speed than by using the method explained in steps 2 to 4. Place the blade on the side of the artichoke, the point at a slight angle facing the center of the leaves. <u>Roll the artichoke, cutting the leaves all around without getting into the heart.</u>

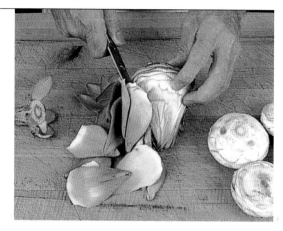

6. <u>Trim the center leaves off at the level of the choke,</u> as explained in step 3.

7. <u>Using a sharp paring knife or vegetable peeler (as shown in photograph 4), trim the remaining leaves from the bottom of the heart</u>

8. <u>and on the top to expose the choke</u>. Rub with lemon to prevent discoloration.

9. Combine the cooking stock ingredients (3 cups/710 milliliters water, 1 tablespoon flour, 2 tablespoons olive oil, ¼ cup/59 milliliters fresh lemon juice, and ½ teaspoon salt) thoroughly, making sure the flour is dissolved, and add the bottoms. Bring to a boil and boil gently for 20 to 25 minutes, until the bottoms are tender but still firm to the touch. Let cool in the liquid. When cold enough to handle, <u>remove the chokes from the bottoms</u> and place the bottoms back in the cooking liquid until ready to be used.

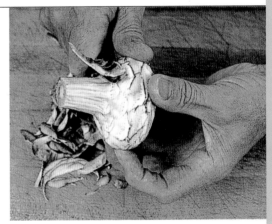

10. As a vegetable accompaniment to meat or fish, the artichoke heart can be cooked in pieces. About 2 inches (5 centimeters) of the stem can also be left on the heart, providing the artichoke is young enough for the stem to be tender. <u>Trim all around the heart, as explained above, and around the stem</u>.

11. Cut the trimmed heart into 4 pieces and <u>remove the choke with the point of a knife</u>. Rub with lemon juice to prevent discoloration. Cook the hearts according to instructions above.

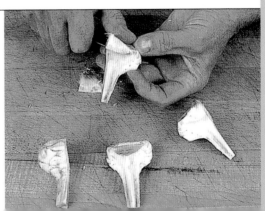

Hollowing Out and Stuffing Artichokes

(Vider et Farcir l'Artichaut)

YIELD: 7 artichokes

7 artichokes

STUFFING

2 tablespoons (28 grams) unsalted butter

¼ cup (59 milliliters) olive oil

⅓ cup (48 grams) chopped shallots

3 or 4 chopped garlic cloves

2 cups (120 grams) bread crumbs

¼ teaspoon freshly ground black pepper

¼ teaspoon salt

2 tablespoons olive oil

1 cup (237 milliliters) water

1. FOR THE ARTICHOKES: Cut about 1¼ inches (3 centimeters) off the top of the artichokes and cut off the stems. <u>Peel the fibrous skin from the stems</u> and reserve the centers. Rub cut parts with lemon to prevent discoloration.

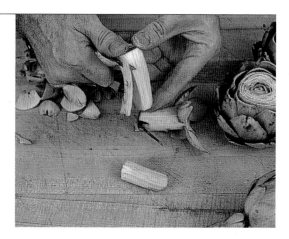

2. <u>Using scissors, cut off the top third of each artichoke leaf.</u> These leaf tips are tough, and each has a "needle" in the center. Wash the artichokes under cool water. Bring 2 quarts (1.9 liters) of water to a boil in a stockpot. Add the artichokes, cover, bring to a boil again, and boil gently for 30 minutes. They will not be completely cooked. Drain in a colander and rinse under cold water.

3. When cool enough to handle, grab the center of each artichoke and <u>pull out the center leaves in one clump.</u>

4. <u>Using a spoon, remove the choke,</u> the hairy material inside at the base. The artichokes are not yet completely cooked and may require some scraping to remove the choke.

5. <u>The centers of the artichokes are clean.</u>

6. STUFFING: Melt the butter and olive oil in a large skillet. When hot, add shallots, garlic cloves, and bread crumbs, and sauté, stirring almost continuously, for 4 to 5 minutes over medium to high heat, until the bread turns a nice brown color. Add pepper and salt. The base of the center leaves is tender. <u>Cut away the tender parts</u> and add to the stuffing.

7. <u>Spoon the stuffing into each artichoke</u>, placing some in the cavity and some in between the leaves. When they are stuffed, place the artichokes side by side in one layer in a saucepan. Sprinkle with olive oil, add water, and place the stems around the artichokes. Cover, bring to a boil, reduce heat, and cook for approximately 20 minutes. By then, most of the moisture should have evaporated and only the olive oil will remain with the gently stewing artichokes. If there is still liquid in the pan, remove the lid and continue boiling until the remaining moisture has evaporated.

8. <u>Arrange the artichokes on a platter with the stems around</u>. The artichokes can be served alone as a first course or as a side dish with meat or poultry.

Preparing Celery for Braising

(Céleri en Branche)

When braising celery, it is important to use celery stalks with the whitest possible hearts, as they will be tender and sweeter. Braised celery can be used as an accompaniment to most roasts, sautéed meats, and poultry.

YIELD: 4 servings

2 or 3 whole celery stalks, depending on the size, as white as possible (about 2 pounds/.9 kilograms trimmed)

1 teaspoon salt

2 tablespoons (28 grams) unsalted butter

½ cup (188 milliliters) *demi-glace*

1. Trim the celery, keeping about 6 inches (15 centimeters) of the root and heart. Reserve the trimmings for stock or soup.

2. Using a vegetable peeler or small knife, remove most of the fiber from around the outside of the celery stalks and trim around the base. Cover the celery with cold water and half the salt, and bring to a boil. Cover and simmer gently for 30 minutes. Drain and cool. (The cooking liquid can be used in stocks or soups.)

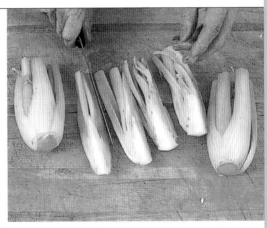

3. Cut each celery stalk lengthwise into fourths (for standard celery) or sixths (for larger celery).

4. Melt the butter in a large skillet. When hot, sauté the pieces of celery for about 2 minutes on each side. Add the *demi-glace* and remaining salt, cover, and simmer for 7 to 8 minutes, until some of the *demi-glace* is reduced and coats the celery. Uncover and cook for 3 to 4 minutes to further reduce the demi-glace and coat the celery by rolling and turning it in the liquid.

Celeriac or Celery Root

(Céleri-rave)

Celeriac or celery root, usually available at certain times of the year, is not the root of the common stalk celery. Though it tastes like celery, it is a different plant. It is excellent cooked and also served raw in julienne with an oil and mustard sauce.

1. <u>Peel the celeriac with a knife</u> or a vegetable peeler.

2. Cut the celeriac in half through the root. Remove the spongy flesh in the center near the stem end. <u>Using a knife or a mandoline, slice into ⅛-inch (3-millimeter) slices.</u>

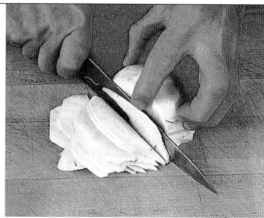

3. <u>Stack a few slices together and cut into a fine julienne.</u> To make a salad, make a mayonnaise (see page 53), but triple the amount of mustard and double the vinegar. Mix with the celeriac and add more salt and pepper. Make the salad at least one hour in advance. Serve cool, but not ice cold.

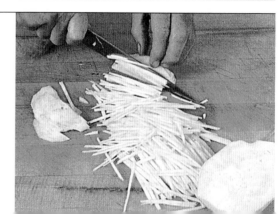

Preparing Kohlrabi

(Préparation du Chou-Rave)

Kohlrabi can be boiled, puréed, made into soup, or just sautéd raw like potatoes. When young and freshly picked, they can be eaten raw in salads.

1. Peel the kohlrabi, removing the thick, fibrous skin. The flesh should be firm and white and should not smell strong.

2. Cut the kohlrabi into ⅛-inch (3-millimiter) thick slices. You should have 5 to 6 cups (625 to 750 grams). In each of 2 skillets, heat 1½ tablespoons olive oil and 1½ teaspoons (7 grams) butter. When hot, sauté half the kohlrabi slices in each skillet over medium heat for about 15 to 20 minutes, tossing occasionally to brown somewhat uniformly. They should be tender but still firm.

Cucumber Salad

(Salade de Concombres)

Cucumbers are widely used in the United States as well as in many European countries and India. Cucumbers can be served raw as a salad, cooked or stuffed as a vegetable, or pickled to use as a condiment. However, it is raw in a summer salad (or as a salad ingredient) that cucumbers are most frequently served.

YIELD: 6 to 8 servings

3 cucumbers
1 tablespoon kosher salt
4 tablespoons sour cream
1½ tablespoons fresh lemon juice
½ teaspoon freshly ground black pepper
2 tablespoons olive oil
2 tablespoons chopped fresh dill

1. Storebought cucumbers are often coated with a chemical to retard spoilage, and it is better to peel them using a vegetable peeler. You don't have to peel the cucumber if you grow your own.

2. Cut into halves lengthwise. You may slice the cucumber with the seeds, season it and serve that way. However, it is more elegant to remove the seeds. Work the edge of a dessert spoon along the seeds, close to the flesh, making a type of incision. When you are through with one side, turn the cucumber and loosen the seeds on the other side. Finally, using the bowl of the spoon, scrape out all the seeds in one stroke.

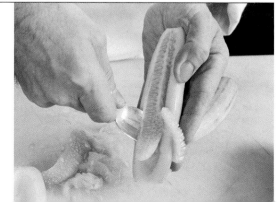

3. <u>Slice into ⅛-inch (3-millimeter) or ¼-inch (6-millimeter) slices</u>. You should have about 5 cups (1 kilogram).

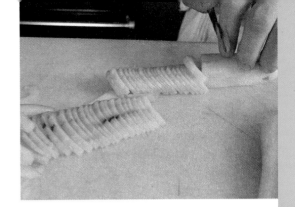

4. <u>Place in a colander and sprinkle with salt</u>. Mix well. Let the cucumber macerate for at least 1 to 2 hours at room temperature. The salt, you will discover, draws the juices from the cucumbers, making them limp, and, paradoxically, very crisp at the same time.

5. <u>Drain, rinse under cold water and press lightly to extract excess moisture</u>. Combine the sour cream, lemon juice, and freshly ground pepper in a bowl. Add the oil, beating with a wire whisk. Combine with the cucumber and the fresh dill. Do not use more salt. Prepared this way, the cucumbers will stay crisp for several days.

Deep Fried Zucchini

(Courgette Frite)

YIELD: 6 servings

4 medium zucchini

2 cups (120 grams) fresh bread crumbs

1 cup (170 grams) stone-ground cornmeal

¼ teaspoon cayenne pepper

2 large eggs

2 tablespoons all-purpose flour

½ teaspoon salt

¼ teaspoon freshly ground black pepper

Oil for frying

1. Cut the zucchini into 2- to 3-inch (5- to 7.6-centimeter) long chunks. Cut the chunks into ½-inch (1.3-centimeter) lengthwise slices. Stack the slices together, then cut them into sticks ½ inch (1.3 centimeters) thick. Combine the bread crumbs, cornmeal, and cayenne together in a shallow bowl. Mix the eggs with the flour, salt, and pepper until smooth. Dip the sticks into the egg mixture, then coat with the bread crumb mixture and drop into the oil heated to 375 degrees (191°C). Cook for 3 to 3½ minutes. Remove to a cookie sheet lined with a wire rack. Sprinkle lightly with salt. Serve immediately.

Preparing Okra

(Préparation de l'Okra)

Okra is sometimes used in stew (like New Orleans gumbo or lamb stew in Africa) since the viscous juice it exudes tends to thicken sauces.

YIELD: 2 servings

½ pound (227 grams) okra

1 cup (237 milliliters) white distilled vinegar

2 quarts (2 scant liters) water

1 tablespoon (14 grams) unsalted butter

1. Remove the tips of okra and slice it in half and then quarters lengthwise. To eliminate some of the sliminess, place in a plastic bag and add the vinegar. Leave for 30 minutes. Remove the okra and rinse well under cold water. Bring water to a boil, add the okra, and return to the boil. Boil for 5 minutes uncovered. Strain in a colander and refresh under cold water. At serving time, heat butter in a skillet, add the okra, and sauté gently, just enough to heat through.

Roasting and Peeling Peppers

(Griller et Peler les Poivrons)

Roasted peppers can be served whole or stuffed; cut into strips and seasoned with garlic, salt, pepper, and olive oil; and in salads and sandwiches.

1. Arrange 8 peppers on a broiler pan and place them under a hot broiler, no more than 1 inch (2.5 centimeters) from the heat source, turning until the peppers blister all around, from 13 to 15 minutes. Alternatively, burn the peppers directly on a gas burner until they are charred all around. Immediately place the peppers in plastic bags. Close the bag and set aside for 10 minutes. Steaming in their own heat in the plastic bag will help the peppers release their skin.

2. Remove the peppers from the bag and peel off the skin; it will come off fairly easily. Tear the peppers open carefully, scoop out the seeds, and scrape off the membranes on the inside. Use as needed.

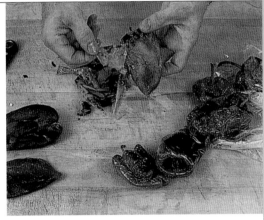

Preparing Sugar Snap Peas

(Préparation des Pois Mange-tout)

Snap peas are one of the pleasures of spring, fresh from the garden.

1. <u>Cut off the pointed end with your fingernail and pull</u>. You will see the string that runs all the way up the side.

2. Pull the string the length of the pea to the stem end, and break off the stem end; <u>pull the string on the other side of the length of the pea and remove it</u>. The strings should be removed from both sides. Cook in boiling water for a couple of minutes, drain, toss with butter and salt and pepper, and serve.

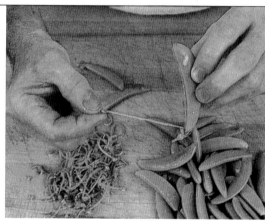

Preparing Sea Beans

(Préparation des Pousse-Pierre)

Sea beans are also called glasswort or saltwort salicorne and grow in abundance along the coast of New England. Only the young, very tender shoots should be picked.

1. <u>Notice that only the tender green shoots are used</u>. For approximately 3 to 4 cups (360 to 480 grams) of sea bean sprouts, bring 3 quarts (2³/₄ liters) of water to a strong boil. Add the sea beans, bring the water back to the boil, and let it boil, uncovered, for approximately 1 to 2 minutes. Remove the beans to ice water to cool and stop the cooking until ready to use. Sauté in oil or butter when needed.

Shelling Fava Beans

(Écosser les Fèves)

When shelled, fava beans can be served raw as crudités or hors d'oeuvre with a bit of salt, or a little vinegar and oil.

1. <u>Remove the beans from the pods</u>. You will notice that even after the beans are out of the pods, there is still a shell on them.

2. With your fingernail or <u>the point of a sharp knife, slit this skin and pull it off</u>. See how the beans inside are more tender and delicate, and a brighter green. For a faster way, blanch the beans in boiling water for 20 seconds and transfer to cold water. Press the skin and the beans should pop out. Use as needed.

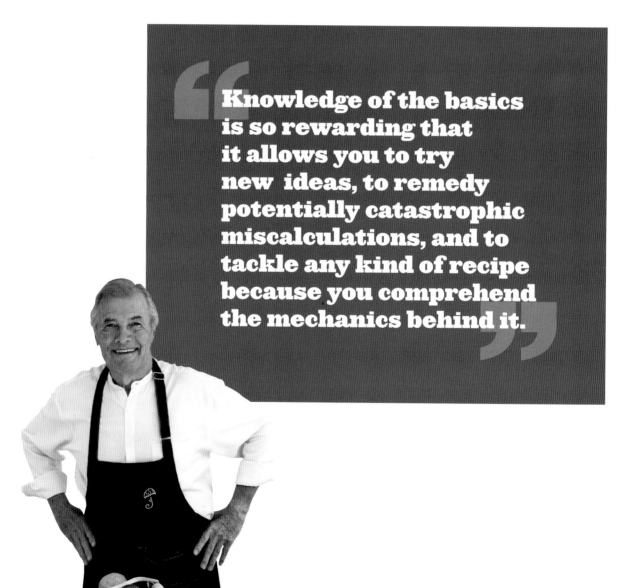

" **Knowledge of the basics is so rewarding that it allows you to try new ideas, to remedy potentially catastrophic miscalculations, and to tackle any kind of recipe because you comprehend the mechanics behind it.** "

Cleaning Salad

(Préparation de la Salade)

Lettuce is one of the most delicate and delectable salad greens. Bibb, oak leaf, or Boston lettuce go well with a light oil and vinegar or a cream dressing because they are very tender and mild. Escarole, curly endive, and the like can support a stronger, mustard-garlic dressing.

1. Holding the lettuce upside down, <u>cut around the center to remove the core and loosen the leaves.</u> Remove the spoiled leaves.

2. <u>The larger, tougher outside leaves should have the top and center rib removed.</u> Only the tender pieces on both sides of the rib are used.

3. With the larger leaves removed, <u>cut through the center rib to separate each leaf into halves.</u>

4. <u>Separate the small leaves of the heart and leave them whole</u>. Wash the lettuce in a lot of cold water. Lift up from the water and place on a towel.

5. <u>Dry the leaves gently, a few at a time</u>, to avoid bruising.

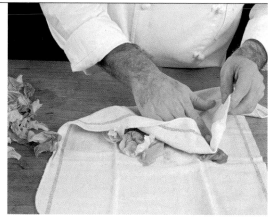

6. Or, <u>place in a salad dryer and spin</u> to extract as much water as possible from the salad.

7. <u>The lettuce should be dry and fluffy</u>. Remember that the best dressing will be ruined if watered down by a salad not sufficiently dried. Keep refrigerated in a towel until serving time. A tender lettuce, such as Boston, is never tossed with dressing ahead of time because it becomes wilted very fast.

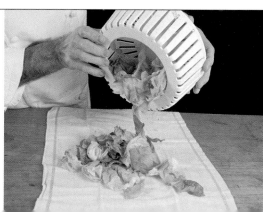

Braised Lettuce

(Laitues Braisées)

Boston lettuce makes a splendid and unusual cooked vegetable which goes well with veal, as well as chicken and beef. Although classically lettuce is braised with carrots, onions, and herbs, it is excellent simply boiled in water and finished with butter. One large head of lettuce will serve 2 as a garnish.

1. Remove any bruised leaves from the lettuce and wash the heads of lettuce in cold water, spreading the leaves gently under the stream of the water to remove any sand. Drop the lettuce heads into a large kettle of boiling, salted water and cover until it comes to a boil again. Uncover; if left covered, the lettuce will lose its vivid green color and turn yellowish. Place a wet paper towel on top of the lettuce; this will keep the lettuce underwater and help cook it evenly all around.

2. Let boil for 15 to 20 minutes, until the core of the lettuce feels tender to the point of a knife; it should be tender, not mushy. Immediately submerge the lettuce in iced water. When cold, remove the lettuce.

3. Be sure not to disturb the natural shape of the lettuce. Squeeze gently to extrude the excess water.

4. <u>Cut the smaller heads into 3 equal-sized pieces.</u> For a larger head, cut in quarters.

5. Place a piece, outside down, on the table and flatten the leafy end gently with a knife. Turn the leafy green part onto the center of the lettuce and, <u>holding it with the point of the knife, fold the core end over it.</u>

6. <u>Trim the core.</u> You should have a nice little package, slightly triangular. Sprinkle lightly with salt and pepper. Melt some butter in a large skillet. When hot, place the lettuce pieces, folded side up, one next to the other, in the skillet. Do not crowd the skillet. Cook on medium heat 4 to 6 minutes until slightly brown. Turn gently and cook 3 to 4 minutes on the other side.

7. <u>Arrange on a serving platter, folded side down.</u> You may coat the lettuce with a *demi-glace*, 1 tablespoon per lettuce, and sprinkle some butter cooked to a hazelnut color (*beurre noisette*) on top just before serving.

How to Prepare Endives

(Cuisson des Endives)

Belgian endives make a great salad. (Separate the leaves, pile them together, cut lengthwise into a fine julienne, then put in ice water to curl.) Endives are good cooked. They can be served plain or in their broth or with a white sauce. (Wrap a slice of ham around each head or half a head, cover with a white sauce, sprinkle with cheese, and brown under the broiler.) Cooked endives can also be sautéed in butter, covered with melted butter and chopped parsley, or they may be puréed and finished with cream and seasonings. The basic way to cook endive follows.

YIELD: 6 to 8 servings

3 pounds (1.4 kilograms) endive (medium size), approximately 12 to 15 pieces
½ tablespoon sugar
1 teaspoon salt
Juice of 1 lemon (approximately ¼ cup/59 milliliters)
⅓ cup (79 milliliters) water

1. Wash and clean the root of the endive very lightly if brown and discolored. Do not cut enough to separate the leaves. Trim any discolored leaves. Rinse carefully under cold water and arrange in layers in a sturdy stainless or enameled pan.

2. Add the sugar, salt, lemon juice, and water and cover the endive with a round of parchment paper. <u>Place a plate on top of the paper</u> and then the regular lid on top. The paper helps the endive steam better and the weight of the plate gently presses them down into their own juices. The top lid prevents the steam from escaping during cooking. Notice that the recipe has just a bit of liquid; the endive will render liquid of its own while cooking.

3. Bring to a boil on top of the stove and either simmer on top of the stove or place in a preheated 400 degree (204°C) oven for 25 to 30 minutes. The endives should still be firm when cooked. Let cool in the broth. When cool enough to handle, remove, arrange in a terrine or bowl, <u>pour the juices on top</u>, cover and keep in the refrigerator until ready to use.

How to Prepare Spinach
(Equeutage des Epinards)

There are two basic ways of preparing spinach: in purée, *when both leaf and stem are finely ground, and left whole with just the stem removed from the leaves. A purée of spinach is usually made with a light cream sauce, seasoned with nutmeg, salt, and pepper and served with fried croûtons and hard-cooked eggs. It is a very good accompaniment to a roast of veal or a roasted chicken. Spinach prepared whole is used in* timbale *or as a bed for poached eggs, fish, oysters, or veal. When using baby spinach, the stem is left in. It can be sautéed for a couple of minutes in a skillet with a bit of olive oil.*

LEAF SPINACH (EPINARDS EN BRANCHES)

1 pound (454 grams) fresh spinach

¼ inch (6 millimeters) water in a large saucepan (not aluminum) with a cover

½ teaspoon salt

1. Note how the long stem runs along the underside of the spinach leaf.

2. Take hold of the leaf on both sides of the stem and pull the stem out. The stems can be used in soups or mixed with other whole leaf spinach if the whole mixture is to be used for a *purée*. Wash the spinach carefully.

3. Bring the water and salt to a strong boil and pile the spinach on top. Cover and cook on high heat for 2 to 3 minutes. The water will barely come back to a boil. The spinach will wilt but still remain green.

4. Drain in a colander and run under cold water until cool enough to handle. <u>Press into a ball, squeezing out the water,</u> then cover with plastic wrap and keep in the refrigerator until needed.

SPINACH MOLD (TIMBALE D'EPINARDS)

YIELD: 6 servings

1 pound (454 grams) fresh spinach
   (prepared as above)

1 teaspoon salt

½ teaspoon freshly ground black
   pepper

⅛ teaspoon freshly grated nutmeg

2 tablespoons (28 grams) unsalted butter

2 teaspoons all-purpose flour

¾ cup (178 milliliters) milk

3 large eggs

½ cup (118 milliliters) heavy cream

6 slices firm white bread, cut into 2½-inch
   (6.5 centimeter) rounds and fried in a
   skillet with butter and vegetable oil until
   golden brown

6 ½-cup (118-milliliter) ramekins, buttered

Cook spinach as explained in steps 3 and 4 and chop coarsely. Sprinkle with the salt, pepper, and nutmeg. Melt the butter in a heavy saucepan and let it cook until it is brown. Add the spinach and mix with a fork. The dark brown butter gives the spinach a very nutty taste. Sprinkle the spinach with the flour, mix it in well, add the milk and bring to a boil, stirring constantly. Let it boil for ½ minute, take off the heat and let it cool off on the side for 10 to 15 minutes. Beat the eggs, mix in the heavy cream and stir the whole mixture into the spinach.

5. Preheat the oven to 350 degrees (177°C). <u>Fill the prepared molds with the mixture,</u> dividing the solids and liquids equally, and place in a pan of tepid water. Bake for 25 to 30 minutes, or until set. The water should not boil. The timbale should rest for at least 15 to 20 minutes before being unmolded. To serve, run a knife around the inside of the mold to loosen the timbale. Unmold each timbale on a piece of bread and arrange around a roast, or serve plain or with a light cream sauce.

Swiss Chard au Gratin

(Côtes de Bettes au Gratin)

Swiss chard and cardoon are excellent vegetables. Cardoon stalks are peeled the same way as are the Swiss chard. The pieces of stalks are cooked in water or in a blanc (a mixture of water and flour) and sometimes served with marrow, in gratins, or with cream sauce or red wine sauce. Swiss chard can be steamed and sautéed in butter or cooked in the juice of a roast. The green of the Swiss chard can be eaten and cooked like spinach. The Swiss chard is often finished with parsley and garlic and, at other times, is cooked in a gratin—which is what we make below—to serve with a roast chicken or broiled steaks.

YIELD: 6 to 8 servings

3 pounds (1.4 kilograms) chard with the widest possible stalks

1 tablespoon (14 grams) unsalted butter

1 tablespoon all-purpose flour

1½ cups (355 milliliters) milk

½ cup (118 milliliters) heavy cream

½ teaspoon salt

¼ teaspoon freshly ground white pepper

½ cup (50 grams) grated Swiss cheese

1. Cut the leaves off on each side of the stalk. The 3 pounds (1.4 kilograms) of Swiss chard when cleaned will yield approximately 1¾ pounds (795 grams) of stalks. As you get toward the end of the stem, <u>remove the green with the end of the stem</u>. Keep the greens for soups or cook as you would spinach.

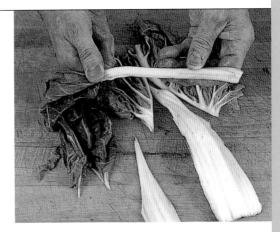

2. The stems are sometimes very wide and often not flat. <u>Cut the stem in strips so the stalks are more manageable and easier to peel.</u> To peel, cut a piece approximately 2 inches (5 centimeters) long from the stem. Do not cut completely through.

3. Break the "cut" piece and <u>pull off. Note the fibers that hang from the large part of the stem.</u>

4. <u>Take the fibers and pull them off so that a complete side of the stem is clean.</u> Repeat the same procedure on the underside of the stem. Removing the fibers makes the chard much more tender and is especially necessary when the vegetable is large and a bit old. As they are peeled, drop the stems in cold, lemony water to prevent discoloration.

5. Preheat the oven to 375 degrees (191°C). Drop the white stems into salted boiling water. Bring to a boil and boil for approximately 6 minutes. Drain in a colander. The pieces should be tender but still firm. For our white sauce, melt the butter in a saucepan over medium heat and add the flour. Whisk and cook for about 1 minute, then add the milk and, still whisking, bring to a boil. Boil for about ½ minute. Remove from the heat and add the cream, salt, and pepper. Mix well. Butter a 6-cup (1.4-liter) au gratin dish and arrange the chard in it. <u>Sprinkle with the grated cheese and pour the sauce on top.</u>

6. Place on a cookie sheet in the oven for about 40 minutes. If not brown enough after this time, place briefly under the broiler. <u>Let the gratin rest at least 10 minutes before serving.</u>

VEGETABLES

Fried Parsley

(Persil Frit)

Parsley should be fried in clean fat that is not too hot and there should be enough fat to cover the parsley completely. In classic French cooking, fried parsley is served with fried fish, fried eggs, or fried croquettes.

YIELD: about 1 cup

2 cups (120 grams) curly parsley, washed and well dried
3 cups (710 milliliters) canola oil
Dash of salt

1. Bring the oil to 275 degrees (135°C) and drop the parsley into the hot oil. Stir with your skimmer. Fry for about 1 minute. Lift out and dry on a paper towel. Sprinkle lightly with salt and serve immediately.

Dandelion Salad

(Salade de Pissenlits)

Dandelion salad announces the coming of spring and, although there is some cultivated dandelion, it does not approach the taste of the wild one. Dandelion should be picked early in the season. Look for plants growing in gravel or soft earth or under leaves. You want stems that have been covered half way up, and will have had a chance to turn white like endive, with the same tender and slightly bitter and stringent taste. Although dandelions are commonly eaten in the French countryside, our recipe is a specialty of Lyon. The fat of the lardons of unsmoked bacon, also known as pancetta, is used with olive oil in the dressing for the salad. The salad is served on lukewarm plates with crusty bread and with a light Beaujolais.

YIELD: 6 servings

1 pound (454 grams) cleaned, washed
   and dried dandelion greens

½ cup (150 grams) small sticks
   (*lardons*) pancetta

3 slices of toast

1 large garlic clove, peeled

2 hard-cooked large eggs, shelled

2 cloves garlic, peeled, crushed
   and chopped fine

1 small can (2 ounces/57 grams)
   anchovies in oil

1½ teaspoons good red
   wine vinegar

½ teaspoon salt

½ teaspoon freshly ground
   black pepper

2 tablespoons extra virgin
   olive oil

1. The dandelion greens should be picked before the flower stage or they will be tough and bitter. Use your knife to dig into the ground and remove the whole plant along with the root. Scrape the root of any dirt, removing any black parts but preserving as much of it as possible so the dandelion leaves still hold together by the root. Split the large plants in half so they can be washed properly. Wash several times in cold water, drain well and dry.

2. Cut the pancetta into ½-inch (13-millimeter) slices and then cut each slice into small strips (*lardons*). Place the *lardons* in cold water and bring to a boil. Boil for 8 minutes, drain, and rinse under cold water. Set aside.

3. Rub the toasted bread with a whole peeled clove of garlic on both sides. In order for the bread to "abrade" the garlic, it must be well toasted. Cut each slice of bread into 6 *croûtons*. Cut the 2 hard-cooked eggs into 6 segments each.

4. Place the anchovy fillets on the table and using the blade of a knife, crush and smear them down into a purée. Chop the 2 cloves of garlic very fine and add to the anchovies. Purée until smooth with the blade of a knife. Place the *lardons* in a skillet and fry them on medium heat until crisp. Meanwhile, place the purée of anchovies and garlic into a salad bowl, add the vinegar, salt, pepper, and olive oil and mix well. When the *lardons* are ready, add them with their fat to the mixture and stir well.

5. Add the washed and dried greens and mix thoroughly. Sprinkle the *croûtons* and the eggs on top. The salad should be room temperature. Serve immediately. This recipe is also good made from very thinly sliced red or white cabbage.

Glazed Onions

(Oignons Glacés)

Glazed onions are extensively used as a garnish in French cooking for coq au vin, boeuf bourguignon, *veal chop* grandmère, *chicken* Boivin, *and the like.*

YIELD: 4 servings

24 small white onions (the size of jumbo olives)
1 tablespoon (14 grams) unsalted butter
¼ tablespoon salt
1 teaspoon sugar
Water

1. Use tiny, white onions or shallots the size of a jumbo olive. Peel the onion by removing a small slice at the stem and one at the root end and removing the onion skin.

2. Place the onions in a saucepan in one layer. They should not overlap. Add enough water to barely cover the top of the onions. Add the butter, salt, and sugar. Place on high heat and boil uncovered until all the water is evaporated (about 12 minutes). Reduce the heat to medium and shake the saucepan or turn the onions to brown them on all sides.

3. Boiling the water is necessary because it cooks the onions. When the water has evaporated, what is left is butter and sugar. The onions will glaze in that mixture in a few minutes. If they do not glaze properly on direct heat, place for a few minutes under the broiler. <u>Transfer the glazed onions to a plate until needed.</u>

Potato-Cheese Stuffed Onion

(Oignon Farci au Fromage et Pommes de Terre)

YIELD: 6 servings

6 medium onions

2 cups (300 grams) onion trimmings (from onions listed above)

2 tablespoons (28 grams) unsalted butter

1 tablespoon olive oil

1 large baking potato, (about 12 ounces/340 grams), cooked with skin on

½ teaspoon salt

¼ teaspoon freshly ground black pepper

4 ounces (120 grams) cream cheese

2 tablespoons chopped chives

1 tablespoon grated Parmesan cheese

1. <u>Peel the onions but leave the root ends.</u> Cover the peeled onions with water, bring to a boil, and simmer at a gentle boil for about 30 minutes, until the onions are tender but still a bit firm. Drain and set aside to cool.

2. When cool, cut off a ½- to ¾-inch (1- to 2-centimeter) slice from the top of each onion so the opening will be larger. Reserve the tops. Using a small spoon, scoop out the inside of each onion, leaving about 2 or 3 outside layers for strength. Remove the root ends. You now have a receptacle for the stuffing.

3. For the stuffing: Chop the onion trimmings coarse. Melt the butter and add the oil to it in the skillet. When hot, add the chopped onions. Sauté over medium to high heat 4 to 5 minutes. Peel the cooked potato and chop coarse. Add to the onions in the skillet and continue cooking, tossing occasionally, for 5 minutes longer. Add the salt, pepper, cream cheese, and chives, and crush the mixture with a fork so it is well mixed. Remove from the heat.

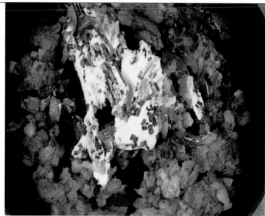

4. Preheat the oven to 400 degrees (204°C). Place the onions in a gratin dish. Using a spoon, stuff the hollowed out onions with the stuffing mixture. Sprinkle with the Parmesan cheese and bake for about 15 minutes if the stuffing is still hot when placed in the onion receptacle. If cold, leave the onions in the oven for at least 25 minutes under the broiler to create a nice brown crust.

Onion Soup

(Soupe à l'Oignon)

Onion soup is widely served all over France, sometimes gratinée, that is with a crust on top, sometimes just as a broth. It can be served in a large terrine, as well as in individual crock pots. In a brasserie or bistro, it is usually served gratinée. The onions are sometimes sautéed lightly and left in the soup, as in our recipe; other times they are browned to a dark stage, then slightly singed with flour, cooked, then pushed through a food mill, as in the Lyonnaise version, which is made with water rather than stock.

YIELD: 6 servings

- 4 cups (600 grams) thinly sliced onion (3 to 5 onions, depending on size)
- 1 pound (454 grams) good Swiss cheese (Emmenthaler or Gruyere), grated
- 3 tablespoons (42 grams) unsalted butter
- 10 cups (2.4 liters) chicken stock, or a mixture of chicken and beef stock, or a mixture of water and stock
- 1 teaspoon crushed, peeled and finely chopped garlic
- 1 teaspoon salt (to taste)
- 1 teaspoon freshly ground black pepper (to taste)

- 2 dozen (24) slices of a baguette, cut very thin and toasted in a 400 degree (204°C) oven until brown

1. Use sweet yellow onions, making sure you remove all the skin and the roots. Cut them in half across and slice very thinly. Melt the butter and brown the onions on medium heat in a large saucepan for 10 to 12 minutes, until brown. Stir in the stock, garlic, salt, and pepper, and boil for 10 minutes.

2. <u>Grate the cheese.</u> Preheat the oven to 400 degrees (204°C). Brown the bread for about 10 minutes.

3. <u>Place 4 to 5 slices of bread in each individual ovenproof bowl (use 12-ounce/340-gram bowls)</u>. Use a bowl with a lip or rim, which prevents the cheese from sinking into the soup as it cooks. Add a third of the cheese.

4. <u>Add the stock until the bowls are filled evenly and to the top.</u> This is very important because the cheese crust must not sink into the bowl if it is to brown in the oven. Sprinkle the cheese on top without pushing it into the liquid. You will need at least 2½ ounces (71 grams) of cheese per bowl.

5. <u>Press the cheese around the edges of each bowl</u> so that when it melts it sticks to the sides and forms a crust that will stay put instead of sinking into the liquid. Sprinkle the rest of the cheese over the tops.

6. Place the bowls on a cookie sheet and bake for approximately 35 minutes, until <u>nicely browned all around</u>. Serve right away, one bowl per guest.

Stuffed Mushrooms

(Champignons Farcis)

Mushroom caps can be stuffed with meat, fish, shellfish, vegetables, or most anything. Snails with garlic butter are often served in mushroom caps. The caps are cooked before they are stuffed. Our mushrooms are stuffed with a light, delicate mixture of shallots, raisins, and coriander.

YIELD: 3 servings

6 large mushrooms (about 12 ounces/340 grams)

1 tablespoon (15 grams) unsalted butter

¾ cup (80 grams) chopped shallots

2 tablespoons raisins

¼ teaspoon salt

¼ teaspoon freshly ground black pepper

2 tablespoons chopped parsley

1 tablespoon chopped fresh coriander (also called Chinese parsley or cilantro)

1 small, thin slice of bread, crumbed in processor

1 teaspoon olive oil

1. Preheat the oven to 400 degrees (204°C). Use large mushrooms, at least 1½ ounces (115 grams) each. Do not clean the mushrooms ahead, but when ready to use, wash them under water at the last moment if they are dirty. If washed ahead, they will discolor and become spongy. <u>Cut off the stems of the mushrooms with some of the underside of the caps.</u>

2. <u>Using a teaspoon, scoop out the inside of each mushroom, removing the stem and gills and leaving the cap as a receptacle.</u> Place the caps, open side down, in a roasting pan and bake for about 10 minutes so they render their juices. Meanwhile, chop the trimmings of the mushrooms coarse. Melt the butter in a skillet. When hot, add the chopped shallots, sauté about 30 seconds, and add the chopped mushrooms and raisins. Sauté for about 1 to 2 minutes, until the juices of the mushrooms have been released and evaporated.

3. When the mushrooms start sizzling again, add the salt, pepper, parsley, and coriander. Let cool for 10 minutes. Gently combine the bread crumbs with the oil, stirring with a fork. The bread should remain fluffy but still be slightly moist from the oil, which will make it brown better in the oven. <u>Stuff the mushroom receptacles with the raisin-coriander mixture and pat the bread crumbs on top.</u> Place under the broiler for 3 to 4 minutes, until nicely browned.

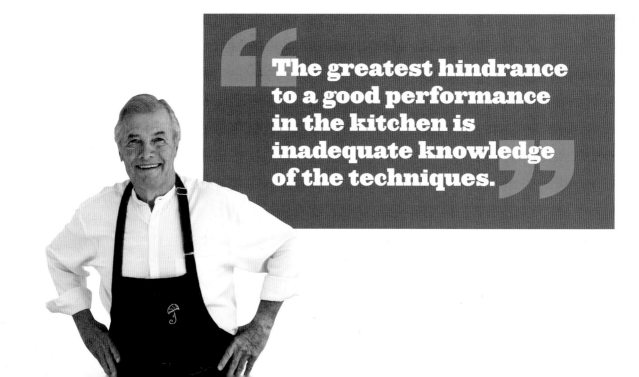

> **The greatest hindrance to a good performance in the kitchen is inadequate knowledge of the techniques.**

Identifying and Preparing Truffles

(Préparation des Truffes)

A truffle is a subterranean mushroom that grows through the root systems of certain trees in symbiosis with the host tree—primarily oaks, hazelnuts, and elms. The truffle matures in six to ten years and the precious fungi is usually found by a sow or a trained dog.

Fresh black truffles freeze better than white, which tend to turn brown and get mushy. When buying truffles, be sure—if they have not been brushed—to scrape the dirt off them before weighing. Unscrupulous sellers have been known to pack dirt into the holes and uneven surfaces of truffles to add weight to them. Fresh black truffles should have a strong aroma, be plump rather than wrinkled, and be firm and heavy. White truffles should also exude a strong perfume, be beige rather than brown, and be firm and plump.

Truffles spoil fairly rapidly: White truffles can be kept for five to six days, or up to 10 days if wrapped in paper or stored in rice; black truffles may keep a few days longer but will eventually shrink and spoil. Most of their flavor may spread through the refrigerator unless they are used as soon as possible or placed in oil or brandy or frozen. Truffles are best served with fast-cooked dishes such as scrambled eggs or omelets, or in potato dishes where the potatoes and truffles form a harmonious, delicate, and flavorful combination. A truffle salad flavored with walnut oil is also excellent made with an extra virgin olive oil.

1. The white Oregon truffle, on the left, is found in medium or small sizes and ranges from a pale beige to a darker brown. It has a musty, strong, woody aroma. Inside, it is basically the same in terms of color and design as the prized truffle of Italy, the *Tuber magnatum*, on the right, but does not have the same pungent aroma and taste.

2. The white truffle, *Tuber magnatum*, the most expensive of all truffles, should be brushed under lukewarm water to remove any dirt from the crannies and holes on the surface and then dried. The surface is smooth and need not be peeled. It should have a dry, strong, pungent aroma. Store, refrigerated, for only a few days, embedded in rice. The truffle can also be sliced and kept in oil or brandy. It's best served raw in slices or grated on pasta or risotto.

3. From left to right: The *Tuber magnatum*, the summer black truffle (*Tuber aestevum*), and the Oregon white truffle. The truffle being brushed is the large *Tuber melanosporum*, the prized "black diamond" and best of the black truffles. This specimen is quite large and weighs approximately 6 ounces. It has a rugged, tough outside, as opposed to the white truffle, which has a smooth exterior.

4. A brushed and cut summer black truffle *Tuber aestevum*. Like the *Tuber brumalle*, it will get darker when cooked. Uncooked, it will have a dark brownish interior with the striation of the white mycelium.

5. The large *Tuber melanosporum*, the most expensive and best of the black truffles, cut in half. The inside is a dark gray, rather than brown like the summer black truffle.

6. Cut the *Tuber melanosporum* into 4 pieces and <u>trim off the outside skin of each piece</u>.

7. <u>Finely chop the skin, which is tougher</u>. The trimmings can be used in pâtés and sauces, or kept in Cognac.

8. <u>Cooked and canned truffles stored in alcohol</u>. As a result of cooking, they are darker in color than the fresh truffle. Keep them in the refrigerator immersed in brandy. The liquid can be used for flavoring pâtés or sauces.

Potato and Truffle Cake

(Pommes Sarladaise)

This dish is named after Sarlat, a town in the southwest of France where a great many truffles are marketed during the winter months. The truffle and potato combination works extremely well, and the entire dish picks up and retains the strong, heady smell and taste of the truffles. For the cook who cannot find or afford expensive truffles, the potato cake can be done the same way, omitting the truffle, and it then becomes Potatoes Anna.

YIELD: 4 servings

1½ pounds (680 grams) baking potatoes (6 cups peeled and
  sliced)
1 large truffle or several small ones
5 tablespoons (70 grams) unsalted butter
4 tablespoons peanut oil
½ teaspoon salt

1. Peel the potatoes and round off the sides of 3 of them to create cylinders of about the same size. Thinly slice (about ⅛-inch or 3-millimeter thick) the trimmed potatoes by hand or with an automatic slicer. Wash the slices in cold water, drain, and set aside. You should have 2 cups (300 grams). The slices of potato from the cylinders will be round, uniform, and of equal size. They are lined up in the skillet to create a design. The unequal-sized pieces of potato are used for the inside of the cake. Thinly slice all the other potatoes, including the trimmings from the 3 rounded potatoes. Wash in cold water and set aside.

2. Trim the truffle(s) of all the rough fibrous skin on the outside and chop the skin into small pieces. Thinly slice the centers of the truffles and set aside. Butter a large skillet, preferably non-stick, with 2 tablespoons (28 grams) of the butter. In another skillet, place 1 tablespoon of the oil and, when hot, add the 2 cups (300 grams) of sliced potatoes of equal size and a dash of salt. Sauté for about 30 seconds, just long enough to coat the potato slices with oil and soften them a bit. Place on a cookie sheet to cool.

3. In the bottom of your no-stick buttered skillet, <u>arrange the slices of sautéed potatoes, placing a slice of truffle between every 2 or 3 slices of potatoes</u>. Remember that this will be unmolded and served upside down, so this layer will be the top of the dish. The truffles should be completely covered underneath by potato slices so they don't dry out during cooking. (The truffles will be visible through the thinly sliced potatoes.) Arrange the first layer so the whole bottom of the skillet is covered with the slices of potatoes and truffles.

4. In the other skillet, <u>add the remaining 2 tablespoons of oil and sauté the additional 4 cups (600 grams) of sliced potatoes (including the trimmings) with a dash of salt</u>. Sauté for about 1 minute and add the chopped peelings of the truffles.

5. Preheat the oven to 400 degrees (204°C). Place this potato-truffle mixture on top of the arranged slices of potatoes and truffles. Cook on top of the stove over medium to high heat for 2 to 3 minutes to brown the potatoes. <u>Using a large, flat spatula, press the potatoes so they are well packed against the bottom of the pan</u>. Dot the potatoes with the remaining 3 tablespoons (42 grams) of butter and cover with a piece of parchment paper or aluminum foil, cut to fit the skillet. With the spatula, press the paper onto the potatoes.

6. Place in the oven for 30 minutes with the paper in position, pressing the paper with the spatula again after 10 minutes to pack the potatoes more tightly. When the potatoes are cooked, set them aside for 4 to 5 minutes to cool and set. Then remove the paper and <u>invert onto a serving platter</u>.

Fried Potato Balls

(Pommes Parisienne)

The potato is probably the greatest food contribution that the New World made to the Old. It was introduced in France in the second half of the seventeenth century, but was first used as a decorative plant. It was popularized by an agronomist named Parmentier during the eighteenth century.

YIELD: 6 servings

4 or 5 large Idaho potatoes, peeled
2 tablespoons (28 grams) unsalted butter
1 tablespoon canola oil
3 tablespoons *demi-glace*
Dash salt

1. Peel the large baking potatoes. Keep in cold water to avoid discoloration. <u>Push a round melon ball cutter down into the potato with your thumb as far as it will go.</u>

2. <u>Still pressing the tool into the potato, pivot the cutter in a downward motion to scoop out a ball.</u> Repeat, using as much of the potato as you can. The trimmings are used in soup or mash. Place in cold water again to avoid discoloration. When ready to use, drain the potatoes, cover with fresh cold water, bring to a boil, and boil 2 minutes. Drain. This blanching of the potatoes will prevent them from discoloring when out of the water and will put some moisture into them. With the additional moisture, the potatoes will cook faster when sautéed in butter and have a softer, nicer consistency.

3. When ready to serve, melt the butter and oil in a skillet and, when hot, add the potato balls. They should be in one layer. Sauté for about 10 minutes over medium to high heat, shaking the skillet so the potatoes brown evenly on all sides. When they are tender, drain the fat out of the skillet and add *demi-glace*. Continue to cook the potatoes over high heat, shaking the pan occasionally so the *demi-glace* reduces and forms a glaze that coats the potatoes. Salt lightly. Serve immediately.

Potato Ovals

(Pommes Cocotte et Anglaise)

There are many ways of shaping potatoes for a fancy party. Nothing goes to waste as the trimmings can be used for soup or mashed potatoes or croquettes.

COCOTTE

1. Cut large potatoes in half. Cut each half into two pieces.

2. Cut the quarters into equal elongated pieces.

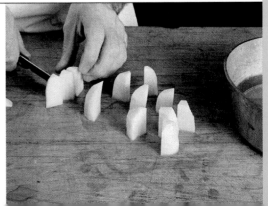

3. <u>Trim or "turn" each piece into a little football-shaped potato</u>. These are *pommes cocotte*. They are blanched for 1 minute in boiling water, drained, and sautéed in butter and oil and served as garnish for roasts, steak, and the like.

ANGLAISE

1. Trim potatoes at both ends and <u>cut into large elongated chunks</u>.

2. <u>Trim each piece into a football-shaped potato</u>. Classially it should have 7 sides. These potatoes can be steamed or boiled (*pommes à l'anglaise*), blanched and fried (*pommes château*), or cooked with butter and a little bit of water (*pommes fondantes*).

3. Left to right: <u>groupings of *pommes poisson* to serve steamed with fish or meat, *pommes cocotte*, *pommes à l'anglaise*, *pommes parisienne*</u>. Shaping the potatoes ensures proper cooking but is essentially done for aesthetic reasons. These kinds of potatoes should be cooked as closely as possible to the moment they will be eaten. If cooked ahead, they will taste reheated.

Deep Fried Potatoes

(Pommes Pailles, Allumettes, et Pont-Neuf)

Deep-fried potatoes take on different names depending on the shapes they are cut into before cooking. Though three kinds of potatoes shown here are all cut into sticks, the sizes are different and hence, the names.

1. Peel each potato and trim to look like a parallelepiped (a rectangular block). All trimmings are used in soups or in mashed potatoes.

2. Cut it into ⅜-inch (9.5-millimeter) thick slices.

3. Stack the slices together and cut into ⅜-inch (9.5-millimeter) sticks for matchstick potatoes (*allumettes*) or into ¾- to 1-inch (19-millimeter to 2.5-centimeter) sticks for the *pont-neuf*.

4. The straw potatoes (*pommes pailles*) can be cut by hand or with a _mandoline_.

5. Left to right: <u>straw, *pont-neuf* and matchstick potatoes</u>. The straws are cooked in 400 degree (204°C) oil until crisp. The *pont-neuf* and matchstick (French fried) are blanched first in 325 degree (160°C) oil until tender but still soft and white. At serving time, they are finished in 400-degree (204°C) oil for a couple of minutes until brown and crisp.

Straw Potato Cake

(Pommes Paillasson)

Pommes paillasson (*which translates to "doormat"*) *are made from potatoes that are peeled, washed, and then cut into a fine julienne with a mandoline (a slicer) or by hand. Once the potatoes have been cut into julienne, they have to be cooked right away or kept in water to prevent discoloration. The water bath washes off some of the potato's starch. If the potatoes are not kept in water but are cooked right away, the starch left in the potatoes will make them "cake" or hold better. On the other hand, they will be slightly gooey inside. If they have been washed, they will be less starchy in taste but more fragile in construction—the potatoes will be more likely to disentangle. The starch acts like a glue. Whichever method you use, the taste is the same, only the texture is slightly different. Use large Idaho potatoes. One large potato will give you approximately 1 cup (150 grams). These potatoes are known as rosti in Switzerland and also Darphin potatoes in France.*

YIELD: 4 to 6 servings

3 cups (450 grams) julienned potatoes (use baking potatoes)
2 tablespoons (28 grams) unsalted butter
4 tablespoons olive oil
¼ teaspoon salt
Dash of freshly ground black pepper

1. Peel and wash the potatoes, then cut into julienne. Wash the julienne and dry in paper towels or cook right away. In a non-stick skillet, heat half the butter and oil. When very hot, add potatoes, salt, and pepper and coat well with fat by stirring. Use a fork to spread the potatoes around.

2. Use a large, flat spoon to press the potatoes down so the strips cohere together into a cake. Cook on medium heat for 4 to 5 minutes, pressing once in a while. Flip the pancake over and cook another 4 to 5 minutes on medium low heat. The pancake should not be more than 1 inch (26 millimeters) thick, crunchy on the outside and soft in the middle. If you cannot flip it in one stroke, place a plate on top, turn it upside down and slide back into the skillet. Serve as soon as possible.

Straw Potato Nest

(Nid en Pommes Paille)

The potato nest is done with julienne potatoes and is usually used as a garnish filled with tiny pommes soufflés or potato croquettes. To make the nest, you need a special double wire basket available in specialty stores. For each nest, you need approximately 2 cups (250 to 300 grams) of loose julienne potatoes. Washing the potatoes julienne will give you a nest which won't hold together as well as the one with unwashed potatoes which, however, won't release as well from the metal nest because the starch will stick to the metal wires. However, it works both ways.

1. Using a knife or a *mandoline* (vegetable slicer), slice the potatoes into slices $1/16$-inch (1.6 millimeters) thick. Pile them together and cut into a thin julienne. Wash and dry, if desired.

2. Dip the wire basket in the hot oil. Then fill the bottom part of the basket with potato strips. Make a hole in the center and place the smaller basket inside to create a nest.

3. Secure both parts with the clip.

4. Drop the potatoes in 400 degree (204°C) vegetable oil and cook for 4 to 5 minutes on high heat. Be sure that the potato nest stays completely immersed during cooking by holding it down into the oil.

5. To unmold, remove the clip and trim away the pieces of potato sticking through both the outside and inside of the nest. This makes it easier to release the potatoes from the mold.

6. Jiggle the smaller wire basket and lift it up from the potatoes.

7. The potatoes may still be hard to remove. <u>Turn upside down, and using a towel, press the mesh to bend it and help the potatoes release.</u> Use a small knife to pry it out.

8. <u>The potato nest released, and ready to be served.</u>

Waffled Potatoes

(Pommes Gaufrettes)

1. The *gaufrettes* potatoes are cut with the *mandoline*, which is a special vegetable cutter. Using the side with the wrinkled or "teeth" blade, <u>hold the potato with the palm of your hand or a towel and cut straight down.</u>

2. Turn the potato 90 degrees. Your fingers are now facing the other direction. Cut straight down. Turn the potato 90 degrees for the next slice. <u>You are crisscrossing the slices, to achieve the waffle shape.</u> If the holes are not evident, the slices are too thick. If the potato slice does not hold together, but is all stringy, the slices are too thin. Adjust the thickness accordingly.

3. Wash the potato slices, dry, and <u>deep fry in 375 degree (191°C) oil.</u> Unlike *pont-neufs* or *allumettes*, which are cooked twice, *gaufrettes* are cooked only once, until nicely browned and very crisp.

Waffle Potato Nest

(Nid en Pommes Gaufrettes)

1. Using the *mandoline*, cut the waffle potatoes. <u>Arrange slices of waffle potatoes in the bottom layer of the wire basket</u> to simulate a tulip.

2. Place the smaller basket on top, secure with the clip and dip in 400 degree (204°C) vegetable oil. Make sure that the whole nest is immersed. It will take approximately 3½ minutes to cook. Remove from the oil, unclip and start jiggling the two parts of the nest to separate them. <u>The nest may remain attached to the top part</u> or may stick to the bottom part. (In our case, the nest stuck to the top.)

3. <u>Using a knife, pry all around and trim the inside to release the nest</u>. The waffle nest is even more fragile than the straw potato nest.

4. The potato nest can be filled with straw potatoes or soufflé potatoes and served as a garnish for roasted poultry.

Puffed Potato Slices

(Pommes Soufflées)

Making the puff, or inflated potato, called pommes soufflées, *is a delicate operation. If the potatoes have too much moisture, as new potatoes often have, they will not puff. If they are soft and marbled, as old potatoes frequently are, they will not puff either. Often 15 to 20 percent of any one batch stays flat. In restaurants, the flat ones are served as regular fried potatoes.*

According to Larousse Gastronomique, the recipe was discovered accidentally in 1837 at the inauguration ceremonies for a railroad service to a small town near Paris. A local restaurant prepared a meal, including fried potatoes, for the official delegation. The train was late and the chef removed the potatoes from the fryer half cooked. At serving time, he was stupefied to see they puffed as he dipped them back in the hot oil. The chemist Michel-Eugène Chevreul worked out the reasons and a recipe was compiled.

1. In restaurants, the first cooking of the potatoes takes place during the morning or afternoon preparation. They are dipped again in hot oil to re-inflate and crisp just before serving. <u>Peel the potatoes and trim each one into the shape of a cylinder.</u> (They can also be trimmed into a tube or a rectangle.) Use the trimmings in soup, purée, hash browns, and the like.

2. Trim the ends of the potatoes. The slices should be the same size and shape to insure proper cooking, and for aesthetic reasons. <u>Here they are cut into straight slices approximately ³/₁₆-inch (4 millimeters) thick.</u>

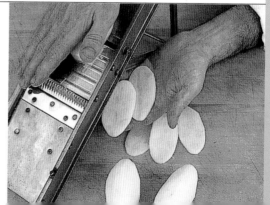

3. For another look, the slice also can be cut on the crinkle side of the blade <u>into slices about ⅜-inch (9.5-millimeters) thick</u>.

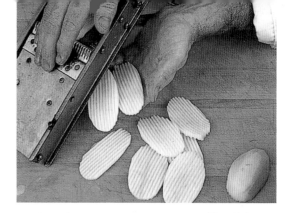

4. Pour vegetable oil, about 2½ to 3 inches deep, into two saucepans. Heat one to 325 degrees (163°C) and the other to 375 degrees (191°C). <u>Drop 15 to 20 slices into the 325 degree (163°C) fryer</u> and shake back and forth on the heat for 6 to 7 minutes (an asbestos pad will make the shaking easier by helping the pan to slide). Be careful not to splash oil on your hands while shaking the pan. You have to get a rhythm going. After 4 to 5 minutes, the slices should come to the surface and blisters should start to appear on them. Keep shaking another minute.

5. Stop shaking the pan. Using a skimmer, remove a few slices at a time. Let drain and soften for 5 to 6 seconds, then dip into the 375 degree (191°C) fryer. <u>The potatoes should swell instantly. Do not let them brown unless you are serving them at this point</u>. As they puff up, transfer to a pan lined with a paper towel to drain. Finish the whole batch in this manner. You will notice they deflate as you place them on the towel. Pick out the ones that puffed up and arrange them on the pan. Eat or discard the other slices. Covered with a paper towel, the good ones will keep at room temperature for several hours.

6. At serving time, <u>drop the slices in the 375 degree (191°C) fryer</u>, moving them around with a skimmer so that they brown evenly. They should be very crisp to stay puffed. (During the first cooking, the surface of the slices becomes watertight. When the slices are dropped into hot oil, the water "imprisoned" inside tries to escape, pushing from the center, <u>making the potato puff up</u>.)

7. Sprinkle with salt and serve immediately on folded napkins. Here are some straight and crinkled *pommes soufflées*.

Potato Flats

(Galette de Pommes de Terre)

In this fried potato pancake, the potatoes are processed raw in a food processor. There are many variations of potato pancakes.

YIELD: about 20

2 potatoes (12 ounces/340 grams)

½ cup (75 grams) all-purpose flour

2 large eggs

½ pound (227 grams) ricotta cheese

2 tablespoons chopped chives

2 teaspoons baking powder

½ teaspoon salt

¼ teaspoon freshly ground black pepper

2 tablespoons canola oil and 1 tablespoon (14 grams) unsalted butter per skillet

1. Peel 2 potatoes, cut into pieces, and place in a food processor with the flour. Process until smooth and add 2 eggs and the ricotta cheese. Process until well mixed. Transfer the mixture to a bowl and add the chopped chives. Sprinkle baking powder on top with salt and pepper, and mix just enough to combine. Heat corn oil and butter in a large skillet and, when hot, add 2 good tablespoons of the potato mixture per pancake, cooking 6 to 8 at one time if your skillet is large enough. Sauté for approximately 2 minutes over medium to high heat on one side. Turn and cook 2 minutes on the other side. These are best when served as soon as possible after cooking. They will be nicely browned with the edges darker and crunchier.

EGGS

Separating Eggs

(Séparation des Oeufs)

When you use eggs, you often end up with an excess of yolk or white. The egg whites, almost pure albumin, freeze well. Defrosted egg whites whip as well as fresh egg whites, and they do not pick up odors. The yolk, however, high in fat, does not freeze well. Unless the temperature goes as low as -20 degrees (-29°C), bacteria will grow in the egg yolk. In addition, yolks easily become freezer burnt. However, they can be kept for a day in the refrigerator covered with a layer of water to prevent a skin from forming on top. Pour the water off before using. For all of our egg recipes, use organic fresh eggs from a farm.

1. To separate the yolk from the white, crack the egg on a flat surface. Cracking it on a sharp edge tends to push some shell inside the egg, introducing bacteria. Open the egg, keeping one half upright to hold the yolk. Let the white drop into the bowl.

2. Pour the yolk into the empty half shell, letting more white drop into the bowl as you are transferring the yolk from one shell to the other.

3. An alternative method is to <u>pour the egg into your hand</u> and let the white drip through your fingers.

Poaching Eggs

(Oeufs Pochés)

When making poached eggs, the fresher the eggs are the better. The older the eggs, the more the whites will tend to spread in the water. A dash of vinegar (distilled white vinegar) is added to the water to help firm the egg white. Salt is omitted because it has the reverse effect and tends to thin down the white. Poached eggs lend themselves to an infinite number of combinations, from the very simple poached egg on toast, to the sophisticated eggs Benedict, served with ham, hollandaise sauce, and truffles. Eggs can be poached several hours, even a day, ahead (as most restaurants do) and kept refrigerated in a bowl of cold water, eliminating any last-minute panic when you want to serve several people at once.

1. To poach 8 eggs, pour 3 quarts (3 scant liters) of water and ¼ cup (59 milliliters) white vinegar into a large saucepan, preferably no stick. Bring to a boil; then, reduce to a simmer. Break one egg at a time on a flat surface. Holding it as closely as you can to the water (to avoid splashing), <u>open it with both thumbs and let it slide into the water</u>. Drop your eggs at the place where the water is simmering so that they don't go down into the water too fast and stick to the bottom. If you are afraid of burning

your fingers, break the eggs in a saucer or bowl and slide them into the water. Go as fast as you can so that the difference in cooking time is not too great between the first and the last egg.

2. As soon as all the eggs are in the water, <u>drag a large slotted spoon across the surface of the water</u> to move the eggs about a bit and keep them from sticking to the bottom of the pan. Once some of the whites have hardened, the eggs will not stick any more.

3. Large eggs take approximately 4 minutes to cook. If you like them more runny or more set, the timing should be changed accordingly. Check the eggs by lifting them, one at a time, with a slotted spoon and pressing them slightly with your fingers. The whites should be set, but the yolks soft to the touch. <u>As soon as an egg is cooked, transfer it to a bowl of iced water.</u> This stops the cooking and washes off the vinegar.

4. When the eggs are cold, lift each one from the water and <u>trim off the hanging pieces with a knife</u> or a pair of scissors. Place in a bowl of fresh cold water.

5. Drain well if you use them cold, or keep refrigerated in cold water. They will keep for at least a couple of days. To use hot, place in a strainer, lower into boiling water for approximately 1 minute, drain, and serve immediately.

Omelets

(Omelettes)

There are different types of omelets, from the classic French version to the country or flat types. There is not one better than another; they are all good in their own way. Omelet making is both simple and difficult. A perfect omelet is golden in color on top, delicate and creamy in the center. In addition to fresh eggs and unsalted butter, there are three other major ingredients: the right pan, practice, and high heat. It is essential to have an 8- to 10-inch (20- to 25-centimeter) no stick omelet pan, with rounded, sloping shoulders that give the omelet a nice shape and help it slide easily onto the plate when cooked. Be sure to use high heat, and do not use too much butter, or the omelet will be wrinkled. The whole operation should not take you more than a couple of minutes.

CLASSIC OMELET *FINES HERBES*

YIELD: 1 omelet

3 large eggs
Dash salt and freshly ground black pepper
2 tablespoons fresh herb mixture (finely chopped parsley, chervil, tarragon, and chives)
1 tablespoon (14 grams) unsalted butter

1. Beat the eggs with salt, pepper, and the herb mixture in a bowl with a fork until well combined; that is, when you lift up the fork, pieces of egg white should no longer separate from the yolk. For a classic French omelet, place the butter in a non-stick skillet 6 to 8 inches in diameter and melt over high heat. Swirl the butter in the pan and, when foaming, add the eggs. Holding the fork flat, stir the eggs as fast as you can while shaking the pan with your other hand. Continue shaking and stirring without stopping so the eggs coagulate uniformly.

2. Still stirring, notice that the eggs are still moist in the center. Incline your pan forward so most of the eggs gather toward the far end of the pan as they set. Now stop stirring while the eggs are still moist in the center.

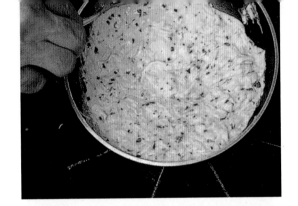

3. Using your fork, bring the near lip over toward the center of the omelet. Note that as the mass of eggs has moved toward the far end of the pan, it has thinned out around the edges. Only the two thin lips are flipped over, first from one end, then the other, to enclose the thick, moist center.

4. Press the fold into place. Note: this motion should create a roundish edge.

5. Run your fork between the edge of the pan and the far lip of the omelet to loosen it. Using the palm of your hand, tap the handle of the pan gently to shake the omelet and make it lift onto itself, so the far lip rises above the edge of the pan.

6. Fold the far lip back toward the center of the omelet, meeting the other lip. Press with the flat of the fork to make sure the omelet comes to a point at each end. While holding the serving plate in your left hand, first bang the end of the pan gently so the omelet pulls together against the edge of the pan. Then, invert the omelet onto the plate and serve immediately.

7. The omelet should be very moist, creamy, and wet in the center.

COUNTRY-STYLE *FINES-HERBES* OMELET:

1. Melt the butter in the omelet pan. Mix together the eggs, salt, pepper, and herbs. When the butter is hot and the foaming has subsided, pour the egg-herb mixture into the center of the pan and cook over medium heat, allowing the eggs to set into large curds and curl at the edges. Then, with the tines of your fork, stir the eggs so the runny part fills the areas between the set curds.

2. When most of the eggs are set but still slightly liquid inside, the omelet is ready.

3. <u>Fold the omelet in half.</u> You will notice that the outside will have a nice brown color as opposed to the classic omelet, which is pale yellow. Invert onto a plate and serve immediately.

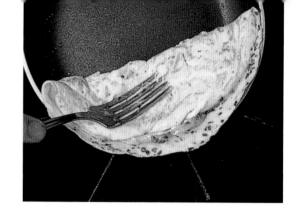

STUFFED OMELET HUNTER-STYLE

YIELD: 1 omelet

2 teaspoons (10 grams) unsalted butter
1 medium mushroom, diced
1 chicken liver, cut into ¾-inch (2 centimeter) dice
Salt and freshly ground black pepper
2 tablespoons tomato sauce
1 teaspoon chopped chives
3 large eggs

1. Heat 1 teaspoon (5 grams) of the butter and, when hot, sauté the mushroom for about 30 seconds. Add the chicken liver and dash of salt and pepper. Sauté another 30 seconds and <u>add the tomato sauce and chives.</u> Set aside.

2. Mix the eggs and dash of salt and pepper with your fork. Heat the remaining 1 teaspoon (5 grams) butter in an omelet pan. When hot, add the eggs and <u>stir, following the techniques used to make a classic omelet.</u>

3. Fold the near lip onto the omelet. <u>Arrange most of the</u> <u>solids from the liver-mushroom mixture down the center of</u> <u>the omelet</u>, saving the remainder for the garnish, pushing lightly with your fork to hold them in place.

4. Tap on the end of the handle gently to bring the far lip up. <u>Press the far lip of the omelet over the stuffing, making</u> <u>sure that the ends of the omelet are pointed.</u> Bang the end of the omelet pan gently so the omelet sits on the far edge of the pan. Invert onto a serving plate. Place a little extra sauce around the omelet and a bit of the liver-mushroom mixture at each end. Serve immediately.

FLAT OMELET, FARMER-STYLE

YIELD: 1 omelet

2 slices salted bacon, cut into ³/₄-inch (2 centimeter) strips
½ Idaho potato, cut into 12 unpeeled, very thin slices
2 tablespoons minced chives
3 large eggs
Dash freshly ground black pepper

1. Cook the bacon strips on both sides for a few minutes, until nicely browned. Add the potato slices and sauté for another 4 to 5 minutes, <u>until the thin slices are nicely</u> <u>browned.</u> <u>Add the chives.</u> With a fork, beat the eggs with a dash of pepper (salt is not necessary because of the bacon).

2. Add the eggs and <u>drag the tines of a fork between the curds</u> to expose the runny eggs to the cooking surface.

3. When the eggs are set, <u>still slightly creamy and liquid in the center</u>, the omelet can be flipped over (if you feel dexterous enough), or you can slide or invert it directly onto a plate. Serve immediately.

4. The 4 omelets: From the top left, clockwise, the flat omelet farmer-style, the country-style *fines-herbes* omelet, the classic stuffed omelet hunter-style, and the classic *fines-herbes* omelet.

Eggs "Cocotte" with Cream

(Oeufs Cocotte Bressane)

These eggs are simple to make. The eggs are cooked in small soufflé molds or ramekins in a water bath and eaten as a first course for dinner or for a light breakfast or brunch. Many variations can be made by adding ingredients—from mushrooms to herbs to shrimp or cream—to the top or bottom.

YIELD: 6 servings

6 jumbo eggs, very fresh
Salt and freshly ground black pepper
6 tablespoons heavy cream

1. Use small ramekins or soufflé molds, no more than ½ cup (118 milliliters) in size. <u>Butter the molds</u> and sprinkle salt and pepper in the bottom.

2. <u>Break an egg into each ramekin.</u>

3. Place the ramekins in a skillet with tepid water around (a *bain-marie*) and cover. Place on top of the stove and let the water boil for approximately 4 minutes. The cover holds in the steam, which makes the top glaze. The eggs should be barely set and still soft in the center.

4. Note that the eggs are shiny and glazed on top. Remove from the *bain-marie* and serve garnished or plain. With a bit of heavy cream on top, they are called eggs *Bressane*; with peas, they will become eggs *Clamard*, etc. They can also be unmolded on a crouton.

5. Sometimes the garnish is placed in the bottom of the mold and the egg is broken directly on top. In this case, put 1 tablespoon of heavy cream in the bottom of the mold, break the egg on top and cook, covered, as indicated above.

Scrambled Eggs

(Oeufs Brouillés)

In classic French cooking, the scrambled eggs are whisked into a very smooth purée and finished with cream and butter. They can be cooked in a double boiler using a wooden spatula, or on a low to medium heat using a whisk. Use a heavy, sturdy saucepan to obtain even heat. The eggs can be garnished with a bit of brown sauce or with a sauce Périgueux (a brown sauce with chopped truffles), or a fresh purée of tomatoes and grated Parmesan cheese, or peas, or sautéed chicken livers, etc. They can also be served plain. The eggs acquire a different name with each different garnish. They can be served as a first course, as well as for breakfast or lunch.

YIELD: 2 to 3 servings

5 large eggs
Salt and freshly ground black pepper to taste
1 tablespoon, plus ½ tablespoon (21 grams) unsalted butter
2 tablespoons heavy cream or sour cream

1. Break the eggs into a bowl and add salt and pepper. Beat the eggs with a whisk to mix well. Set ¼ cup of the raw eggs aside to be used at the end of the cooking time. Melt the butter in a heavy saucepan. When foaming, pour in the eggs and cook over medium heat, stirring gently with the whisk. Be sure to get around the bottom edge of the pan with your whisk, since the eggs will have a tendency to set and harden there first. Keep cooking and whisking gently until the mixture gets very creamy.

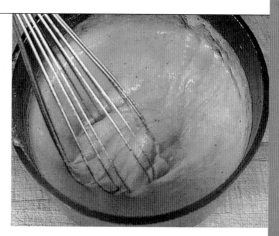

2. The eggs should have the smallest possible curds. Continue cooking until you can see the bottom of the pan as the whisk is drawn through the eggs. Remove the pan from the heat; the eggs will continue cooking, especially around the edges of the pan. Add the reserved raw eggs and the cream and keep mixing; the uncooked eggs and cream will absorb the heat still generated by the pan. Transfer to a serving dish and serve immediately.

Deep-Fried Eggs

(Oeufs Frits Américaine)

This is a different way to prepare eggs. Instead of poaching them in water, they are poached in oil. The centers are runny and soft, just like regular poached eggs. Only one egg can be done at a time, and it must be cooked very fast so that the white is wrapped around the yolk and nicely browned. Deep-fried eggs are usually served with bacon and fried tomatoes for lunch or breakfast.

YIELD: 3 servings

2½ to 3 cups (592 to 710 milliliters) canola or peanut oil
6 large eggs, very fresh

1. Pour the oil into a 2-inch/5-centimeter-deep no stick skillet. (There should be at least 1½ inches/5 centimeters of oil so the eggs can be immersed.) Heat to 360 degrees (180°C) and warm two wooden spatulas in it (to prevent the eggs from sticking to the spatulas). Break one egg at a time into the oil, or break into a cup and slide it into the oil if you are afraid of being splashed with hot oil.

2. Then, use the two spatulas to gather the egg white around the yolk.

3. "Squeeze" the egg slightly (between the spatulas, against the side of the skillet) for a few seconds to keep the egg white contained—so it doesn't spread as it cooks. If the egg sticks to one spatula, scrape it off with the other spatula. Turn the egg in the oil and cook it for about 2 minutes altogether. Remove the egg with a slotted spoon, drain on paper towels and serve immediately. When the egg is taken out of the oil it will be nicely puffed. If kept a few minutes, it will deflate slightly.

4. Notice that the center has the consistency of a poached egg. Like the preceding egg recipes, this dish can be served with a variety of garnishes and with each different garnish, it changes its name. Here it is served on a cooked slice of eggplant garnished with sautéed red pepper and cilantro.

> **Repeat and those techniques will become so much part of yourself that you will never forget them.**

FISH
&SHELL

FISH

Oysters

(Huitres)

Aficionados prefer oysters raw on the half shell with a dash of lemon, or a mignonnette sauce made by mixing together ½ cup (118 milliliters) good red wine vinegar, ¼ cup (36 grams) chopped shallots, ½ teaspoon coarsely ground black pepper and a dash of salt. (Crushed peppercorn is called mignonnette; hence, the name of the sauce.) These fine mollusks should be used, as all shellfish, only if they are alive and fresh. Despite the fact that restaurants sometimes wash oysters to get rid of any lurking bits of shell that might present problems to their patrons, once oysters are opened, they should not be washed. Oysters are often larger and fatter in the United States than they are in France. The "green" flat oysters of France, the Belons and Marennes, are now grown in Maine. Oysters are usually poached in their own broth. Be sure not to overcook these delicate shellfish or they will toughen. As soon as the edges of the oyster whiten and curl up, they are cooked enough.

1. Some of the oysters available from good markets are, top 2 rows, from left to right, closed and open: Apalachicola, Cotuit, Pacific oysters; and bottom 2 rows, from left to right, closed and open: Wellfleet, Blue Point, Belon, Chincoteague. Other well-known varieties include the Louisiana, Kent Island, Cape Cod, and the tiny, delicious Olympia, all of which can be bought in good markets, depending on the time of the year and availability.

2. Wash the oysters under cold water. Use special sturdy oyster knives with pointed tips like the ones shown here. Hold the oysters in a thick towel or pot holder to prevent an accident.

3. Shucking oysters: With the oyster held firmly in the palm of your hand, <u>pry and push the tip of the blade into the pointed end</u> at the "hinge," between the top flat shell and the convex bottom one. You may have to exert a great amount of pressure to insert the knife between the shells at the hinge, but that is the place where you can make the cleanest opening, free of fragments of shell.

4. When you have inserted the point of the knife, press down to pop open the lid. Then move your knife back and forth, <u>making the blade slide against the top shell inside to sever the muscle that holds both sides together. Lift up the lid.</u>

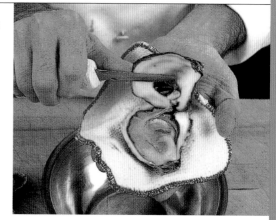

5. If the oyster shell crumbles and cannot be opened at the hinge, <u>insert the point of the knife on the curved side of the oyster between the shells</u>. Pry it open and sever the muscle.

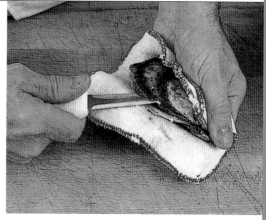

6. This technique tends to break little pieces of shell loose inside the oyster. <u>Be sure to remove them after the muscle is opened.</u> Do not wash the oysters under water as this flushes out the juices and the best taste of the oysters. Open the oysters over a bowl and retrieve the extra liquid to use in soups or sauces. At a time when a lot of oysters are opened, the extra juices can be used to rinse the oysters after opening to eliminate possible pieces of shell. Then add 1 tablespoon of the juice to each oyster after the rinsing, leaving the bits of shell in the bowl.

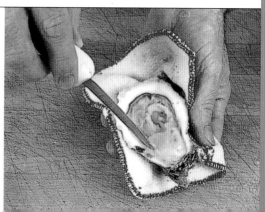

7. Oysters on the half shell: The oyster should be left in the deep shell. <u>Slide your knife under the oyster to sever the muscle and free the oyster.</u>

8. <u>Arrange the oysters on a bed of seaweed or shaved ice. Serve with lemon or sprinkled with lemon juice.</u> They are good served with mignonnette sauce and black pumpernickel bread.

Clams

(Palourdes)

Where the oyster knife is pointed and the tip is usually curved, the clam knife is straight, rounded at the tip, and sharp on one side. Personally, I prefer to use a regular paring knife to open clams. Cherrystones and little necks (the smallest of the hard clam clan) are commonly served on the half shell, although they are often cooked in the shell (clams casino and Rockefeller), or outside the shell (clam fritters, spaghetti and clam sauce). Like oysters, clams should not be overcooked. There are only two alternatives when it comes to cooking clams: to poach them only a minute or so to avoid toughening, or to cook them a couple of hours to have them tender. Cooked in between the two, they will be very rubbery. This principle applies to meat as well. Beef should be cooked rapidly (a steak) or braised (a stew); in between, the meat is, paradoxically, overcooked and undercooked at the same time.

1. Holding the clam firmly in the palm of your hand, place the sharp side of the knife blade at the seam, slightly on the "bulged" side where it is easier to open, and, using the tips of your fingers in back of the blade, tighten your grip, "pulling" the blade up through the seam. The muscle has to be severed for the clam to open.

2. Force the clam open. Run the knife along the top shell to free the meat.

3. Break the top shell off by twisting it. Discard. You may work over a bowl to salvage the drippings. To free the clam completely from the shell, run the knife under the meat and sever the muscle. Place on a flat plate. Do not wash.

4. The clams are presented on seaweed to keep them cool and steady, although they can be served on ice. Serve with lemon, mignonnette, or a cocktail sauce and buttered bread.

Soft-Shell Clams

I discovered soft-shell clams in America. They are now one of my favorites for soup or fried clams.

YIELD: 6 servings

4 pounds (1.8 kilograms) soft-shell clams (about 6 dozen)

2 cups (120 grams) fresh bread crumbs (made in the food processor)

1 cup (125 grams) stone-ground cornmeal

¼ teaspoon cayenne pepper

2 large eggs

2 tablespoons flour

½ teaspoon salt

¼ teaspoon freshly ground black pepper

Oil for frying (at least 3 cups/711 milliliters)

1. Wash the clams under cold water several times, lifting them up from the water to leave behind as much sand as possible. Place in a saucepan, preferably stainless steel, and cover. Place on high heat. Within 2 to 3 minutes the clams should open and release their juices. <u>Drain in a colander.</u>

2. Remove the clams from the shells, reserving the liquid (after straining through paper towels) for another use. <u>Be sure to pull the black skin off the long necks.</u>

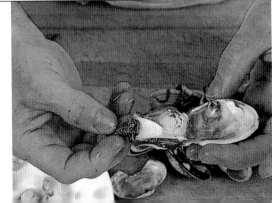

3. Combine the bread crumbs, cornmeal, and cayenne together in a shallow bowl. Mix the eggs with the flour, salt, and pepper until smooth. <u>Dip the clams into the eggs mixture</u> and then into the bread crumb mixture, making sure they are coated well all over. Heat the oil to 375 degrees (191°C) in a deep skillet or fryer. Drop the clams in, a few at a time, and cook for about 2 minutes. Drain and serve immediately.

Preparing Razor Clams

(Couteau)

The razor clam is very tender and meaty but tends to be quite sandy and must be washed carefully several times to ensure that all traces of sand are removed. The liquid from the clams must be strained through a paper or cloth towel to be usable. There are long narrow razor clams on the East Coast and short wider ones on the West Coast, shown below.

1. Wash the razor clams several times in cold water, <u>lifting them up from the water</u> after you finish washing so any sand remains in the bottom of the washing receptacle. If you feel they are very sandy, toss a handful of salt into cold water and let the clams soak in the salted water. It tends to help them disgorge some of the sand. Lift them out of the salted water and rinse again under fresh water. Place the clams in a saucepan, preferably stainless steel, cover (no liquid necessary), and cook over medium to high heat on top of the stove for about 5 minutes at the most, just until all the clams open.

2. Open up the clams completely. Save the juices and strain through paper or cloth towels to remove all the sand. You should have approximately 1 cup (237 milliliters) of juice. Set aside. <u>Remove the clams from the shells</u>, and taste one to determine if they are sandy. If so, wash them carefully inside and outside one by one under lukewarm running water to remove all the sand. Use as needed in its broth with melted butter or sautéed with herbs and garlic or in stuffing.

Sea Urchins

(Oursins)

Unfortunately, this sea delicacy is rarely available in fish stores or restaurants except Japanese restaurants, even though it is commonly found off the coasts of the United States. They are popular in Mediterranean countries, and are usually eaten raw with bread and butter. They exhale a prevalent odor of iodine, and the roe (the only part eaten) are reminiscent of nuts, butter, and salt all together.

1. Bottom and top of a sea urchin.

2. The needles are straight and hard in fresh sea urchins.

3. Hold the sea urchin with a potholder. <u>Insert the point of a pair of scissors into the "mouth"</u> (the soft depression in the center of one side). Cut one-third down the shell, then, turn the scissors and cut around the shell.

4. <u>Lift up the "lid."</u>

5. The mouth of the sea urchin is attached to the lid. <u>Discard</u>.

6. <u>With a teaspoon, lift up the roe and eat with bread and butter</u>. (They can also be used to make mousse or as a garnish.) Fishermen in France open the sea urchin and immerse it in seawater, shaking it to clean the inside. Everything washes out except the roe which is attached to the "wall" of the shell. They dip sticks of buttered bread into the roe and eat them.

7. <u>Plate of sea urchins.</u>

Mussels

(Moules)

We have mussels in great abundance all along the New England and mid-Atlantic shores. The best mussels are the ones found in cold waters. They are sold by weight—about 12 average-sized mussels to a pound (454 grams)—and any aficionado can easily consume at least 1½ pounds (681 grams).

There are a number of ways to serve mussels. The simplest and easiest way to prepare them is marinière (sailor-style), page 170. This is how you frequently find them in bistros in France—plain and in the shell. For something a little more sophisticated and richer, you can try them poulette (with a cream sauce), page 171. For this dish, the shell is separated and only the half shell with the meat in it is kept. In some recipes the meat is removed entirely from the shell after cooking and used to make a pilaf de moules, page 171 or combined with a rémoulade or a light well-seasoned mayonnaise and served as a salad for a first course. Billi-bi, one of the best possible soups, can be made from the broth the mussels cook in, with the addition of wine, cream and herbs. Nowadays, mussels bought in stores are often cleaned. If you fish your own, clean as explained below.

CLEANING MUSSELS

1. Mussels are attached to one another by a "cord" or "beard" which looks like old wet hay or grass. Nowadays, commercially grown mussels are often sold cleaned (that is, with the beard removed).

2. With a small paring knife, scrape off the dirt and most of the encrustations that are on the shell. Cut or pull off the beard. Place in cold water and rub the mussels against each other to clean the shells further.

3. Press each one on a bias to determine if it is full of mud or sand. If so, the shells will slide open and, obviously, these are to be discarded.

4. Certain mussels are open. This does not mean that they are bad. The spoiled ones smell strongly, contrary to the fresh mussels which smell pleasantly of iodine and seaweed. If you touch the inside muscle and edge with the point of a knife

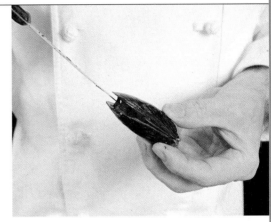

5. the fresh mussel will close immediately. As long as the shell is moving the mussel is still alive. Place the mussels again in a lot of cold water with salt (a handful of salt per gallon/3.8 liters of water), and let them sit for 1 hour so that they throw off any sand that escaped the first washing.

6. Wash again one or two more times. The mussels are now ready to cook.

MUSSELS SAILOR-STYLE (Moules Marinière)

YIELD: 6 servings

5 pounds (2.25 kilograms) clean mussels

2 cups (310 grams) chopped onion

1 tablespoon finely chopped garlic

½ cup (18 grams) chopped parsley

½ teaspoon freshly ground
   black pepper

2 sprigs of fresh thyme

Dash of salt

2 tablespoons olive oil

2 tablespoons (28 grams) unsalted butter

1½ cups (356 milliliters) dry white wine

1. Combine all the ingredients in a large pot, cover, place on high heat and bring to a boil.

2. Keep cooking for approximately 10 minutes. Twice during cooking, lift the kettle with both hands, your thumbs holding the cover, and shake the kettle in an up-and-down motion to toss the mussels. They should all open. Do not overcook or they will toughen. Serve in large deep plates or in bowls with some of the broth on top.

MUSSELS WITH CREAM SAUCE (Moules Poulette)

1. Cook as for *moules marinière*. Separate the shells, arranging the halves with the meat on plates. Melt 2 tablespoons (28 grams) butter in a saucepan and mix in 2 tablespoons flour. Add the broth, leaving any sandy residue in the bottom, and bring to a boil, mixing with a whisk. Let simmer for 2 minutes. Add ½ cup (118 milliliters) heavy cream and bring to a boil again. Add salt and pepper if needed. Cook a few minutes and spoon sauce over the mussels.

PILAF OF MUSSELS (Pilaf de Moules)

1. Cook as for *moules marinière*. When the mussels are cooked, remove the meat from the shell and trim (optional, see trimming mussels, page 173). Prepare the sauce *poulette* and set aside. Preheat the oven to 400 degrees (204°C). In a saucepan, sauté ⅓ cup (50 grams) chopped onion in 1 tablespoon (14 grams) butter for 1 minute. Add 1½ cups (322 grams) Carolina type rice, stir, add 3 cups (710 milliliters) chicken stock, salt and pepper and bring to a boil. Cover and bake for 20 minutes. Butter small bowls (each should hold about 1½ cups).

2. Put approximately ½ cup of rice in the bottom and up the sides, making a "nest."

3. Add about 8 to 10 mussels, 2 tablespoons of the *poulette* sauce and

4. <u>cover with more rice, enough to fill up the bowl</u>.

5. <u>Press the mixture with a spoon</u> to pack it together well.

6. <u>Place a serving plate on top of the bowl and</u>

7. <u>invert so the bowl now rests on the plate</u>.

8. <u>Remove the bowl by lifting it</u> off the food.

9. <u>Pour some of the sauce around the pilaf and decorate with a piece of fresh parsley. From right to left:</u> *pilaf de moules, moules poulette* and *moules marinière*.

TRIMMING MUSSELS

1. When the mussels are very large and serve as garnish, the edge tends to be tough. It can be removed. Starting at the top of the mussels, <u>pull to remove the brown edge.</u> Use as needed.

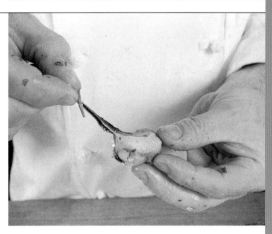

Crabs

(Crabes)

The common, blue hard-shell crab is usually boiled in a well-seasoned broth and eaten on newspapers directly at the table. (In summer, when the crab discards his shell, the soft-shell crab is one of the best delicacies to be found in the United States.) Hard-shell crabs are inexpensive, tasty and readily available. They are also excellent in stew, sautéed with hot oil Chinese style, provençal with garlic and tomatoes, or américaine with a peppery wine and tomato sauce.

HARD-SHELL CRAB WITH WINE

YIELD: 6 servings

6 tablespoons (90 milliliters) olive oil
1 cup (155 grams) coarsely chopped onions
1 dozen (12) hard-shell crabs
1 cup (237 milliliters) dry white wine
1 tablespoon chopped garlic
½ teaspoon salt
½ teaspoon freshly ground black pepper
1 cup (60 grams) coarsely chopped Italian parsley

1. The difference between the male and the female crab is seen by examining the underside of the crab. <u>The crab on the left with the larger skirt or apron is the female; the male, on the right, has a narrow, pointed skirt or apron.</u> When the female is full of roe during the summer (she is sometimes called a "berry crab" at that time), she is most flavorful.

2. To kill and clean the crab, hold it with a towel so it doesn't pinch your hands with its claws; lift up the apron or skirt and twist to remove. The two large claws can also be twisted out prior to removing the apron to prevent pinching.

3. Starting at the pointed corner of the crab, lift the flap or pointed end of the shell. Remove it and retrieve any roe or liquid inside to add to the stew. Discard the upper shell.

4. Notice in this she-crab all the beautiful roe and tomalley in the center. Keep this (along with any liquid), as it imparts delicious flavor to any dish.

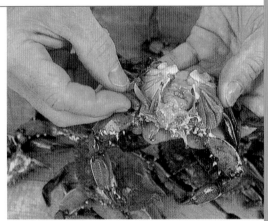

5. Next to the roe you will notice the lungs, which are the spongy appendages on each side. Pull them off and discard, as they are not edible.

6. Crack the body in half in the center and, using a meat pounder, <u>crack the large claw so the meat inside is more accessible</u> when the crab is cooked.

7. Heat the oil. When hot, add the onions and sauté for 1 minute. Then, add the crab (including roe and liquid), wine, garlic, salt, and pepper. Bring to a boil, cover, and cook at a high boil for about 3 minutes. Toss the mixture well, add the parsley, and serve immediately.

Preparing Soft-Shell Crabs
(Préparation des Crabes Mous)

More expensive and very seasonal, this delicacy is well worth its price. Make sure to get crabs as freshly shed as possible. A few days after shedding, a tougher skin forms on top of the crab.

1. <u>Lift up the skirt or apron and twist</u> or cut it off with scissors.

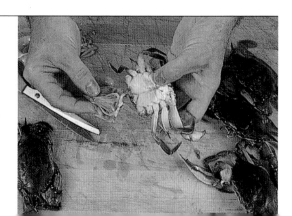

2. <u>Cut a strip off the front part of the shell</u>, which includes the eyes and antennae and is tough. Discard.

3. Lift up the top shell at both ends where it is pointed to expose the spongelike appendages on either side. Although edible in the very fresh soft-shell crab, most of the time they should be removed. <u>Remove by pulling them off</u>.

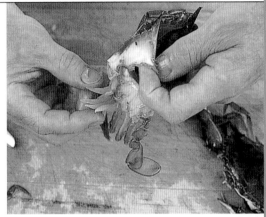

4. Mix ½ cup (100 grams) flour, ½ teaspoon salt, and ¼ teaspoon freshly ground black pepper together and dust lightly on both sides of 4 or 5 crabs. Place 2 tablespoons (28 grams) of butter in a skillet. Dust the crabs with the flour mixture again, shaking off the excess. When the butter is hot and foamy, place the crabs, top side down, in the skillet. Do not crowd them or they won't cook properly. Sauté on medium to high heat for 1½ minutes. <u>Turn, cover the pan, and continue cooking</u> on low to medium heat about 2 minutes longer. Sprinkle the crabs with 1½ teaspoons fresh lemon juice. Serve immediately.

How to Prepare Shrimp

(Préparation des Crevettes)

Shrimp (in the markets this refers usually to shrimp tails) are available in different sizes and prices. The large ones are very expensive. The smaller the shrimp, the less expensive they usually are. They always have the best flavor bought fresh and unshelled. For a shrimp cocktail, simply poach the shrimp with their shells in a vegetable stock (boiled water, carrots, onions, thyme, bay leaf, parsley, celery, Tabasco, and black peppercorns) for about 10 minutes. Drop the shrimp into the boiling stock. Cover, barely bring back to a boil, then remove from the heat. Allow the shrimp to cool in the liquid, where they will take on the flavor of the stock. The stock can be re-used to make a consommé of shrimp or a soup.

1. Peel the shells from the tail: Hold the tail end of the shrimp with one hand and, with the thumb and index finger of the other hand, peel off the shell from the thickest part. It will come off easily. Holding the shelled part, pull gently on the flap of the tail so the shell comes off. It will come away easily. In this recipe, the shells are not used, although they are excellent for stocks and soups and can be frozen.

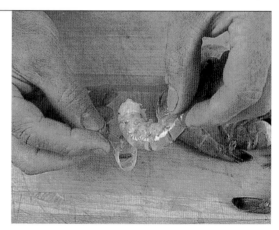

2. Shrimp should be deveined if you see a strip of dark color through the flesh. This indicates that the intestinal tract is full and should be removed. Make an incision approximately ⅛ inches (3 millimeters) deep down the back of each shrimp to expose the intestinal tract, as shown in the picture on the right, and rinse under cool water to clean. The shrimp on the left has been cleaned.

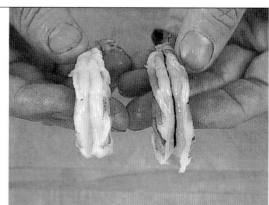

SHRIMP SALAD (Salade de Crevettes)

YIELD: 4 servings

1 pound (454 grams) fresh shrimp tails, shelled (16 to 20)

½ pound (227 grams) onions, peeled and very thinly sliced (about 2 cups loose)

⅓ cup (80 milliliters) dry white wine

2 tablespoons good red wine vinegar

½ teaspoon salt

1 teaspoon freshly ground black pepper

½ teaspoon grated orange rind

1 cup (60 grams) coarsely chopped Italian parsley

¼ cup (60 milliliters) good olive oil, preferably extra virgin

1. Place all the ingredients for the shrimp salad, except the orange rind, parsley, and oil, into a large skillet. Cook for 2 to 3 minutes on medium heat, stirring with a wooden spatula. The mixture should not even reach a complete boil. As soon as the shrimp stiffen and whiten, remove from the heat, let set at room temperature for 10 minutes, and pour the whole mixture into a bowl. Add the rest of the ingredients, toss all together and let it cool and marinate for at least 1 hour before serving. The shrimp should be served at room temperature as a first course with toast or regular bread.

Snails

(Escargots)

Eaten by the Roman Sybarites who knew how to fatten them, escargots are a delicacy, which are sometimes available fresh in the United States. Although most snails come from snail farms, wild ones are still available at local markets in the countryside throughout France. The two varieties eaten are the succulent "big white" from Burgundy, called vineyard snails because of their fondness for grape leaves and vines, and the smaller garden snails, called the "small gray." The best and most tender snails are picked up at the end of winter. They are called les dormants, *the sleepers, because they spend the winter in hibernation. Fresh snails are starved for at least 48 hours before they are eaten, in case they have eaten herbs which may be toxic to people.*

1. To cook the small gray or "petit gris" snails: These small gray garden snails are tiny and at least 2 dozen are required per person when they are served out of the shell. Adjust the quantity if the snails are larger.

2. Wash the snails in cold water two or three times, lifting them out of the water. Cover with cold water and bring to a boil. Boil about 1 minute <u>and drain in a colander</u>. Again, wash in cold water two or three times. Notice how green this cooking water often is.

3. With a snail fork or needle, <u>remove the snails from</u> <u>the shells</u>.

4. <u>Remove the snails' black lower part, which looks like a</u> <u>coil</u>. This dark, twisted end, the cloaca, will separate easily. Wash the snails again in cold or lukewarm water to remove any remaining mucus. Put them in a pan and barely cover with chicken stock and white wine. Add salt and pepper and boil gently for 1 hour. Remove the scum that forms on the surface every 10 minutes. The snails should be cooked and tender but still firm when pierced with a fork. For larger or tougher snails, increase the cooking time until the snails are tender. Cool them in their own liquid (there should be enough liquid remaining to barely cover the snails).

ESCARGOTS BOURGUIGNONNE

YIELD: 6 servings

3 sticks (³⁄₄ pound/340 grams) unsalted butter, softened

4 cloves garlic, peeled, crushed and chopped very fine (1 tablespoon)

4 tablespoons chopped Italian parsley

1 teaspoon Pernod or Richard (or another anise-flavored liqueur)

¼ cup (60 milliliters) dry white wine

1½ slices fresh bread, crumbed in the blender

1 teaspoon salt

½ teaspoon freshly ground black pepper

3 dozen (36) large cooked snails, fresh or canned (if the small ones from the preceeding technique are used, put two in each shell)

Mix together all of the ingredients except the snails.

You can vary the recipe by adding chopped shallots, almonds, chives, and so on. You could omit the anise liqueur, the wine, and the bread.

1. There are two kinds of shells, <u>the real snail shells pictured in the foreground, and the porcelain imitations shown in the back</u>, which are washed and reused in restaurants. The real shells are often washed and reused, but it is not an easy job to wash them properly, and they often smell rancid. Mushroom caps, as well as artichoke bottoms, are also used as receptacles for snails.

2. Preheat the oven to 400 degrees (204°C). <u>Place 1 teaspoon of the butter mixture</u> in the bottom of each shell and

3. <u>push the snail in</u>, rounded side first.

4. <u>Cover with more of the butter mixture</u>, at least 2 teaspoons more.

5. <u>When using the porcelain shells, proceed in the same manner.</u>

6. Snails in porcelain and real shells, oven ready.

7. Place in the oven and bake for 12 to 14 minutes. Be extra careful not to burn the garlic butter. Bring the snails, bubbling hot, to the table.

8. The snails are served on a plate from the special escargotière (snail dish) in which they were cooked. To eat snails, a special fork and tongs are used.

9. Hold the snail shell with the tongs and pull the snail out with the thin, narrow fork.

10. Pour the extra butter left in the shell into the snail dish, and use your bread to soak up the butter.

Preparing Whelk
(Préparation des Gros Bûlots)

Whelk is a relative of the tiny periwinkle and the conch and, in texture and type, is similar to the land snail. It has the same lower twist or coil as a land snail; the coil is usually removed. Whelk can be found along the Atlantic coast. In the New York area it is often known as scungilli.

Because whelk meat can be quite tough, cooking times vary, depending on size. If it is cooked at a very gentle boil in plenty of water, an hour is usually long enough for medium-sized whelk to be tender. Even when cooked, the meat will always remain a little chewy and elastic, which is characteristic of whelk.

1. Notice that the whelk has a very thick lip and some are redder inside than others. Note also that on top of the meat there is a leathery piece (called the operculum), which protects the meat.

2. Pour boiling water over the whelk and set it aside for 5 minutes. This is long enough to "set" the whelk so it can be removed from its shell.

3. Using a large kitchen fork, pry the meat out. It should come out in one piece.

4. <u>Pull off the operculum on top of the meat</u>. It may be hard to pull off; if so, cut it off.

5. <u>Pull out the coil or twisted part at the end of the meat</u>. This contains the liver and intestines and tends to be pasty and bitter, so discard it.

6. Split open each whelk on the rounded side to <u>remove the long reddish-black appendage</u>, which is part of the gut.

7. The meat is now trimmed and <u>should be brushed to remove some of the black around the foot</u>. Dip a strong-bristled brush in lukewarm water and scrub to remove most of the exterior black covering. The whelk is now ready to be cooked.

8. Place the meat in a large saucepan, cover with 2 quarts (2 scant liters) cold water, and add a dash of salt. Bring to a boil and simmer gently for 1 hour and 15 minutes. The whelk, when pierced with a fork, should be tender but still firm. Drain and <u>cut into ¼-inch (6-millimeter) slices</u>. Use as needed in salad or pasta.

Crayfish

(Écrevisses)

These tiny sweet water lobsterlike crustaceans are native to just about every part of the world except Africa. In the United States they come from Louisiana, well known for its crayfish, and California. The Pacific crayfish is usually quite clean, while crayfish from Louisiana sometimes require scrubbing to rid them of mud. There are many different species of crayfish and some too small to be eaten. To be edible they should be at least 4 to 5 inches (10 to 13 centimeters) from tail to head. Only the tail meat gets eaten (the body can be used to make soups, sauces and seasoned butter). Count on a dozen (12) tails per person as a first course. Like all shellfish, crayfish should be handled live. Two different, classic ways of preparing crayfish follow—one in a hot broth, the other a crayfish au gratin—both are usually served as a first course.

CRAYFISH IN BROTH (Écrevisses à la Nage)

YIELD: 2 servings

2 dozen (24) crayfish (about 2 pounds/908 grams)

2 tablespoons (28 grams) unsalted butter

1 large leek (white part only), cut into julienne (1 cup/150 grams)

1 large onion, peeled, cut in half and thinly sliced (2 cups/300 grams)

2 small celery ribs, peeled and cut in julienne (½ cup/75 grams)

1 carrot, peeled and thinly sliced (½ cup/75 grams)

2 cups (473 milliliters) dry white wine

1 cup (237 milliliters) water

½ teaspoon thyme

3 bay leaves

4 strips lemon rind (use a vegetable peeler)

1½ teaspoons salt

½ teaspoon freshly ground black pepper

½ teaspoon red pepper flakes or a good dash cayenne pepper (optional)

1 small bunch Italian parsley, stems removed, very coarsely cut (1 cup/37 grams)

1. The central intestinal tract has to be removed or the crayfish will taste bitter. Hold the crayfish down as shown, <u>grab the center flap of the tail and twist gently back</u> and forth to loosen it.

2. <u>Pull and the intestinal tract attached to it should come out.</u> (If it breaks, try to pull it out with the point of a knife, but don't worry if you can't get it. The crayfish is still edible.)

3. Melt the butter in a large frying pan. Add the leek, onions, celery and carrots. Sauté on medium heat for 1 minute. Add the wine and water, thyme, bay leaves, lemon, salt, pepper, and optional pepper flakes. Bring to a boil and boil on high heat for 2 minutes. Add the crayfish and parsley, stir to mix, cover and bring to a boil. Simmer gently for 1 minute. <u>Remove from the heat and let the crayfish cool in the broth.</u>

4. When cool, arrange the crayfish on a platter with all of the vegetable garnish on top. Optimally you can *troussé* a few crayfish to decorate the top of the dish. To *troussé*, <u>take one of the front claws, turn it upside down being careful not to break the claw at the joint, and gently push the smaller "pincer" part into the shell of the tail</u> to hold the claw in place.

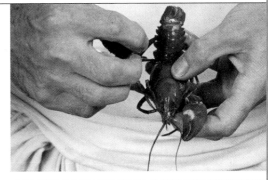

5. <u>Repeat with the other claw.</u> The crayfish are ready to be "seated." To enjoy the crayfish, you have to use your fingers, which means this is not a dish for a formal dinner party.

CRAYFISH TAILS AU GRATIN (Gratin de Queues d'Écrevisses)

This dish is served in some of the best restaurants. It is time-consuming, elegant, and very rich. To make the crayfish go a bit further, you can reuse the shells to make a bisque of crayfish. (After you strain the crayfish in step 3 and remove the tail, cover the shells and strained solids with water and boil for 1 hour, then strain. Adjust to 2 quarts/2 scant liters and use as a base for sauces, consommés or thicken with tomatoes and cream for the bisque.)

YIELD: 2 servings

2 dozen (24) crayfish (about 2 pounds/908 grams), gutted (see steps 1 and 2, previous technique)

2 tablespoons (28 grams) unsalted butter

2 tablespoons good cognac

3 tablespoons chopped shallots

½ cup (75 grams) coarsely chopped leek

1 tablespoon chopped celery

3 tablespoons coarsely chopped carrots

1 large tomato, peeled and chopped (1½ cups/300 grams)

1 cup (237 milliliters) dry white wine

2 cups (473 milliliters) light fish stock

½ teaspoon thyme leaves

1 teaspoon salt

½ teaspoon freshly ground black pepper

1 tablespoon tomato paste

⅓ cup (80 milliliters) heavy cream

1. Separate the body from the tail of the crayfish. Melt the butter in an extra large skillet or saucepan, until very hot. Add the crayfish tails and sauté for about 1 minute, until they turn red. Remove from the heat and let cool.

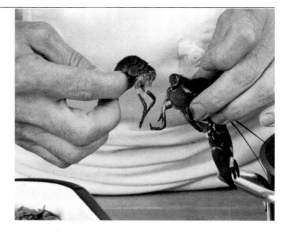

2. Remove the meat from the tails and set aside.

3. <u>Chop the bodies coarsely</u>. Place, with the tail shells, in the butter and continue sautéing on high heat for 2 to 3 minutes until the bodies turn red. Add the cognac and ignite. When the flame subsides, add the shallots, leek, celery, carrots, tomato, white wine, fish stock, thyme, salt, pepper, and tomato paste. Cover and bring to a boil. Lower the heat and simmer for 30 minutes. Remove from the heat and strain through a food mill fitted with a large-holed disk. Press all the solids to extrude as much of the liquid as possible, then strain the juices again through a finer sieve. You should have approximately 1 cup (237 milliliters) of liquid left. If not, reduce to the right amount, or add water to adjust. Add the cream, bring to a boil and reduce by half. Arrange the tail meat in two small baking dishes (about 12 per person) and heat in a 400 degree (204°C) oven for 2 minutes. Pour the hot sauce on top and serve immediately.

Stuffed Squid Poulette

(Calamars Farcis)

Squid is inexpensive and easily obtainable. Like a lot of other shellfish, it is tough only if overcooked. It should be either cooked very briefly or braised a long time in order to be tender. It's the in-between cooking that makes it as hard as rubber. The Basques as well as the Spaniards prepare calamari or squid using the ink that is contained in a bag inside the tentacles. The ink is not needed in our recipe. In fact, the small saclike appendage full of ink is usually removed before the squid reaches the marketplace. For our recipe, we used small tender squid about 6 inches (15 centimeters) long. After being cleaned as explained in the technique below, squid can be sliced, breaded and deep-fried or sautéed briefly, or blanched and marinated in oil, lemon or lime juice and served partially raw as a seviche.

YIELD: 6 servings as a main course

About 3 pounds (1.4 kilograms) squid (12 medium sized squid)

STUFFING

1 tablespoon (14 grams) unsalted butter

$\frac{1}{2}$ cup (100 grams) finely diced or coarsely chopped carrots

1 cup (135 grams) coarsely chopped, loosely packed leeks

1 teaspoon peeled, finely chopped garlic (2 cloves)

$\frac{1}{4}$ teaspoon salt

Dash freshly ground black pepper

9 ounces (255 grams) coarsely chopped tentacles from the squid (see below)

$\frac{1}{2}$ pound (227 grams) shrimp, peeled

1 large egg

TO COOK THE SQUID

1 tablespoon (28 grams) unsalted butter

$\frac{3}{4}$ cup (115 grams) diced onion

1 cup (237 milliliters) white wine

1 teaspoon salt

1 teaspoon freshly ground black pepper

TO FINISH THE DISH

1 tablespoon (14 grams) unsalted butter

1 tablespoon all-purpose flour

$\frac{1}{2}$ teaspoon peeled and finely chopped garlic

$\frac{1}{2}$ cup (119 milliliters) heavy cream

2 tablespoon chopped chives

1. Wash the squid in water to clean. Pull out the head and the tentacles; these will come out of the body in one piece.

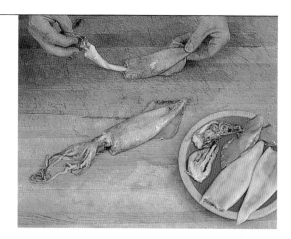

2. Pull the pen out of the body. The pen, which looks like a long piece of plastic, is the central cartilage and should be discarded.

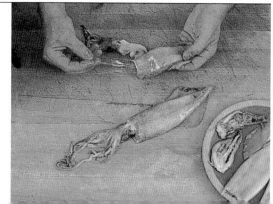

3. Remove the flap on each side of the body and <u>pull the black skin off</u>. Discard the skin.

4. <u>Pull off and discard the black skin from the flaps also</u>, and set aside.

5. <u>Cut off the tentacles</u> at the head and eyes.

6. <u>Press on the round part where the tentacles come together</u> and a knotty beak will come out of the center. Discard it. Place the tentacles in cold, salted water and rinse carefully. Lift them out of the water, leaving behind any residual sand. Coarsely chop the tentacles into small pieces. (You should have about 9 ounces/255 grams of tentacles.)

FOR THE STUFFING: Melt the butter in a large saucepan. When hot, add the carrots and leeks, and sauté on high heat for 1 minute. Add the garlic, salt, pepper and the pieces of tentacles and cook for about 1 minute on high heat. Remove from the heat and lift out the mixture with a slotted spoon, reserving in the saucepan any remaining juice. Let the squid mixture cool in the refrigerator. Place the shrimp in the food processor and process briefly (about 10 seconds). Add the egg and process until the mixture is smooth. Remove and combine the shrimp paste with the cooled tentacle mixture.

7. Place the stuffing in a pastry bag without a tip. Rinse the bodies of the 12 squid, inside and out, under cold water and dry briefly with paper towels.

8. Insert the end of the pastry bag into the body of each squid and stuff the cavity. Press gently with your hand to distribute the stuffing evenly inside. Notice that the squid are stuffed only about half full because the stuffing has a tendency to expand and the squid itself will shrink considerably during cooking.

9. To cook the squid: Melt the butter in the saucepan containing the juice from the stuffing preparation. When hot, add the onions and place the stuffed squid on top in one layer. Place the flaps from the squid around the stuffed squid and top with the wine, salt, and pepper. Cover with a buttered round of parchment paper, cut to fit the saucepan. Place on high heat and bring to boil. Turn the heat to very low, cover the saucepan with a lid, and simmer the mixture very gently for 20 minutes.

10. Remove the cooked squid to a tray or cookie sheet. Place the round of parchment on top and keep warm. Strain the juice, pushing the solids through with a spoon to obtain the most of the cooked onion and reduce the liquid to 1½ cup (355 milliliters). In a small bowl mix the butter and flour together with a whisk to make a kneaded butter. With the whisk, stir in the reduced juice and bring the mixture to boil, stirring constantly. Add the garlic and cream and return the mixture to boil. Add the chives. <u>Place the squid on a platter and serve, coated with sauce, with a grain, in this case kasha.</u>

KASHA

YIELD: 8 servings

2 tablespoons (28 grams) unsalted butter
⅓ cup (50 grams) chopped onions
1 cup (195 grams) kasha (roasted buckwheat kernels)
1 large egg
2 cups (474 milliliters) chicken stock
½ teaspoon salt (if chicken stock is unsalted)
⅛ teaspoon freshly ground black pepper

Melt the butter in a saucepan and remove from the heat. Add the onions and the kasha and mix well with the butter to coat the kasha. Add the egg and mix in thoroughly with a fork. Place back on the stove and cook, stirring, over medium to high heat until the egg scrambles and mixes with the kasha and onion and the mixture becomes granulated and separated. Add the chicken stock, salt, and pepper, and bring to a boil. Reduce the heat to very low, cover tightly, and cook for 15 minutes.

Preparing Octopus

(Préparation des Poulpes)

Octopus is delectable when properly cooked. When cooked either too long on too high a boil, however, it can be mushy and grainy. Brought to a gentle boil from a cold-water start and cooked gently for 30 to 45 minutes, it will be firm yet tender.

1. <u>Turn the head of the octopus and the sac inside out, if the ink sac is still there.</u> In this recipe it is discarded. Wash the octopus carefully under cold running water. Place it in a pot filled with 5 to 6 quarts of cold water and bring to a boil. When it begins to boil, lower the heat to maintain a gentle boil (so it doesn't toughen the protein) and cook for 30 minutes.

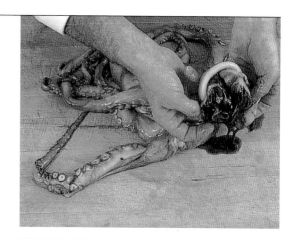

2. Lift the cooked octopus out of the water and place immediately in a pan of cold water. The reddish-purplish gummy skin can now be removed. <u>Just rub and push it off under the cold water.</u> Most of it will come off, except on the suction cups. (Note: Only a few minutes of blanching is not enough; the octopus needs longer cooking before the gelatinous skin can be slid off.)

3. <u>Cut the meat into ½-inch (1.25-centimeter) pieces.</u> You should have about 4 cups (620 grams) of meat and it should be firm but tender. Use as needed in salad or sauté.

Lobster

(Homard)

Freshness is extremely important with lobster and other shellfish, and the only way to assure a lobster's freshness is to buy it alive. There are three basic ways of cooking lobster: boiling or steaming, stewing, and broiling. The lobster is cut differently depending on which way you cook it.

BROILED LOBSTER

YIELD: 4 servings

4 lobsters (1¼ pounds/567 grams each) including 1 cup (165 grams) of the insides and liquid

5 tablespoons (75 grams) unsalted butter

1 cup (155 grams) chopped onions

1 cup (110 grams) cornbread crumbs

½ cup (30 grams) chopped herbs (combination of tarragon, parsley, and chives)

¼ teaspoon freshly ground black pepper

¼ teaspoon salt

Olive oil and Tabasco, for cooking

KILLING, SPLITTING LOBSTER

1. On the left, as indicated by the knife, is the male lobster. Notice that the first two appendages on the underside of the body under the rib cage are longer and go between the rib. The female, on the right, has a wider body and tail, and those same two appendages are much smaller and do not extend up to the rib cage. A female is often more tender and the roe is delicious.

2. To kill and split a lobster in half, place the point of a large, sturdy knife in the middle of the body, directly on the line that runs down the center of the shell. Push down with the knife to split the front and kill the lobster.

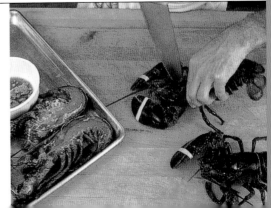

3. Turn the lobster around and, following the same cut, <u>continue cutting down with the sturdy knife to split the lobster into 2 halves.</u>

4. <u>Be sure to remove and discard the little sac</u> (at this point, split in half), which is the stomach, just next to the eye at the point of the head. Remove on both sides.

5. <u>Save the liquid, the roe (if any), and the tomalley (liver).</u>

6. Heat the butter in a skillet. When hot, add the chopped onions and sauté for about 2 minutes, until they begin to soften, then add all the liver and roe and stir over the heat, cooking for about 1 minute. <u>The green liquid will turn a reddish color.</u>

7. <u>The mixture now has turned harder and is set.</u> Remove it from the stove and combine it in a bowl with the cornbread crumbs, chopped herbs, pepper, and salt. Mix lightly so it doesn't get pasty. Cover the claws of each lobster with a towel to prevent splashing and, using a meat pounder, crack them to make it easier to extract the meat after cooking.

8. Then arrange all the lobster halves flesh side up on a cookie sheet, making certain they are approximately flat. Spoon about ⅓ cup (35 grams) of the stuffing onto each, filling up the cavity and covering the flesh of each lobster thinly so it doesn't dry out during cooking. Sprinkle each half lobster with approximately ½ teaspoon of olive oil and a few drops of Tabasco. Place the lobsters under a preheated broiler for 10 to 12 minutes, turning the sheet around so they cook evenly all over, including the tails and claws.

STEAMING LOBSTER, EXTRACTING MEAT

1. Place 2 lobsters 1½ pounds (680 grams) each, in a steamer, 2 per deck, over 6 cups (1½ liters) of boiling water, and steam for about 12 minutes. Remove the lobsters to a tray, setting aside the cooking liquid in the steamer for a sauce or soup.

2. When the lobsters are cold enough, separate the tail, pressing the tail to crunch the shell. Remove the shell at the end of the tail and set it aside for decoration. Reserve the other shells for soup.

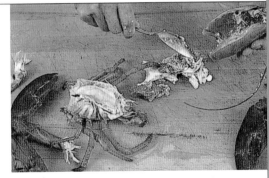

3. Pull the meat off the tail and set aside. Pull the small legs off the body and set aside. Lift the top part of the shell from the body and, using a spoon, empty the entire shell. Reserve the shells for soup.

4. The red roe is in the center, the tomalley on the left, and the little sac (the stomach), which should be discarded, is held in the background.

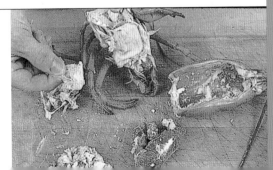

5. Cover the claws with a towel to prevent splattering, and crack with a meat pounder.

6. Separate the meat, preferably in one piece, from the shell of the claw.

7. Be sure to remove the little piece of cartilage from the center of each claw.

8. The aficionado considers the meat in the joints just above the claw the best part of the lobster. Extract this meat from the shell. Reserve shells for soup.

9. Cut the tail crosswise into ¼-inch (7-millimeter) wide slices. The lobster meat is ready to use in a salad or served with butter.

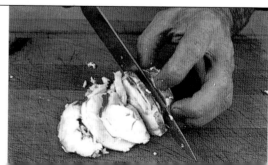

Shellfish Sausage

(Boudins de Fruits de Mer)

As its name implies, this is a purée of shellfish formed into the elongated shape of a sausage. The sausage can be small or it can be large—one sausage to serve one person or one sausage for 2 or 3. We chose not to use regular sausage casings and mold our sausage in foil. The foil allows you to choose the size and shape of your sausage, and because the sausage are skinless they are easier to manage on the plate. The sausage can be prepared ahead of time, kept in foil until ready to serve, then reheated in hot water in the foil. Serve with boiled salted cucumbers or tiny boiled potatoes.

YIELD: 8 to 10 servings

SAUSAGE

½ pound (227 grams) scallops

½ pound (227 grams) raw shrimp, with the shells

1 pound (454 grams) fillet of sole, preferably gray or lemon sole, trimmed and cut into ½-inch (13-millimeter) pieces. Ask your fishmonger for a cup worth of trimmings. (See note.)

1½ cups (355 milliliters) heavy cream

1 teaspoon salt

¼ teaspoon freshly ground black pepper

1 tablespoon fresh herbs, chopped finely, a mixture of tarragon, parsley, chives, chervil, etc.

SAUCE

½ cup (25 grams) celery leaves

½ cup (112 grams) onion, sliced thin

1 bay leaf

¼ teaspoon thyme leaves

½ teaspoon salt

½ teaspoon crushed peppercorns

½ cup (118 milliliters) dry sherry

3 cups (710 milliliters) fish stock or water

1¼ sticks (½ cup plus 2 tablespoons/142 grams) unsalted butter

(Note: The fish should be very fresh so it has texture and albumin to hold the cream. If the fillets are burned by ice or defrosted, the mixture will lack albumin and will bleed or separate.)

1. Cut scallops into ½-inch (13-millimeter) pieces. Peel the shrimp and <u>cut into ½-inch (13-millimeter) pieces</u>. Keep the shells to flavor the sauce. Purée the sole in the food processor for a few seconds. Push pieces of fish back into the purée with a rubber spatula, and blend again for a few seconds until you have a smooth mixture. Add ½ cup (118 milliliters) of cream and blend for a few seconds more. Whip the remaining cream until it holds a soft peak. (Do not overwhip.) Whisk the fish purée into the lightly whipped cream. Fold in the scallops, shrimp, salt, pepper, and herbs.

2. Cut 3 large pieces of aluminum foil (about 14 inches/ 35.5 centimeters long) and butter. <u>Place one-third of the mixture in each.</u>

3. Roll the mixture to enclose it and <u>twist the ends to tighten.</u>

4. Place the "sausages" in a large skillet. Cover with cold water and <u>use a small lid as a weight to hold the sausages down and keep them immersed.</u> Cover with a normal lid, bring to 180 degrees (82°C), and cook for about 20 minutes. (If you are making smaller sausages, cook for less time.) Don't let the water boil or even simmer. Remove from heat and let the sausages sit in the water for about 10 minutes.

5. Remove the sausages from the water and <u>unwrap carefully</u>. Transfer to a buttered dish, cover with wax paper and keep warm in a l60-degree (70°C) oven while you make the sauce.

6. Put the trimmings from the fish in a saucepan. Place the shrimp shells in the food processor and purée for a few seconds. Add to the trimmings with the celery leaves, onion, bay leaf, thyme, salt, peppercorns, sherry, and fish stock. Bring to a boil. Boil gently for 20 to 25 minutes. Strain, then reduce the liquid to ½ cup (118 milliliters). Place on low heat and add the butter, piece by piece, beating between each addition. Add salt and freshly ground pepper if needed. <u>Coat the sausages and serve immediately</u>.

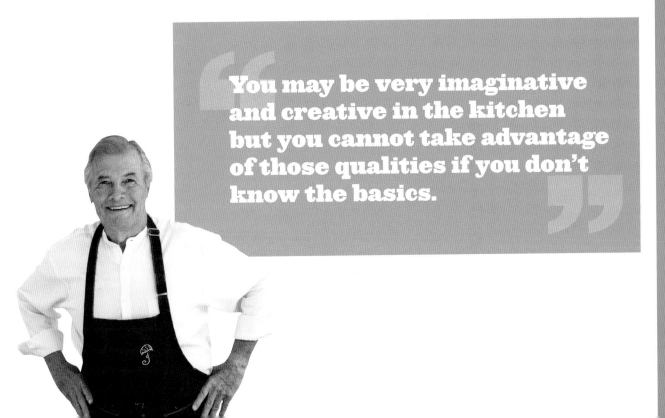

> "You may be very imaginative and creative in the kitchen but you cannot take advantage of those qualities if you don't know the basics."

Salt-Cured Salmon

(Gravlax)

Gravlax, or gravlaks, was originally a Scandinavian salmon dish. Customarily made by boning out a fresh salmon and pickling it with lots of sugar and a dash of salt, it is heavily seasoned with dill. After a day or so, the fillets are sliced and served raw with a sweet mustard and dill sauce. Our version is pickled with more salt than sugar and is served with fresh herbs, capers, extra virgin olive oil, and fresh lemon juice. One 7- to 8-pound (3.2- to 3.6-kilogram) salmon will serve about 30 people.

1. Bone out the salmon, using a long, strong, very sharp knife. <u>Start by sliding your knife under the front gill</u> toward the head.

2. Twist the knife so the blade faces the other way and cut down in one swoop, through the rib cage bones <u>right on top of the main central bone, to remove the whole fillet in one piece.</u> Turn the salmon upside down and remove the other fillet in the same manner.

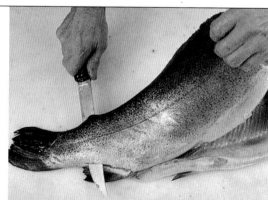

3. Do not worry if you leave some of the salmon flesh on the bones. Using a spoon, scrape the bones of the salmon and inside the gill and the corner toward the head to remove as much of the flesh as possible. That purée of flesh can be used for salmon tartare or mousse.

4. Using a thin knife, slide the blade beneath the rib cage to remove the ribs on each of the fillets.

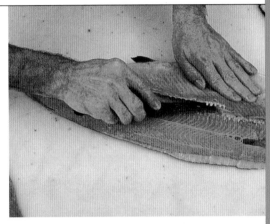

5. There is a central line of bones that extends straight down into the fillet that must be removed. Using a strawberry huller or a small pair of pliers, pull each of the small bones, one by one, to remove. There are more than 30 of these small bones and they extend from the neck three-quarters down the fillet.

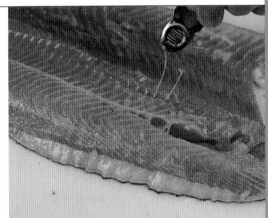

6. With a large knife, remove the skin of the salmon. Using your knife at a 45-degree angle, push the knife forward, cutting gently back and forth in a jigsaw motion with the right hand, while pulling the skin with the left hand.

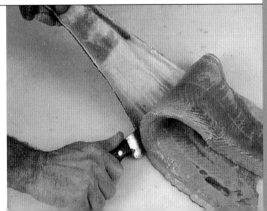

7. Using your knife horizontally, <u>gently cut off all the dark flesh on top of the fillet</u>, just under the skin. That dark flesh is mostly fat and should be discarded. In a poached salmon, it is the part under the skin that turns black and slides off after cooking.

8. Although the whole half side of salmon can be used for gravlax, if you intend to make salmon tartare or to poach pieces of salmon for aspic, <u>cut away the thin section of the belly</u> and the end of the tail and save them for these dishes, using only the thickest part for the gravlax.

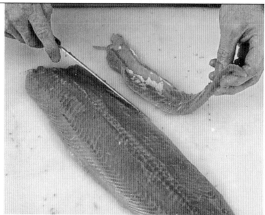

9. For each fillet, each about 1 pound (454 grams), mix together ¼ cup (80 grams) coarse (kosher) salt and 2 tablespoons granulated sugar. Place the fillets on a large piece of aluminum foil. <u>Rub the salt and sugar mixture on both sides of the fillet</u>. Reduce the salt and sugar mixture if the fillets are smaller. Cover with another sheet of foil and fold the edges carefully. Cure for at least 6 hours. When ready to serve, slice thinly (see page 426). Serve sprinkled with fresh herbs, capers, and a dash of olive oil and fresh lemon juice. Serve with buttered toast.

Poached Salmon Glazed with Aspic

(Saumon Poché en Gelée)

There is nothing more glorious than a large, decorated, glazed salmon for a buffet. For a 6½-to 7-pound (approximately 3 kilograms) salmon, the fish poacher should be 28 to 30 inches (71 to 76 centimeters) long. Make the vegetable stock and poach the salmon in it one day ahead. (If there's any salmon left over, the meat can be molded in aspic and served very attractively with vegetable garnishes.)

YIELD: The salmon will serve 15 to 18

FOR POACHING SALMON

2 cups (300 grams) coarsely chopped
green of leek

2 cups (300 grams) diced carrots

2 cups (300 grams) coarsely chopped
leafy celery

2 tablespoons salt

1 teaspoon black peppercorns

4 bay leaves

2 fresh thyme leaves

1 salmon (6½ to 7 pounds/3 kilograms)

VEGETABLE FLOWERS

Blanched strips of leek

Cooked carrots, sliced thin

Hard-cooked egg

Black olives

ASPIC

5 large egg whites

3 cups (150 grams) greens, a mixture of
leeks, scallions, parsley, and celery

5 to 6 envelopes unflavored gelatin
(4 tablespoons)

10 cups (2.5 liters) strong poaching liquid

GARNISHES

Artichoke bottoms

Vegetable salad

4 tomatoes

2 hard-cooked eggs

Lettuce leaves

1. Place all the poaching ingredients in a large kettle, cover with water and boil on a high heat for 30 minutes. Pour the stock and vegetables into the fish poacher.

2. <u>Place the perforated rack on top of the vegetables.</u> Lay the fish on top and fill with cold water, enough to cover the fish. The stock should be barely lukewarm. Bring to a simmer on medium to high heat. As soon as the stock starts simmering, reduce the heat to very low and let the fish poach (just under a simmer) for 30 minutes. (This is equal to 10 minutes per inch/2.5 centimeters of thickness at the thickest point.) Remove from heat and let the fish cool off gently in the broth overnight.

3. Lift the fish from the broth. (The salmon should be intact. If it is split, it boiled too fast.) Let it drain and set for a good hour. Then slide the salmon onto the working table. <u>Cut through the thick skin in a decorative pattern near the head.</u>

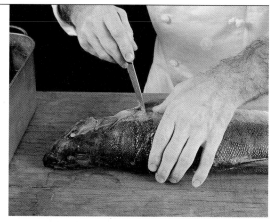

4. <u>Pull the skin off.</u> It should come easily.

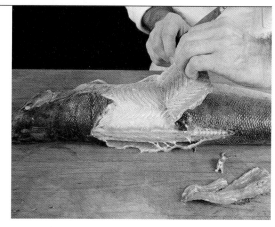

5. Using a small pair of pliers or tweezers, <u>pull off the bones that stick out along the back of the fish.</u>

6. <u>Scrape off the top of the flesh, especially along the middle line to remove darkish brown fatty flesh</u>. The salmon should be nice and pink all over. When the salmon is all cleaned, slide it onto a large serving platter. If you do not own a platter large enough to accommodate the salmon, cut an oval piece of plywood, pad with a towel, cover with a piece of white cloth and staple underneath.

7. Using vegetable "flowers," decorate the salmon. First, place long strips of blanched green of leeks near the head and tail to outline the edge of the skin. Next, <u>place strips down both sides of the salmon</u> to frame the area to be decorated.

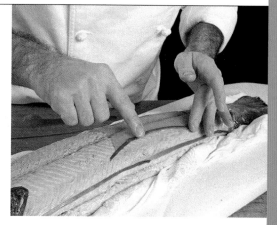

8. <u>Make a flowerpot</u> with thin slices of cooked carrots and green of leek.

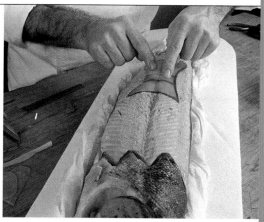

9. <u>Make flowers using your imagination</u>. Simulate the eye of the fish with the white of a hard-cooked egg and the black of an olive. Refrigerate the salmon. It should be cold for the aspic to stick to it.

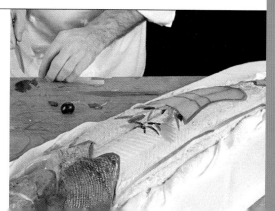

10. Make an aspic by thoroughly mixing together egg whites, greens and gelatin. Add the poaching liquid. Bring the mixture to a boil, stirring to avoid scorching. Let it come to a strong boil; then shut the heat off. Let the mixture settle for 10 minutes, then pour through a sieve lined with wet paper towels. Chill the mixture on ice until syrupy, and <u>glaze the whole salmon</u>.

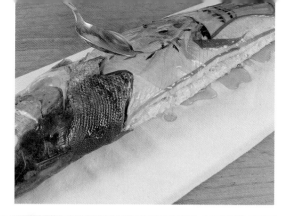

11. Prepare the garnishes. <u>Fill artichoke bottoms with your favorite vegetable salad.</u>

12. Slit, without going through, a large wedge of tomato. <u>Pull open and</u>

13. <u>set a quarter of a hard-cooked egg in the opening</u>.

14. Cut two tomatoes in half. Squeeze the seeds and some juice out. Compress the flesh inside to make a receptacle and <u>fill it with the vegetable salad.</u>

15. <u>Decorate the top of the garnishes with strips</u> or cutouts of tomatoes, leeks, eggs, and the like.

16. <u>Decorate around the salmon with lettuce leaves and the garnishes.</u>

Preparing Sole

(Sole: Entière, Filets, Paupiettes)

You will find sole, sometimes Dover sole, featured in fine fish stores and restaurants, and rightly so, for this is probably the most versatile of fish. Dover sole is imported, fresh or frozen, from Europe, the best being caught in the English Channel. It is the best of the small "flat" fish family (which includes grey sole, lemon sole, flounder, fluke, and dab, to cite the most known), and it can be prepared in more than a hundred different ways. It is excellent broiled, poached whole, or filleted, in mousses, paupiettes, sautéed in butter, deep-fried, and baked, to give you a few examples. If Dover sole is not available in your market, apply the recipe to its kin, especially the grey or lemon sole which are the firmest, though they are not firm enough to be char-broiled as the Dover sole could be. A 1-pound (454-grams) fresh sole will give you approximately 6 ounces (170 grams) of flesh after cleaning and filleting.

WHOLE DOVER SOLE

1. Cut the head off on the bias.

2. Grasp the black skin at the head and pull off. (If grey sole, flounder, etc., are used, be sure to pull the skin slowly and carefully to avoid pulling the flesh off with it.)

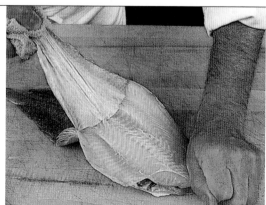

3. With the rounded handle of a knife, bear down on the flesh and "push" the guts out.

4. Scrape the white side with a knife or scallop or clam shell, as illustrated, to remove the scales. Wash under water thoroughly. Since the white skin is tender and holds the shape of the fish, it is generally left on, especially when the fish is to be grilled.

5. With sharp scissors, cut off the fins and bones on each side of the fish. Grill or sauté whole.

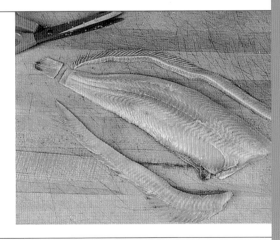

TO REMOVE THE FILLET:

1. Remove the head, black and white skin as explained in preceding technique. <u>Slide a knife, which has a special thin, sharp and very flexible blade, under the central bone</u> in the middle (apply pressure to flex the blade so that it slides along the central bone) and detach the fillet from underneath. Repeat with the other side, sliding the blade on the flat ribs. You now have 2 single fillets taken from the top of the sole.

2. Turn the sole over and fillet the other side. The correctly filleted sole yields 4 single fillets, 2 on each side. <u>The cleaned, central bone and fins are excellent for stock or fish *fumet*</u>.

3. For *paupiettes,* the fillets are rolled, starting with the <u>thickest end</u>. Be sure that the white, fleshy side which touched the central bone, is on the outside of the *paupiette*. Rolled this way, the *paupiette* will contract during cooking and keep its shape. Rolled the wrong way, it will open during cooking.

4. When served flat, the fillets are *ciselés* to retain their natural shape; i.e., <u>little slits are made on top to prevent them from contracting while they cook</u>.

5. Cut only the top layer of the fillets on the sinewy side.

6. Fillets, stuffed or unstuffed, can be folded in half with the slits inside and served poached, with or without a sauce.

7. Fillets should be pounded when used to line a mold. Pound gently to avoid tearing the meat apart. The motion should be down and toward you.

8. Arrange in a *savarin* mold to make a lining for a mousse or a quenelle mixture.

Baked Sole with Mushrooms and Parsley

(Sole Bercy)

YIELD: 2 servings as a first course

2 tablespoons (28 grams) unsalted butter

2 tablespoons chopped shallots

¾ teaspoon salt

¼ teaspoon freshly ground black pepper

1 1¼-pound (568-gram) Dover sole

4 large mushrooms, sliced (1 cup/80 grams loosely packed)

3 tablespoons chopped fresh Italian parsley

⅓ cup (79 milliliters) dry white wine

1 teaspoon all-purpose flour

⅓ cup (79 milliliters) heavy cream

5 or 6 drops of fresh lemon juice

Following the technique for whole sole (page 210), steps 1-5, clean the sole, leaving the white skin on.

1. Preheat the oven to 450 degrees (232°C). Rub a gratin dish with ½ tablespoon (7 grams) butter. <u>Sprinkle the shallots over the butter</u>, along with salt and pepper.

2. Arrange the sole on top, and <u>add another ½ tablespoon (7 grams) butter</u>.

3. Top with the mushrooms, 2 tablespoons parsley, <u>and the wine</u>.

4. <u>Place a buttered piece of wax paper on top</u> and place in the oven for 10 minutes.

5. At this point, the sole should be done. <u>Lift the sole up with a large spatula and place on a plate.</u>

6. Using the blade of a knife, <u>"push off" the lines of bones from the fins on either side of the fillets</u>. They should come off easily.

7. Lift up the top fillets of the sole from the central bone and

8. place in a gratin dish or serving platter.

9. Remove the central bone in one piece and

10. place the second half of the sole on top of the first half. The sole is now completely boned and reconstituted. Cover the sole with the wax paper and keep warm in the oven.

11. Melt the remaining 1 tablespoon (14 grams) butter in a saucepan, add the flour and cook for 10 seconds on high heat. <u>Add the drippings of the sole</u> and bring to a boil, stirring with a whisk. Add the cream, bring to a boil and simmer for 1 minute. Correct seasonings with salt and pepper, if needed. Add 5 or 6 drops of lemon juice to the sauce.

12. Remove the sole from the oven and <u>the wax paper from the fish</u>. Coat with the sauce.

13. <u>Sprinkle with remaining parsley</u> and serve immediately.

Sole Sautéed in Butter

(Sole Meunière)

Whereas the sole bercy is cooked with the little side bones intact (they are removed after cooking), sole meunière is cooked without them. The reason is that where the trimmings enhance the stock for the sole bercy, they just absorb the butter used to sauté the sole meunière, without adding any extra flavor to the meat of the sole. Therefore, it is preferable to remove the side bones before cooking.

1. Clean the sole leaving the white skin on. <u>With a pair of scissors, remove the bones on the side of the fillets.</u> The trimmings can be used in stock.

2. Sprinkle the sole with salt and a small dash of pepper. <u>Dredge in flour.</u>

3. Melt 2 tablespoons (28 grams) of unsalted butter and 1 tablespoon of olive oil in a skillet. <u>Place the sole in the pan, skin side down</u>, and cook on medium to low heat for about 3 minutes on each side.

4. Bring the skillet directly to the table. <u>Using a spoon and fork, lift up the top fillets and place on each side of the sole.</u>

5. <u>Remove the central bone and discard.</u>

6. <u>Place the bottom fillets on a hot plate and cover with the top fillets</u>. The sole is reconstructed and completely boned.

7. <u>Add 1 tablespoon of warm brown stock all around</u> (optional) and the drippings of the skillet.

8. Cover with slices of lemon dipped in chopped parsley and <u>serve immediately</u>.

Goujonnettes of Sole

(Goujonnettes de Sole)

Goujon is a small fresh water fish that's called gudgeon in English. In France it is deep fried and eaten like French fries. Goujonnette is made from larger fillets of fish and cut into small goujonlike strips and deep fried.

Fried fish is usually coated with flour or bread crumbs and either pan fried or deep fried. Deep-fried fish is usually soaked in beer and then coated with flour or bread crumbs. Pan-fried fish is usually soaked in milk and then coated with flour.

Fillet of sole is often used for goujonnettes. Serve with mayonnaise or tartar sauce.

1. <u>Cut the fillets in long strips</u> about ¼-inch (6-millimeters) wide by 4 to 5 inches (10 to 13 centimeters) long.

2. Place the fish strips in a small bowl and cover with beer. Lift the pieces of fish from the beer and dip them into flour. <u>Shake well.</u>

3. Place the flour-coated strips of fish into a colander and <u>shake well to eliminate excess flour</u>. Heat vegetable oil to 375 to 400 degrees (190 to 204°C) and dip the *goujonnettes*, a handful at the time, into the fat. Fry for 6 to 8 minutes on high heat, until nicely browned all around.

4. Lift the *goujonnettes* from the oil with a slotted spoon. Sprinkle lightly with salt and <u>arrange on a platter or in a folded towel</u>. Serve with lemon wedges, lemon butter, or tartar sauce.

Stuffed Brill

(Barbue Farcie)

The brill is a type of small turbot from the flat fish family. It is similar to an extra large sole. Other kinds of flat fish can also be boned and stuffed in the same manner.

YIELD: 4 to 6 main course servings or 8 to 10 first course servings

1 brill or very large lemon sole or small halibut, approximately 3 pounds (1.4 kilograms), neither gutted nor trimmed

STUFFING

2 tablespoons (28 grams) unsalted butter

1¼ cups (75 grams) fresh bread crumbs (3 to 4 slices white bread)

2 tablespoons freshly chopped parsley

6 shallots, peeled and finely chopped (⅓ cup/50 grams)

¾ cup (170 grams) coarsely chopped shrimp, peeled, deveined and briefly cooked

½ teaspoon salt

¼ teaspoon freshly ground black pepper

TO COOK THE FISH

½ tablespoons (7 grams) unsalted butter

1 small leek, finely chopped (½ cup/75 grams)

2 cups (160 grams) sliced mushrooms

¼ teaspoon freshly ground black pepper

½ teaspoon salt

1 cup (237 milliliters) dry white wine

TO FINISH THE SAUCE

2 tablespoons heavy cream

½ stick unsalted butter (¼ cup/56 grams)

Salt and freshly ground black pepper to taste

1 tablespoon chopped fresh herbs (parsley, tarragon, chives, etc.)

1. Trim away the outside bones of the fish and place it flat on a chopping board, white-ish side up. With a sharp knife, cut along the central line.

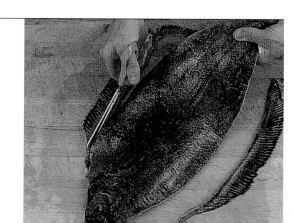

2. Using a flexible bladed fish knife, separate the flesh from the bone by sliding the blade along the central bone. <u>Repeat on the other side</u>. Do not cut through the skin. You will notice that the flesh stops near another layer of bone.

3. Turn the fish black side up and repeat the same procedure on this side. <u>Using a large pair of shears, cut the bone away from the fish on both sides.</u>

4. Cut the central bone as close as you can from the tail and from the head. It should come out in one piece. <u>The fillets are now completely loose, but still held together by the head and the tail</u>. To prepare the stuffing, melt the butter in a skillet and add the bread crumbs. Cook, stirring, until the crumbs are nicely browned. Transfer to a bowl and add the parsley, shallots, shrimp, salt, and pepper.

5. Preheat the oven to 425 degrees (218°C). Butter a roasting pan with ½ tablespoon (7 grams) of butter. Line the pan with the leek and mushrooms. Place the fish over this mixture, arranging the bottom fillets so they touch. <u>Place the stuffing inside</u> and cover with the two top fillets. Sprinkle with salt and pepper and pour the white wine on top.

6. Cover with a piece of buttered parchment paper and place the roasting pan on top of the stove. Bring to a boil and place in the oven for 15 minutes. Remove from the oven and, <u>using a knife, remove the black skin and discard</u>. Remove the solids around the fish and place in a bowl.

7. <u>Using a small knife, pull away the layer of bones</u> next to the fillets. It slides out easily. Discard the bones.

8. <u>Holding the fish in place with the lid, pour the cooking liquid into a saucepan</u> and set aside for the sauce. You should have about ½ cup (118 milliliters) of liquid.

9. <u>Place a serving platter on top of the fish</u> and turn upside down. Arrange the solids around the fish.

10. <u>Pull off the skin on the white side and discard</u>. Cover the cleaned fish with parchment paper and keep warm in a 160 degree (70°C) oven while you make the sauce. Add heavy cream to the reserved cooking liquid and bring to a boil. Reduce, if necessary, to ¾ cup (178 milliliters). Add the butter, piece by piece, whisking between each addition as you would for a *beurre blanc*. Taste for seasonings and add salt and pepper if necessary. Remove the fish from the oven. Blot off any juices that may have accumulated around the fish.

11. <u>Pour the sauce over the fish</u>. Sprinkle with fresh herbs and serve immediately.

> **Start with the simple techniques and work gradually toward the more involved and complicated ones.**

Whiting Breaded "En Colère"

(Merlan "en Colère")

Whiting is a very good, inexpensive fish. It has only a large central bone, which means it is easy to eat. It is extremely delicate provided it is well cleaned. Whiting can be served plain, poached or sautéed in butter, as well as deep fried. In our recipe, it is twisted into a crown shape called "en colère," "angry-style," so-called because its tail is secured in its mouth.

YIELD: 2 to 3 servings

2 to 3 whiting

BATTER

1 large egg, slightly beaten

1 teaspoon vegetable oil

1 tablespoon water

¼ teaspoon salt

Dash of freshly ground white pepper

2 tablespoons all-purpose flour

2 cups (120 grams) fresh bread crumbs

Vegetable oil for frying

COLBERT BUTTER

YIELD: A generous ½ cup (112 grams)

1 stick (½ cup/112 grams) unsalted butter

1 tablespoon fresh tarragon leaves

2 teaspoons fresh lime juice

¼ teaspoon freshly ground black pepper

¼ teaspoon salt

1 tablespoon meat glaze (see page 27), diluted and melted

2 tablespoons white wine

1. Each whiting should weigh approximately ¾ pound (340 grams) before gutting. Make sure you remove the gill as well as the thin black skin inside the cavity on both sides of the wall of the abdomen. If the black veil is left in, it will make the fish bitter. Trim the fins, and wash under running water. Dry the whiting with paper towels.

2. <u>Twist the fish to place the tail between the jaws</u> and squeeze them to close and hold the tail in place. To prepare the batter, mix together the egg, oil, water, salt, and pepper.

3. Coat the whiting lightly with flour and pat all over to shake off the excess. Dip into the egg batter to coat well and push off the excess with your fingers. <u>Roll the egg-coated whiting in the breadcrumbs.</u> Pat firmly so the crumbs stick to the fish.

4. <u>Hollow out the centers of 6 large mushrooms caps,</u> reserving the trimmings for stocks and sauces. Brush the caps with lemon juice to prevent discoloration.

5. Heat at least 3 inches (7½ centimeters) of oil to about 350 degrees (177°C). Lower the fish into the oil and cook for 8 to 10 minutes. It should be well browned outside. To check if the fish is done, insert a fork or knife along the back bone of the thickest part of the fish-the flesh should separate from the bone easily. Drain the fish and <u>serve on a platter with fried parsley (page 113)</u>, <u>lemon wedges,</u> and Colbert butter spooned into hollowed-out mushrooms.

Cleaning and Boning Trout

(Préparation de la Truite)

Fresh trout can be gutted from the gill, opened, and the fish boned out. It can be sautéed with the head on, or the tail slid through the mouth for a different presentation.

1. Clip off the fins—but not the tail—with scissors and <u>cut the underside of the fish from just above the tail</u> to the head.

2. The fish can be gutted from the underside or from the gill area. <u>To remove the gills, insert your index finger into the gill cavity, moving it from one side of the cavity to the other, and remove the gills with your fingers by pulling on them.</u> Most of the guts will come out attached to the gills. Wash the trout thoroughly inside and out under cold water. The trout is now ready for grilling or even poaching.

3. <u>Cut at the tail end, below the rib cage,</u> on each side of the central bone to loosen the two fillets.

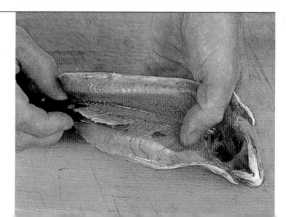

4. When one side is finished, repeat on the other, starting at the head. <u>Slide your knife behind the rib cage until the central bone is loose and the rib cage exposed</u>. Place the trout on its back and, holding a small, pointed, sharp knife, cutting side up, slide the point of the blade behind the rib cage on the right side of the trout. Keep cutting behind the rib cage to expose the central bone.

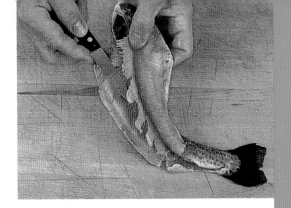

5. Now that the rib cage is exposed, <u>cut behind it and down, to free the two fillets completely</u> from the central bone.

6. Using your thumb and index finger, <u>pry out the bone to loosen it and break it at the head</u> as close as possible to the inside of the gill area.

7. <u>With scissors, cut the bone at the tail</u> and cut off any extra fins and bones that are visible. The trout could now be cooked flat like a steak in just a couple of minutes.

Trout with Almonds

(Truite Amandine)

1. Another way of using the boned out trout is to <u>fold the trout inward</u> and pull the tail through the mouth.

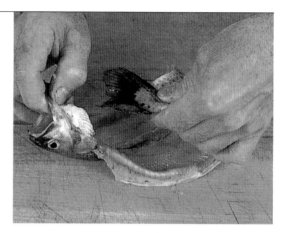

2. <u>The trout is now ready to be sautéed.</u>

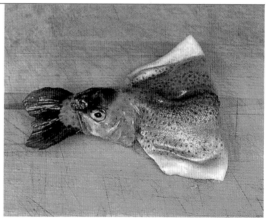

3. Sprinkle the trout with salt, freshly ground black pepper and dredge lightly in flour. Melt 3 tablespoons (42 grams) butter in a heavy skillet, and when hot, place the fish in a skillet, skin side down, and cook on medium to low heat for about 3½ minutes on each side. <u>The skin should be crisp and nicely browned.</u>

4. Place the trout on a warm plate and add 1 tablespoon sliced almonds to the drippings. Cook the almonds for about 1 minute in the hot butter. <u>Spoon almond and drippings mixture over the trout.</u>

5. Sprinkle with a few drops of lemon juice and decorate with slices of lemon dipped in chopped parsley. <u>Serve immediately.</u>

Rolled Trout

(Paupiettes de Truites)

Another use is to roll the fillet of trout (stuffed or unstuffed) and cook it with its head on.

1. <u>Separate the fillets from the central bones by cutting each side of the bones.</u>

2. <u>Remove the central bone near the head</u>.

3. <u>Roll each fillet so that the skin shows on the outside</u>.

4. <u>Rolled up trout, ready to cook</u>. Trout are often prepared this way when they are to be poached and served cold in aspic.

Smoking Fish

(Fumage des Poissons)

Commercially smoked fish is expensive and often not as good as fish smoked at home. The commercial product is usually more salted and more smoked than the homemade product because the manufacturers want the fish to have the longest shelflife possible.

Smoking your own fish is fun and rewarding. There are only a few smoked fish available on the market—such as white fish, sturgeon, trout and salmon—but you can smoke practically any type of fish at home. We have had great results with mullets, porgie, eel, pike, etc. There are two basic ways of smoking: the hot and cold methods. The hot method partially cooks the fish as it smokes. The cold method smokes the fish but leaves it raw.

If you have one of the small home smokers, you will be able to hot smoke but not cold smoke. If you have no smoker, you can make one yourself from an old refrigerator or metal locker. It can be used for both the hot and cold methods. Hot smoking is done at temperatures between 200 to 225 degrees (93 to 107 °C). Cold smoking temperatures shouldn't go above 90 degrees (32°C).

Before you smoke—whichever way you choose—you have to cure the fish with salt. Here, too, there are two different methods: You can cure it in a liquid brine (salt and water), or with dry salt. The salt leeches all the moisture out of the fish, thereby depriving the bacteria of the medium necessary for its survival. It is in this way that salting preserves. Use the kosher coarse salt which has larger crystals to better cure the fish.

Both meat and fish are smoked by being exposed to the smoke given off by smouldering wood chips. Different types of woods can be used—hickory, maple, alder, juniper, and most woods from fruit trees. Resinous woods such as pine, spruce, etc., or pressure-tested wood should be avoided. Herbs such as bay leaves or thyme, rosemary, oregano, or dry basil stems can be added to the wood chips to flavor the smoke.

In the first technique we are hot smoking trout in a little home smoker. In the second, we will cold smoke salmon in a converted ice box smoker. Hot smoking is necessary with a tight, firm fleshed fish such as sturgeon, eel and even trout. The tougher the flesh, the higher the temperature should go; 200 degrees (93°C) will be sufficient for trout, but it should go up to 225 degrees (107°C) for eel. Because of its particular texture, salmon is cold smoked. If subjected to temperatures above 90 degrees (32°C), it will cook through. The proteins coagulate around 120 degrees (49°C) and force out the moisture of the fish (it is visible as a white custard-like sediment); the flesh will flake and the salmon cook.

SMOKED TROUT (Truites Fumées)

YIELD: 12 first course lunch or brunch servings

4 cups (1 scant liter) water
2 cups (640 grams) kosher salt
1 tablespoon sugar
6 trout, 12 ounces (340 grams) each, gutted and cleaned
Vegetable oil
Hickory or alder chips

1. Put the salt and sugar in tepid tap water. Mix to dissolve and let cool. (The saltiness of the brine can be checked with a hydrometer—the specific gravity should be 1155 at 60 degrees Fahrenheit (15°C)—or by floating an egg on top of the brine; a bit of eggshell the size of a 50 cent coin should emerge from the water.) Place the trout in the brine for 2 hours. Remove, wipe dry with paper towels inside and out, and rub lightly with vegetable oil.

2. Skewer the trout, three at a time, through the gills and mouths. (We used sticks of wood as skewers.)

3. Hang the trout in the smoker. Plug in the hot plate, fill up the little tray with the wood chips, return to the smoker, and put the cover back on the smoker. Leave the trout in the smoker for approximately 1 hour. (It will take 15 to 20 minutes before the chips are hot enough to produce smoke.)

4. After 1 hour, unplug the smoker and leave the trout inside for another hour to cool and set. <u>Take the trout out</u>. They will have a nice yellowish color, be slightly warm to the touch and a little soft.

5. Refrigerate for at least 1 day to allow the trout to set and the taste to develop. Then remove the skin: <u>Start at the belly and "unwrap" to the back</u>. Continue unwrapping to the other side. The skin will come off in one piece.

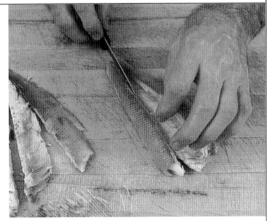

6. Remove the head and <u>split the top fillet in half following the line down the center of the trout</u>. Pull out the back fillet, which is the thickest and the nicest. It should slide off the bone easily. Then push away on the other side to separate the belly fillet from the bone.

7. <u>Remove the central bone which should come out in one piece</u>. The trout is now ready and is usually served with toast and butter. For an elegant first course serve lukewarm, boned-out fillet of trout rolled and filled with scrambled eggs.

SMOKED SALMON (Saumon Fumé)

Use a large thick salmon. Ours weighed 10 pounds/4.5 kilograms (gutted, head on). If you don't want to smoke a whole fillet, you can smoke half a fillet as long as the flesh is thick. Take your piece from the thickest part of the fillet. The instructions that follow are for one side of salmon, 3½ pounds (1.6 kilograms) with skin on but boned, and head and tail removed.

YIELD: about 10 servings as a first course

½ **of a 10-pound (4.5-kilogram) salmon, scaled, washed, and filleted**

2 cups (640 grams) kosher salt mixed with ⅓ cup (75 grams) sugar

2 tablespoons peanut oil

1. Clean and fillet the salmon. Your fishmonger can do this for you or you can do it yourself following the instructions on page 202.

2. Using a pair of tweezers or small pliers, pull out the tiny bones which run down the center of the fillet. The bones can also be removed after smoking, too. If left, they make carving difficult.

3. Spread some of the salt mixture on a large rectangular piece of aluminum foil and place the salmon, skin-side down, on top. Spread the rest of the salt mixture on top, sprinkling just a little on the tail because it is thin and shouldn't absorb too much salt. There should be about ⅛ inch (3 millimeters) of salt mixture on top of the fillet except for the tail end.

4. Pack the salmon tightly in the aluminum foil and refrigerate for 6-8 hours or overnight, during which time the salmon will cure. Adjust the curing time for larger or smaller slabs of salmon. Remove from the aluminum foil, wash under cold water, and dry carefully with paper towels.

5. Place the salmon on a wire rack and let it dry for approximately 6 hours or overnight in front of a fan. A thin veil will form on top of the skin which should be dry to the touch. Rub the fillet generously all around with peanut oil. (At this point the salmon could be served in thin slices as gravlax.) To smoke the salmon, place in the smoker.

6. We use an electric barbecue starter to get the wood chips smoking. Note that an aluminum gutter elbow was fitted to go through the old refrigerator retrofitted as a smoker. This leaves the source of the heat on the outside so that only the smoke enters the refrigerator. With this method the temperature will not exceed 90 degrees (32°C) inside the box.

7. Embed the barbecue starter into the wood chips. <u>Wrap the opening with aluminum foil</u> to contain the smoke and force it through the pipe into the refrigerator. Plug the starter in for 3 minutes. <u>The chips will start smoking after about 1 minute</u>. After 3 minutes of smoke, unplug. The chips will continue to smoke for a few minutes. Let the salmon "rest" (without opening the door) for 1 hour.

8. <u>Repeat the same procedure twice more</u>. This gives a total of 9 minutes of intense smoke and about 3½ hours in the smoker.

9. <u>The salmon in the smoker</u>. Let the slab dry and settle under refrigeration for at least 1 day before slicing. Slice thin on a slant and serve plain with a dash of lemon juice and thin, buttered slices of black bread. The salmon can also be seasoned with capers, olive oil, and ground black pepper.

Boning Out and Filleting Black Bass and Gravlax

(Bar en Gravlax)

Black bass has firm white flesh and is excellent sautéed, poached, or raw in gravlax. This recipe serves 6 to 8.

1. To bone the fish, insert a long, sturdy, sharp knife under the gill toward the head. Twist the knife so the blade faces out and, in one swoop, <u>cut down through the rib cage</u> and along the top of the central bone to remove the whole fillet in one piece.

2. Turn the fish on the other side and <u>repeat this procedure to remove the other fillet</u>. You will notice that the line of rib bones is still attached to each of the fillets.

3. <u>Slide the point of your knife under the rib bones</u> on each of the fillets and remove the rib cage bones.

4. To remove the skin, make a cut at the tail end down through the fillet to the skin. <u>Hold the end of the skin with one hand and pull while pushing your knife in the other direction</u>, moving your knife forward in a jigsaw motion with the blade at about a 45-degree angle. The fish fillet will slide off the skin.

5. Notice that in the center of the fillet, on the side of the head, there is a line of bones about one-third of the way down. <u>Cut a strip down the center to remove those bones.</u> The fillets should be completely free of skin, bones, and sinew. Use as needed or make gravlax.

GRAVLAX (Gravlax)

Although gravlax made with salmon, a fatty fish, will be very moist and rich, it can also be made with waxy, very firm, thinner, white-fleshed fish. Red snapper, black fish, and black bass all work particulary well for this type of gravlax.

YIELD: 12 servings as a first course

CURING

1½ tablespoons sugar

2½ tablespoons kosher salt

2 black bass (each weighing about 1½ pounds/680 grams), cleaned (each fillet weighing about 5 to 6 ounces/142 to 170 grams)

FLAVORING

1 tablespoon gin

½ teaspoon freshly ground black pepper

1 teaspoon grated lime rind

2 teaspoons chopped fresh mint

1 tablespoon chopped fresh dill

3 tablespoons chopped fresh Italian parsley

1. Mix the sugar and salt together. Place the fillets on a piece of plastic wrap on top of a piece of aluminum foil. Sprinkle the salt and sugar mixture over them, patting it all around the fillets. Wrap in the plastic wrap and aluminum foil, and refrigerate on a tray for 5 to 6 hours to cure. When cured, you will notice that the fillets have absorbed most of the sugar-salt mixture and are firm. Rub the fillets with the gin. Mix the pepper, lime, mint, dill, and parsley together, and pat this over the fillets. Wrap again and refrigerate with a 3- or 4-pound weight on top to press the fish down and make the flesh more compact. Refrigerate for a few hours or overnight.

2. Remove the wrappings and place the fillets flat on the table. Using a long, thin knife, cut on the bias into thin slices about 2 to 3 inches long and the width of the fillet. Each of the slices should be bordered with a thin layer of the green.

3. Mix together 2 cups (350 grams) diced cucumbers, 2 cups (240 grams) chopped hard-cooked eggs, 1/2 cup (125 grams) sour cream, and ¼ teaspoon each salt and pepper (you should have about 4 cups). Toast 12 bread ovals until nicely browned. Cover each slice with approximately 1/3 cup (75 grams) of the sour cream-cucumber-egg mixture and cover with 3 or 4 slices of cured fish.

4. Arrange on a platter. Notice that the fish should be arranged on the bread so the border of the fish remains on the outside, forming a design. Decorate by placing a piece of parsley, mint, or dill in the center of each and serve as soon as possible.

Preparing Ray or Skate Wings

(Préparation des Ailes de Raies)

Buying a whole skate is not common, as most fish mongers only sell the wings. The ray is excellent poached, sautéed, or grilled. If it is to be grilled or sautéed, as in our Ray Meunière, the skin must be removed prior to cooking. The black skin, especially, tends to be quite tough and is full of needle-like prickers. When it is poached, the skin is left on and removed after cooking. Vinegar is always added to the water to eliminate the sliminess.

RAY MEUNIERE WITH MUSHROOMS

YIELD: 4 servings

2 small rays (each about 1½ pounds/680 grams), whole and not gutted, or
  1 large wing (about 2 pounds/907 grams
¼ teaspoon salt
⅛ teaspoon freshly ground black pepper
⅓ cup (50 grams) all-purpose flour, for dredging
2 tablespoons (28 grams) unsalted butter
2 tablespoons olive oil
4 ounces (180 grams) mushrooms, sliced (about 2 cups)
Dash of salt and freshly ground black pepper

TO FINISH THE DISH
2 tablespoons (28 grams) unsalted butter
1 tablespoon lemon juice
1 tablespoon chopped fresh Italian parsley

1. The ray on the left is shown on its side with the tough, prickly black skin. On the right, it is turned over to show the white underside of the ray, where the mouth is and the skin is softer and smoother.

2. <u>Cut the wings from the ray by following the bone on each side of the belly.</u> The wings are the edible portion of the fish.

3. A large ray's wing bought at the market is approximately 1½ inches (3 centimeters) thick and weighs 2 pounds (1 kilogram). <u>Cut the wing into 4 slabs about 5 ounces (141 grams) each.</u> The pieces can now be poached or sautéed.

4. <u>To sauté, use a sharp knife to remove the black skin,</u> holding it with a towel if too prickly.

5. <u>Remove the white skin underneath,</u> using the technique shown to remove skin from fish fillets.

6. Salt and pepper the pieces of ray and dredge with flour, shaking off any excess. Heat the butter and oil in a large, sturdy skillet. When hot, add the ray. Cook over medium to high heat for about 6 minutes on one side, turn, and cook approximately 6 minutes longer on the other side, a total of 12 minutes. It should be cooked through but not overcooked. The meat should separate from the bone when pulled but still be slightly moist and pink in the center.

7. Place the cooked ray on a serving platter or, as here, on a copper dish. Add the sliced mushrooms to the drippings in the pan and cook briefly (1 minute), as they should still be firm. Season with a dash of salt and pepper, then lift the mushrooms out of the pan and scatter them on top of the ray. Heat the remaining 2 tablespoons (28 grams) of butter in a clean skillet until it is foamy and brown. Sprinkle the lemon juice on the ray, pour the hot butter on top, garnish with chopped parsley, and serve immediately.

Cleaning Frogs

(Nettoyage des Grenouilles)

As a child, I used to go fishing for frogs with my father and brothers. In France, the green frog is commonly eaten and is about half the size of the bull frog that we use in the United States. The bull frogs are quite large and tender when young. The meat is usually pale beige and plump. If you come across darker-colored meat or stringy-looking flesh, it is likely that the frog is older and will be tough.

1. Frogs can be caught with a net during the day or at night with the help of a flashlight. Hold the frog by the hind legs and hit its head with a rock to kill it. Using large scissors, cut the dead frog just under the head and front leg. Grasp the skin with one hand and pull it while holding the frog with the other hand. It will peel off easily. With scissors, cut above the feet. With a small frog, only the meaty back legs are used.

2. With a larger frog, cut the skin on the back and, using both hands, <u>insert your fingers underneath the skin and pull on each side</u>.

3. <u>With a firm pull, the skin will slide off easily</u>. Cut just below the head at one end and above the feet at the other end. Remove and discard the guts.

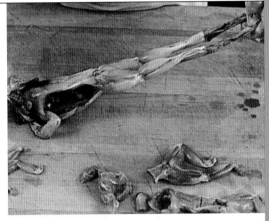

4. <u>Using the scissors, separate the front from the back</u>. For very large frogs, separate the legs. Wash thoroughly under cool water. They can now be sautéed or poached.

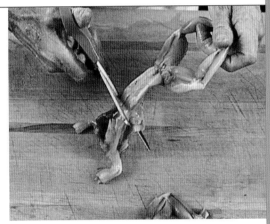

Skinning and Cleaning Eel

(Dépouillage et Nettoyage des Anguilles)

Eel used to be a great favorite, not only in the ancient cooking of the Romans but throughout the Middle Ages and practically up to the twentieth century. It is not, however, very commonly served in the United States. Most of the eels caught in this country are sent to Germany, Holland, and Belgium, which are great eel-loving countries.

Eel is one of the best fish to smoke, as it is very fatty and retains the smoke well, while the meat remains very spongy, moist, and tender. If eel is smoked, it is not skinned. When sautéed or stewed, however, it must be skinned. The best eel for this purpose weighs about 1 to 1 ½ pound (450 to 680 grams), at the most. Although a second skin underneath, a fatty layer on top of the flesh, is not always removed, in my opinion removing it greatly improves the taste. The first skin is pulled off and the eel is blanched. This sets the fat layer on top, which can then be scraped off or removed with a knife, and the eel is then sautéed or used in stew.

EEL WITH POTATO MIETTES

YIELD: 6 servings

TO COOK THE EELS

2 eels (1¼ pound each/567 grams)

All-purpose flour

3 tablespoons peanut oil

2 tablespoons (28 grams) unsalted butter

Dash salt

TO COOK THE POTATOES

2 pounds (907 grams) potatoes,
   (about 6 potatoes)

1 tablespoon (14 grams) unsalted butter

3 tablespoons olive oil

5 scallions, coarsely chopped
   (about ½ cup/60 grams)

Dash each salt and freshly ground
   black pepper

TO FINISH

3 tablespoons (42 grams) unsalted butter

1 teaspoon chopped garlic

1 tablespoon red wine vinegar

½ cup (100 grams) chopped fresh sorrel

1. Cut all around the head of the eel just under the side fin to loosen the skin.

2. Hold the slippery head with a towel. <u>Using pliers, pull the skin, which should come off easily.</u>

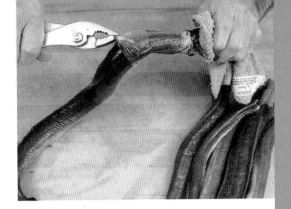

3. Cut off the head and, with scissors, <u>cut off the fin on each side</u>.

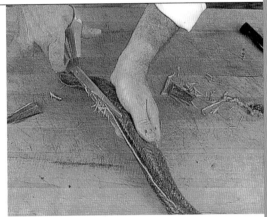

4. <u>Using a sharp knife, open the belly of the eel from the anus to the head</u> and clean the inside, removing all the guts and blood. Cut each eel into about 5 pieces, each about 4 inches (10 centimeters) long.

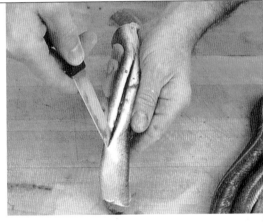

5. Bring 2 quarts of water to boil. Drop the eel pieces into the boiling water, bring it back to the boil, and boil 2 to 3 minutes. Drain the eel in a colander and rinse well under cold water until cold. <u>When cold, peel or scrape off all the black surface, which is mostly fat, until the eel is practically clean of all that second skin and fat.</u>

6. To cook the eels: Dry the eel pieces with a paper towel and sprinkle them with flour, coating well. Divide the oil and butter between 2 large skillets and, when hot, add the floured pieces of eel. Sprinkle lightly with salt and brown over medium to low heat for 7 to 8 minutes, <u>turning the pieces after 3 to 4 minutes to brown evenly.</u> Cover the skillets and set the eel aside to continue cooking and softening in its own heat for another 3 to 4 minutes.

7. For the potatoes: Peel the potatoes, cut into ¼-inch (7-millimeter) slices and then into ¼-inch (7 millimeter) dice. Wash in cold water and drain. Heat the butter and oil in a large skillet, preferably no stick. When hot, add the well-drained potatoes. Sauté over high heat for 12 to 15 minutes, <u>stirring occasionally, until nicely browned and cooked.</u> Add the scallions, sprinkle with a dash of salt and pepper, and continue cooking for 2 to 3 minutes longer.

8. At serving time, arrange the potatoes and scallions on individual plates. Place 1 or 2 pieces of cooked eel on top. Melt the 3 tablespoons (42 grams) butter in a skillet. When foaming but not too hot, add the garlic, cook for a few seconds, and then add the red wine vinegar. Heat through and spoon onto the eel. Sprinkle with the fresh sorrel (or, if not available, another type of herb). (The acidity of the sorrel tends to go well with the richness of the eel.) Serve immediately.

Identifying Caviar
(Caviar: Différentes Sortes)

1. The most common types of caviar available. In the top row, from left to right: natural salmon (from the chum), red salmon (from the king), and whitefish caviar. In the bottom row, from left to right: beluga, osetra, sevruga, and pressed caviar. Notice that the black sturgeon caviar is identified by the color on the lid of the can; blue for beluga, yellow for osetra, green for sevruga, and red/purple for pressed caviar.

2. The best-quality caviars: from left to right, beluga, osetra, and sevruga. Notice the size and color of the beluga and that the osetra is slightly golden/greenish with a very separated grain. The sevruga grains are smaller and a bit lighter in color.

3. The same three caviars displayed on spoons: from left to right, beluga, osetra, and sevruga. Sometimes the color will change from one fish to another, getting lighter or darker depending on the maturity of the eggs, the time of the year it is fished, the length of time it has been kept, the amount of salt in the brine, how long it has been stirred, and so on.

4. Three other types of caviar: from left to right, the red coho, the whitefish, and the natural, from the chum salmon.

5. Served on a plate with mother-of-pearl spoons: from left to right, the red king, the whitefish, and the natural. Notice that the grains should be whole, soft, and sticking together but not broken.

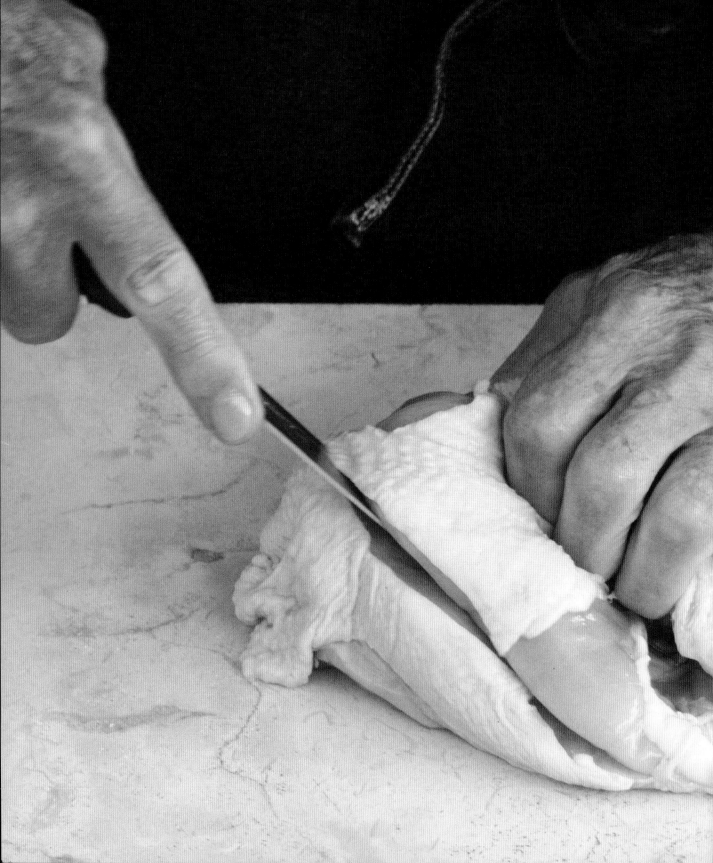

POULTRY

Eviscerating a Chicken or Other Poultry

(Vidage des Volailles)

1. The technique used to eviscerate a chicken is the same as that for eviscerating a pheasant, duck, grouse, or even smaller birds such as quail or squab. The feet, which are very gelatinous, are good used in stock. If you use the feet in a stock, the thick scaly skin that covers them should be peeled off. This is easily done if the feet are passed over the flame of a gas range. Roast the feet all around until the skin starts to blister; then, using a towel to prevent burning your hand, rub the skin off. It will come off easily.

2. For a special presentation, trim each side of the feet, keeping only the center claw with the tip cut off.

3. For aesthetic reasons, trim the ends of the wing tips and the small protrusion, or nubbin, on the side of each wing tip.

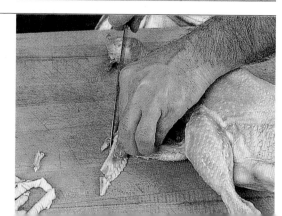

4. Fold the wings as illustrated to hold them in place. To clean out the chicken: Place the chicken on its belly and press the skin of the neck underneath to make it taut on top. Slit the neck skin the length of the neck with a sharp knife.

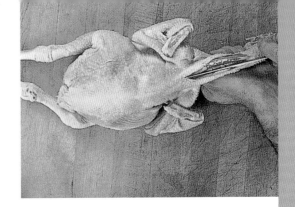

5. Separate the neck from the skin by pulling with both hands.

6. Separate the layer of skin from the trachea and baglike crop (which leads to the first stomach) attached to it.

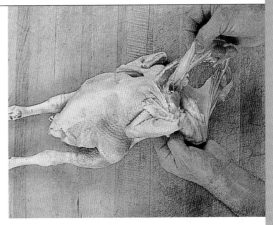

7. Placing the chicken on its back, pull the crop and skin up. Push your finger in along the backbone. On each side of it, run your finger up and down along the rib cage on each side and all around. The object here is to loosen the lungs in the area close to the neck opening.

8. Cut the neck and sac at the opening. <u>Notice how the skin of the neck is nice and clean inside</u> and large enough so that it can be folded back onto the chicken back to cover the whole opening.

9. With the chicken on its back, <u>cut near the tail to enlarge the opening</u>, cutting away the little round pieces of meat on the tail.

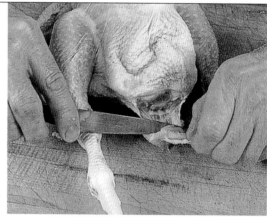

10. Then, using a knife, <u>slit the skin in the center from the tail to the point of the breast</u>, or sternum, to enlarge the opening.

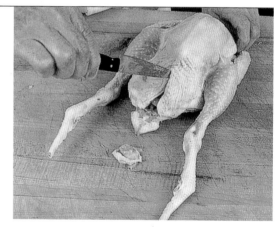

11. Slip your finger inside and remove the 2 large pieces of fat, one on each side of the opening. Loosen completely and <u>pull the entire insides out</u>.

12. If the insides have been properly loosened, they will come out in one piece. <u>To identify these parts, starting at the bottom are the lungs, then the heart and the liver, and, finally, the gizzard, or the second stomach, with the fat around it.</u> Separate these organs to clean.

13. <u>Notice that on top of the liver there is a green bag.</u> This is the gallbladder, and the green liquid bile inside is extremely bitter. Cut off the sac without breaking it. If any of the liquid spills on top of the liver, cut away the areas that have been touched by the bile as they will be very bitter. If store-bought livers are green in spots, it means that bile has spilled there, so be sure to remove contaminated areas.

14. Remove the fat around the gizzard and <u>slit it on the fleshier side to open it.</u>

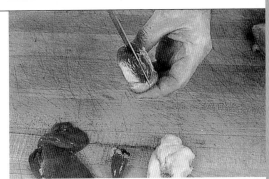

15. <u>Open the gizzard and remove the little sac inside</u> full of gravel. Discard it.

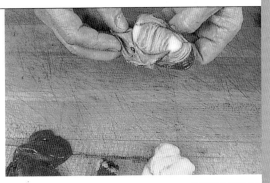

16. <u>The chicken, completely eviscerated.</u> In front, from left to right, the neck, the heart, the liver, the gizzard, and the fat. When you buy a chicken at the supermarket, you should find a package in the cavity with the liver, heart, and gizzard, all cleaned.

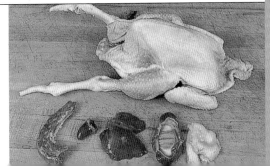

Trussing Chicken and Other Poultry

(Bridage du Poulet et Autres Volailles)

Once a bird is properly tied, it will keep its shape, be easier to manipulate and roast evenly throughout without getting dry. The chicken pictured has a mushroom stuffing under the skin, which accounts for the dark color.

METHOD 1

1. Trussing Method 1, without a trussing needle: Be sure to use a fairly thick cotton kitchen twine so it doesn't cut your fingers or the meat of the chicken. Slide the string under the tail of the chicken and around the tips of the drumsticks. <u>Then cross the string above the chicken.</u>

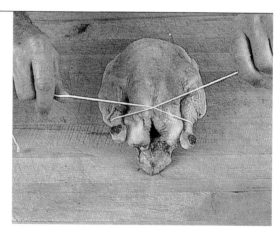

2. <u>Slide both ends of the string under the tips of the drumsticks</u> to create a Figure 8.

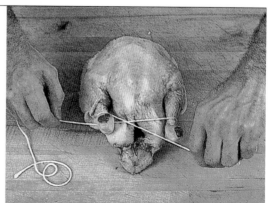

3. Pull the string together, which will tighten and close up the tail opening. Be sure the legs are pushed back snugly against the chicken and the breast is up. <u>Bring the 2 pieces of string around the sides of the chicken</u> until they join at the neck or next to the wing and tighten the string. It should secure the hanging skin of the neck and anchor behind the wing so it doesn't slide off.

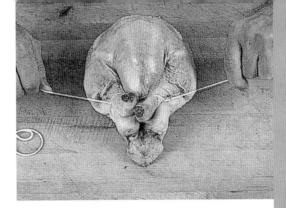

4. <u>Tie a knot, making several loops instead of just one</u>. The object is to make a knot that holds without someone's finger securing it. Secure further with a second knot. In this trussing technique, notice that the string does not go across the top of the breast of the chicken (which would mark the top and make it less attractive); it should just pass around the tips of the legs and extend along the sides and behind the neck and the wings.

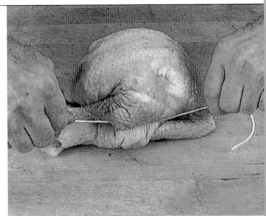

5. Trussing Method 2, with a trussing needle: In the following pictures, the trussing technique actually creates a design like an X with a closed bottom and top. Thread a long, thin trussing needle with string and, <u>starting at the soft spot on the lower part of the thigh near the carcass, push your needle through, coming out on the other side in the middle of the leg</u> between the thigh and the drumstick. Pull through.

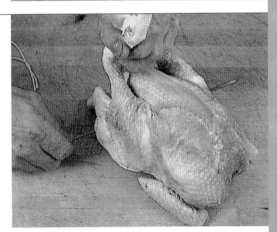

6. Place the chicken breast-side down. With the trussing needle and twine, <u>go through the wing, the skin of the neck, and the opposite wing</u>. Pull through.

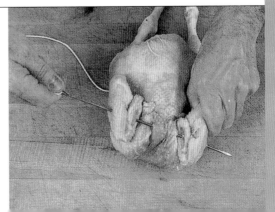

7. Turn the chicken over again onto its back and <u>push the needle from the center of the leg to the lower part of the thigh on the opposite side</u>, a reverse of what was done in step 6.

8. Be sure that the legs are pressed back against the breast of the chicken, then <u>come across above the leg with the needle and thread</u>. Secure with the same kind of knot used in step 4.

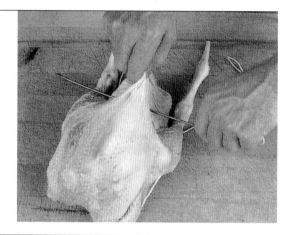

9. <u>Notice that the chicken on the left, with its legs folded, was trussed using the trussing needle, while the chicken on the right was trussed without it.</u>

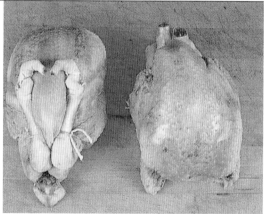

Tying Chicken (Half-Hitch Technique)

(Ficeler la Volaille)

The next four pictures demonstrate how to tie a stuffed, boned chicken using the half-hitch technique. The same technique is used to tie a veal, lamb, or beef roast, as well.

1. Cross the legs of the chicken and attach together with kitchen twine. <u>Tie the twine with a double knot at the drum end of the chicken.</u>

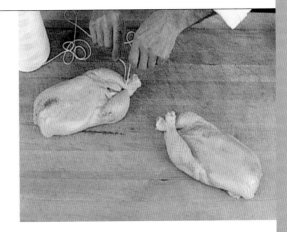

2. Make a loop at the opposite end, <u>then slide it underneath to within 2 inches (5 centimeters) of the drum end</u> and pull to tighten the loop (called the half-hitch).

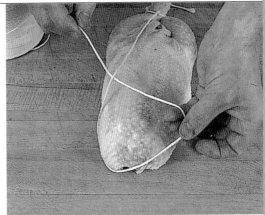

3. Repeat the loops down the <u>whole length of the chicken.</u>

4. When the chicken is secure on top, roll it gently until it is back-side up, and secure it on the back also. Make a loop around each crossing of the twine so it looks the same on the bottom as the top. <u>Finish by tying the twine at the crossing of the legs where the tying began.</u> Notice that the skin on the back is overlapping to hold the stuffing inside.

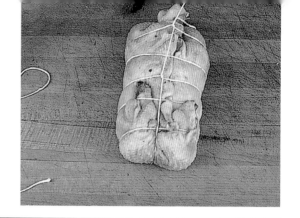

Chicken Stuffed under the Skin

(Poulet Farci sous la Peau)

Stuffing a chicken between the skin and the flesh not only flavors the bird but keeps it moist as well.

YIELD: 4 to 6 servings

STUFFING

1½ tablespoons olive oil

12 ounces mushrooms (about 3 cups loose/345 grams), sliced

½ teaspoon salt

¼ teaspoon freshly ground black pepper

1 tablespoon chopped Italian parsley

2 cloves garlic, peeled, crushed and chopped fine (1 teaspoon)

1 3½-pound (1.6-kilogram) roasting chicken

1 tablespoon (14 grams) soft unsalted butter

SAUCE

2 tablespoons finely chopped onion

2 to 3 cloves garlic, peeled, crushed and chopped (1 teaspoon)

2 cups (300 grams) fresh, coarsely chopped tomatoes (peeled and seeded)

Salt and freshly ground black pepper to taste

½ cup (75 grams) oil-cured pitted olives

1 tablespoon chopped Italian parsley or other fresh herbs (chives, tarragon, etc.)

1. Heat the oil in a saucepan, add the mushrooms, salt, and pepper. Cook on medium heat for 4 to 5 minutes, until the liquid given off by the mushrooms has evaporated. Add the parsley and garlic and mix well. Set aside and let cool. Preheat the oven to 400 degrees (204°C). Remove the wishbone from the chicken (see page 266, step 1) and slide your finger between the flesh and the skin to loosen the skin from the breast.

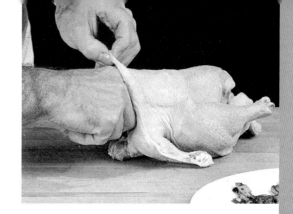

2. Keep pushing your fingers between the skin and the flesh to separate the leg meat from the skin. Slowly loosen the skin all around the chicken except along its back.

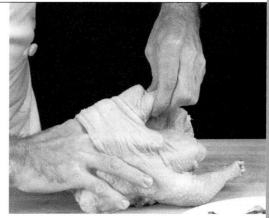

3. Lift the skin from the flesh and using a spoon or a spatula push the seasoned mushrooms inside.

4. Press the chicken back into shape and truss with or without a trussing needle. See trussing techniques, page 256.

5. Rub the skin of the chicken with softened butter, sprinkle lightly with salt and pepper and place the chicken on its side in a roasting pan or skillet. Roast for 1 hour, turning from side to side after the first 25 minutes and finally placing it on its back during the last 10 to 15 minutes of cooking. Baste every 5 minutes during the last 10 to 15 minutes of cooking.

6. Lift the chicken from the roasting pan, trim the ends of the drumsticks and keep the chicken warm on a platter, uncovered, in a 160-degree (70°C) oven. Pour out most of the clear fat in the roasting pan; add the onions and sauté for 1 to 2 minutes on medium heat. Add the garlic and mix for a few seconds, then the tomatoes. Bring to a boil and simmer gently, stirring with a wooden spatula to melt the solidified juices. Season the sauce with salt and pepper. At serving time, pour the sauce on top and around the chicken, sprinkle with the olives and the herbs, and serve immediately. The chicken can be carved in the dining room or cut into portions in the kitchen and arranged on plates with the olives, sauce, and herbs. The olives are not added to the dish prior to serving because they tend to blacken the sauce and make it taste bitter.

Creation in the kitchen follows your mood. Some days are clear and sunny, some dark and cloudy. The only control is technique.

Preparing Chicken for Broiling

(Poulet pour Griller)

Chickens that are to be broiled or grilled should be cut in the way that offers maximum surface to the heat.

1. Holding the chicken on its side, <u>cut through the backbone on one side of the neck</u> with a sturdy sharp knife.

2. <u>Pull the chicken open</u> and

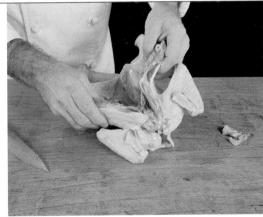

3. <u>separate the backbone by cutting on the other side of the neck bone</u> down to the tail. Reserve the pieces of bone for stock.

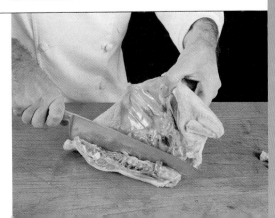

4. Remove the shoulder bones that stick up <u>by cutting at the joint</u>.

5. <u>Remove the rib cage</u> on each side.

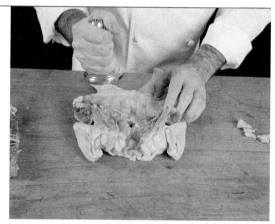

6. <u>Using a meat pounder, flatten the chicken.</u>

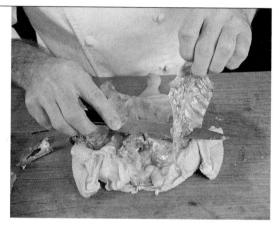

7. <u>Make an incision at the joint which separates the thigh from the drumstick.</u> This helps the chicken cook evenly (the thickest part of the leg would otherwise take longer to cook).

8. <u>Cut a hole through the skin</u> between the point where the breast and thigh meet.

9. <u>Push the tip of the drumstick</u>

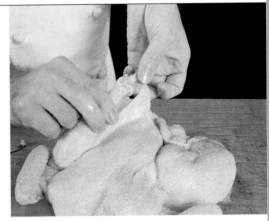

10. <u>through the hole</u> to secure the leg.

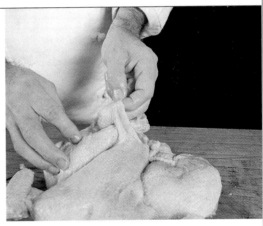

11. <u>Chicken ready to cook</u>. Preheat the oven to 450 degrees (232°C). Sprinkle with salt and pepper and brush with olive oil or softened butter before cooking. Cook skin-side up. For chicken *grillé à la diable*, bake the chicken—a 3- to 3½-pound (1.4- to 1.6-kilogram) roaster won't take more than 35 minutes—then coat with mustard and bread crumbs and finish under the broiler.

Boning a Chicken in One Piece

(Désossage Galantine)

1. Cut the chicken wings, leaving only the first joint at the shoulder. Keep the trimmings for stock. Lift up the skin by the neck and <u>slide a small, sharp paring knife along each side of the wishbone</u>, which forms a pointed triangle. Using your thumb and forefinger, push the bone out, prying at the point where the bone is held in the sternum, or breastbone.

2. Place the chicken on its side and make an incision through the skin on the back <u>from the neck to the tail</u>.

3. With the chicken on its side, lift up the skin at the shoulder joint. Move the wing and you will notice that there is a joint there. Place your knife where the joint is and cut, <u>wiggling the knife so it cuts through the joint</u>. Repeat on the other side at the shoulder.

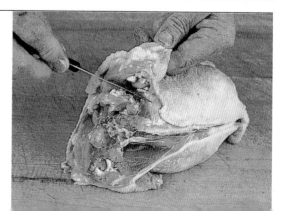

4. Hold the chicken carcass securely through the bone of the shoulder, with the thumb and forefinger of one hand; take hold of the wing at the joint with the other hand and pull. <u>The meat will come off the bone on the whole side of the carcass in the back down to the oyster of meat.</u> Repeat on the other side.

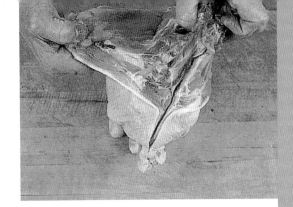

5. The meat is still attached to the bone at the breastbone. <u>Place two fingers on each side of the bone and pull down.</u> The chicken is now completely free from the top and is holding only at the joint of the leg.

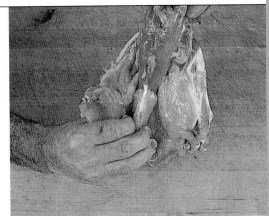

6. With the chicken on its side, <u>cut through the little oyster of meat up to the joint of the hip.</u>

7. Open up the leg and crack at the joint of the hip, then <u>cut through the joint to sever the large sinew.</u> Now pull the leg free from the carcass.

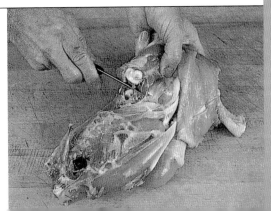

8. Repeat on the other side and, finally, <u>pull the whole carcass free of the meat</u>.

9. The only things left attached to the carcass are the fillets on each side of the breastbone. <u>Slide your thumb or finger underneath and pull them off</u>.

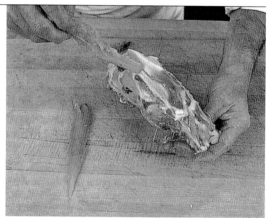

10. Holding one of the fillets flat on the table, with a knife scrape the meat free from the sinew that runs through the fillet, <u>pushing the meat off so the sinew comes out in one place</u>. Repeat with the other fillet.

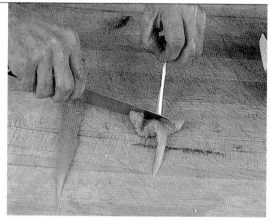

11. To remove the leg bone, cut around the tip of the thigh bone so it can be held. Holding the blade of the knife perpendicular to the bone, start scraping the meat down off the bone until you get down to the joint. <u>Cut around the joint with the knife</u> and, again, scrape the bone of the drumstick down to the tip of the leg.

12. <u>Break the bone at the end from the inside</u> so the outside skin is not torn and the knuckle at the end of the drumstick is left intact. (This end knuckle will be trimmed off after cooking because the meat would shrink if cut before cooking.)

13. <u>To remove the wing bones, cut around the joints where they are held and pull the bones off.</u>

14. Place the two fillets on the skin where there is no meat. Most of the surface should be lined with meat. Roast, poach, or stuff as needed.

Chicken Sausage
(Poulet en Saucisse)

A galantine is a boned bird, usually a duck or chicken, filled with a forcemeat mixture and alternate layers of liver, truffles, and the like. The boned, stuffed bird is poached in broth, cooled off and served with its own aspic. A ballottine is essentially the same except the stuffed bird is roasted instead of poached and served hot with a sauce. A simplified version, the poulet en saucisse, *is not quite a galantine or a ballottine, but it partakes of both.*

YIELD: 6 to 8 servings

1 boned-out chicken, pages 266

THE POACHING BROTH
Wings, bones, neck, and gizzard from chicken
1 carrot, peeled and coarsely sliced
1 onion, peeled and coarsely sliced
1 celery rib, coarsely sliced
2 bay leaves
¼ teaspoon dried thyme
½ teaspoon salt

Place the wing pieces, bones, neck, and gizzard in a kettle, cover with cold water and add the remaining ingredients. Bring to a boil and simmer for 1½ hours.

STUFFING AND COOKING
2 tablespoons (28 grams) unsalted butter
½ cup chopped onion

5 ounces (142 grams) mushrooms, chopped fine (1½ cups)
1½ teaspoons salt
½ teaspoon freshly ground white pepper
2 large chicken livers
Same amount or weight of chicken fat as of chicken livers (lumps from inside the bird)
8 ounces (227 grams) ground pork
1 tablespoon sherry

Melt the butter in a saucepan, add the onion, and sauté for 1 minute. Add the mushrooms, salt, and pepper. Cook until all the liquid is evaporated from the mushrooms and the mixture starts to stick in the pan (about 5 minutes). Set aside and let cool. Cut the livers and chicken fat in small pieces. Place in a food processor and process until smooth. Add the ground pork and sherry. All ingredients should be well blended and the mixture should be smooth.

1. Spread the purée of mushrooms evenly on the meat.

2. Then place the liver mixture on top, <u>spreading it with wet fingers</u>. (Wet your fingers by dipping them into cold water.)

3. <u>Bring both sides of the skin toward the center.</u>

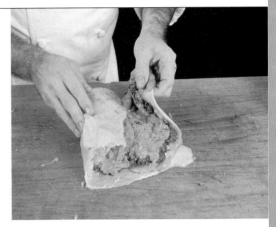

4. <u>Pull the skin of the neck to enclose the stuffing</u>.

5. At this point the chicken can be trussed, as explained on page 256, or poached for a galantine, which follows. <u>Place the chicken on a piece of cheesecloth</u> and

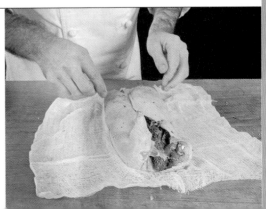

6. wrap carefully. <u>Tie with a string and secure both ends</u>, using the half-hitch technique, as explained on pages 259.

7. Using 2 tablespoons olive oil, <u>brown the chicken</u> (it will brown through the cheesecloth) in a large skillet on medium to low heat. It will take about 20 minutes.

8. Strain the prepared poaching broth. You should have 5 to 6 cups (1.2 to 1.4 liters) If you don't, add water as necessary. Place the browned bird in a deep casserole and <u>pour the stock on top</u>. It should come almost to the top of the bird.

9. Bring to a boil, lower the heat and simmer slowly, just below the boil, for 1½ hours. Let the chicken cool in the stock, overnight if possible. <u>Remove from stock</u>

10. <u>and unwrap.</u>

11. <u>Trim the meat around the drumstick bone</u> and pull the drum up.

12. Strain the cold stock through a fine sieve to remove the fat. Bring to a boil and reduce over medium heat until you have about 1¼ cups (296 milliliters) left. It should be reduced enough to make a concentrated natural aspic. Place the reduced stock on ice and mix while cooling. <u>Cut the "sausage" into ½-inch (13-millimeter) slices.</u>

13. Arrange on a large tray and <u>coat with the aspic when it is oily</u> and almost set. Place paper frills on the legbones.

Preparing Chicken for Stews

(Poulet pour Sauter)

There are literally hundreds of recipes that call for cut-up chicken. Chicken can be cut "off the bone" (the backbone) or cooked with the bone in.

OFF THE BONE

1. A chicken can be cut off the bone into quarters (2 legs and 2 single breasts), into 5 pieces (2 legs, 2 wings, 1 whole breast), or into 7 pieces, if the chicken is large enough (about 3½ pounds/1.6 kilograms), by separating the legs into thighs and drumsticks. Begin by cutting the wing at the second joint, leaving only the first section attached to the chicken.

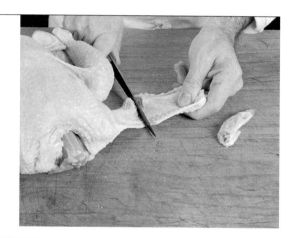

2. Place the chicken on its side and, with a small sharp knife, cut the skin all around the leg.

3. Open the leg to expose the joint where the thigh is attached to the body. Cut through the joint.

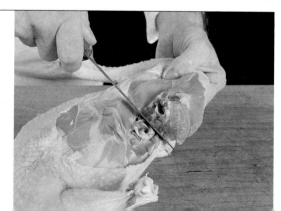

4. Holding the chicken firmly with one hand, <u>pull the leg until it separates from the body</u>.

5. <u>Cut off the tip of the drumstick</u> and

6. <u>push down on the meat to expose the bone</u>. Separate the thigh and drumstick at the joint. Cut the other leg in the same manner.

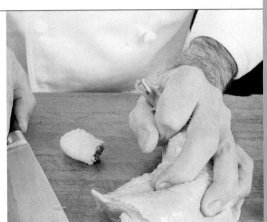

7. With the chicken on its side, pull back the wing. With your knife, find the joint where the wing is attached to the body and <u>cut through with the point of your knife</u>.

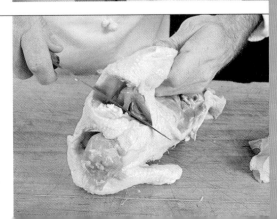

8. <u>Cut down along the breast</u> so part of the white meat is attached to the wing.

9. Then, holding the chicken firmly with one hand, <u>pull the breast section out</u>. Repeat on the other side.

10. <u>Trim the end bone of the wings.</u>

11. <u>Separate the breast</u> (in fact, the sternum; *bréchet* in French) from the carcass. Use the carcass, neck, and tip of bones for stock or sauces.

12. <u>Chicken ready to sauté</u>.

BONE IN

1. Remove the first joint of both wings. Then, with a heavy knife, <u>cut through the center of the breast</u> and through the back on one side of the backbone to separate the chicken into halves.

2. <u>Remove the backbone and tail</u> from the half it is attached to.

3. <u>Separate the leg from the wing</u>, going right through the bones with the large knife.

4. <u>Cut each breast and leg into halves</u>.

5. <u>Chicken ready for stewing or frying</u>.

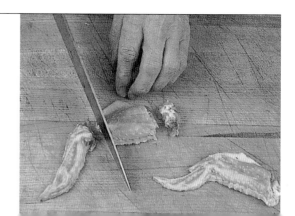

Stuffing Chicken Wings

(Farçir l'Aile de Poulet)

1. Cut the chicken wings above the wing tip joints on one side <u>and above the joint at the other end</u>, keeping only the middle segment. The object is to loosen the bones so they can be pulled out.

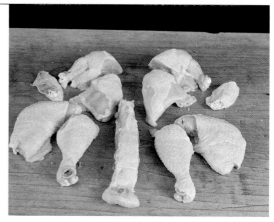

2. <u>Trim off the strips of fatty skin</u> that run along either side of the wing. It tends to be tough. (The trimmings can be frozen to use in stock or soup.)

3. Using a towel for a better grip, <u>pull out the 2 bones</u>; they should come out easily now that the wings have been cut at both ends.

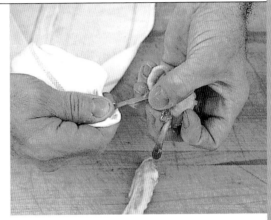

4. To stuff 12 to 16 wings: Place the 5 ounces (110 grams) of chicken meat, 2 ounces (56 grams) chicken fat, ¹/₄ cup (15 grams) parsley, a dash of nutmeg, and 1 teaspoon salt in the bowl of a food processor and process for 15 to 25 seconds, until well blended. Place the mixture in a pastry bag fitted with a ½-inch (13-millimeter) plain tip and <u>stuff the wings until they take on a roundish, balloon shape</u>. Don't worry if the stuffing is still visible. In a saucepan, cover the wings with cold water, bring to a boil, and cook at a gentle simmer for 30 minutes. Use as needed in consommé or stew.

Boning Out and Stuffing Chicken Breasts

(Désossage et Farçir de la Poitrine de Volaille)

1. <u>Cut off each wing close to the shoulder joint,</u> leaving only a tiny piece of bone on the body for looks. The wings can be used in stew or stock.

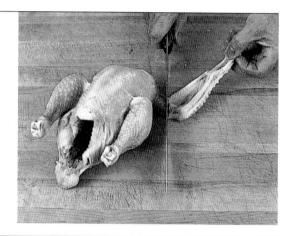

2. <u>Slide a knife along each side of the wishbone.</u> Insert your thumb and finger to loosen the wishbone and pry it loose.

3. Slide your thumb behind the wishbone and <u>pull it out</u>.

4. <u>Cut along the breastbone on each side</u>, slicing the skin of the neck in half. The object here is to divide the chicken in half and keep the longest possible pieces of skin. Place the chicken on its side and cut the skin alongside the backbone.

5. Lift up the skin at the shoulder joint and place your knife on the joint where the wing is attached to the body. (You can find out where the joint socket is by moving the little piece of wing tip that remains.) <u>Cut right through the joint of the shoulder.</u>

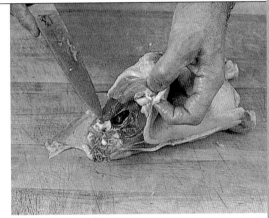

6. Grab the joint of the shoulder and the wing stump and pull, holding the carcass flat on the table with one hand and pulling with the other until the meat comes off the bone as far as the thigh joint. Remove the little oyster of meat near the back and break the leg-thigh at the joint, which will open. <u>Cut through the joint (there is a large sinew there)</u> and pull this half of the chicken completely loose.

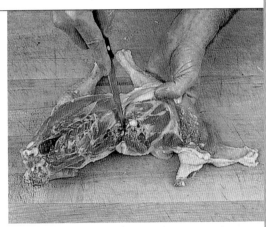

7. <u>Separate the leg from the breast,</u> being sure to cut the skin so that more of the skin stays on the breast than the leg. Repeat with the other side of the chicken. The only pieces of meat left now are the little fillets still attached to the breast. Slide your finger behind the fillets and pull them off the carcass on both sides. Remove the sinew from the fillets. Remove as much skin from the breast as you like and use as needed.

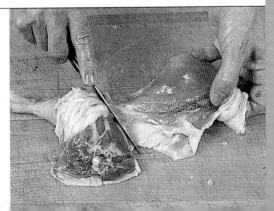

8. <u>Lift up the skin of the breast all around</u>, using the point of the knife if necessary, so the skin is completely loosened except where it is attached at the wing stub. If there is a lot of fat on the inside of the skin, scrape more of it off with the flat edge of the knife blade.

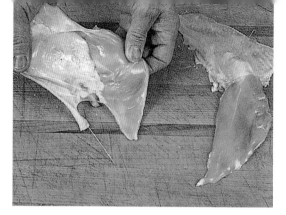

9. Place the chicken breast skin-side up on the work surface, pull back the skin, and <u>spoon about ½ cup (115 grams) of your favorite mousse on top of each breast</u>. Arrange a piece of fillet meat on one side of each of the breast, pressing it into the mousse.

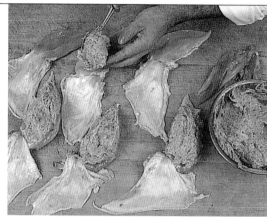

10. <u>Bring the skin back on top of the mousse, so it encases the whole surface.</u>

11. <u>Hold the stuffed breast skin-side down in the palm of one hand and try to bring the edges of the skin around to the underside of the breasts.</u> The skin will not wrap all around. Repeat with each breast. Refrigerate, skin-side down, covered, until ready to cook.

12. To sauté the chicken breast, sprinkle the chicken with ½ teaspoon salt and heat 1 tablespoon (14 grams) unsalted butter each in 2 skillets, preferably non-stick. When hot, add the chicken skin-side down, and sauté for about 4 minutes over high heat. Cover, reduce the heat, and cook gently for 10 minutes. Note that the chicken is cooked only skin-side down so the meat doesn't toughen. Remove the cover from the chicken and continue cooking until the juices are reduced and the chicken is sizzling again in the fat. <u>The chicken should be nicely browned. Remove to a platter.</u> Remove the fat and deglaze the pan with ½ cup of brown stock. Bring to a boil, strain, and serve with the chicken.

Chicken with Morels

(Poulet aux Morilles)

Morels are wild mushrooms that can be found along the edges of the woods and on hillsides in early spring. Fresh-picked morels are toxic eaten raw in salad but fine when cooked. They are also perfectly safe after they have been dried, which is the way they are usually bought in specialty stores. Dry morels are very expensive but one ounce goes quite a long way. Use the tiny, pointed black-headed type, which is the best morel.

YIELD: 4 to 6 servings

1 ounce (28 grams) dried morel mushrooms

1 3½-pound (1.6-kilogram) chicken

½ teaspoon salt

¼ teaspoon freshly ground black pepper

2 tablespoons (28 grams) unsalted butter

½ cup (118 milliliters) dry white wine

6 shallots, peeled and finely sliced
  (2 tablespoons)

⅓ cup (79 milliliters) dry sherry

½ cup (118 milliliters) heavy cream

Small cube *glace de viande* (optional)

1. <u>One ounce of tiny dried black-headed morels.</u>

2. Soak the morels in 2 cups of tepid water for at least 15 to 20 minutes. If they are whole, split them in half lengthwise to dispose of the sand. <u>The inside is like a hollow furrow.</u> Cut the tips off the stems.

3. Lift the morels gently out of the water so as not to take the sand with them. Drain and press gently to extrude some of the water. Pour the soaking water slowly from the bowl as <u>there will be sand at the bottom of it.</u> Reserve the soaking liquid (stock) for the sauce.

4. Cut the legs from the chicken and separate into drums and thighs. Pull the skin off the meat. Remove the wishbone from the breast. Cut at the shoulder joint (arrow) and along the breastbone (arrow). <u>Pull the breast meat off in one piece.</u> Repeat on the other side.

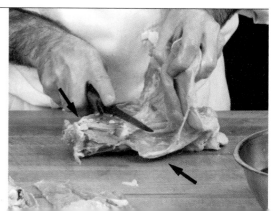

5. <u>Remove the skin from the breast</u>. Trim the wings. (Use the carcass, trimmings, etc., to make a stock for future use.) Cut each individual breast into 2 pieces. You now have 8 pieces of chicken with all fat and visible skin removed. Sprinkle the chicken pieces with salt and pepper.

6. Melt the butter in a skillet. <u>When foaming, place the pieces of chicken in it.</u> Gently sauté on medium heat for 4 minutes. The chicken should be browned lightly, but a crust shouldn't form on the flesh. After about 2 minutes on one side, turn and brown 2 minutes on the other side. The butter should be foaming nicely, but not burning. Add the white wine, cover and simmer another 2 minutes, then remove the lower 2 pieces of the breasts. These boneless pieces of white meat will be cooked first. After another 2 minutes, remove the other 2 pieces of white meat where the wing is attached. Leave the dark meat simmering gently for another 5 to 6 minutes, then remove and set aside with the breast meat. Add the shallots to the pan drippings and cook for about 1 minute. Add the sherry, morels, and reserved soaking liquid, bring to a boil and reduce to simmer on high heat for 6 to 8 minutes, or until the mixture is reduced by three quarters.

7. Add the cream. Bring to a boil and cook for about 1 minute on high heat. The sauce should be glossy and should just coat a spoon. Add salt and pepper to taste and a small cube of *glace de viande*, page 27, if you have any. <u>Pour over the chicken and serve immediately</u>. This is an elegant dish, ideal as a main course for a dinner served with braised endives or potatoes and green vegetables.

Chicken Pie

(Fricassée de Poulet en Feuilletage)

Chicken pie is a stew made of boned chicken combined with a vegetable garnish and a cream sauce and topped with puff paste. It is then baked.

YIELD: 6 servings

BRAISING THE CHICKEN

1 3½-pound (1.6-kilogram) chicken, quartered

Salt and freshly ground black pepper

½ cup (75 grams) thinly sliced onions

1 bay leaf

1 pinch dried thyme leaves

1 cup (237 milliliters) dry white wine

1 cup (237 milliliters) chicken stock

GARNISHES

2 carrots, peeled and cut into 2-inch (5-centimeter) chunks, split into ¼-inch (6-millimeter)-thick sticks, blanched 3 to 4 minutes in boiling water and drained

½ cup (62 grams) fresh or frozen baby peas, blanched 30 seconds in boiling water and drained

1 or 2 stalks celery, peeled, cut into 2-inch (5-centimeter) chunks and then into ¼-inch (6-millimeter) sticks, blanched 1 minute in boiling water and drained

12 pearl onions, peeled and blanched 3 minutes in boiling water and drained

1 cup (150 grams) fresh snow peas, cleaned, blanched 1 minute in boiling water and drained (Note: The vegetables can, of course, be varied at will.)

SAUCE

1 teaspoon (5 grams) unsalted butter

1 teaspoon all-purpose flour

¾ cup (178 milliliters) heavy cream

Salt and freshly ground black pepper to taste

CRUST

1 pound (454 grams) of puff paste, page 590

2 large egg yolks, beaten, for the wash

1. Sprinkle the chicken with salt and pepper. Brown in a saucepan, skin-side down, without fat on medium heat for 8 to 10 minutes. There is enough fat in the skin to brown the pieces without adding extra fat. Add the onions, bay leaf, thyme, wine, and stock to the chicken. Cover and simmer for 25 minutes. Remove from heat and, when cool enough to handle, remove the skin and take the meat off the bones. Cut the meat into 1- to 2-inch (2.5- to 5-centimeter) chunks.

2. For the sauce: Knead the butter and flour together (a *beurre manié*) and, using a whisk, whip the mixture into the juices vigorously. Bring the sauce to a boil, stirring, and simmer for 1 minute. Add the cream, bring to a boil again, taste for seasonings, and add salt and pepper if needed. Divide the meat and all the vegetable garnish among 6 crocks and pour the sauce over them. The crocks should not be more than two-thirds full.

3. Roll the puff paste dough into ¹/₈-inch (3-millimeter) thick rounds large enough to cover the top of the crocks andpartway down the sides of the crocks. Brush them with the egg yolk.

4. Place the dough on top of the crocks, egg-washed side down. Be sure to stretch the dough on top of the crock so it does not sink in the center. Press to assure that the dough adheres firmly to the sides of the dish.

5. Brush the top and sides of the dough with egg yolk. Refrigerate for 1 hour, or place in the freezer for 15 to 20 minutes to firm up the dough.

6. Preheat the oven to 375 degrees (191°C). Place the crocks on a cookie sheet and bake for 30 minutes. Serve immediately, one crock per person. Or, make one large pie for several people. For a large pie, make a hole in the crust and serve the stew from the crock, with a piece of puff paste and some vegetables in each portion. The chicken pie is a complete main course with crust, vegetables, meat, and sauce.

Cleaning Squab and Other Poultry

(Préparation du Pigeon et Autres Volailles)

A squab is a young domesticated pigeon, about 4 weeks old, which has not yet flown and has been specially fed to be plump and tender. An older pigeon is tougher and should be braised, but a dove (which is a wild species of pigeon) is quite tender.

Cleaning squab is similar to eviscerating a chicken, as shown on page 252.

1. Cut the feet off the squab just under the joint. Holding it on its back, <u>cut the tips sticking out at the first joint of each wing</u>. This is primarily for aesthetics.

2. Holding the skin tightly squeezed around the neck, <u>make a long incision</u> to expose the bone.

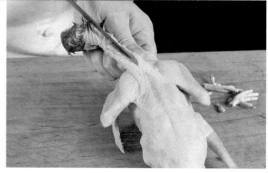

3. <u>Separate the neck from the skin</u> and crop (the loose baglike first stomach) by pulling with both hands.

4. <u>Cut the neck at the base, near the body</u>, and the skin next to the head. Separate the neck from the head.

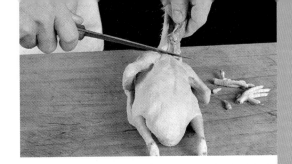

5. <u>Pull out the crop and the viscera</u> from the skin of the neck.

6. Lifting up the crop and viscera in the direction opposite the backbone, <u>slide one finger underneath the crop</u>. Slide the finger along and on each side of the backbone to loosen the guts and lungs.

7. Sever the crop near the opening and <u>fold the neck skin onto the back of the bird</u>.

8. <u>Cut a piece from the opening above the tail</u> and

9. <u>slit the skin open to the tip</u> of the breastbone.

10. <u>Pull the insides out</u>. All the entrails should come out easily in one long piece.

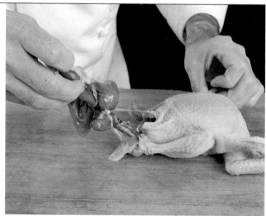

11. Reserve the little lumps of fat on each side of the opening. Separate the heart and the liver. (Squab liver does not contain a gallbladder, although most other poultry does.) <u>Slit the gizzard (the second stomach) on the thick and fleshy side</u> until you feel the inside which is harder.

12. <u>Open it and remove the pouch inside the gizzard.</u>

13. <u>Make a hole on each side of the opening</u> and slide the tip of the drumstick inside to hold the leg.

14. <u>Squab, oven ready.</u> From left to right: fat, cleaned gizzard, heart, and neck. (The liver is in front.)

Boned Stuffed Squab

(Pigeons Désossés et Farcis)

The squab is a good transition between regular poultry and real game, such as pheasant, woodcock, etc. It is dark meat and though it doesn't have a gamey taste, it is probably as close as you can get to game if you have never had it. Squab liver, unlike other poultry livers, does not have a gallbladder (the little green sac filled up with bile that is removed from the liver). Squabs generally weigh between 10 and 18 ounces (283 to 510 grams). The squabs shown here weighed 1 pound (454 grams) each, cleaned. It is easier to eat the squabs if they are boned, particularly if you are going to stuff them. The same instructions for boning squab also apply to cornish hens and other small birds.

YIELD: 6 servings

6 squab (about 1 pound/454 grams each), eviscerated (boned and cleaned)

STOCK

Carcasses, necks, gizzards, wings

½ cup (75 grams) sliced onion

½ cup (80 grams) coarsely sliced carrot

2 cloves garlic, skin on

1 cup (237 milliliters) dry white wine

¼ teaspoon dried thyme

4 quarts (4 scant liters) water (approximately)

SAUCE

½ teaspoon arrowroot, dissolved in 1 tablespoon water

½ teaspoon salt

¼ teaspoon freshly ground black pepper

STUFFING

(You may change the fruits in the stuffing, using figs, dates, raisins, etc.)

3 slices French bread, well toasted and blended into fine crumbs (about 1 cup/60 grams)

¾ cup (169 grams) finely chopped mild boiled ham

1½ cups (142 grams) loose, finely chopped mushrooms (about 5 ounces)

½ cup (105 grams) (about 4) sliced dry, pitted prunes

½ cup (about 4) (65 grams) sliced dry, pitted apricots

¼ cup (59 milliliters) melted unsalted butter

½ teaspoon salt, depending on the saltiness of the ham

¼ teaspoon freshly ground black pepper

1. Lift the skin at the neck of the squab and run your knife along each side of the wishbone. Push your thumb and index finger along the bone on each side to pry it out. Pull it out.

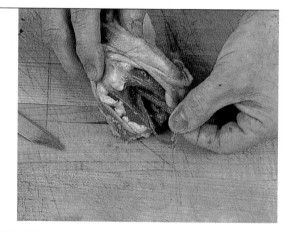

2. Cut at the joint of the shoulder on each side of the wishbone. Push your index finger and the side of your thumb through the opening made by the knife. The object is to loosen the meat all around the central carcass.

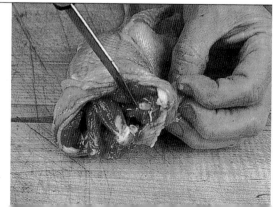

3. The most delicate part of the operation is to separate the skin from the back of the bird, as it adheres very tightly there and tends to tear. <u>Using the tip of your index finger, push between the skin and the back carcass to loosen the skin.</u> Go slowly to avoid tearing the skin.

4. After the meat has been separated from the back and around the shoulder, <u>lift out the breast meat, prying to separate it from the top of the breastbone without tearing the skin.</u> The fillets are still attached to the central carcass.

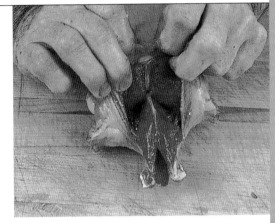

5. When it is loose from the carcass, <u>turn the flesh inside out,</u> pulling the meat down to separate it from the carcass. The fillets are still attached to the central carcass.

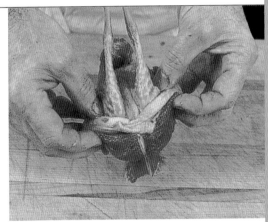

6. Keep pulling down until all the breast meat is separated and <u>most of the carcass—up to the joint of the hip on each side—is visible.</u> Notice that the fillets are still attached to the carcass.

7. <u>Holding the squab by the thigh bone, cut right through the hip joint</u> and pull so the leg separates from the carcass. Repeat on the other side.

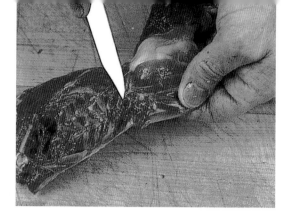

8. To remove the bones of the leg: With the squab still inside out, scrape the meat from the thigh bones with a knife and cut all around the knee joint. Keep scraping to loosen the meat from the drumstick bone and <u>break the drumstick bone just above the tip.</u>

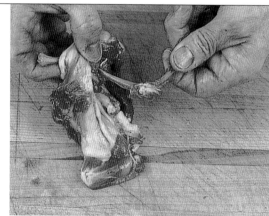

9. <u>Turn the squab right side out again.</u> The only bones left are the first joint of the wings. Place the neck, gizzards, heart, carcass, trimmings, etc., in a large saucepan without any fat. Brown on high heat for 1 to 2 minutes, then on medium to low heat for 25 minutes, stirring once in a while with a wooden spatula. (There is enough fat in the skin to brown the bones.) The saucepan should be large enough to hold the bones in one layer.

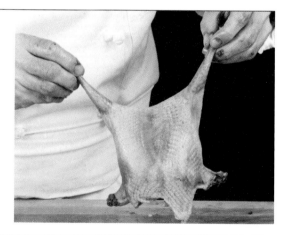

10. When the bones are nicely browned all around, and a nice crust of solidified juices has formed at the bottom of the pan, add the onions, carrots, and garlic, and cook, still browning, for another 10 minutes. Add the white wine, thyme, and approximately 2 quarts (2 scant liters) of water. Bring to a boil, lower the heat and simmer slowly for 1 hour. Remove the scum with a skimmer. After another hour, add another 2 quarts (2 scant liters) of water and

cook for another hour. Strain the liquid through a fine strainer. You should have approximately 4 cups (1 scant liter) left. Remove as much fat as possible then reduce the liquid to 1¼ cups (296 milliliters). This reduced stock will be the base of the sauce.

11. While the stock cooks, prepare the stuffing. Toss together all the ingredients of the stuffing gently and using a pastry bag, your finger, or a spoon, <u>stuff the squabs</u>.

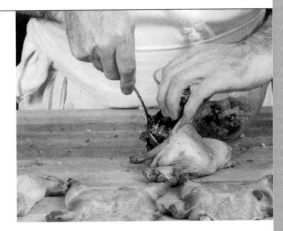

12. <u>Cover the opening at the neck and tail by wrapping the loose skin under the body</u>. Gently press the squab back into its original shape.

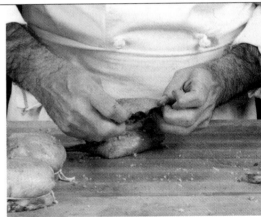

13. To truss, place a piece of string under the squab at the tail opening and <u>cross above the drums</u>.

14. Bring the string back under the tip of the drumsticks in a Figure 8. Pull gently on both ends of the string to close the opening at the tail and <u>bring around the sides of the bird to tie in front.</u>

15. Preheat the oven to 400 degrees (204°C). <u>Make a knot under the breast.</u> Trussing holds the squab in shape while cooking. Truss all of the squabs. Sprinkle the squabs with salt and pepper and place in a roasting pan breast-side up. To brown properly, the squabs should not touch one another, and the sides of the roasting pan should not be too high. Because squabs are fatty enough, you don't have to rub them with butter before roasting. Roast in the oven for 20 minutes. After 15 minutes, baste with the fat which has melted from the birds, and then cook another 5 minutes.

16. Untie and <u>trim the ends of the drumsticks</u> and the ends of the wing bones. Place the squabs on a platter and keep warm uncovered in a 160-degree (70°C) oven while you finish the sauce. If the pan drippings are separated into solidified juices and clear fat, pour the fat out and retrieve the solidified juices by dissolving with stock. If not, cook the juices on top of the stove until the fat separates completely from the solidified juices. Pour the fat out and add the 1¼ cups (296 milliliters) of stock. Boil the mixture for a few seconds while stirring with a spatula to dissolve juices. Strain into a small saucepan and add the dissolved arrowroot, stirring. Season with salt and pepper. You should have a generous cup of sauce. Serve on a large platter or on individual plates which are very hot. Coat each squab with about 2 to 3 tablespoons of sauce.

Boning Out Quail

(Désossage de la Caille)

1. Cut the skin along the back of the quail. <u>Sever the joint of the shoulder on either side of the neck</u>. See the boning out of chicken and squab. A knife is needed to cut the back skin and shoulder joints, but the rest of the boning can be done with the fingers.

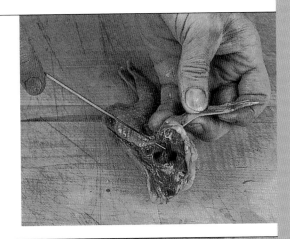

2. Holding the wing bone, <u>pull out the wing on each side of the neck to separate the carcass from the meat</u>. Although still held at the breastbone, most of the quail meat should be separated from the carcass.

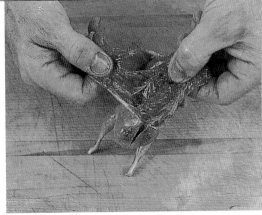

3. <u>Pull the breast to separate it from the sternum</u>. Notice that the little fillets are still attached to the bone. They will be removed later.

4. Break the leg bone at the hip joint and pull it off. As you break and pull, the leg will separate from the back carcass. Pull the carcass off. The only 2 pieces left on the carcass now are the fillets; slide your finger between the meat and the bone and remove the fillets. Set aside. The quail is now opened flat, with the bones of the legs and wings still in place.

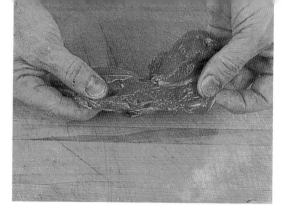

5. Using your finger, stand the thigh bone up so the joint is on the table, and grasping the bone as you would a pencil, push your fingers down the length of the bone, scraping the meat off as you go down. The thigh bone is now clean. Continue pushing and separating the meat from the knee joint. Now push down along the drumstick bone to separate the meat. Break the bone off at the joint of the foot.

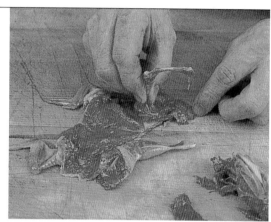

6. Trim the wings and remove the little piece of bone in each. The quail is completely boned out with the fillet separated (in front) and the bones (on the side). It can be stuffed or sautéed.

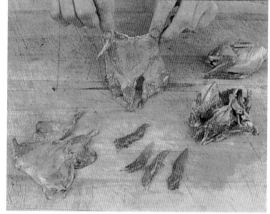

7. To sauté the quail: Heat 1 tablespoon (14 grams) unsalted butter in each skillet. Sprinkle the quail with salt and freshly ground pepper on both sides. When the butter is hot, place the quail skin-side down and cook covered over high heat for 5 minutes. The quail are cooked only on the skin side. The heat generated in the covered pan will be enough to cook the meat and the skin. Serve with the natural juices.

Boning and Cutting up a Duck

(Découpage du Canard)

1. In this technique, the duck is cut into 4 pieces. The neck skin is kept for cracklings and the bones for stock. Remove the wing tips (the first joint), which will be used for the stock. Keep the second joint, which will be braised with the duck. Lift up the skin of the neck and cut from one side of the wishbone to the other—which is like a half circle—and slide your thumb underneath and pry to remove it. (It is always good to remove the wishbone, even when roasting a whole duck, since doing so facilitates carving.)

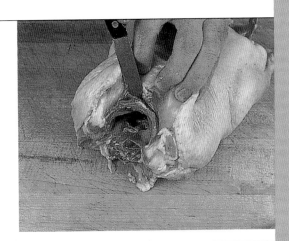

2. Place the duck on its side, grab a leg, and lift it until the duck is almost lifted off the table. In this manner, the weight of the duck is used and helps in separating the leg from the carcass. With the tip of your knife cut the skin around the leg, which will separate from the body. Keep cutting the skin all around until you touch the backbone.

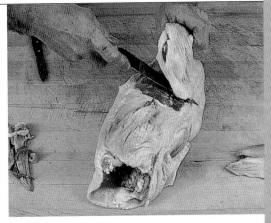

3. Place the leg so the thigh bone is parallel to the backbone and lift up to crack it open at the joint. Cut right through the sinews of the joint of the leg, and keep pulling and cutting to separate the leg entirely from the body. Repeat with the other leg.

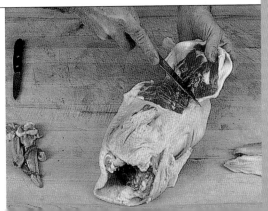

4. To separate the breast halves, place the duck on its back and, with a sharp knife, <u>cut along the breastbone on each side to separate the 2 halves.</u> Notice that the flesh is not very thick at the breastbone.

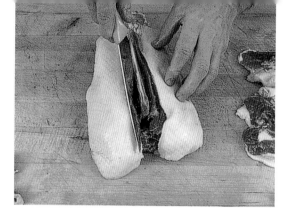

5. Place the duck on its side, hold the wing bone and move it with one finger. Place your finger under the skin on the shoulder joint. As you move the wing bone, you will feel the articulation. <u>Cut with your knife through the joint</u>, wiggling the blade to make it slide into the joint. Repeat on the other side, through the joint of the other breast.

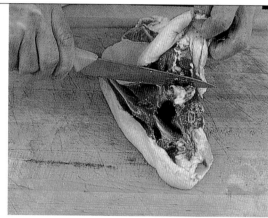

6. Grab the wing at the joint with one hand and, holding the carcass through the bones with the other hand, <u>pull the breast off in one piece.</u> Repeat on the other side with the other half.

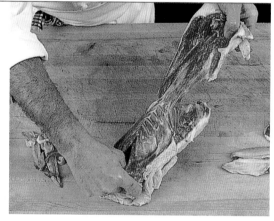

7. The only things to be removed now are the 2 small fillets on the sternum, or breastbone. <u>Slide your finger underneath and pull each fillet off the sternum.</u>

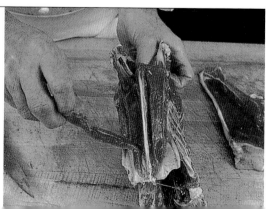

8. Inside each fillet, there is a long sinew. Holding the sinew at the end, <u>scrape the meat from it with the knife</u>. Repeat with the other sinew.

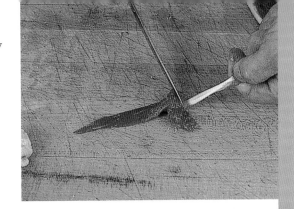

9. <u>Remove some of the fat around the meat of the breast and legs</u> and cut off the tips of the drumsticks for use in the stock.

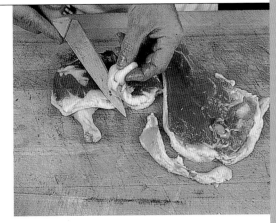

10. <u>The cut duck</u>: In the back on the left are the bones cut into 1½- to 2-inch (4 to 5 centimeters) pieces; the extra fat from the inside and the skin, cut into 1-inch (2.5-centimeter) pieces for use as cracklings; and the 2 pieces from the wings. Underneath are the 2 breast halves with the fillets next to them and, below, the 2 legs.

MEAT

Trimming and Cooking Meat

To ascertain the exact degree of doneness when roasting or broiling meat, you need a thorough, practical knowledge of cooking. The professional chef knows by touching, or rather pushing into the meat with his fingers. How the meat springs back clearly reveals the degree to which the meat is cooked. An underdone roast feels soft and mushy; when rare, it feels soft with some bounce; when medium, it feels hard and springy; and when well-done, it feels hard with almost no bounce. However, variations due to differences between cuts, quality and method of cooking make this system difficult for the untrained. Another method—cooking meat so many minutes to the pound or gram—is also unreliable because it doesn't take into account the temperature of the oven, or the cut, shape, quality, or preparation of the meat. For instance, a 6-pound (2.7-kilogram) rib roast will take close to 2½ hours in a 325-degree (163°C) oven to be rare and about 1½ hours in a 420-degree (215°C) oven. At the same temperature, a 3-pound (1.4-kilogram) piece of top round will take twice the time required for a 3-pound (1.4-kilogram) flank steak because of the difference in shape. One meat may be porous, another may be tight; one may be fatty, the next one may be lean; one is boned out, another is cooked bone in, and so on and on. All these factors modify the cooking of the meat and alter the timing.

It is *imperative* that the meat "rest" before being carved (from 5 to 10 minutes for a small rack of lamb, to 25 minutes for a large rib roast). As the meat rests, the juices can settle, ensuring a nice pink color throughout the meat. A roast beef sliced as soon as it comes out of the oven will be mushy, lukewarm, practically raw in the middle, and grey and dry 1 inch (2.5 centimeters) all around the outside. The same piece of meat will be uniformly pink throughout if allowed to settle in a lukewarm place for 15 to 20 minutes.

You will really come to understand meat once you begin trimming it yourself, relying less on your butcher and more on your own skills. It requires some practice, but it will save you money and you will be able to have your meat trimmed the way you like it without extra expense.

Once you get to know the principal cuts in one animal, they become quite easy to recognize in other animals, even if the cuts are handled differently. For example, after you have worked on a saddle of lamb, you will know that the lamb loin chops come from the saddle. You will also recognize veal saddle, veal loin chops, pork loin chops, and, in the beef, the shell steak, the tenderloin and the porterhouse steak, all of which come from the same part of the animal. Whether you are served a saddle of venison or a "rabble" (back) of hare, you will recognize where it comes from in the animal.

Spring lamb—the 8- to 12-month-old animal—is preferred for saddle of lamb. It has more taste and flavor than baby lamb and hasn't yet acquired the strong flavor of mutton. Baby lamb (which weighs under 20 pounds/9 kilograms with skin and head) is usually served around Easter and is always cooked medium, unlike mutton which is cooked well, and spring lamb which should be served pink.

Trimming a Saddle of Lamb

(Parer une Selle d'Agneau)

1. A saddle, the piece between the ribs and the legs, comprises the T-bone with the two loins and two tenderloins. The kidneys are underneath the saddle. This saddle is 9½ pounds (4.3 kilograms), untrimmed.

2. This is the saddle of lamb as viewed from the top.

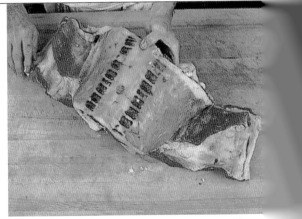

3. Remove the kidneys, including their lumps of fat, by cutting and pulling. Remove each kidney from its envelope of fat.

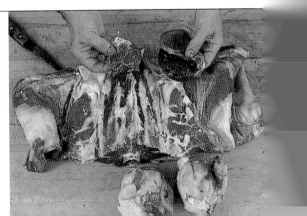

4. <u>Cut the flank or skin on both sides of the saddle.</u> With the saddle still upside down, trim the strip of sinews and fat along the central bone. Keep trimming the fat on both sides of the tenderloin.

5. Turn the saddle right side up and <u>trim the skin and fat off the back</u>. Keep trimming on both sides of the loins, leaving only a very thin layer of fat on top of the meat.

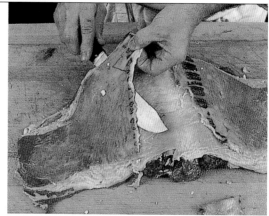

6. <u>Fold the skirt back onto the tenderloin</u>. (This protects the choice tenderloin from drying during cooking.)

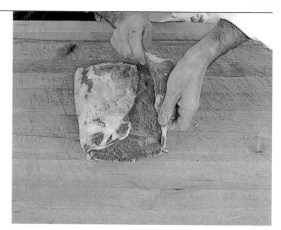

7. <u>Tie the saddle</u> to secure the skirts underneath.

8. <u>Saddle, oven ready</u>. The trimmed saddle weighs 3½ pounds (1.6 kilograms), and the trimmings and kidneys combined weigh 2 pounds (908 grams). The trimmings make a delicious stew. The kidneys can be broiled or sautéed. The fat is discarded.

Boning, Stuffing, Tying, and Cooking a Saddle of Lamb

(Désossage Selle d'Agneau)

The saddle is comprised of the two loins, the two tenderloins, the flanks, and the kidneys. An expensive cut of meat, it can be roasted whole and carved, as well as boned out and cut into small médaillons or stuffed. The loin (which is a half saddle) can be cut into loin chops or boned out and stuffed. Lamb fat is strong and cannot be used in any dish. The bones can be used for stocks or soups.

1. Place the saddle on its back, and <u>cut off the two fillets by following the contour of the central bone</u>. They should come off easily.

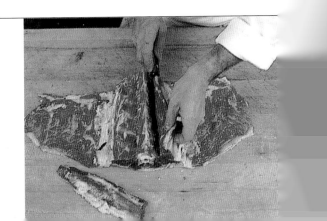

2. <u>Slide your knife flat underneath the bone where the fillets sat and cut</u>, following the contour of the bone, to loosen one loin.

3. Repeat on the other side and, finally, <u>lift up the central bone and separate it from the meat</u>. The rim in the center of the bone is against the top skin part of the saddle. Be careful not to make holes in the top of the saddle while boning.

4. If you have left some meat on the bone while boning, <u>use a spoon to scrape it off</u> and set it aside for the stuffing.

5. <u>Clean up the two fillets</u>. Notice that each fillet separates into two pieces, the fillet and the "chain" of the fillet, which should be scraped with a knife or spoon to separate the meat from the sinews. (This scraped-off meat can be used in the mousse.) The fillets themselves can be cut in half. Keep the thicker part of the 2 fillets to place in the center of the saddle. The tails can be kept for stuffing.

6. After the fillets have been arranged in the center of the saddle where there is a space from the removal of the bone, <u>place the 2 extra pieces of flank on either side of the loins</u>.

Stuffed Saddle of Lamb

(Farcir et Ficeler une Selle d'Agneau)

YIELD: 8 to 10 servings

LAMB-SAGE MOUSSE

½ cup (70 grams) ½-inch (1.25-centimeter) sliced leeks

½ cup (80 grams) peeled and very thinly sliced carrots

½ cup (119 grams) water

2 ounces (138 grams) spinach, washed

1 pound (454 grams) meat (12 ounces/340 grams lamb trimmings, 4 ounces/114 grams chicken meat)

2 large eggs

1 teaspoon salt

½ teaspoon freshly ground black pepper

½ cup (120 milliliters) heavy cream

6 to 9 sage leaves

1. FOR THE MOUSSE: Cover the leeks and carrots with water, bring to a boil, cover and cook 3 minutes. Then add spinach and cook about 1 minute longer. Most of the moisture will be evaporated, and the mixture should be almost dry. Spread on a large platter or cookie sheet to cool quickly and thus retain the color of the vegetables. Put the lamb and chicken into a food processor and process for about 5 seconds. Clean the meat from the sides of the bowl with a rubber spatula.

2. Add the eggs and process for 10 seconds, until very smooth. Add salt and pepper, and while the machine is operating, add the cream through the feed tube. Process about 30 seconds to blend. Pile the sage leaves together and shred them into a fine julienne. Combine the mousse with the shredded sage. Press the cold vegetables with your hands to extract more liquid (too much liquid will make the mousse break down) and mix with the mousse.

3. Sprinkle the saddle and fillets with ¼ teaspoon salt and ¼ teaspoon pepper and spread the mousse on top. The filling should be about 1 inch (2.5 centimeters) thick.

4. Bring back the extra pieces of flank from above and below to cover the mousse and fold in the 2 flanks from either side to enclose the mousse entirely on 4 sides.

5. Using kitchen twine and the half-hitch technique (see page 259), tie the saddle without squeezing it too much so there is room for the stuffing to expand.

6. When the saddle has been secured, add 2 extra pieces of string the length of the saddle to hold the stuffing in place during cooking.

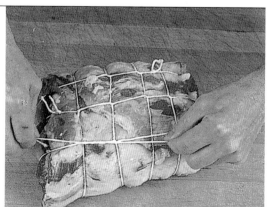

7. Lift the saddle up by the string and place in a roasting pan on top of the stove, stuffed side down. Cook in this position for 25 minutes, first over high heat for about 1 minute and then over low heat for the remainder of the cooking time. This step will cook the flank and mousse, so the loin is not overcooked at the end. <u>Spoon some of the drippings on top of the saddle and place in a preheated 400 degree (204°C) oven for 30 to 35 minutes.</u>

8. <u>The saddle is now cooked</u>. Lift it out of the roasting pan and place on a platter to rest in a 130 degree (54°C) oven or on the side of the stove where it's warm. Let it rest for at least 20 to 30 minutes before carving.

9. Meanwhile, make the sauce: Remove most of the fat from the roasting pan and add 1 cup (155 grams) chopped onions. Sauté for about 5 to 6 minutes, until the onions are quite brown. Add 1 cup (237 milliliters) white wine, 2 cups (300 grams) chopped tomatoes, 2 teaspoons chopped garlic, and 2 cups (473 milliliters) water, and bring to a boil. Boil gently for 8 to 10 minutes on top of the stove. Add 2 teaspoons potato starch dissolved in 2 tablespoons water and strain. You should have approximately 1³/4 to 2 cups (414 to 437 milliliters) of sauce remaining.

When ready to serve, <u>slice the saddle in pieces about ¹/2 to ³/4 inch (13 to 19 millimeters) thick. Hold the slices with one hand while you cut from behind with the other hand. This will help the slices to hold their shape.</u> The saddle can be cut into 8 to 10 nice slices.

Stuffing a Loin of Lamb

(Farcir un Faux-filet d'Agneau)

The loin is half the saddle and can be stuffed and cooked like a saddle.

1. Make the Lamb-Sage Mousse (see page 309). Arrange all the flat pieces of the lamb wrapper on the table, one slightly overlapping another, and <u>spread the mousse on top of them</u>. The mousse will, in a sense, be the cement that will hold everything together. Sprinkle the loin with salt and pepper, and place in the center of the mousse.

2. Using a dough scraper or a spatula, gently lift up the wrapper, now covered with mousse, and <u>encase the loin with both sides</u>. Using the half-hitch trussing technique (see pages 259), secure the loin with kitchen twine. Do not tie it too tight since the stuffing will expand during cooking. Cover any areas where the mousse is visible with aluminum foil to hold it inside.

3. Preheat the oven to 400 (204°C) degrees. <u>Gently lift up the roast by the string and place it in the center of the skillet.</u> Brown it over medium heat for approximately 5 minutes, rolling it over gently so it browns on all sides. Place the roast in the oven for about 20 minutes, basting it after 10 minutes. Then lift it out of the roasting pan and place it on a platter to rest in a warm oven (about 150/66°C) for at least 15 to 20 minutes before serving.

Trimming a Rack of Lamb

(Préparation du Carré d'Agneau)

The double rack in our picture is a "primal" cut (a piece as it comes directly from the slaughterhouse) and extends from the shoulder blade to the saddle or the last rib. That double rack is complete here with the breasts, and sometimes this piece takes on the name of "bracelet." It usually has 8 ribs and weighs approximately 10 to 11 pounds (4½ to 5 kilograms) whole for a spring lamb. Without the two breasts, it weighs approximately 7½ pounds (3.4 kilograms) untrimmed. Each single rack, completely trimmed (a double rack yields 2 single racks), will weigh approximately 1¼ pounds (567 grams) and serve 3 to 4 people. Although racks of lamb are usually bought split and trimmed, the professional cook may want to prepare it from the beginning.

1. This is the double rack seen from the shoulder side. As you may notice, there are layers of fat in the meat and the shoulder blade, which should be removed.

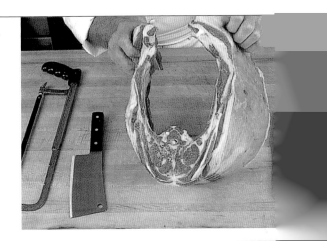

2. This is the double rack seen from the saddle side. It is a solid piece of meat without fat. When buying lamb chops that are cut from the rack, the preferred choice is the chops cut from the side of the saddle.

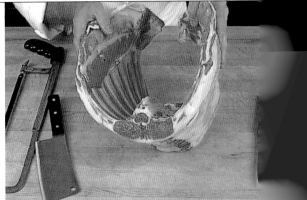

3. Using a hacksaw, <u>remove the breast on each side of the rack</u>. The breasts will weigh approximately 1¾ pounds (794 grams) each.

4. Using a sharp, pointed knife, <u>cut straight down on each side of the backbone, or chine bone</u>, going as deep as you can. The tip of the knife should touch the bone underneath. Keep cutting so the backbone is well separated from the meat on each side.

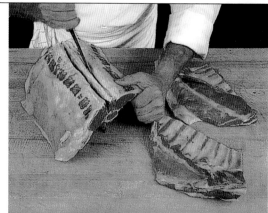

5. Place the rack so the ribs are facing you, and using the point of a sturdy cleaver, <u>start cutting on each side of the backbone where the ribs join</u>. Keep cutting to separate the rack completely from the backbone. If the double rack is split right in the center, each of the single racks will have the chine, or backbone, underneath, and every time one cuts between the ribs, the backbone must be cut also. The object is to remove the backbone completely so that the only bones remaining are the ribs, which are easy to cut apart.

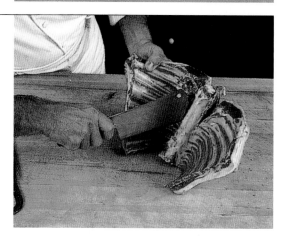

6. Lift the layer of meat and fat from the top of the loin with your hand. It should separate easily. <u>Then slide a knife between the layer and the loin to separate the entire top in one piece and expose the loin and the ribs.</u>

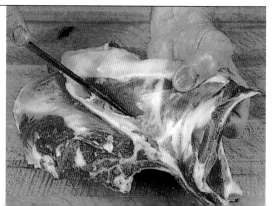

7. <u>Trim the surface of the ribs</u> where there is still some fat remaining.

8. The layer removed from the top of the rack can be used. Insert your finger between the meat itself and the top layer of fat and <u>pull the meat</u>. It should separate into one layer of meat plus the shoulder blade. Set it aside. It can be used in stuffing or in stew. Discard the fat.

9. To dress up the rack, the meat can be trimmed away from between the top of the ribs. <u>Remove approximately 1 inch (2.5 centimeters) of meat and fat from between each of those ribs</u> and scrape the point of the ribs to make them clean. Reserve scraps.

10. <u>Complete division of the whole rack</u>: On the left, the 2 single racks, one with the ribs dressed up and the other without; in the center background, the backbone, which can be used in soup or stock; in the center, the layer of meat from the top of the racks, which can be used in stuffing and stew; and, on the right, 2 breasts of lamb, 1 stuffed and 1 unstuffed, which can be used in stew or broiled.

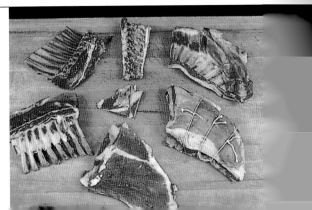

Lamb Chops

(Côtes d'Agneau)

1. Trim and separate a double rack as explained in the preceding technique. <u>Separate each rack into individual chops by cutting between each rib.</u>

2. For thin chops, make one chop from each rib. For thicker chops, cut one chop with 2 ribs, <u>then remove one of the ribs.</u>

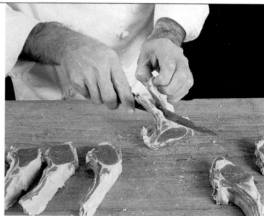

3. <u>Cut the layer of fat along the rib.</u>

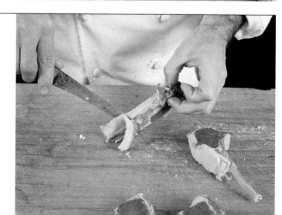

4. Holding the chop in one hand, <u>cut the fat above the "eye"</u> all the way around the rib.

5. <u>"Scrape" it off with your knife</u> to expose a clean bone.

6. <u>Flatten the chop slightly</u>.

7. <u>Trim a chunk of the fat above the eye</u>.

8. <u>Chops from one rack</u>. Note the 2 chops in front. The one on the left is cut from the end of the rack that is near the saddle. It is called the "first" or "prime" chop. The other chop on the right is cut toward the shoulder and is called the "second" or "lower" chop. It is customary, as shown in front, to serve one first and one second chop to each guest.

Trimming a Leg of Lamb

(Préparation du Gigot)

A glorious roasted leg of lamb is an ideal menu course for a special party for 10 to 12 guests.

1. <u>A whole untrimmed leg of lamb</u> with the hipbone weighs approximately 7½ to 8 pounds (3.4 to 3.6 kilograms). Use a spring lamb, i.e., a lamb from 8 to 12 months old.

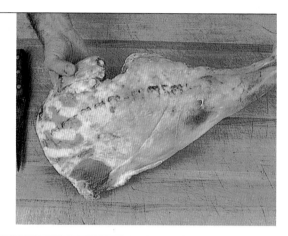

2. <u>The untrimmed leg of lamb, as seen from underneath.</u> There is a lot of fat on the outside of the leg, and most of it should be removed. Place the leg on its back and insert a thin, sharp, sturdy knife along the hipbone. Follow the bone as closely as you can.

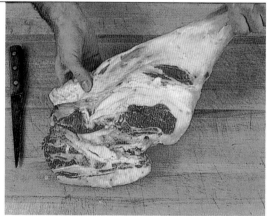

3. <u>Cut inside the socket of the hip joint</u> (you will see the tip of the femur). Remove the tail and the hipbone in one piece. Keep for stock and discard the fat.

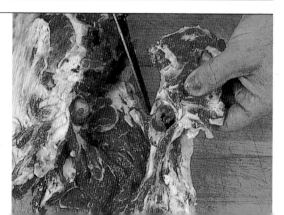

4. Trim the fat along one side of the leg.

5. Next trim the fat along the other side.

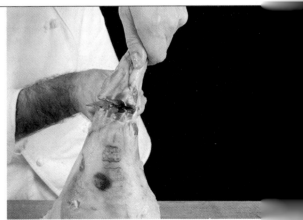

6. Holding the leg by the shank, cut the meat all around the bone.

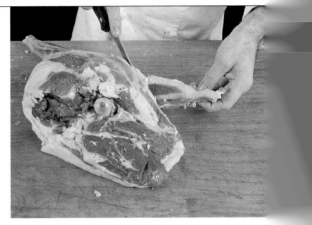

7. With the leg flat, remove the meat from the tip of the bone. You should have 2 or 3 inches (5 or 7.6 centimeters) of exposed bone.

8. <u>Using a saw, cut off the knotty tip of the bone.</u> The bare bone is decorative and serves as a handle, which makes carving easier.

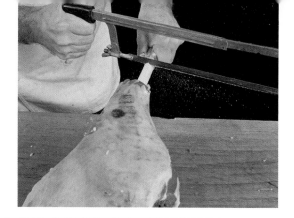

9. <u>Trim the top of the leg of fat</u>, leaving a layer about ¼ inch (6 millimeters) thick.

10. The leg can be roasted whole or <u>a piece from the hip side can be removed and used for stew.</u> (This shortened leg is called *gigot raccourci* in French.)

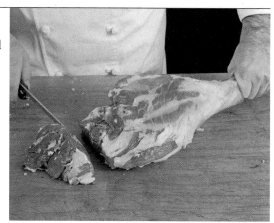

11. <u>Leg of lamb, oven ready</u>.

Skinning and Cutting Up a Baby Lamb

(Dépiauter et Découper l'Agneau de Lait)

1. Here is the whole baby lamb, just gutted. The meat does not need to age more than a couple of days. The omentum is a lacy membrane that connects the stomach to other organs. It can be used to wrap pâtés or crépinettes. The organs are, starting at the left front: the round sweetbread (pancreas gland) and, above, the 2 small kidneys, used in the stuffing. In the second row are the lungs, which are excellent stewed with red wine. In the third row front is the spleen, also good in stew, and, above, the heart, used in the stuffing. Finally, there is the liver, excellent sliced and sautéed. Total weight of the offal is about 2 pounds (907 grams).

2. To remove the skin, place the lamb on its back and cut through the skin the length of the leg with a pointed knife. Pull off the skin. It should come away from the flesh easily. To help release the skin, cut the membrane between the skin and the flesh with the point of a knife as you are pulling. After the legs are free, pull off the skin along the back.

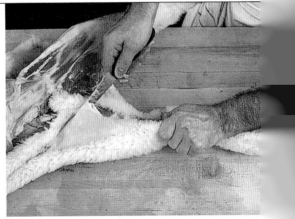

3. Continue to pull until the front shoulders of the lamb are uncovered. Pull the skin down the front legs and cut at the joint of the knee. Cut at the neck. The head can be kept or discarded. If the head is kept, remove the skin and eyes.

4. <u>Remove both front legs at the shoulder joints by pulling and cutting between the shoulders</u> and the body of the lamb. The front legs should separate easily.

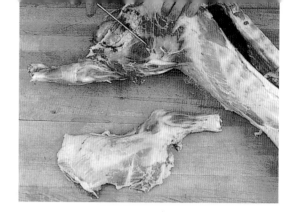

5. With the baby lamb on its back, <u>cut with a knife and a cleaver through the bones just above the 2 back legs</u> to separate the legs from the rest of the body.

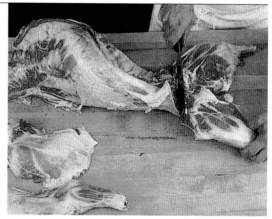

6. <u>Cut across the first rib to remove the saddle.</u> It is the piece that extends from the back legs to the ribs. The fillets, which are inside the saddle, extend from the back legs (head of the fillet) to the first rib (tail of the fillet). The length of the fillets is the same as that of the saddle.

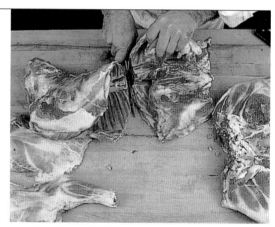

7. <u>Cut the breast off the rack</u>, leaving approximately 2 inches (5 centimeters) of bones on the ribs. The breast can be cut, bones and all, into 2-inch (5-centimeter) pieces and used for stew.

8. <u>Separate the double rack from the neck</u>.

9. <u>Remove the pelvis bone</u>, which holds the back legs together.

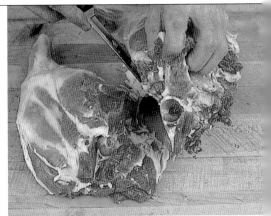

10. Bone out the saddle (see Stuffed Saddle of Lamb, page 309). Remove the 2 fillets first and, following the bone, <u>cut so that the whole central bone comes out in one piece</u>. Lift the bone off the saddle and cut in the center to have 2 single loins.

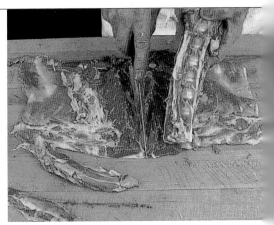

11. Bone out the front legs or shoulders: <u>Follow the bone of each shoulder blade, cutting around it</u> to separate it from the flesh.

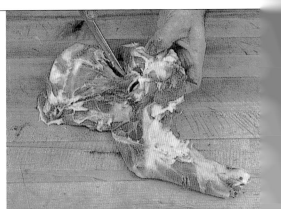

12. When loose on top and around, <u>pull the bone out</u>. Continue to remove the bones of the front legs so the shoulders are completely boneless.

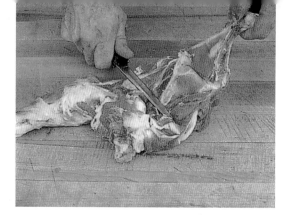

13. To separate the double rack into 2 single racks, place the rack on the table and <u>slide your knife along each side of the chine bone</u>.

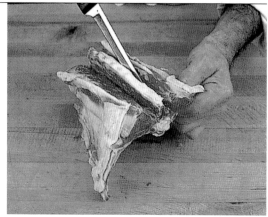

14. <u>Cut with a cleaver down the chine bone on each side to separate both racks.</u> The racks are completely boned out except for the ribs and can be cut through easily at serving time.

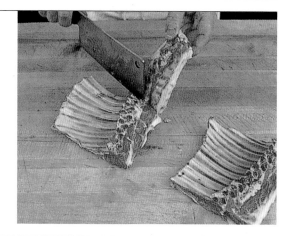

15. <u>Here is the whole baby lamb, boned out.</u> From left to right, first row front, the chuck meat from around the neck, (about 1 pound/454 grams). Behind the breast, cut (bones and all) into 2-inch (5-centimeter) pieces (about 1 pound/454 grams). Next the 2 boned-out shoulders (2³/4 pounds/1.25 kilograms for both). Next are the 2 racks, ready to cook (1¹/4 pounds/567 grams for both) and, next to them, the saddle, cut in half (about 1³/4 pounds/794 grams for both). On the far right are the 2 back legs, (about 4¹/2 pounds/2 kilograms for both). In the back row are the bones and sinews, to be used in stocks and soups (about 4 pounds/1.8 kilograms).

16. <u>The lamb's head, spilt in half, and the brain and tongue</u> <u>(about 2 pounds/907 grams total)</u>. Not pictured is the skin or fleece, which weighs approximately 4¾ pounds (2.2 kilograms) for a total weight of about 23 pounds (10.4 kilograms) for the whole baby lamb.

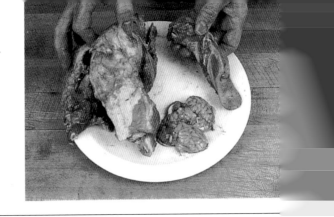

Stuffing and Cooking a Baby Lamb Shoulder

(Farçir l'Épaule d' Agneau de Lait)

YIELD: 6 servings

4 tablespoons (56 grams) unsalted butter
1 cup (100 grams) finely sliced leeks
1 cup (155 grams) coarsely chopped onions
1 cup (60 grams) bread crumbs (made in food processor from 2 slices bread)
1 cup (225 grams) diced lamb offal (mixture of sweetbreads, kidneys, and heart)
2 tablespoons chopped Italian parsley
¼ teaspoon crushed dried sage or 1 teaspoon shredded fresh sage
½ cup (10 grams) chopped dried morels or other dried wild mushrooms, soaked ½ hour in 2 cups (476 grams) tepid water
½ teaspoon salt
½ teaspoon freshly ground black pepper
Dash salt and freshly ground black pepper

1. TO MAKE THE STUFFING: Preheat the oven to 400 degrees (204°C). Heat 2 tablespoons (28 grams) of the butter in a saucepan. When hot, add the leeks and onions and sauté over medium heat for about 5 minutes. Place bread crumbs on a cookie sheet in the oven or under a broiler and cook for 4 to 5 minutes until nicely browned. <u>Add diced offal to the leek-</u> <u>onion mixture and sauté for 1 to 2 minutes</u>. Add parsley, sage, bread crumbs, drained mushrooms, salt, and pepper. Toss gently and cool.

2. Place the loin and the shoulder on the board and sprinkle both pieces with 1 teaspoon salt. <u>Divide the stuffing</u> between the 2 pieces of meat.

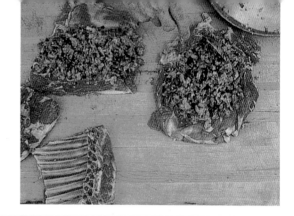

3. <u>Roll up the loin and the shoulder so the stuffing is held inside.</u> If some of the loose stuffing falls out at the ends, a small piece of aluminum foil placed at either end will help hold it in.

4. Tie the shoulder and the loin with string, <u>using the half-hitch technique</u> (see page 259). Don't tie too tight; the stuffing should have room to expand a little.

5. <u>Here are all the pieces, ready to be cooked.</u> (This will be enough for 10 to 12 servings.) From left to right: the leg, the rack, the boned-out stuffed loin, and the boned-out stuffed shoulder.

6. To cook the meat: The pieces of meat are first browned in butter on top of the stove in a large skillet. Next, they are roasted in the oven, for different lengths of time, depending on size and length of cooking required. They all come out of the oven at the same time. Preheat the oven to 400 degrees (204°C). Place 2 tablespoons (28 grams) butter in a very large sauté pan. Sprinkle the meat with 1 teaspoon salt and a dash of pepper. When the butter is hot, brown the pieces all around over high heat. The rack should be just lightly browned for 2 to 3 minutes and removed to a plate. The 2 stuffed roasts should take 6 to 7 minutes and the leg about 8 to 9 minutes to brown. Keep the leg (the largest piece) in the sauté pan and place in the oven for about 20 minutes. Then add the stuffed roasts in a separate pan and cook at the same temperature for another 20 minutes. Baste the pieces, then add the rack and cook for 10 minutes longer. Total roasting time is 10 minutes for the rack, 30 minutes for the stuffed roasts, and 50 minutes for the leg. Remove from the oven. The internal temperature of the lamb should be approximately 140 to 150 degrees (60°C to 66°C). Remove to a pan and allow the meat to rest in a warm place (150-degree/66°C oven) and continue cooking in its own juices.

7. For the brown shallot sauce: To the drippings in the pan add the ½ cup (119 milliliters) of liquid the mushrooms and bring to a boil while stirring to loosen all the solidified juices. Boil for 1 minute and strain. You should have about 1½ cups (356 milliliters).

Heat 2 tablespoons (28 grams) of butter in a skillet. When hot, add ½ cup (55 grams) chopped shallots and sauté for 3 to 4 minutes. Add ½ cup (15 grams) chopped Italian parsley and the reduced sauce (above). If the sauce is too thin, thicken with ½ teaspoon of potato starch dissolved in 1 tablespoon of water.

Remove the string from the roasts and cut into ½-inch (1.25-centimeter) wide slices. Arrange on a serving plate and spoon some sauce on top.

On the plate, from left to right: the stuffed shoulder, the leg, the stuffed loin, and the sliced rack.

Loin of Veal

(Carré de Veau)

The loin is divided by a "T" bone with the tenderloin (fillet) on one side and the loin on the other. The loin as well as the tenderloin is the choicest, tenderest, and most expensive piece of veal. The loin is sometimes roasted whole, stuffed, or unstuffed. It is also boned out, trimmed of all fat and sinew, and divided in small mignonnettes (small scallopine) or grenadins (larger steaks). The fillet is usually roasted whole or used in pâtés. The bones and trimmings should be kept for stock and the sinewy piece of the flank steak ground used in stews, pâtés, or stuffing.

1. One single loin (sometimes called half a saddle) weighs approximately 14 to 15 pounds (6.35 to 6.8 kilograms) (depending on the size of the animal) untrimmed, with fat, kidney, flank, and bone in.

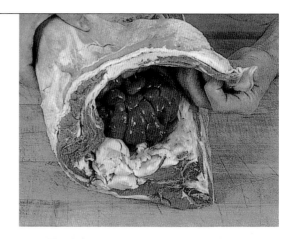

2. Pull off the whole block of fat that encases the kidneys and remove the kidneys from the fat. This white, waxy fat is sometimes rendered. It is good for deep-frying potatoes and can be used in mousse as well as fish mixtures.

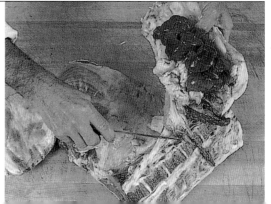

3. <u>Cut approximately 6 inches (15.25 centimeters) from the flank</u>. This extra piece can be used in stew but can also be butterflied and placed at the ends of a roast to hold in the stuffing.

4. <u>Run your knife around the bone</u> to remove the fillet in one piece. Separate the chain from the fillet. The chain is that long, narrow strip of meat attached to the fillet, and it is full of sinews; scrape it with a knife to remove as much meat as possible.

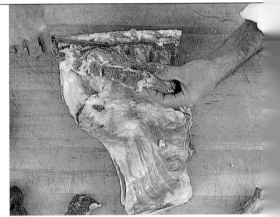

5. <u>Run your knife behind the ribs and central bone</u> to loosen the loin.

6. <u>Remove most of the fat from the inside of the veal</u>.

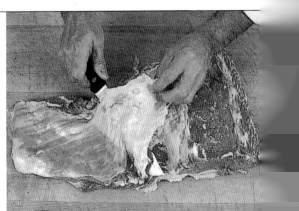

7. When the bone is loose, <u>use a spoon to scrape any remaining meat from it.</u>

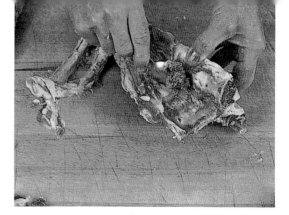

8. In this roast, the flank is narrower than the loin, and it should be as wide in order to encase the stuffing and overlap the loin. <u>Butterfly the flank and open it until it is approximately as wide as the loin.</u> Split the fillet and kidneys in half lengthwise.

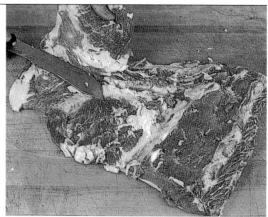

9. <u>The whole loin is now boned out</u>: In the back row, from left to right are: 3 pounds (1.3 kilograms) of fat, 2 pounds (907 grams) of bone and sinews together, and about 1 pound (454 grams) of extra flank, cut into pieces, on the right. In the front, on the left, are the trimmed roast and flank together (about 4 pounds/1.8 kilograms), the kidneys (12 ounces/340 grams), and the fillet of veal (about 6 ounces/170 grams), with about 10 ounces (283 grams) of trimmings, behind.

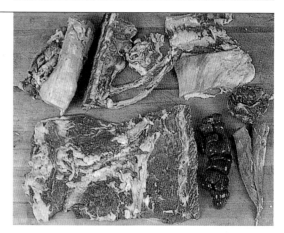

10. To make the mousse: Soak the 2 slices of white bread in ⅓ cup (79 milliliters) of milk for a few minutes. Place 10 ounces (283 grams) of veal trimmings and 3 ounces (85 grams) of fat in the food processor and process for about 15 seconds. Add 1 egg and process for another 5 to 10 seconds. Add the soaked bread, 1 chopped garlic clove, 3 tablespoons of chives, 1 tablespoon of fresh or 1 teaspoon dried oregano, ¼ teaspoon black pepper and ½ teaspoon salt, and process just to mix well.

Sprinkle ¼ teaspoon of salt and ¼ teaspoon of black pepper on the meat and kidneys. Spread a layer of the mousse (using about half) where the flank joins the loin. Place the kidneys on top of it and the fillet alongside with some mousse in between.

11. Place the 2 pieces of butterflied extra flank one on each side (top and bottom in this photograph), tucking them under the kidneys. Spread the remainder of the mousse on top and bring these two pieces of meat back over the mousse to encase it with the kidneys. Bring the flank back over the stuffed loin to encase it completely.

12. To tie: Attach one loop of the twine at one end of the roast to secure. Then, using the half-hitch technique (see page 259), secure across and lengthwise to hold the stuffing inside. The weight of the roast should be approximately 8½ pounds (3.85 kilograms) now.

At cooking time, preheat the oven to 400 degrees (204°C). Arrange the bones and the sinews from the saddle in a roasting pan and cook in the oven for 30 to 45 minutes.

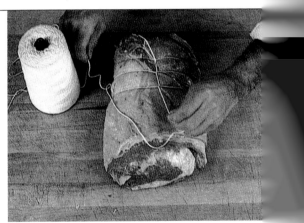

13. When the bones are browned, push them to the sides and position the roast in the center of the pan. Sprinkle it with ½ teaspoon salt and rub 1 tablespoon (14 grams) of butter on top. Place in a 400 degree (204°C) oven for 30 minutes.

14. <u>Turn the roast over</u>, reduce the oven temperature to 350 degrees (177°C), and continue cooking for 1 hour.

15. Turn the roast over again and continue cooking 45 minutes longer (about 2 hours and 15 minutes total). <u>The roast should have an internal temperature of 130 to 140 degrees (54°C to 60°C) as it comes out of the oven</u>. The temperature will continue to rise 5 to 10 degrees as it rests. Lift up the roast, place it in another roasting pan, and set it on the side of the stove or in a 140 degree (60°C) oven to keep warm and relax.

16. Pour off as much of the clear fat as possible from the drippings in the roasting pan and discard it. Place the remaining drippings and bones in a saucepan, add 1 quart (1 scant liter) water to the roasting pan, and <u>scrape with a wooden spatula to melt the solids</u>. Add these to the saucepan with the bones, bring to a boil over high heat, and boil gently 25 to 30 minutes.

17. Notice that after the meat has rested for 15 to 20 minutes a lot of juice has come out of it. <u>The juice is red because of the kidney inside, which has been resting and releasing juices</u>. Add the juices to the bones, which are being boiled for the sauce.

After the bones have been boiled for about 30 minutes, strain the stock, let it rest for a few minutes, and remove most of the fat from the top. Return the stock to high heat and reduce it to 2 cups (474 milliliters). Add 1 teaspoon potato starch dissolved in 1 tablespoon water to the reduction and bring to a boil. Add salt and pepper, if needed, and serve with the sliced roast.

Breaded Veal Scaloppine

(Escalope de Veau Viennoise)

For veal scaloppini, you should use first-quality veal, usually the cuts from the top sirloin or the loin. The meat should be without fat or gristle. Each scaloppine should weigh about 5 to 6 ounces (142 to 170 grams) and should be pounded paper thin into a slice about 10 inches (25 centimeters) in diameter.

1. Use a long sharp knife. Hold your hand flat on the meat to direct the knife, and <u>cut on a slant</u>.

2. <u>Slice about ¼ inch (6 millimeters) down the meat</u>. Do not separate the slice from the meat.

3. Open the first slice and <u>cut another slice through</u>, separating it from the bulk of the meat. Both scallops should hold together. (You can also cut a ½-inch/13-millimeter-thick slice, place it flat on the table, and butterfly it to obtain the same result.)

4. <u>Using a meat pounder, thin out the veal</u> by pounding down and out from the center toward the edges. The meat should not be crushed, but thinned down. Wetting the pounder with cold water helps it slide on top of the scallops without making holes in the meat.

5. Pounding is the most delicate operation in the recipe. If you do not have a good meat pounder, or if you do not feel confident about the procedure, ask your butcher to prepare the scallops for you. <u>You can place two small scaloppine overlapping to create one large one</u>.

6. <u>Pound the pieces gently where they overlap to make them adhere to one another.</u>

7. After it is pounded, dip the meat in flour lightly, shaking off any excess. Beat together 1 egg, 1 tablespoon vegetable oil, 1 tablespoon water, salt, and pepper and <u>dip both sides of the floured scallop in the mixture</u>. Squeeze out excess with your fingers. Prepare fresh bread crumbs in the blender and spread on the table. Dip the veal on both sides into the crumbs, pressing on it slightly to make them adhere well. Shake off any excess.

8. Pat the breaded veal with the flat side of a large knife. <u>Mark a crisscross lattice on top with a knife</u>. Refrigerate until cooking time. The breaded veal is cooked in a large frying pan in a mixture of butter and vegetable oil. Start with the marked side down. After 3 to 4 minutes on medium heat, turn and cook for the same amount of time. In the *viennoise* style, it is served with melted butter and decorated with chopped hard-cooked eggs, capers, lemon slices, and anchovies.

Rolled Veal

(Paupiettes de Veau)

A paupiette is a thin piece of meat or fish that is pounded, rolled, and usually stuffed and then braised. Paupiettes de veau are sometimes called oiseaux sans tête (headless birds) because of the resemblance to stuffed quail or woodcock.

YIELD: 4 servings

THE STUFFING

¾ pound (340 grams) chopped veal

4 ounces (113 grams) veal fat

2 tablespoons chopped fresh tarragon

¼ cup (35 grams) crushed ice or small cubes

1 large egg

¼ teaspoon salt

⅛ teaspoon freshly ground black pepper

THE VEAL

1. Holding your hand flat on the meat to direct the knife, cut 8 scaloppines, about 2½ ounces (71 grams) each. Pound each piece into a paper-thin slice about 6 to 8 inches (15 to 20 centimeters) in diameter.

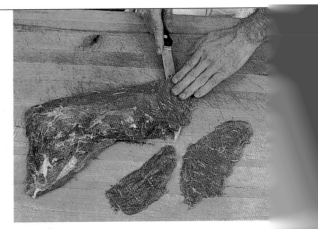

2. Place the chopped veal, fat, tarragon, and ice in the food processor and process for 10 to 15 seconds, until the ice is incorporated and the mixture is smooth. Add the egg along with the salt and pepper. Process for 15 seconds longer, just enough to make the mixture smooth and bind it together. Transfer the mixture to a bowl.

3. Place about ⅓ cup (50 grams) of the stuffing mixture in the center of each scaloppine. <u>Fold the edges around the stuffing, wrapping as securely as possible.</u> Tie the stuffed packages with string, knotting them on the top or the bottom. If the meat has been cleaned of all fat and sinews and is well pounded, it won't shrink or move during cooking.

4. Heat 2 tablespoons (28 grams) butter in a large skillet and, when hot, add the *paupiettes* and <u>brown gently all around</u> for 5 to 6 minutes.

TO COMPLETE THE DISH

2 tablespoons (28 grams) unsalted butter

1 cup (155 grams) thinly sliced onion

3 cloves garlic, peeled, crushed, and chopped

½ cup (118 milliliters) dry white wine

1 teaspoon salt

½ teaspoon freshly ground black pepper

1 teaspoon arrowroot

2 tablespoons cold water

1 tablespoon chopped parsley

Melt the butter, add the onion, and sauté for 3 to 4 minutes. Add the garlic and sauté 1 minute longer. Pour the onion mixture over the *paupiettes*, then deglaze the skillet with the wine and add this liquid to the casserole with the salt and pepper. Bring to a boil, then reduce the heat and simmer, covered, over low heat for 25 minutes. With a slotted spoon, transfer the *paupiettes* to a platter and remove the strings. Keep warm.

Mix the arrowroot and the cold water into a smooth paste and stir into the braising liquid. Bring to a boil and taste; add salt and pepper, if needed. Pour the sauce over the *paupiettes*, sprinkle with parsley and serve immediately, two to a person.

Stuffed Veal Breast

(Poitrine de Veau Farcie)

Veal breast is an inexpensive and versatile cut of meat. It can be roasted; it can be divided into short ribs (tendrons) and braised; and it can be stuffed as shown here. Most recipes for stuffed veal call for a boneless piece of meat. However, the meat is easier to bone after cooking. The ribs slide off effortlessly, which helps you recognize when the meat is cooked. They also keep the roast from shrinking and add to its flavor.

A veal breast can weigh from 4½ to 8 pounds (2 to 3.6 kilograms) and run from about 18 to 25 inches (46 to 63 centimeters) long. The stuffed veal can be braised in the oven or cooked, covered, in a large, deep roasting pan over a flame. If you do not have a pan large enough to accommodate the breast, you may cut it in half. Each piece is then stuffed and tied before braising. Use your favorite stuffing, or the vegetable stuffing suggested below.

YIELD: 8 to 10 servings

1 10-ounce (283-gram) package fresh spinach

1 3-ounce (85-gram) piece fresh salted pork (called pancetta), cut into ¼-inch (6-millimeter) sticks (small lardons)

1 carrot (½ cup/75 grams), peeled and coarsely chopped

1½ cups chopped onions (225 grams)

1 celery rib (1 cup/150 grams), peeled and coarsely chopped

1 or 2 small eggplants (4 cups/376 grams), peeled and cut into ½-inch (13-millimeter) slices

1 cup (127 grams) green pepper, seeded and chopped

½ cup (118 milliliters) water

1 teaspoon salt

1 teaspoon freshly ground black pepper

¼ teaspoon dried thyme leaves

4 hard-cooked eggs, coarsely chopped

1 tablespoon garlic, peeled, crushed, and chopped fine

⅓ cup (12 grams) chopped Italian parsley

7 cups (420 grams) fresh bread crumbs

Cook the spinach in salted, boiling water for 8 to 10 minutes. Drain, run under cold water, and press to extrude the water. Chop coarsely.

Place the lardons in a large saucepan and cook on medium heat until the pieces are browned and crisp and all the fat is rendered (about 5 minutes). Add the carrots, onion, and celery and cook for 3 to 4 minutes. Add the eggplant, green pepper, and water. Mix well, cover, and let cook until all the water is evaporated and the mixture starts to sizzle again (about 5 to 6 minutes). Add the salt, pepper, thyme, and mix well.

Remove from the heat. Add the chopped eggs, spinach, garlic, parsley, and bread crumbs. Stir just enough to blend the ingredients together.

1. A whole breast of veal weighs approximately 16 pounds (7.25 kilograms). This cut is from a milk-fed veal, the calf weighing approximately 300 to 320 pounds (136 to 145 kilograms) when slaughtered. The breast is divided into pieces and used for roasts, stews, or braises. <u>Cut the breast in half</u>.

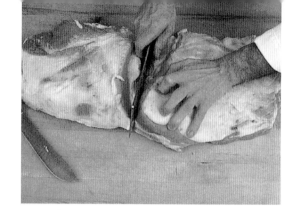

2. <u>Cut off the thick part of one half</u> to leave a thin piece weighing approximately 6 pounds (2.72 kilograms) The thick part, which I am not using here, is opposite the ribs and has large bones and cartilage. The meat can be frozen, used for stewing and braising, or boned out for pâté, and the bones and sinews used for stock.

3. From one side of the piece to be stuffed, <u>remove the hanging piece of meat</u> that is part of the skirt steak.

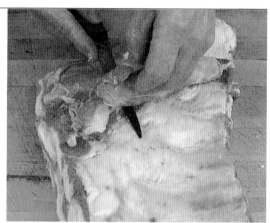

4. <u>Remove any skin from the skirt.</u> Trim other pieces of fat and/or meat from the breast.

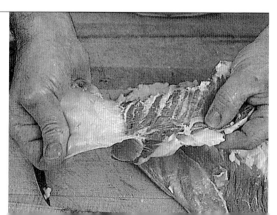

5. To create a pocket in the veal breast, place it rib-side down on the table. Holding your knife so the blade is parallel to the table, <u>cut directly on top of the bones</u> to create the largest possible pocket.

6. Note that I have not cut through the breast at either end or in the back; <u>only the front is opened up</u>. There should be approximately 1 to 1½ inches (2.5 centimeters to 3.75 centimeters) left intact on three sides.

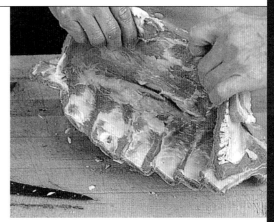

7. <u>Stuff the spinach mixture into the breast</u>, pushing it inside to make certain it goes into all the corners.

8. Place a strip of aluminum foil around the opening and <u>tie it in place with cotton kitchen twine at 1- to 2- inch (2.5- to 5-centimeter) intervals</u> with separate loops and knots using the half-hitch technique (pages 259).

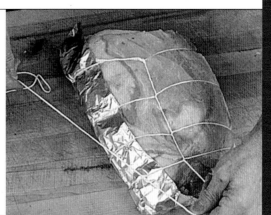

9. To braise the meat: Melt the 2 tablespoons (28 grams) butter in a large saucepan or roasting pan. Sprinkle the roast with 1½ teaspoon salt and, when the butter is hot, place the roast, stuffed-side down, in the skillet, and sauté over medium heat for about 10 minutes. It should be nicely browned. Turn the roast over and <u>add the 2 chopped carrots, 2 chopped onions, and head of garlic cloves.</u> Brown for about 10 minutes, bone-side down.

10. Turn the meat again, bone-side up, and add the 4 pieces of pig's foot, 2 cups (474 milliliters) chicken stock, and 1 cup (237 milliliters) white wine. Cover the roast with a large piece of aluminum foil or, if the pan is deep enough, with a lid. Bring to a boil, reduce the heat, and continue cooking at a very slow simmer for approximately 2½ hours. The internal temperature of the stuffed breast should be 160 to 170 degrees (71°C to 77°C). Let cool to lukewarm before handling.

11. Place the roast on a baking sheet and remove the string and foil. Cut along the bones and <u>twist them out; they should pull out easily.</u> (This can be done while the meat is lukewarm or when it is completely cold.) The roast could be served hot at this point with the braising liquid.

Boning Out a Leg of Veal

(Désosser le Cuisseau de Veau)

The purpose of boning out the leg is to divide the different muscles. Some muscles are more tender than others, and the fiber of the meat goes in one direction for one muscle and in the other direction for another. When all of the pieces are separated, each can be cut properly, usually against the grain, and used in different ways: The most tender part is best for steak or a sauté of escalope, the drier, tougher parts are better braised. The gelatinous, moist pieces are good for stew as well as for boiling or roasting.

The veal leg can weigh between 35 and 50 pounds (16 to 22.5 kilograms). The veal leg I am cutting up here weighed about 38 pounds (17 kilograms). The same boning technique can be used for a leg of beef, a leg of pork (a whole ham), and even a leg of lamb, some parts of which can be used for a shish kebab and some for roasting or for stew.

1. Here is the whole leg of veal as seen from the top.

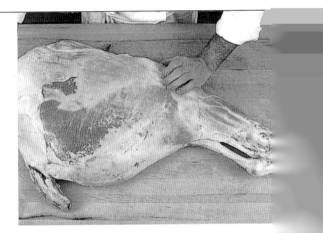

2. Here is the whole leg of veal as viewed from the inside. Notice on the inside by the tail and the pelvic bone the thick, white, waxy, hard fat and the pink, pale color of the flesh, both of which are signs that the meat is of high quality.

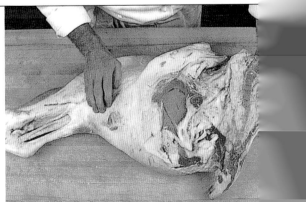

3. <u>Remove the shank by cutting with a sturdy knife through the first joint at the knee.</u> To make *osso bucco*, cut the unboned shank into pieces about 1½ to 2 inches (4 to 5 centimeters) thick (about 3 or 4 per shank). The shank can also be braised whole with the bone in and then brought to the table and carved. In this instance, the carving will be done the long way, standing the bone straight up and cutting down to remove the shank. This will make a very tender, moist piece of braised meat.

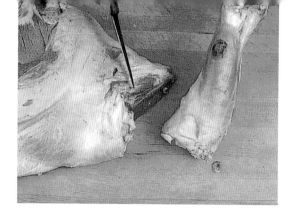

4. To make the stew, bone out the shank, sliding your knife around the bone. It will come out in one piece. <u>This piece of meat (weighing approximately 2 pounds/907 grams) can be rolled on itself</u> and roasted or braised or cut into serving-size pieces. As you bone out the leg, be sure to set the bones aside. They can be cut into pieces and used for stock or frozen for later use.

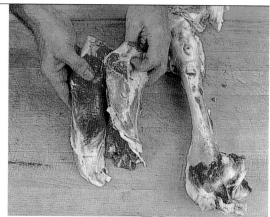

5. Along the inside of the pelvic bone by the tail, the tip of the fillet is lodged within the pelvic area. <u>Run your knife all around to dislodge it.</u> This piece of tenderloin, weighing approximately 1 pound (454 grams), is only the head or top of the fillet and is the tenderest part of the whole back leg. Clean the piece of fillet of any sinews and fat, and set aside for the veal escalope. The rest of the fillet is part of the loin or saddle and is not shown in our picture.

6. To remove the pelvic bone, <u>run a sturdy, sharp-pointed knife along the bone to loosen it from the flesh.</u> Cut gently and work slowly to make certain that you don't cut into the meat too much and that you follow the contours of the bone.

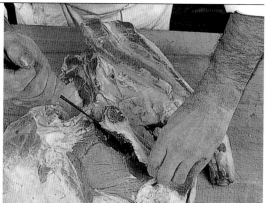

7. When the bone is loose all around, pry it out. Notice that in the socket, where the end of the femur bone is lodged, there is a large sinew. Gut the sinew to remove the bone more easily. Keep pulling and cutting until the entire pelvic bone is separated from the leg. Cut the bone into pieces and set aside for stock or soup.

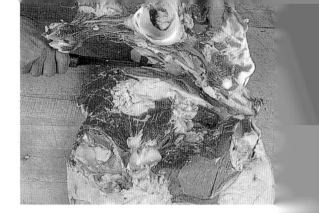

8. To remove the largest muscle of the leg—the top round—place the leg of veal inside up flat on the table. Cut next to the head of the femur bone (where the bone is closest to the surface of the meat), and continue cutting with your knife along the bone. As you cut and pull on the meat, you will see that the meat separated by itself into different muscles. Follow the separation of the meat to scoop out the large rounded muscle called the top round.

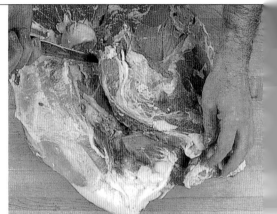

9. Lift the top round from the meat and separate. This is one of the choicest parts of the back leg and weighs between 4¼ and 4½ pounds (1.9 to 2 kilograms).

10. The top round has an upper layer of skin and meat, which should be separated from it. As you start cutting, you will see the separation. This layer of meat and skin closest to the surface of the leg is tougher. However, braised or cleaned and ground, it can be used for *paupiettes* or for making pâté as well as quenelles or stuffings. Clean the entire surface of the top round and set aside.

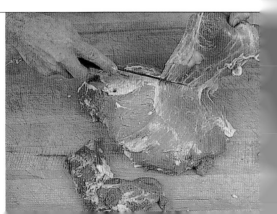

11. Now that the top round has been removed, you will notice that on the lower part of the leg, where the shank was removed, there is still a rounded, sinewy piece of meat. This is also a part of the shank and should be separated from the leg. Weighing about 2 pounds (907 grams), it is moist, gelatinous, and ideal for braising or stewing.

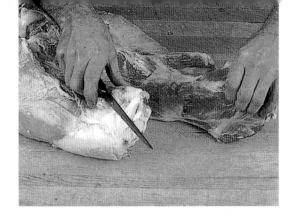

12. The large bone, being now almost completely visible, is easy to remove. Cut on each side, sliding your knife underneath and cutting gently all around the bone until it is completely separated from the meat. Cut the bone into pieces by sawing or breaking with a hammer, and set the pieces aside for stock or soup.

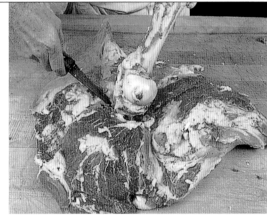

13. Remove the top knuckle (a round, moist piece of meat close to the shank). This tender piece is used for roasting. Start pulling and cutting around the muscle to remove the entire large, roundish piece of meat, weighing about 4½ pounds (2 kilograms). The top knuckle can be used for escalopes or steaks.

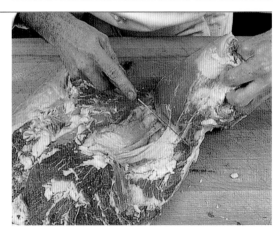

14. On the side of the hip, remove the top sirloin or hip steak, the tenderest part of the leg except for the fillet. This piece of meat will be smaller, weighing approximately 2 pounds (907 grams), and will be cut into steaks.

15. Finally, remaining on the table is the bottom round to be divided into two parts: the roundish, long, cylindrical muscle called the "eye round" and, attached to it, a flatter, wider piece called the "flat." The eye round is the toughest part of the leg and is often braised with stock or wine to give it some tenderness. It can also be ground for use in pâté. The flat, a tenderer piece, is often braised or roasted. The bottom round of the veal is used for pot roast or for the escalopes. (The whole flat weighs about 2 pounds/907 grams.)

16. Here are all the muscles of the leg, divided into pieces. From the left to right in the front are the pieces of shank together, the fillet, the cleaned top round, and the roundish, solid top knuckle. In the back, on the right above the top knuckle, is the hip or top sirloin, to be used for steak, and, next to it, the bottom round divided into the eye round (the small cylindrical piece) and, below it, the flat.

Preparing a Shoulder of Veal for Grilling

(Épaule de Veau á Griller)

1. The whole leg of veal as seen from the top, including the shank. It will weigh approximately 15 pounds (6.8 kilograms).

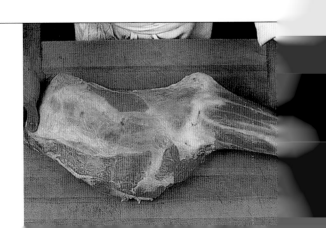

2. <u>Here is the inside of the shoulder</u>. You can recognize the shoulder blade by the lump of the fat in the center. Except for that lump of fat in the center, near the shoulder blade joint, there is basically nothing to remove or trim except the shank, should you decide to remove it.

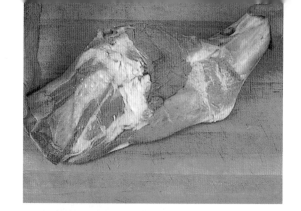

3. <u>Cut the shank off at the joint</u>. The shank will weigh approximately 4 pounds (1.8 kilograms) with the bone in. Of those 4 pounds (1.8 kilograms), 2 pounds (907 grams) will be meat, and 2 pounds (907 grams) will be bones. The bones can be cut and frozen or reserved for stocks or soups.

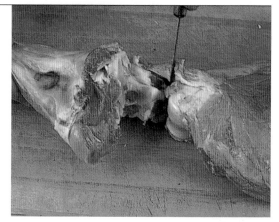

4. Have a strong fire going on the grill that can last and withstand long cooking. Push the hot coals to the side so that where you cook the shoulder is not too terribly hot. (Otherwise, the exterior will get too dark during cooking.)

Place the shoulder top-side down and cook approximately 30 minutes, <u>then turn to brown on the other side</u>. Continue cooking, turning the roast every 30 to 45 minutes, for 2 to 2½ hours longer. When finished, the internal temperature should be approximately 125 to 130 degrees (52°C to 55°C).

Remove the veal from the grill, place on a tray, and keep in a 140 degree (60°C) oven to continue cooking slowly in its own juices and resting for 45 minutes longer. If you can't transfer it to an oven, you can place it covered with a piece of aluminum foil in a warm place off to the side of the barbecue to continue cooking. Serve in slices with herb butter and vegetable garnish.

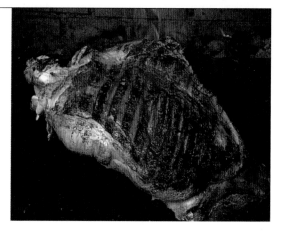

Beef Rib Roast

(Côte de Boeuf)

1. This rib roast has 4 ribs and weighs about 9 pounds (4 kilograms) untrimmed. <u>A rib roast is fatter on the large side</u> which is closer to the "chuck" or the neck.

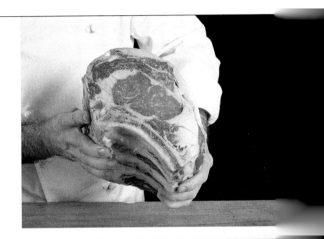

2. <u>It is leaner on the smaller end</u> which goes toward the "sirloin" or the lower back. Hence, it is preferable to buy the ribs closest to the sirloin.

3. Using a sturdy sharp knife, <u>lift up the top layer of fat from the whole roast</u>.

4. <u>Keep cutting down the back of the roast to remove the flat bones</u>. The only bones left should be the ribs.

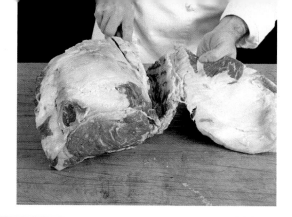

5. <u>Remove the nerves and large sinews covering the meat.</u>

6. <u>Place the top layer of fat on the roast</u>. This is an optional step. The meat can be roasted with or without this top layer.

7. <u>Tie it with string</u>. When the meat is cooked (110 degrees/43°C internal temperature), remove the layer of fat and brown the top of the roast under the broiler for a few minutes.

Trimming Shell Steak

(Préparation du Contre-filet ou Faux Filet)

1. Slide your knife between the bone and the meat and, standing the roast on the end of the chine bone (backbone), <u>continue cutting alongside the chine bone to separate it from the meat.</u>

2. Following the contour of the bone, <u>separate the bones from the meat.</u> Trim away most of the fat underneath and on top of the meat. (There are approximately 5½ pounds/ 2.5 kilograms of fat and about 2½ pounds/1.1 kilograms of bones on this piece of meat.)

3. At one end of the strip, there is a triangular piece of meat lodged on top of the strip and separated from it by a large sinew. Although this triangular piece is often left in place and the steaks cut directly through it, it is preferable to remove it because the connecting sinew is tough. <u>Following the contour of the sinew, cut off the triangle of meat.</u>

4. <u>The triangular piece of meat is being removed</u> and can be used as a steak. (It weighs approximately 8 ounces/227 grams, more or less, depending on the size of the shell.)

5. Now the top of the strip can be cleaned of the large gelatinous sinews, which are excellent in white as well as brown stock. <u>Remove by pulling on a strip of sinew with one hand while cutting and sliding the knife against the sinew with the other hand</u> to get it off with as little meat attached as possible.

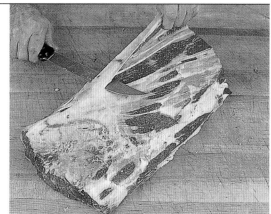

6. When the whole shell is trimmed (there is still a little bit of the front flap and chain attached to it), most of the fat and sinews have been removed. <u>Cut off about a 3-pound (1.4-kilogram) piece of the shell for a roast.</u>

7. <u>Cut the rest of the shell into ¾- to 1-inch (2- to 2.5-centimeter) thick steaks of approximately 10 ounces (283 grams) each.</u> Depending on the size of the shell, it will yield approximately a dozen steaks in addition to the 3-pound (1.4-kilogram) roast, bones and sinews (which can be used for stock), and fat. The steaks can be wrapped in plastic wrap and then in aluminum foil and frozen individually for later use. If the steaks are frozen, be sure to defrost them slowly, still wrapped, in the refrigerator.

Pepper Steak

(Steak au Poivre)

Pepper steak is usually made with an expensive cut such as a shell steak from the beef loin. However, it is quite good made from a hip steak or a shoulder blade steak (also known as a "chicken steak"). An 8- to 10-ounce (227- to 283-gram) boneless, well-trimmed steak serves one.

1. If the shell steak is bought ready-cut, trim the fat all around the meat. Crush whole black peppercorns with a rolling pin or the edge of a heavy saucepan by spreading them out and pushing down and forward. You can hear them crack. Repeat until all the little corns are broken. Crushed peppercorn is called *mignonnette* in French cooking. Black peppercorns are preferred, being more flavorful and less pungent than white.

2. Salt the steak on both sides. Spread the *mignonnette* on the working surface and press the steak onto the pieces on both sides.

3. Sauté the steak in hazelnut-colored butter, 3 or 4 minutes on each side.

4. The classic way to prepare steak *au poivre* is to deglaze the skillet with cognac, add some brown sauce, and finish it with little bits of fresh unsalted butter. However, red wine is often added, as well as shallots and sometimes cream. Find your own variations.

Trimming Fillet or Tenderloin

(Préparation du Filet de Boeuf)

1. <u>Here is the whole fillet in Cryovac</u>. This is how it comes from the butcher or slaughterhouse. Remove the plastic.

2. Separate the long strip called the "chain," <u>pulling it from the fillet proper</u>. Cut it off.

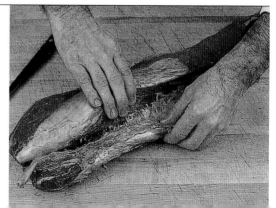

3. The chain is full of sinews and it would be difficult to remove them one by one, but, because the meat is very tender, it can simply be scraped from the sinews. Holding the chain at one end, scrape the meat from the chain with a knife or a spoon. The meat can be transformed into delicious hamburger. Use the sinews for stock.

4. Remove the small layer of fat from the top of the fillet. Remove the layer of thick sinew under the layer of fat and reserve it for stock. The fillet is now completely cleaned on top. Turn it over and trim the underside, if necessary. Discard the fat and reserve the sinews and tendons for stock.

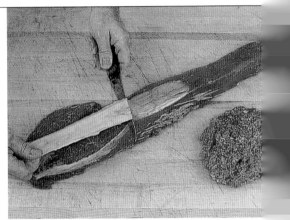

5. If you want to cook the whole fillet, fold the thin tail in on itself. To do so, tuck the tail under and then secure the thin end of it with a string before cooking. Tied this way, the fillet is the same thickness throughout and will cook evenly.

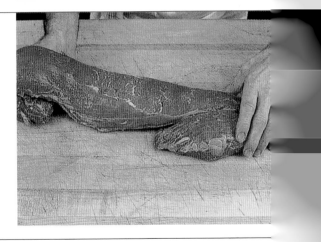

Cuts of Fillet

(Division du Filet de Boeuf)

1. The fillet is usually divided into pieces. Here the large tip of the fillet, which is slightly pointed, is cut into one large steak called a *chateaubriand* (see below), weighing from about 1¼ to 1½ pounds (567 to 680 grams). This piece of meat will serve about 3 people. Next, the whole center of the fillet, which is the same thickness, is cut into "hearts of fillets," or tournedos, about 7 to 8 ounces (198 to 227 grams) each.

2. From left to right is: the head of the fillet, the *chateaubriand*; seven *tournedos*; 2 smaller fillets (*filets mignons*), about 3 ounces (85 grams) each; and, finally, the tail of the fillet, cut into strips 2 to 3 inches (5 to 7.5 centimeters) long by ½ inch (1.25 centimeters) thick, which are usually used in a sauté like Beef Stroganoff.

3. For the *chateaubriand*, stand the large piece of fillet pointed side up and place a towel around it.

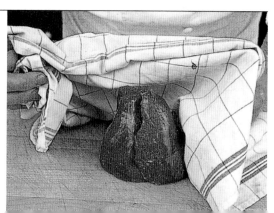

4. Gather the towel around to hold the fillet and, using a meat pounder, <u>pound the meat so it flattens and takes on a roundish form as you hold its shape with the towel.</u>

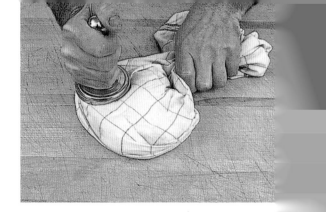

5. The *chateaubriand* is now ready to be cooked. It is an oval shape about 7 inches (17.75 centimeters) long by 5 inches (12.7 centimeters) wide and approximately 1¼ inches (3.2 centimeters) thick. Set aside in the refrigerator until ready to cook.

> **Techniques put with talent equal great food. With love it brings forth extraordinary dishes. One cannot cook indifferently.**

Preparing Skirt, Flank, and Hanging Tenderloin

(Préparation du Flanchet (diaphragme) Bavette et Onglet)

1. For the skirt steak: <u>Pull off the layer of skin on both sides.</u> You will notice that the skin on both sides is not removed lengthwise but rather from side to side, following the fiber of the meat. Trim the excess fat from the meat. An untrimmed 2-pound (207-gram) skirt steak yields approximately 1¼ pounds (567 grams) of trimmed meat.

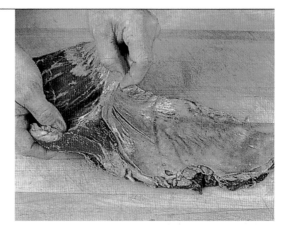

2. For the untrimmed flank steak: <u>Pull off the skin on both sides.</u> Notice that the skin will separate from the thicker, meatier side lengthwise and should be pulled down and off. Most of these pieces of meat, unless purchased directly from a slaughterhouse, will come trimmed from your local butcher. They may, however, not be as trimmed as they are in this photo. If so, trim further until completely clean for grilling.

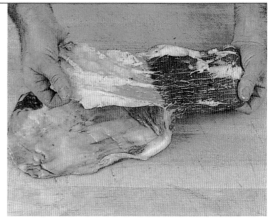

3. The thin end of the flank steak is mostly fat. <u>Trim the steak into an oval shape, removing most of the fat, especially at the tail end.</u> A 2½-pound (1.13-kilogram) untrimmed flank steak will yield a trimmed steak of about 1¾ pounds (794 grams) and approximately ¾ pound (340 grams) of fat and sinew.

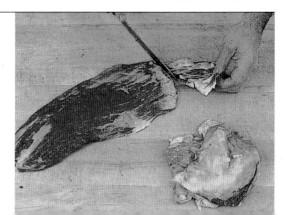

4. For the hanging tenderloin: When untrimmed, this piece of meat is covered by a thick skin, especially at the tail, where there is a big lump of fat. <u>Clean off the excess fat</u>, pulling the layer of skin and fat from the meat. A 3-pound (1.4-kilogram) hanging tenderloin yields approximately 1½ pounds (680 grams) of completely trimmed meat.

5. <u>Here are 3 pieces of meat, trimmed</u>: the skirt steak on top, the flank steak in the center, and the hanging tenderloin on the bottom.

Stuffed Flank Steak

(Bavette Farcie)

Flank is a popular cut of meat and not too expensive. It is usually roasted or charcoal broiled and served thinly sliced, as London broil. The meat is fibrous and will be tough if not cut against the grain. However, properly prepared, flank is tasty and juicy. This stuffed flank is served hot, but it is also good cold, cut in thin slices and served without the sauce on a bed of lettuce decorated with tomato wedges, sour French pickles (cornichons) and good mustard. A 3- to 3¼-pound (1.4- to 1.5-kilogram) untrimmed flank steak (about 2¼ to 2½ pounds/1 kilogram trimmed) will serve 6 people when stuffed.

YIELD: 6 servings

THE STUFFING

2 tablespoons olive oil

2 tablespoons (28 grams) unsalted butter

2½ cups (325 grams) ¼-inch
  (6-millimeter) bread cubes

1 pound (454 grams) lean ground beef

2 large eggs

1 onion, peeled and chopped, (¾ cup/112
  grams)

½ celery rib, chopped (½ cup/75 grams)

2 cloves garlic, peeled, crushed and
  chopped fine (1 teaspoon)

2 tablespoons chopped Italian parsley

1½ teaspoons salt

½ teaspoon freshly ground black pepper

¼ teaspoon crushed thyme or savory

Heat the oil and butter in a skillet and brown
the bread cubes. Combine the remaining
ingredients in a large bowl and then add the
bread cubes, mixing lightly to avoid making
a mush.

1. You will probably buy the flank trimmed, or ask
the butcher to trim it for you. However, if you buy it
untrimmed, your first step is to pull off the thin "skin" on
one side and

2. then the fatter skin on the other side. Trim off excess fat
at the end.

3. Pressing gently on the flank with one hand to keep it flat, <u>cut into the steak lengthwise with a small, sharp paring knife</u> to make a pocket for the stuffing.

4. <u>Lift up the upper "lip" and cut, keeping your blade horizontal</u>. Be careful not to come out at either end.

5. <u>Cut deeper into the steak</u>, but do not cut through to the other side.

6. <u>If you cut through the flank by accident,</u>

7. <u>slice a thin piece off an end</u> where it won't affect the pocket

8. <u>and use it as a patch to plug the hole</u>; the stuffing will keep it in place.

9. Once your cavity is ready, <u>push the stuffing into the opening</u>, making sure the corners are filled.

10. <u>Bring the lower lip of the flank against the stuffing</u>.

11. Then <u>bring the upper lip down on top</u> to form a nice loaf.

12. <u>Tie the roast.</u>

COOKING THE STUFFED FLANK STEAK

1 tablespoon (14 grams) unsalted butter

1 tablespoon olive oil

1 medium carrot, peeled and diced fine (about ¾ cup/112 grams)

1 onion, chopped (about ¾ cup/112 grams)

2 bay leaves

1 tomato, coarsely chopped (about 1 cup/150 grams)

1 teaspoon thyme leaves

1 cup (237 milliliters) water or stock

1 cup (237 milliliters) dry red wine

2 teaspoons arrowroot, dissolved in ¼ cup (59 milliliters) cold water

Salt and freshly ground black pepper

You will need a deep, heavy casserole with a cover. Heat the butter and oil in the casserole, and then brown the stuffed meat on all sides. Add the carrot, onion, bay leaves, tomato and thyme and cook over moderate heat, uncovered, for 5 minutes. Add water or stock and wine, bring to a boil, cover and braise on a very low heat on top of the stove, or in a 350 degree (177°C) preheated oven for 1½ hours. Lift the meat to a platter, remove the strings, and keep warm while making the sauce.

Spoon out most of the fat from the surface of the braising liquid in your casserole. Stir the dissolved arrowroot into the liquid left in the casserole. Bring to a boil and cook, stirring constantly, until the sauce thickens slightly. Add salt and pepper to taste.

To serve, cut the meat in ½-inch (13-millimeter) slices (if cut too thick, the meat is tough), one per person, and arrange on a platter with the uncarved part of the roast. Pour 2 or 3 tablespoons of sauce over each serving.

Stuffed Pork Chops with Sour Sauce

(Côtelettes de Porc Farcies Charcutière)

Although in our recipe we use the pork chops from the rack, loin chops can be used as well. The chops do not have to be stuffed and can be broiled or sautéed in different ways; for example, Normandy-style with apples, cream, and Calvados.

YIELD: 6 servings

6 pork chops, center cut (6 to 7
  ounces/170 to 198 grams each)

STUFFING

1 tablespoon (14 grams) unsalted butter

1 cup (100 grams), cleaned and diced finely,
  (white and light green parts only) leek

½ cup (60 grams), peeled and
  finely diced celery

1 pound (454 grams) blanched spinach,
  coarsely chopped

½ cup (80 grams) finely diced boiled ham

½ teaspoon salt

¼ teaspoon freshly ground black pepper

SAUCE CHARCUTIÈRE

½ cup (80 grams) finely chopped onions

1½ cups (300 grams) peeled, seeded,
  and coarsely chopped tomatoes

1 tablespoon crushed and chopped garlic

¾ cup (178 milliliters) *demi-glace*, page 27

½ cup (118 milliliters) dry white wine

½ cup (90 grams) sour French gherkins
  (*cornichons*), thinly sliced

Salt and freshly ground black pepper,
  if needed

2 tablespoons chopped fresh herbs
  (parsley, tarragon, chives, etc.)

1. When you buy a whole rack or a piece of rack you will find that it usually comes with the backbone (chine bone). This makes it difficult to cut into chops or to carve in the dining room if it is roasted whole. To remove the backbone, place the rack flat and <u>cut all along the bone to separate from the meat</u>.

2. Standing the rack up and using the front part of a cleaver, <u>cut through the end of the rib to sever the whole backbone.</u>

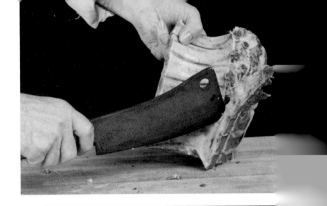

3. <u>The backbone is now separated from the rack.</u> The rack at that point could be roasted whole, seasoned with carrots and onions, and served with natural juices. Prepared this way, it is easy to carve in the dining room.

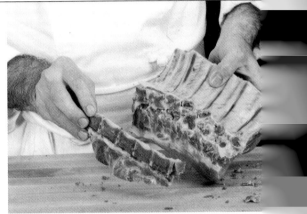

4. <u>Cut in between each rib to make individual chops.</u> The chops should weigh approximately 6 to 7 ounces (170 to 198 grams) each.

5. <u>Trim each chop along the rib of sinews and fat.</u> Trim if the pork is a few days old, as this is where the meat usually spoils first. In addition, trimming makes the chop a bit more elegant.

6. To make the chop still more attractive, <u>clean the end off the rib</u>. (Use the trimmings in stocks or soups.) Cut the meat all around the bone (it will be mostly fat), and scrape it off to expose the end of the rib.

7. Place the chop flat and, holding it down with one hand, <u>slice it through the middle with the point of a knife</u>. Do not slice the ends. It should form a pocket. Cut deep enough to touch the rib with the knife.

8. <u>Open the chop and flatten each half with a meat pounder</u> to make it a bit larger so it can hold more stuffing and form a better pocket.

9. For the sauce: Melt the butter in a small skillet, add the leek and sauté for 1 minute on medium to low heat, then add the celery and sauté for a few seconds. Mix the spinach in with a fork and sauté for another minute. Combine with the ham and season with salt and pepper. Mix well. Let the stuffing cool, <u>then divide among the chops</u>.

10. Push the stuffing in the cavity and <u>close the meat on top</u>. If the chops are not overstuffed and if the meat has been pounded nicely, it doesn't need to be tied or secured with a skewer.

11. Sprinkle the chops with salt and pepper. Melt 2 tablespoons (28 grams) of butter in a wide skillet with a cover. Add the chops and cook, uncovered, on medium heat, for 4 minutes on one side. When browned, turn, cover and cook on medium heat for another 5 minutes on the other side. <u>The pork chops should cook slowly</u> or they will become dry and stringy.

12. Place the chops on a platter and keep warm, uncovered, in a 160 degree (71°C) oven. Add the onions to the drippings and sauté for 1 to 2 minutes on medium heat, then add the wine. Boil for a few seconds, stirring to melt all the solidified juices. Add the tomatoes and garlic and cook for 1 minute. Add the *demi-glace* and wine, bring to a boil and reduce for 2 to 3 minutes until it coats the spoon and has the consistency of a sauce. Add salt and pepper if necessary. Stir in the cornichons, <u>pour the sauce over the chops</u>, sprinkle with herbs and serve.

Rabbit Blanquette

(Blanquette de Lapin)

A rabbit stew in cream sauce is ideal for a large party; it doesn't need much more than an hour of cooking if the rabbit is young (about 3 months old). If the rabbit is larger and older, increase the cooking time until the meat feels tender, just a bit firm when pierced with the point of a fork.

The rabbit stew, or blanquette, and the dumplings can be done several days ahead. Do not add the mushrooms, pearl onions, or cream until the last moment when reheating to ensure a fresher, better taste. In case your rabbit has the skin still on and is not eviscerated, steps 1 through 4 of this recipe will show you how to prepare it for cooking. Otherwise, pick up at step 5.

YIELD: 8 to 10 servings

2 young rabbits, 2 ¾-pound (1.25-kilo grams) each

3 tablespoons (42 grams) unsalted butter

2 cups (310 grams) coarsely chopped onions

3 tablespoons all-purpose flour

1 tablespoon chopped garlic

8 to 10 sprigs fresh thyme or 1½ teaspoons dried thyme

1 sprig fresh oregano or ½ teaspoon dried oregano

2 cups (474 milliliters) water

2 cups (474 milliliters) chicken stock

½ teaspoon freshly ground black pepper

2 teaspoons salt

FOR THE DUMPLINGS

2 rabbits' livers, hearts, and kidneys (about 6 ounces/170 grams total)

¾ pound (340 grams) pork, at least ⅓ fat, from the shoulder, cut into ½-inch dice

1 large clove garlic, chopped

½ cup (30 grams) chopped Italian parsley

¼ teaspoon freshly ground black pepper

½ teaspoon salt

¾ pound (340 grams) tiny white pearl onions (40 onions), peeled

¾ pound (340 grams) oyster mushrooms, chanterelles, or cultivated mushrooms

1 cup (237 milliliters) heavy cream

1. Make an incision with a knife through the skin in the middle of the rabbit's back. Place both hands in the incision and pull on each side to separate the skin from the flesh. You need strength but the skin should come off easily.

2. As you pull the skin off and expose the meat, you will notice that <u>it is almost completely free of fat</u>.

3. Pull off the skin toward the tail to expose the back legs. Cut at the tail, then <u>break the foot bone with the back of a large knife</u>, and cut through.

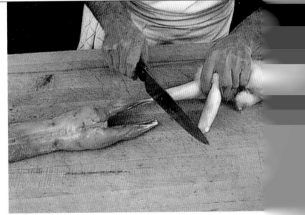

4. <u>Proceed in the same manner with the front legs.</u> Pull the skin toward the head and cut at the neck.

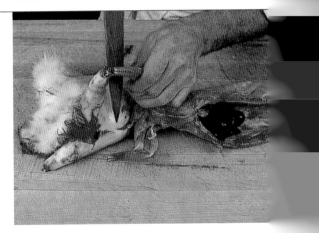

5. <u>Cut each rabbit into 7 or 8 pieces, depending on size.</u> You should have 2 back legs, the front legs with some of the rib part, and the back cut into 3 pieces. Sprinkle with salt and pepper.

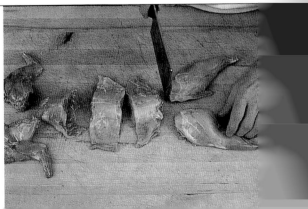

6. Melt the butter in 1 very large saucepan or 2 skillets and, when hot, place the pieces of rabbit in one layer in one or both skillets. Brown for 10 minutes over medium to high heat, turning the rabbit pieces so they are nicely browned all around. Add the chopped onions and cook briefly for 2 to 3 minutes. Remove the rabbit to a plate. Sprinkle with the flour and stir to mix well. Finally, stir in the garlic, thyme, oregano, water, stock, pepper, and salt. Mix well and bring to a boil, stirring to ensure that the mixture doesn't stick to the bottom of the pan. Add the rabbit pieces and bring to a boil. Lower the heat, cover partially (leaving an opening just large enough to allow some of the steam to escape), and cook over very low to medium heat for 1 hour, boiling very gently.

7. FOR THE DUMPLINGS: While the rabbit is cooking, place the livers, hearts, and kidneys in the food processor and process until smooth. Add the pork and chopped garlic clove, and keep processing until the mixture is smooth again, for about 1 minute. Add the parsley, pepper, and salt, and process again, just enough to mix. Remove and place in a bowl.

Place 1½ inches (3 centimeters) of water in a large, flat saucepan and bring to a boil. Lower the heat to stop the boiling and, using a large spoon, drop the equivalent of 2 tablespoons of the liver mixture into the hot water. You should have approximately 1 dozen liver dumplings. The water should not boil. Keep cooking the dumplings in the water (heated to approximately 170 degrees/77°C) for 10 minutes. Remove with a slotted spoon and set aside.

8. <u>When the rabbit is cooked, remove with a slotted spoon and place in a large clean saucepan.</u>

9. <u>Strain all the sauce from the rabbit through a fine sieve directly onto the pieces of rabbit.</u> In a separate pot, cover the pearl onions with cold water, heat on top of the stove, and boil gently for 5 minutes. Drain. Clean the mushrooms.

10. <u>Add the dumplings, the pearl onions, the mushrooms, and cream to the rabbit.</u> Place back on the stove, bring to a very light boil, and simmer gently, covered, for 10 to 12 minutes.

11. Serve the Rabbit Blanquette.

CHAR

OFFAL & CUTERIE

Chicken Liver Custards

(Gâteau de Foies Volailles)

The chicken liver custard is a specialty of the French area of Bresse, which is known for the superiority of its chicken and their pale, pink, fatty livers, which are considered the best. The custard is a refined dish, which is generally served as a first course for an elaborate dinner or as a main course for brunch or a light dinner. You can make it in individual molds or in a large one with or without the carrot decoration on top. The sauce is a reduction of chicken stock with cream. A tomato sauce with a mushroom garnish is excellent with it, too.

YIELD: 6 to 8 servings

CUSTARD

3 chicken livers, cleaned of filaments and any greenish parts

1 large clove garlic, crushed, or 2 small cloves

1 teaspoon (5 grams) unsalted butter

½ teaspoon freshly ground white pepper

1 teaspoon salt

1 teaspoon cornstarch

1 cup (237 milliliters) milk

6 large eggs

1 cup (237 milliliters) heavy cream

2 to 3 large carrots, peeled, optional

SAUCE

2 cups (473 milliliters) chicken stock

1 cup (237 milliliters) beef stock

¾ cup (178 milliliters) heavy cream

Salt and freshly ground black pepper

1 tablespoon (14 grams) unsalted butter

1 tablespoon coarsely minced fresh chives

1. Preheat the oven to 350 degrees (177°C). Puree the livers and garlic in a food processor until smooth. In a skillet, melt the butter until hot and add the liver mixture. Using a rubber spatula, stir the livers for 1 minute or so until they solidify and hold. Return the mixture to the food processor and blend again with pepper, salt, and cornstarch and then add the milk. Blend until smooth and add the eggs and the cream. When well blended, strain into a bowl through a fine sieve.

2. Butter several small soufflé molds or a large 4- to 5-cup (1- to 1.2-liter) mold. Fill the molds with the liver mixture and <u>place in a pan with tepid water</u>. Bake for about 35 minutes for the small molds, 60 minutes for the large mold. The water around the custard should not boil. If it gets too hot, add some cold water or some ice cubes during the cooking. Remove from the heat and let the custard set for at least 20 minutes before unmolding.

3. Slice the carrots very thin with a vegetable peeler, a *mandoline*, or with a knife. Slice some of them into rounds and some of them into long strips. Drop the carrots into boiling water, bring back to a boil and boil for 30 seconds until wilted. Lift out into a bowl of cold water to stop cooking and retain color. Drain the carrots and place on a paper towel to dry. Set aside until ready to use. <u>Start decorating the custard with the carrots, if desired.</u>

4. For the sauce, reduce the chicken and beef stocks in a saucepan to about ¾ cup (178 milliliters) to obtain a strong, dark *demi-glace*. Add the heavy cream and boil on high heat for 1 minute until it reduces to about 1½ cups (355 milliliters) and is slightly syrupy. Add salt and pepper to taste and place the butter, in small pieces, on top of the sauce to prevent a skin from forming. Set aside. <u>At serving time brush with butter to shine the top and heat slightly in the oven.</u> Arrange sauce around each custard and sprinkle with the chives. Serve immediately.

Making Chicken Cracklings

(Gratons de Peau de Poulet)

1. Preheat the oven to 400 degrees (204°C). Spread the chicken skin on a baking sheet, flesh side down. <u>Sprinkle with ¼ teaspoon salt</u> and place in the oven for 20 to 30 minutes.

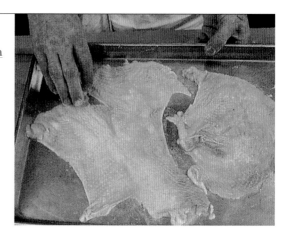

2. <u>The skin should be very crisp</u>. If not, cook a little longer. Transfer to a plate and set aside. The fat rendered by the chicken skin can be used to sauté potatoes or for stew. Use cracklings on salads or in bean stew or soups. The cracklings also can be baked into bread (see page 442).

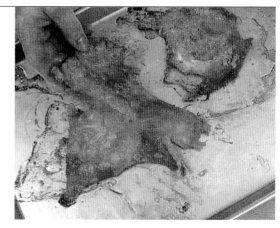

Preparing Beef Tongue

(Préparation de la Langue de Bœuf)

The beef tongue used here is already cured but uncooked. This is how most tongue is sold in markets. If it is not cured, put the tongue in a plastic bag with 2 cups of curing salt. Refrigerate for 5 to 8 days, turning the bag occasionally.

BRAISED BEEF TONGUE WITH LENTILS

Beef tongue cooked with beans, lentils or potatoes makes an excellent winter dish, easy to prepare ahead and flavorful when reheated. The beef tongue itself can also be sliced cold for sandwiches or served at a buffet, glazed in aspic.

YIELD: 8 to 10 servings

1 3¾-pound (1.8-kilogram) cured beef tongue

8 ounces (227 grams) salt pork, cut into ½-inch dice

¾ pound (340 grams) onions, cut into 1-inch chunks (2 or 3 medium onions)

10 ounces (283 grams) carrots, cut into 1-inch chunks (about 3 medium carrots)

2 tablespoons fresh rosemary leaves

1 pound (454 grams) lentils

6 cups (1.4 liters) chicken stock

Salt, if needed, depending on saltiness of the tongue, salt pork, and stock

1. Place the tongue in a kettle and cover with cold water. Bring to a boil and simmer gently just under the boil, about 180 degrees (82 °C), for a good 2½ hours. Remove the tongue and let cool for at least 30 minutes, until cool enough to handle.

2. Peel the tongue and remove the bones toward the throat. (They are the only bones left in the meat.)

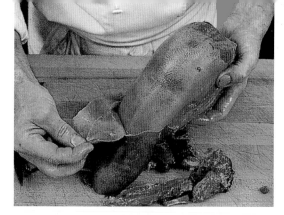

3. Cover the little pieces of salt pork, called lardons, with water. Bring to a boil and boil about 1 minute, drain in a sieve, wash under cold water, and place in a large Dutch oven. Cook over medium to high heat for about 10 minutes, until they are nicely browned and most of the fat has been rendered. Add the onions and carrots and continue cooking for about 3 minutes. Then add the tongue and the rosemary, lentils, and chicken stock to the pot. Simmer gently for 1 hour with the pot covered almost completely except for a slight opening. It is better to cook this dish ahead and let sit for at least 30 minutes before carving.

4. Remove the tongue from the lentils and cut into ½-inch (1.25-centimeter) slices.

5. Arrange the tongue on a large serving platter with the vegetables and lentils. (If any lentils are left over, they can be puréed with some water in the food processor. Some of the tongue can be diced and combined with the pureed lentils to make a very flavorful soup. This also works well with sausage or ham.)

Tripe with Wine and Calvados

(Tripes à la Mode de Caen)

Tripe usually refers to the stomach of ox or beef, although in France certain parts of the intestine are considered to be tripe as well. The pieds paquets is a specialty of Marseille, made from lamb tripe mixed with the feuillet (part of the huge intestine), formed into little packages and cooked slowly for a long time. There are many different recipes for tripe and the one given here is the classic version cooked in Normandy and finished with Calvados. Beef feet are usually added to give a more gelatinous consistency to the dish.

YIELD: Serves 8 to 10 servings

TRIPE
10 pounds (4.5 kilograms) beef tripe (honeycomb)

2 beef or calf feet, 1½ to 2 pounds (681 to 907 grams) each

3 carrots, peeled (about ½ pound/227 grams)

2 large onions, peeled and cut into halves

1 large leek or 2 to 3 smaller ones, cleaned

2 to 3 stalks of celery

3 bay leaves

1 teaspoon dried thyme

1½ tablespoons salt

1½ teaspoons freshly ground black pepper

2 quarts (2 scant liters) light, chicken or beef stock, or a mixture of both

1 bottle dry white wine

2 tablespoons Calvados

TO FINISH THE DISH (optional)
1¼ cups (187 grams) flour

½ cup (118 milliliters) lukewarm water

1 large egg, beaten, for glaze

1. The tripe will come cleaned and already blanched. If you are unable to obtain it fresh, defrost it slowly under refrigeration.

2. <u>Split the beef feet into halves</u>. Cut the meat all around the central bone and in the middle of the hoof. It is not necessary to cut through the bone.

3. Arrange the feet, carrots, onions, leek, and celery and all the seasonings in a large kettle. <u>Place the tripe on top</u> and add the stock and wine. Cover and bring to a boil. Lower the heat and simmer very slowly for 5 hours. Set aside to cool.

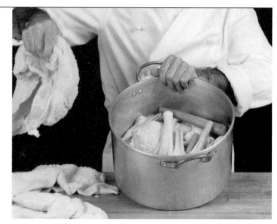

4. When cool enough to handle, lift the tripe, feet and vegetables from the liquid. Reduce the liquid on high heat to 2 quarts (2 scant liters). Meanwhile, bone out the feet and cut the meat into 1-inch (2.5-centimeter) pieces. Discard the bones. <u>Cut the tripe into 2-inch (5-centimeter) pieces</u> and chop all the vegetables coarsely. Combine with the reduced stock. You should have just enough liquid to cover the tripe.

5. Bring to a boil. Taste for seasoning. You may have to add salt and pepper depending on the strength of the stock. It should be well seasoned.

6. At this point, the tripe could be served or divided into containers and frozen. When ready to use, defrost under refrigeration overnight. Boil. <u>Serve with a sprinkling of Calvados</u> (applejack brandy), approximately ½ teaspoon per person. The tripe is customarily served in bowls with boiled potatoes.

7. For a fancier way of serving tripe, place in earthenware crocks, seal the lid with dough so no steam escapes, and bake in the oven. Preheat the oven to 325 degrees (163°C). Make a dough by mixing the flour with water and kneading for 1 minute. <u>Roll pieces of dough into 1-inch (2.5-centimeter)-thick strips,</u> dampen with water and place around the lid. Press to flatten the dough to make sure it adheres well. Brush with the egg wash, and place on a cookie sheet in the oven for 1 hour. Serve as is from the oven. At the table, break the dough and lift the cover in front of your guests. Tripe is customarily served as a main course with boiled potatoes.

How to Prepare Marrow

(Preparation de la Moëlle)

Beef marrow is often used in French cooking. It is removed from the bone, poached, and served on toast or served with a sauce, as we will here. It is sometimes used in place of butter in dumplings or quenelles. When the marrow is removed from the bone it is reddish and bloody. It should be placed in cold water in the refrigerator for at least a day and the water should be changed a couple of times to get rid of the bloody part of the marrow and make it white and firm. If the marrow is not soaked in water it will turn dark during cooking instead of being white.

1. Order a large marrow bone from your butcher and have it cut with a saw above or below the knuckles, so as to have just the part in between, where most of the marrow lies. <u>Use a hammer to break the bone</u>. Be sure to do it on a butcher block or other heavy, sturdy surface. Otherwise the vibration will cause the hammer to bounce.

2. When the bone is broken open, <u>use a small knife to remove the marrow, keeping the pieces as large as possible.</u> Be careful not to cut yourself on the very sharp pieces of bone. Place the marrow in cold water in the refrigerator, if possible overnight. Change the water once or twice.

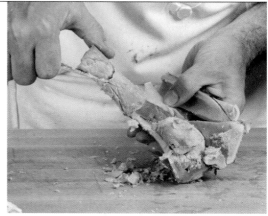

3. <u>Slice the marrow in approximately ⅜-inch (9-millimeter)-thick pieces.</u> Bring a pot of salted water to a boil and drop the marrow in it. Reduce the heat and poach very gently in 190 degree (88°C) water for 4 to 5 minutes until the marrow becomes opaque, which indicates that it has been cooked throughout.

4. Using a slotted spoon, <u>remove the pieces of marrow from the pot</u> (they will float on top). Marrow is often served on toast, with a sprinkling of coarse salt. It also may be served in cooked artichoke bottoms, as shown here, or in a red wine sauce as a classic garnish for a filleted steak.

Peeling and Slicing Calves Liver

(Nettoyer et Trancher le Foie de Veau)

1. Place the calves' liver upside down on the table (the sinewy side on top). <u>Insert your knife and remove most of the large sinews.</u> Then start peeling off the skin.

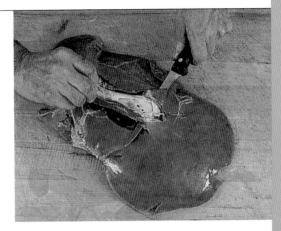

2. When the skin on the underside has been removed, <u>turn the liver over and peel the skin from the top.</u> Although some cooks do not remove this thin veil of skin, removing it makes the liver much more tender.

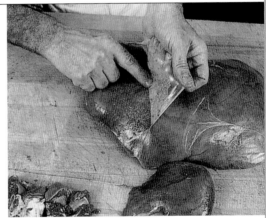

3. <u>The liver can be cut into 24 small (1½-ounce/43-gram) slivers, as in the foreground here,</u> or it can be cut in larger, thicker steaks, each weighing about 5 ounces (142 grams). These can be sautéed in olive oil and butter until medium rare.

Kidneys

(Rognons)

The choicest kidneys are veal and lamb kidneys, which are enclosed in an envelope of fat. Unfortunately, U.S.D.A. regulations require veal kidneys be opened and freed of fat and skin before leaving the slaughterhouse. This means they can never be broiled or braised whole, like lamb kidneys. Beef kidneys are usually used for long-simmered stews such as kidney pie.

1. The envelope of fat protecting the veal kidney is very white and waxy. This high-quality fat is good with ground veal for making dumplings, pâtés, or other hors d'oeuvre. Notice that since the fat is waxy, it can be separated into small pieces. The fat is held together by small membranes, and if it is to be used in dumplings or quenelles, it should be separated from the membranes. <u>Remove the kidneys from their envelope of fat.</u>

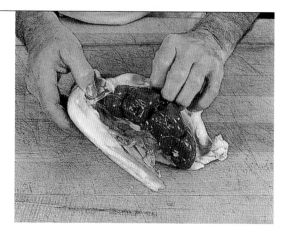

2. <u>Cut the sinew that holds the kidney to the fat.</u> Notice that the kidney will weigh approximately one-quarter of the total weight. There is much more fat than kidney. Set the fat aside.

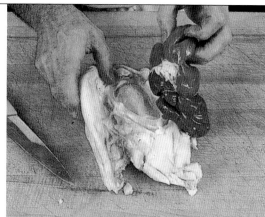

3. Spilt the kidney in half lengthwise. <u>Remove most of the sinews and pieces of fat from the inside of the kidney so that it is practically clean.</u>

4. <u>Cut the kidney into slices</u> if you want to sauté it.

5. <u>On the left: kidney ready to broil or roast whole. On the right: kidney ready to sauté.</u> Kidneys should be cooked a few minutes only at the highest possible heat. They should be pink in the middle. Drain the kidneys in a sieve for a few minutes (pink liquid will run out of the kidneys and should be discarded). After the kidneys are sautéed, a sauce is made with the drippings in the pan. Return the kidneys to the pan only long enough to warm them in the sauce. Do not boil; the kidneys will get tough.

STUFFED VEAL KIDNEYS

In this recipe, kidneys are stuffed and cooked in an envelope of fat, which is discarded after cooking. Stuffed kidneys are often served with sautéed potatoes.

YIELD: 4 servings

2 tablespoons (28 grams) unsalted butter

2 tablespoons chopped onions

1 large clove garlic, peeled and finely chopped

1½ cups (135 grams) diced mushrooms

⅓ cup (40 grams) finely chopped country-cured ham (prosciutto)

⅓ cup (20 grams) chopped flat parsley

⅛ teaspoon freshly ground black pepper

4 1¾-pound (794-gram) veal kidneys, with fat

1. For the stuffing: Melt the butter in a skillet and, when hot, sauté the onions for about 1 minute. Add the chopped garlic and the diced mushrooms, and sauté for 1 to 2 minutes. Add the ham, parsley, and pepper, and toss well to mix. Set aside to cool. When cool, place the 4 whole, split-open kidneys on the table, open them up, and <u>divide the stuffing among them</u>. Fold the kidneys back on themselves, enclosing the stuffing.

2. Place the fat of the kidney on the table and cut and pound it to extend it and make it into a layer approximately ¼ inch (6 millimeters) thick. <u>Wrap the stuffed kidney with that layer of fat.</u> If one layer is not large enough, add several and tie them with string into a package to hold the fat together and protect the kidney inside during cooking.

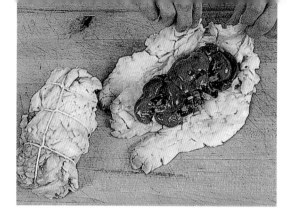

3. Preheat the oven to 400 degrees (204°C). Place the wrapped kidneys in a large ovenproof skillet or shallow saucepan and brown on top of the stove over medium to high heat for about 5 minutes, until the fat is browned all around. Place in the oven for 7 to 8 minutes, turn the kidney package over, and continue cooking for a total cooking time of 15 minutes. Most fat should be melted. At that point, the kidneys should be medium rare inside. If the kidneys are larger, increase the cooking time. Set the kidneys aside, still in their fat envelopes, for at least 5 to 10 minutes so they can relax and continue cooking slowly in their own heat. <u>Then unwrap.</u> Serve as needed.

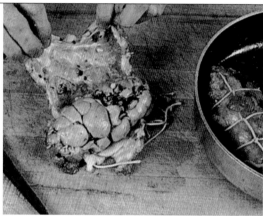

ROGNONS D'AGNEAU (Lamb Kidneys)

1. <u>Remove the kidneys from their casings of fat.</u> Pull and cut off the sinew holding them to the fat. Often the kidneys are damaged by butchers or meat inspectors who slice through the meat to check the condition of the animal. Try to get undamaged kidneys.

2. Place the kidneys flat on the table and, with a sharp knife, <u>cut horizontally from the rounded end down to within a half inch (1.25 centimeters) of the other side.</u> Open to butterfly.

3. <u>Thread the kidneys on a skewer</u>, going down on one side of the fat and coming up on the other side. Rub with oil and sprinkle with salt and pepper. Grill as needed.

4. To sauté: Split the lamb kidneys in half, as shown in picture 2, cutting through completely to separate the halves. Each half will be cut into three pieces. <u>Cut a wedge from one end</u>.

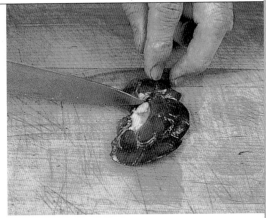

5. Cut a wedge from the other side. <u>Remove the lump of fat from the center piece</u>. The kidneys should be sautéed in one layer in a very hot skillet (2 skillets if necessary). The hotter the skillet the better, as the kidneys should sear on the outside without getting soggy and starting to steam.

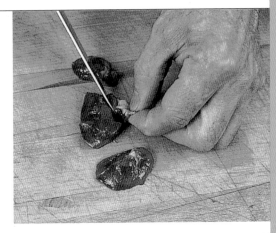

Breaded Sweetbreads with Tarragon Sauce

(Ris de Veau)

Sweetbreads are, for me, the choicest of the offals. The best sweetbreads are from lamb and calves. Sweetbreads are glands. The elongated sweetbread, the thymus, or throat, is at its best in young calves and almost disappears in older animals. The round sweetbread, the pancreas, is considered the better of the two. In old animals, it becomes mushy and pasty, but is still used by some cooks in stew. There are infinite ways of serving sweetbreads: breaded and sautéed, braised with a Madeira sauce, in champagne sauce, in puff paste, in pâté and so on.

YIELD: 6 servings

BREADED SWEETBREADS

- 2½ pounds (1.1 kilograms) pancreas sweet breads, yielding 1½ pounds (680 grams) after blanching and pressing
- 5 slices bread
- 6 tablespoons (84 grams) unsalted butter
- 2 tablespoons peanut oil
- ½ teaspoon salt
- ¼ teaspoon freshly ground black pepper

TARRAGON SAUCE

- 1 cup (237 milliliters) chicken stock
- ½ teaspoon potato starch dissolved in 1 tablespoon water
- 2 teaspoons fresh lemon juice
- 4 tablespoons (56 grams) unsalted butter
- 1 tablespoon chopped fresh tarragon
- ¼ teaspoon salt
- ⅛ teaspoon freshly ground black pepper

1. The sweetbread held is the long, narrow throat or thymus sweetbread, and the one in front on the table is the pancreas sweetbread. Notice that the glands are quite clean and white so there is no need to pull off any sinews or rubbery appendages or to soak to remove blood. These sweetbreads are the pancreas from milk-fed veal and the quality and size are excellent.

2. Cover the sweetbreads with cold water. Bring to a boil, lower the heat, and simmer for 25 minutes. Then place the sweetbreads under cold water, letting the water run over them until they are completely cold. Arrange the sweetbreads flat on a cookie sheet lined with paper towels. Place another piece of paper towel and another cookie sheet over them. Finally, place a 5-pound (2.3-kilogram) weight on top to press overnight or at least for 2 to 3 hours, refrigerated.

3. Pull off any sinews, nerves, or rubbery appendages that may still be attached to the top of the sweetbreads. Cut the sweetbreads into ⅜- to ½-inch (.95- to 1.3-centimeter) -thick slices.

4. Trim the crusts from the slices of bread, reserving the trimmings for other types of bread crumbs. Use only the center of the bread so that the crumbs are completely white. Melt 3 tablespoons (42 grams) unsalted butter. Sprinkle the sweetbreads lightly with salt and pepper on both sides. Dip them in the melted butter, running each piece of meat along the edge of the pan to remove the excess (they should just be lightly coated with the butter). Dip the sweetbreads in the bread crumbs so they are lightly covered on both sides.

5. Melt the remaining butter in 2 large skillets and add the oil. When hot, place the breaded sweetbread slices in the skillets and sauté over low to medium heat for approximately 5 minutes on one side; turn, and continue cooking for 5 minutes on the other side.

FOR THE SAUCE: Place the chicken stock in a saucepan and reduce to ½ cup (119 milliliters). Add the dissolved potato starch and lemon juice, and bring to boil. Whisk in the butter, piece by piece, until thoroughly incorporated. Bring back to the boil. Add the fresh tarragon, salt, and pepper and set aside.

6. Spoon the sauce onto warm individual plates. <u>Place 2 pieces of breaded sweetbreads on top and serve immediately.</u>

Brains

(Cervelles)

Brains are excellent, nutritious, and inexpensive. The best brains are veal and lamb brains. (Pork brain is a bit mushy.) Brains are often poached in a flavorful stock, fried in butter, and served with capers, parsley, and lemon. They are also used in pâtés, salads and sauces, and are sometimes simply breaded and fried. Though this technique is illustrated with veal brain, lamb brain is handled in the same manner.

1. <u>A veal brain weighs approximately 10 to 14 ounces (283 to 397 grams).</u>

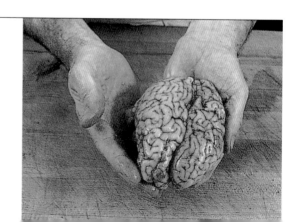

2. <u>Cut each of the brains in half.</u> <u>The half on the right shows the surface of the brain and the half on the left the inside.</u> Soak in cold water for 2 to 3 hours.

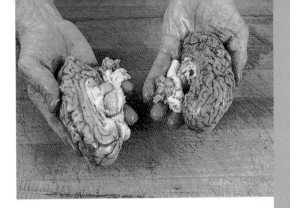

3. <u>Pull off the fine membrane covering the brain.</u> (You can loosen it by sliding the tips of your fingers through the crevices of the brain.) The membrane is tough and the brain will be darker after cooking if the membrane is left on.

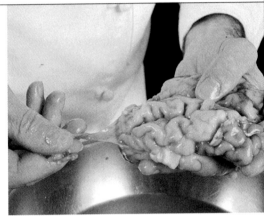

4. <u>Work under water, cleaning the whole brain.</u> Place 2 cups (474 milliliters) water, 2 tablespoons good vinegar, 1 bay leaf, ½ cup (80 grams) sliced onion, 1 teaspoon salt, and 1 teaspoon crushed peppercorns in a saucepan. Bring to a boil and simmer for 15 minutes. Add the brain to the stock and simmer slowly for 10 minutes. Let the brain cool off in the liquid. Refrigerate in the liquid. It is ready to be used when needed.

5. Remove the brain from the cooking liquid and <u>separate into halves with a knife.</u>

6. <u>Split each piece open (butterfly).</u>

7. <u>One brain (both halves) ready to be used.</u> For brains in black butter, probably the most common way of serving it, sprinkle with salt and pepper, dredge in flour and sauté in butter and oil until crusted and nicely browned on both sides. Transfer to a serving platter and sprinkle with drained capers and ½ teaspoon vinegar. Melt some butter in a saucepan until brown. Pour over the brain and sprinkle with chopped parsley. Serve immediately.

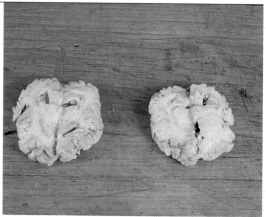

Pork Spread Rillettes

(Rillettes de Porc)

The word charcuterie *implies different manners of cooking meat, but most particularly different pork preparations: pâtés, sausages, galantines, ham, etc. By extension the word* charcuterie *is also the store where these dishes are sold. In addition, most charcuteries sell take-out food ranging from pike quenelles to different salads of fish, shellfish, stuffed tomatoes, smoked fish, salami, rillettes, etc. Rillettes consist of seasoned pork cooked a long time, cooled, shredded into tiny pieces, bound together by fat, and seasoned highly with salt and pepper. They are eaten cold with Dijon mustard and crunchy French bread as a first course or as a snack. The rillettes can also be made out of goose, rabbit, or duck, but even so, most of the time pork will be added to enrich the rillettes with fat and make it the right consistency. The rillettes are usually packed in small crocks and served as such with bread. Rillettes can be seasoned with wine or stock, thyme, bay leaf, etc., but the simple recipe given below and made with water retains the true taste of that country dish. The crocks should be covered tightly with plastic wrap and kept refrigerated up to 10 days. To keep longer the crocks have to be sealed with melted fat.*

2¾ pounds (1.25 kilograms) fresh pork from the chuck, butt, or neck (the meat should have about half fat, half lean)

1 tablespoon salt

½ teaspoon freshly ground black pepper

1 clove garlic, peeled

1 cup (237 milliliters) dry white wine

Water

1. Cut the meat into 2- to 3-inch (5- to 7.6-centimeter) cubes and place in a large heavy saucepan with the salt, pepper, garlic, wine, and enough cold water to reach 1 inch (2.5 centimeters) above the surface of the meat. Bring to a boil and cover. Simmer very, very slowly for 4 hours, covered. Uncover and cook another hour to evaporate the extra liquid. Skim the scum which comes to the top of the liquid every 20 minutes during the first hour of cooking. The meat should poach gently in the liquid.

2. After 4 hours of cooking, nearly all water should have evaporated and the liquid in the pot should be fairly clear. Let the meat fry in the fat for 10 minutes to give it a roasted taste. Let the mixture cool. The pieces of meat should be embedded in a nice, clear, white fat.

3. Scoop out the solids and, using your hands, pick all the bones out of the meat, then break the pieces of meat into fibers. Return the meat to the fat and bring the mixture to a boil, stirring.

4. Let cool again and stir with a heavy metal or wooden spoon to mix well and achieve a homogenized texture. If the quantity is too large or hard to mix, place the mixture in the bowl of a heavy-duty mixer and, using the flat beater, mix on speed 1 for a few seconds, just long enough for the mixture to blend together. Do not overmix or the fat will emulsify and the rillettes will get too white and creamy. Pack into earthenware crocks.

5. Smooth the top. If the rillettes are to be kept more than several days, cover with about ¼-inch (6-millimeter) layer of rendered pork fat, lard, or vegetable shortening. When the fat is cold and hard, cover with plastic wrap and keep refrigerated until serving time.

6. At serving time, scrape the fat from the top, make a cross-hatch pattern with your knife, garnish with parsley, and serve with toast, black bread, or crunchy French bread.

Country Pâté with Pecans and Hot Honey Mustard

YIELD: 12 to 14 servings

FORCEMEAT

½ pound (227 grams) pork or chicken liver

2 ½ pounds (1.1 kilograms) pork shoulder or butt

1 pound (454 grams) veal shoulder or stew

1 cup (100 grams) pecan halves

1 large egg

1 tablespoon cornstarch

⅓ cup (35 grams) chopped shallots

1 large clove garlic, chopped fine (½ teaspoon)

SPICE MIXTURE

(Put the following ingredients in an electric spice grinder or coffee grinder and process into a powder)

2 large bay leaves

1 sprig fresh thyme

½ teaspoon coriander seeds

1 teaspoon black peppercorns

FLAVORINGS

1½ tablespoons curing salt

½ cup (118 milliliters) white wine

½ to ¾ pound (227 to 340 grams) caul fat (or leaf lard cut from hard fatback)

GARNISHES

2 bay leaves (for top of loaf)

¼ teaspoon dried thyme

HOT HONEY MUSTARD

⅓ cup (23 grams) mustard seed

2 allspice berries

¼ teaspoon anise seed

½ teaspoon black peppercorns

3 tablespoons honey

¾ teaspoon salt

3 tablespoons white wine

3 tablespoons red wine vinegar

1. Clean the liver of any sinews and trim the pork shoulder and veal shoulder, cutting the lean pieces into a ½-inch (1.3-centimeter) dice. (Here, from a 2¼-pound/1 kilogram pork shoulder, 1 pound/454 grams of the meat is cut into ½-inch/1.3-centimeter pieces and the remainder ground. The 1 pound/454 grams of veal shoulder yields ½ pound/227 grams of ½-inch/1.3-centimeter pieces and the remainder is ground.) Push the pork liver twice through a meat grinder fitted with the fine screen so it is well-puréed.

(This could also be done in a food processor.) Then, grind the remaining 1¼ pound (567 grams) of pork and the ½ pound/227 grams of veal. Mix it with the ground liver along with the diced veal and pork. Add the pecan halves, egg, cornstarch, chopped shallots, garlic, the spice mixture, salt, and wine, combining it well with the sliced and ground meat.

2. Place the caul fat in tepid water to make it easier to handle (it tends to tear when very cold). <u>Line a 5- to 6-cup (1.4-liter) mold with the caul fat</u>, letting the edge of the fat extend over the sides of the mold.

3. <u>Pack the pâté mixture into the mold.</u>

4. <u>Bring up the edges of the caul fat to cover the pâté,</u> trimming away any excess. Place 2 bay leaves on top of the pâté and sprinkle with thyme.

5. Cover with plastic wrap and a lid and let macerate a couple of hours or overnight, if possible.

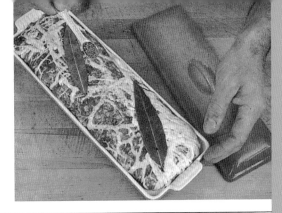

For the hot honey mustard: Place the mustard seed, allspice berries, anise seed, and peppercorns in the bowl of a spice grinder or mini-processor and grind until almost smooth. Combine with the honey, salt, white wine, and vinegar. (Note: At this point the mixture will be soft, but it will eventually thicken.) Allow to macerate at least 3 hours before using.

6. At cooking time, remove the plastic wrap and place the lid back on the pâté mold. Preheat the oven to 325 degrees (153°C). <u>Place the pâté in the center of a deep roasting pan</u>, surround it with lukewarm water, and put it in the oven for approximately 45 minutes. Reduce the heat to 300 degrees (149°C) and cook for 1 hour longer (a total of 1 hour and 45 minutes). The internal temperature of the pâté should be between 150 (65°C) and 155 degrees (68°C). (Remember that our cast-iron mold is fairly narrow and long. If the same amount of meat is cooked in a shallower, thicker loaf pan, the cooking time should be increased until the internal temperature of the pâté reaches 150 to 155 degrees/65 to 68°C.)

7. Remove the pâté from the hot water and let cool, refrigerated, at least overnight. Run a knife around the pâté or place the pot in warm water for a few seconds to warm it and <u>unmold the pâté</u>. Trim off excess pieces of caul fat, dry the pâté with paper towels, and wrap it in plastic wrap.

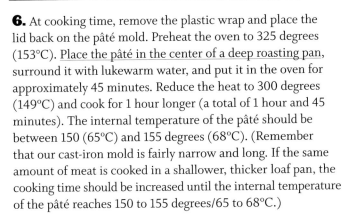

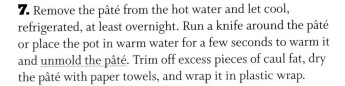

8. Notice the coarse texture and nice color of the pâté.

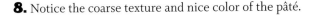

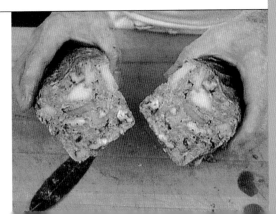

Preparing Fresh Foie Gras

(Préparation du Foie Gras)

The large liver from a force-fed duck or goose is one of the greatest delicacies known to epicureans. Until fairly recently, most foie gras was produced in France, but today much comes from other countries, including the United States. The foie gras produced in this country generally is from ducks and weighs no more than two pounds. The best quality duck liver is pale pink, firm, and has a pleasant, mild odor. Inferior grades tend to shrink and melt during cooking and taste bitter.

Foie gras may be cut into slivers and sautéed, or cut into larger slices, like calves' liver, and served with garnishes. I like to serve it cold in aspic. In my experience, all foie gras should be served within 48 hours of preparing. If it is kept longer, wipe it with a paper towel to remove liquid and fat, return it to the terrine, and cover it with clear fat, preferably a mixture of duck or goose fat and butter. The liver should be completely covered so that no air can get to it. Packed this way, it can be refrigerated for several weeks. When served, the fat should be cleaned off and saved for sautéing potatoes or adding to stews. The foie gras can then be sliced.

YIELD: 8-10 servings

1 Grade A duck liver (about 1 pound 10 ounces/737 grams)
1½ teaspoon salt
1 teaspoon sugar
½ teaspoon freshly ground black pepper
2 teaspoons plain gelatin
3 tablespoons cognac

1. Remove the foie gras from the plastic. You will notice that it has 2 lobes. <u>Separate by breaking it apart.</u> Soak in tepid water for 2 hours. Remove as much of the sinews, veins, and gristle running through it as possible and discard. For my recipe, it does not matter if the liver is broken into several pieces since it will join together during cooking. When the foie gras is to be sliced and sautéed, it is better to slice it before cleaning and remove the pieces of sinews from the slivers afterward.

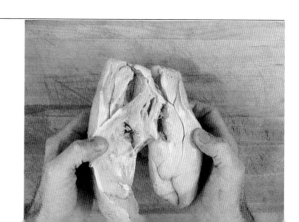

2. Wherever sinews and bloody strips are visible, <u>pull gently to remove, using your fingers</u> and the point of a knife to go deeply into the foie gras.

3. To remove even more sinews and nerves, split open the lobes again and <u>probe with your knife where red strips are visible</u>.

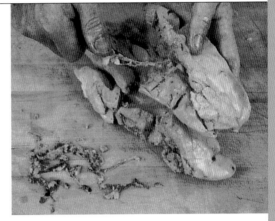

4. If any part of the foie gras looks slightly greenish, it probably indicates that the gallbladder has broken and run slightly onto the foie gras. This liquid is extremely bitter and <u>any green areas should be sliced off and discarded.</u>

Place the broken pieces of foie gras in ice water and leave for at least 3 hours; the object is to drain more blood out of the foie gras to make it whiter. Drain and dry the foie gras with paper towels.

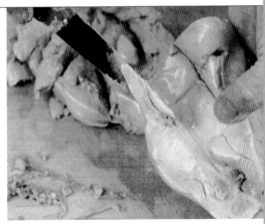

5. Combine salt, sugar, black pepper, and gelatin and sprinkle the foie gras with the mixture. Place some of the large pieces of the foie gras on a kitchen towel, arrange the smaller pieces in the center, and cover with the remaining large pieces. <u>Wrap the towel carefully around the foie gras to compact it into a tight mass.</u>

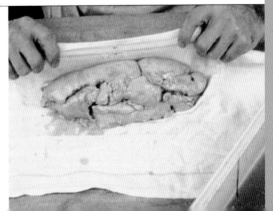

6. Tied the ends of the towel tightly with string and <u>place the foie gras in a terrine</u>. Pour the cognac on top.

7. <u>Cover the terrine with a lid and then with aluminum foil</u>, securing it tightly around the edges. Preheat the oven to 225 degrees (107°C). Place in a roasting pan with tepid tap water around it that comes to at least two-thirds of the way up the outside of the terrine. Cook in the oven for 1 hour.

8. <u>The inside of the foie gras should reach approximately 130 degrees (54°C)</u>. Cut a piece of wood to fit the terrine, and place it on top of the foie gras with a weight of about 1 to 1½ pounds (454 to 680 grams) on top. Let cool, refrigerated, overnight. The weight will press out any remaining blood and juice.

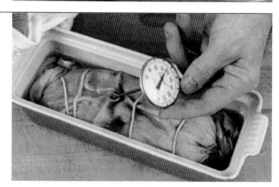

9. The following day, <u>scrape off the surface fat</u> and remove the wood. The fat can be used to sauté vegetables or add to sauces for flavor. Run a knife around the towel-encased foie gras to release it. Pull on the towel to unmold. If it doesn't unmold easily, warm up slightly to release.

10. <u>Unwrap the foie gras and clean by wiping with a paper towel</u>. It is ready to slice and use as you like. The foie gras could be placed back in a clean terrine with enough fat to cover. It will keep in the refrigerator for several weeks.

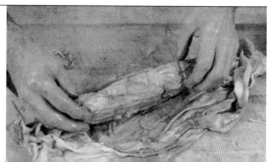

Pistachio Sausage in Brioche with Mushroom Sauce

(Saucisson en Brioche)

Although my sausages are cooked in brioche in this recipe, the same mixture stuffed into a casing and hung to dry makes a conventional salami.

YIELD: 6 servings

PISTACHIO SAUSAGE

1¼ pounds (567 grams) coarsely ground pork, about ⅓ fat and ⅔ lean (the shoulder or Boston butt is ideal)

2 teaspoons curing salt (Morton's Tender Quick)

¾ teaspoon coarsely ground black pepper

½ teaspoon sugar

⅓ cup (45 grams) shelled pistachio nuts, with most of the dry skin removed

2 tablespoons red wine

1 clove garlic, crushed and chopped

BRIOCHE

1 package dry yeast (¼ ounce, 2 teaspoons)

½ cup (119 milliliters) water, warm from the tap (about 100 degrees)

1 teaspoon sugar

½ teaspoon salt

3 cups (450 grams) flour (1 pound all-purpose)

4 large eggs

2 sticks (1 cup/230 grams) unsalted butter, softened

FOR FINISHING THE SAUSAGE

Egg wash made with 1 egg with half the white removed, beaten with a fork

Flour

1 tablespoon (14 grams) butter for buttering cookie sheets and aluminum foil

1 slice bread, crust removed, crumbed in a food processor

FOR THE RED WINE-MUSHROOM SAUCE

1 tablespoon (14 grams) unsalted butter

1 tablespoon olive oil

½ cup (55 grams) peeled, chopped shallots

3 cups (270 grams) diced mushrooms

1 cup (237 milliliters) fruity red wine

1 cup (237 milliliters) *demi-glace*, page 27

Salt and freshly ground black pepper to taste

1. Combine the coarsely ground pork (being sure you have at least one-third fat and two-thirds lean) with the salt, pepper, sugar, pistachios, wine, and garlic, and mix well. Cover the mixture with plastic wrap and store in the refrigerator for at least 3 days to cure. (It can be kept for as long as 1 week.)

2. Using plastic wrap, shape the meat into a long sausage form. Press the meat together thoroughly to make sure there are no air pockets in the center. It should be approximately 12 inches (30.5 centimeters) long by 1½ inches (3.8 centimeters) thick.

TO MAKE THE BRIOCHE:

Mix the yeast, warm water, and sugar together in a food processor bowl and let proof at room temperature for 10 minutes. Add the salt, flour, and eggs, and process for about 1 minute. The mixture will be very elastic, smooth, and shiny. Add the softened butter, squeezing the butter into the dough with your hands just long enough to incorporate it. Don't worry if some of the pieces of butter are still visible; it will not hurt the mixture.

The dough is easier to handle and rises quite well when it is cool and has been allowed to rise slowly overnight. If doing this way, wrap the dough in a plastic bag and place in the refrigerator. If the dough is to be used sooner, however, leave it in the mixer bowl, cover it with a damp towel, and leave at room temperature (about 72 degrees/22°C) to rise for approximately 3 to 4 hours. (It should at least double in size.)

Punch the dough down slowly to eliminate the air inside and use immediately.

FINISHING THE SAUSAGES:

3. Spread the cold dough on a lightly floured board. Roll it with a rolling pin or spread it with floured hands into a rectangle large enough to enclose the sausage (approximately 10 inches/25.4 centimeters wide by 13 to 14 inches/33 to 36 centimeters long). Brush the center with the egg wash and sprinkle with a little flour. Place the sausage on top and brush again with the egg mixture and sprinkle with a little flour. The flour and egg mixture will

form a type of glue, which will tend to hold the brioche tightly against the sausage without separating.

4. <u>Fold one side of the brioche on top of the sausage and brush it again with the egg wash.</u>

5. Then fold up the other side of the brioche, overlapping it on top. Press out the 2 ends of dough to make them thinner, brush with the egg wash, and <u>fold them on top of the package.</u>

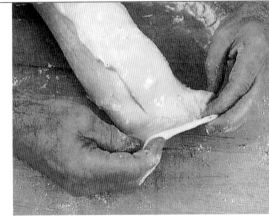

6. Butter a large aluminum cookie sheet and, turning the sausage package over, place it seam side down on the cookie sheet. There is a double layer of dough underneath now, and only one layer on top. By the time the dough has risen, the sausage will have sunk a little and be approximately in the center of the dough when it finishes cooking. Brush the top of the package with egg wash and <u>score the dough with the dull edge of a small knife if you want to make a design on top.</u>

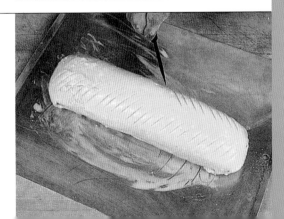

7. Make 3 holes on top of the dough; this will permit the steam to be released and prevent the dough from cracking too much during cooking. Brush the dough all over with an eggwash. Tear off a long sheet of no stick aluminum foil (long enough to go completely around the sausage) and fold it into thirds lengthwise. Butter the strip on one side, and wrap it loosely around the sausage, butter side in. Secure it loosely with a string, being careful you don't make it too tight since the brioche needs room to expand.

8. Sprinkle the top with 2 to 3 tablespoons of bread crumbs to give a nice finish to the top and set aside. Let the sausage-stuffed brioche rise for a good hour at room temperature (about 72 degrees/22°C). Preheat the oven to 375 degrees (191°C). Set the pan in the center of the oven and cook for about 25 minutes. By then, the brioche will have expanded and set. Remove the string and foil and continue to bake for an additional 25 minutes (approximately 50 minutes total baking time).

9. Let the sausage cool in a warm place by the stove for at least 20 to 30 minutes before slicing. Using a serrated knife, cut into 1-inch (2.5-centimeter) thick slices.

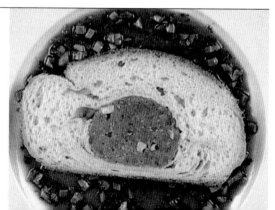

10. TO MAKE THE RED WINE-MUSHROOM SAUCE: Place the butter in a large skillet and, when hot, add the chopped shallots. Sauté for about 1 minute, add the mushrooms, and sauté for 2 minutes, until the mushrooms have rendered most of their juice. Add the red wine and boil down to ⅓ cup. Add the *demi-glace* and bring to boil. Season with salt and pepper to taste. Place 1 slice of sausage in brioche on each warm plate and surround with 2 to 3 tablespoons of sauce. Serve immediately.

Black Pudding

(Boudins)

The black pudding or boudin is a very common country dish in France. Each region has its own variation. Some use apples, some leeks, some spinach, some chestnuts, etc. Regardless of the seasoning used, the boudin is bound with blood and enriched with pork fat.

Pork blood produces the best result but it is sometimes hard to find. The blood can be ordered from your butcher and will very likely come frozen, although, of course, it is better fresh. It is usually packed in half-gallon containers which will make approximately 40 boudins. The casing used for the boudins can be hog casing, approximately 1 to 1½ inches (2.5 to 4 centimeters) in diameter, or a small beef middle casing, as used in our recipe, which is also approximately 1½ to 2 inches (4 to 5 centimeters) in diameter. Casings usually come packed in salt. When served, the natural casing is removed. Serve one boudin as a first course and two as a main course.

YIELD: 16 to 18 sausages

1 pound (454 grams) pork fat

1 pound (454 grams) onions, peeled and sliced

2 leeks, peeled, white and light green parts only, sliced very thin (2 cups/200 grams)

1 quart (1 scant liter) pork blood

1¼ teaspoons salt

½ teaspoon freshly ground black pepper

1 teaspoon cornstarch

8 to 10 feet (2.4 to 3 meters) hog or beef middle casings

1. Cut the fat into 1-inch (2.5-centimeter) chunks. Place fat in a large saucepan and melt for about 10 minutes on medium to high heat. Add the onions and leeks and cook for another 10 minutes on medium heat. Process in the food processor.

2. Let cool for at least 15 minutes or until lukewarm, and stir in the blood, salt, pepper, and cornstarch.

3. Run the dry casings under water. Place the opening of the casing over the end of the faucet and let tepid water run through. Let the casing soak in lukewarm water for about 10 minutes, then squeeze to get rid of the water and place on a large cookie sheet.

4. To tie off the end of the casing so it will remain securely closed (it tends to be very slippery and will untie with a conventional knot), tie a piece of string (with one knot only) around the casing about 3 to 4 inches from one end. Loop the end of the casing over the knot.

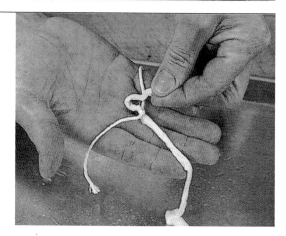

5. Tie the string around again into a double knot, creating a little loop of casing at the end and securing the casing so it won't slip.

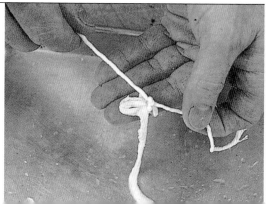

6. Using a funnel, pour the mixture into the casing. When filled, tie the other end of the casing with kitchen string. Leave a few inches (5 to 8 centimeters) of casing empty before the knot. The bit of extra space is for expansion during cooking and to accommodate the amount of casing taken in when you divide the *boudins* into individual portions.

7. Divide the filled casing into 5-inch (13-centimeter) lengths. You can simply twist the casing (reversing the twist for each different sausage) or tie with twine in order to separate the portions.

8. Place the *boudins* in a large saucepan into a coil. Use a wide saucepan that can hold the *boudins* in one layer. Add hot tap water to at least 1 inch (2.5 centimeters) above the meat. Place over high heat and bring the water to approximately 170 degrees (77°C). Do not boil or the *boudins* will burst.

9. Poach at the same temperature for 20 to 25 minutes. Prick the *boudins* with a needle to check the cooking. It is cooked when the liquid coming out of the casing is clear and only a few drops come out and stop. When cooked, cool the *boudins* under cool running water. Lift the *boudins* from the water and let cool completely on a cookie sheet. Separate into serving portions.

10. The *boudins* can be covered and stored in the refrigerator. It is at this stage that they can be bought in a *charcuterie* in France. At serving time, place in a skillet on medium heat. No fat is necessary. <u>For a more delicate dish remove the casing</u>. Cook for about 2 minutes on each side. Reduce to low heat, cover and let cook slowly for 10 minutes. Serve with freshly made mashed potatoes and/or sautéed apples on the side.

"There is nothing more exhilarating than a great chef in action. There is nothing so frightening as a bad chef in charge of the stove."

Salami and Sausage

(Saucisson et Saucisse)

The word saucisson in French refers to large sausages that are usually dry, like salami. Like smoked salmon, prosciutto, and other cured meats and fish, these sausages are not cooked. Saucisse refers to smaller sausages, such as link sausages and even frankfurters and knockwurst. These sausages are cooked and then served. The recipe below can be used to make either sausage—sausage that can be cooked with potatoes, in brioche, and the like, or that can be dried to make salami.

In this recipe, the sausage is cured by the addition of curing salt to the ingredients. Fresh sausage is kept in the refrigerator for a good 2 or 3 days to cure before cooking (dry sausage cures while it dries), and in the process of curing it turns pink.

To dry, the sausage should be hung in a cool cellar or garage. The place should be airy, preferably dark and very dry or the sausage will spoil. The first few days of drying are the most important. The skin of the sausage will become whitish, which is a sign that it is curing. After eight weeks, the sausage can be consumed semi-firm (demi-sec). However, dried it will keep for months.

The fresh pork butt, which is part of the shoulder blade roast, is an excellent cut for sausage, as it is readily available, and has the right proportion of lean to fat.

Use a good commercial curing or pickling salt (Morton Tender Quick Mix, for example, which is available on the internet). Replace the regular salt in your recipe with the same amount of curing salt.

YIELD: 6 to 8 sausages

5½ pounds (2.5 kilograms) fresh pork butt

4 tablespoons curing salt

2 teaspoons freshly ground black pepper (for fresh sausages,
    use 2½ teaspoons and omit the peppercorns)

1½ teaspoons whole black peppercorns (only for dry sausage)

2 large cloves garlic, crushed, peeled, and finely chopped (2 teaspoons)

½ cup (118 millileters) dry red wine

1. To make a coarse sausage, use a large screen with the holes about ³/₈ inch (10 millimeters) wide for the meat grinder. <u>Position the vice first</u>, then the knife (flat side out) and the screen. Screw the lid on. Grind the meat. Then mix thoroughly with the other ingredients.

2. <u>Natural casings come from hogs, right, beef, middle, and sheep, left.</u> Pork casings are 1½ to 2 inches (3.8 to 5 centimeters) in diameter and are used for Italian sausage. Sheep casings are about 1 inch (2.5 centimeters) in diameter and are used for link sausage. The beef casing pictured is about 2½ to 3 inches (6.4 to 7.6 centimeters) in diameter and is the best for large sausages. It comes in bundles preserved in salt and can be kept almost indefinitely, packed in salt in a cool place.

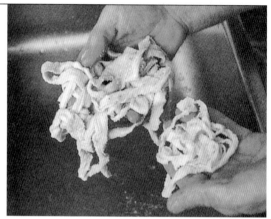

3. Pull the length you need and wash under lukewarm water. Fit the end of the casing to the opening of the faucet <u>and allow tepid water to run through the inside.</u> Then let the casing soak in cold water for 10 minutes. Drain and squeeze the water out.

4. To use the meat grinder as a stuffer, you need a sausage attachment. Remove the knife and screen, leaving only the vice. <u>Screw the funnel into place with the lid.</u>

5. Gather the casings on the funnel. Leave a small piece hanging so air can be "pushed" out of the casing. If air pockets form in the sausage, you will find when you slice it that there are "holes" in the meat and the meat will be gray. <u>Fill the casing</u>, holding the tip of the casing lightly so that it does not unroll too fast.

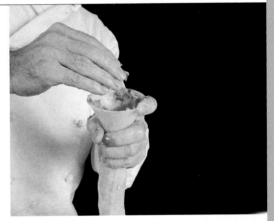

6. To fill the casing by hand, use a large pastry bag with a large plain tube or a funnel with a large opening (at least 1 inch/2.5 centimeters). Slip some of the casing around the tapered part of the funnel to have a good grip. <u>Push the meat into the casing with your fingers.</u>

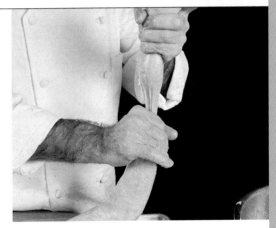

7. <u>Squeeze along the length of the casing</u> to push the meat down.

8. To tie the end, <u>make a simple flat knot first</u>.

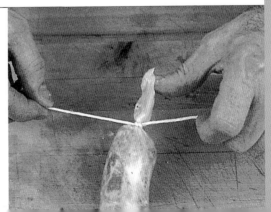

9. Fold the tip of the casing on top of the knot and <u>tie it again with a double knot</u>.

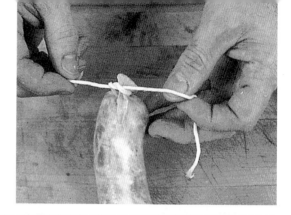

10. With one hand, push the meat toward the tied end. Squeeze the sausage where you want the end to be. <u>Prick with a sharp fork or a skewer wherever you see a little pocket of air</u>. Twist the sausage simultaneously. Be sure that there is no air trapped inside the meat. Tie the end of the sausage. After 3 days in the refrigerator, the sausage can be poached and served with potato salad. It also could be dried.

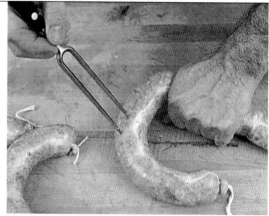

11. Tie the string so that <u>you have a loop to hang the sausage</u>.

12. Let dry 2 to 3 months in a well-ventilated place or in a refrigerator on a rack.

Cured, Raw Country Ham

(Prosciutto/Bayonne-style) (Préparation du Jambon Cru)

The greatest hams in the world, such as Bayonne from the southwest of France, Westphalia, and Czechoslovakia as well as Parma from Italy, and Serano from Spain, are all uncooked hams, served raw in very thin slices with bread and butter or sweet fruits such as melon or figs. Great American hams, such as Smithfield, Virginia, or the Nashville country ham, can be served the same way.

To make a prosciutto-type at home you have to cure a piece of pork, perferably the hind leg of the pig. A shoulder, a piece of the front leg, as well as a piece of chuck (used for Italian coppa), give excellent results. In many parts of Europe farmers cure and dry their own hams as well as smaller pieces of meat and use them either raw (cut in thin slices) or cooked with sauerkraut or beans for a country casserole dish.

There are two basic ways of curing ham: either you immerse it in a liquid brine (mostly salt, sugar, and water), or you cure it in dry salt. The salt drains the liquid out of the meat, depriving the bacteria of the moisture it needs to survive, and therefore preserving the meat from spoilage. After the salting, the meat is sometimes smoked, then it's dried. Professional producers dry at exact temperatures with controlled humidity. Too much heat and humidity can spoil the ham. A home-cured ham—hung in a cellar, a garage, an attic, or refrigerator—should be processed in the winter so it has a chance to cure and start drying before the warmer, more humid months.

YIELD: 50 to 60 servings

1 15-pound (6.8-kilogram) fresh ham
1 3-pound (1.4-kilogram) box kosher salt
1½ cups (330 grams) granulated sugar

2 tablespoons Armagnac or bourbon
⅓ cup (80 grams) coarsely ground black pepper
⅓ cup (24 grams) dry herbes de Provence

1. Remove the pelvic bone from the ham.

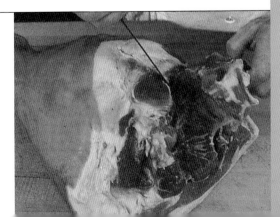

2. Place the ham in a plastic bag. Mix the salt and sugar together and <u>rub over the ham</u>, especially on the areas where there is no rind. Leave in the open plastic bag in a cool place (about 50 degrees or lower), checking on it every couple of days and, with a spoon, pressing any fallen salt mixture back into place on the ham. Let it cure for approximately 18 days, which is at least 1 day per pound.

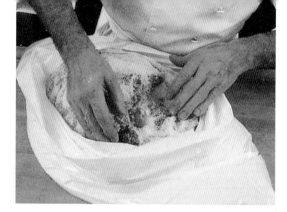

3. After 18 days, some of the salt should have melted around the ham and the meat should be wet and red from the mixture of still-dry salt and brine. Rinse the ham carefully under water and dry it with paper towels. Rub with the Armagnac, <u>then the mixture of black pepper and herbes de Provence</u>, rubbing them over the ham so it is well-covered. Be sure that you push the herb mixture with your fingers around the bone, where there may be little holes, so that you saturate the ham with the seasonings.

4. Place the ham in a piece of canvas or cheesecloth so it is protected from flies and other insects. Secure with twine and <u>hang it to dry for a minimum of 8 months</u>. It should be in a place that is cool (it can range from freezing to 50 degrees/10°C), especially for the first 3 to 4 months and where you have good air circulation to prevent the ham from spoiling. If you have space in your refrigerator, the ham will dry well there, provided it has good air circulation and the ham is placed on a wire rack so it dries from underneath as well as on top.

5. Eight months later: The ham has dried. <u>Remove the wrapping</u>. The ham can be brushed and washed under water.

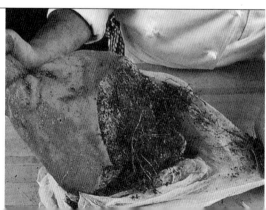

6. The rind as well as the fat is very good and can be kept for cooking with beans, potatoes, and the like. <u>Trim some of the rind and fat from the top.</u>

7. <u>Trim off the hard surface of the ham</u> to expose the meat underneath. Trim only a few inches down and around the ham and start slicing.

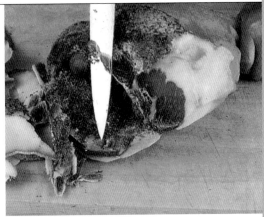

8. <u>Keep slicing until you reach the level at which the ham is untrimmed.</u> Then, trim some more around the ham and continue slicing. To facilitate the carving of the ham, place it in a large container. I have used a pâté mold to hold it securely, making it steadier and easier to slice. Cut into the thinnest possible slices with a long, thin knife (this requires a little practice) or, if you have access to a slicing machine, slice the ham on it.

Cold Parsleyed Ham

(Jambon Persillé)

The jambon persillé *is pieces of ham imbedded in parsleyed aspic. The pink of the ham and the green of the parsley make a very attractive presentation as well as a delicious dish. It is usually served as a first course with a dry white wine or a light red wine, crunchy bread, and cornichons. Pigs feet gives the gelatinous texture that is needed.*

YIELD: 10 to 12 servings

FOR DRY CURING

1 cup (288 grams) curing salt

¼ cup (55 grams) sugar

¼ teaspoon powdered cloves

¼ teaspoon powdered thyme

¼ teaspoon powdered allspice

4 pigs' feet split into 8 halves, about 2½ to 3 pounds (1.1 to 1.4 kilograms) (If you have a choice, choose the front feet, which are fleshier)

PARSLEYED HAM

1½ cups (225 grams) thinly sliced leeks, white and tender green parts (about 1 large leek)

¾ cup (80 grams) sliced shallot (about 6 to 8 shallots)

1½ teaspoon peeled, crushed, and chopped garlic (about 3 to 4 cloves)

½ teaspoon dried thyme

1½ cup (356 milliliters) dry white wine

2 teaspoons freshly ground black pepper

2¾ pounds (1.25 kilograms) ham, cleaned and cut into 1¼- to 1½-inch cubes

1½ cups (56 grams) chopped Italian parsley

RÉMOULADE SAUCE

¾ cup (115 grams) finely chopped onions

½ cup (105 grams) small capers, drained

1 cup (37 grams) coarsely chopped Italian parsley

1 tablespoon Dijon-style mustard

1 teaspoon freshly ground black pepper

½ teaspoon salt

¼ cup (60 milliliters) red wine vinegar

1 cup (240 grams) peanut oil

½ cup (120 grams) good olive oil

FOR THE CURING:

1. Combine the salt, sugar, cloves, thyme, allspice, and pigs' feet in a large plastic bag, and refrigerate for 4 days. The dry ingredients will turn to liquid in a few hours. Twice a day, turn the bag from one side to the other to distribute the brine evenly. Although curing the pigs' feet is not absolutely essential, it improves the flavor and color of the dish.

2. When ready, wash the feet under cold water and place in a kettle. Cover with water. Bring to a boil, cover, and boil gently for 2½ hours. Remove from the stock and pick the meat off the bones as soon as it is cool enough to handle. Cut the meat into ½-inch (1.25-centimeter) pieces. You should have 2 cups (474 milliliters) of leftover broth. If you have more, reduce to 2 cups.

3. Place the meat back in the 2 cups of stock with the leek, shallots, garlic, thyme, white wine, pepper, and ham cubes. Bring to a boil, cover, and boil gently for 15 minutes. Let cool to lukewarm and add the parsley.

4. Pour into a 3-quart mold. Cover tightly with plastic wrap and refrigerate overnight.

5. Meanwhile, make the rémoulade sauce: Place the chopped onions in a sieve and rinse under cold water. This washes off the sulfur molecules, which make the eyes water, and also prevents the onions from turning black and getting too strong in taste. Combine with the capers, chopped parsley, mustard, pepper, salt, wine vinegar, peanut oil, and olive oil, and refrigerate.

When ready to unmold, use a spoon to scrape away any fat from the top and discard it.

6. Unmold the ham (it will weigh about 6 pounds/2.7 kilograms) and serve cold in slices with the rémoulade sauce.

7. Slices of parsleyed ham with the cut ham in the background. You should be able to cut about 25 to 30 slices (about 4 ounces/113 grams each) from the whole parsleyed ham.

Rolled Headcheese

(Hure de Porc)

Headcheese is jellied meat and rind of the pig's head. There are different ways of making headcheese. The meat is sometimes cut into 1- to 2-inch (2.5- to 5-centimeter) pieces, cooked with stock and seasonings, and the whole mixture is placed into molds and allowed to cool and harden in the refrigerator. Then, the "loaf" is cut into slices and served with a vinaigrette. In this recipe, however, the meat and rind are rolled into a large headcheese sausage. It is a bit more work this way but the headcheese is meatier with less aspic. Curing the meat in a brine before cooking makes it tastier and gives it a nicer color. The brine can be used for ham or other pieces of pork, spare ribs (petit salé), shoulder, feet, loin, and the pig's feet recipe that follows on page 421.

YIELD: 16 to 18 servings

1 whole pork head with bone, weighing approximately 12 pounds (5.4 kilograms) (Be sure the head is perfectly cleaned of hair)

BRINE

6 quarts (6 scant liters) water

4 cups (1¼ pounds/568 grams) curing salt

1½ cups (284 grams) brown sugar (about 10 ounces)

1 teaspoon thyme leaves

4 bay leaves crushed

½ teaspoon allspice

½ teaspoon coriander seed

½ teaspoon cloves

FIRST COOKING

½ cup (118 milliliters) dry white wine

1 small leek, cleaned and chopped fine, white only (1 cup/135 grams)

4 to 6 shallots, peeled, chopped fine (¾ cup/108 grams)

¼ cup (18 grams) chopped Italian parsley

Salt and freshly ground black pepper

SECOND COOKING

2 cups (473 milliliters) dry white wine

3 cups (710 milliliters) well-seasoned chicken or beef stock, or a mixture of both

1 teaspoon freshly ground black pepper

½ teaspoon salt

1. To prepare the brine, put the water, salt, sugar, and spices in a large non-aluminum kettle and bring to a boil. Let cool, covered, before using.

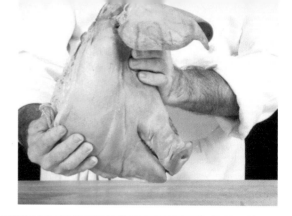

2. <u>Split the skull into halves using a saw or a large cleaver.</u> Remove the brains, which can be poached and fried in brown butter. Do not cut through the skin under the chin.

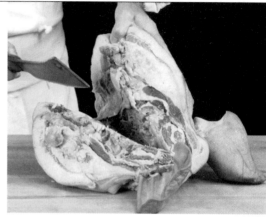

3. <u>Bone the head all around the central bone.</u> Do not worry if some meat is left on the bone because the meat can be removed easily after cooking. You should have approximately 6½ pounds (2.9 kilograms) of meat, rind, and fat plus the remaining bones.

4. <u>Place the meat and bones in the brine solution</u> with a weight on top to keep the meat immersed. Keep in brine for 6 days in a cold place or refrigerate if possible. Wash bones and meat well under cold running water. Cover the meat and bones with cold water (salt is not necessary because the meat has been cured in brine) in a huge kettle and bring to a boil. Keep the meat submerged in the cooking liquid by placing a plate or lid and a weight on top. Simmer slowly for 1½ hours.

5. Let cool for 1 hour and remove the meat and bones to a tray. When the meat is cold enough to handle, start to pick the meat off the bones and discard the bones. <u>Remove as much fat as you can from between the layers of meat and skin.</u> There will be large chunks of fat which must be removed and either discarded or kept to make *rillettes* or used in stews or to sauté potatoes or other vegetables.

6. <u>Spread out the largest pieces of skin on a towel, outside skin side down.</u>

7. Place the wine, leek, shallots, and parsley in a small saucepan. Simmer 4 to 5 minutes until the vegetables are wilted and most of the wine has evaporated. <u>Cover the skin with the mixture</u> and sprinkle black pepper and salt to taste on top of the meat.

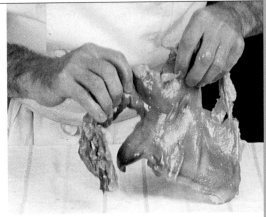

8. <u>Place the remaining pieces of meat on top of the shallot mixture</u> and roll in the towel to form a large sausage with as much skin as possible on the outside. If you do not have a large fish poacher or *pâté* mold to accommodate the headcheese, make two smaller sausages instead of one large one. Smaller headcheese are easier to handle and serve.

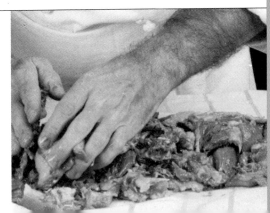

9. Wrap the headcheese in a large towel. <u>Tie the ends and center of the headcheese</u> with sturdy cotton kitchen twine.

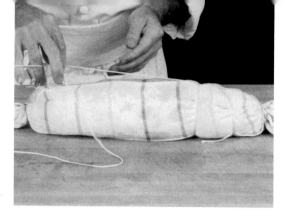

10. Place the sausage in a fish poacher or a large *pâté* mold and <u>cover with white wine, the stock, salt, and pepper.</u>

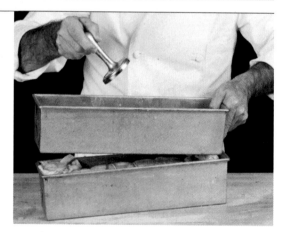

11. To make sure the meat is immersed, <u>weight it down with something heavy.</u> Bring to a boil on top of the stove and simmer very gently for approximately 15 minutes. Allow to cool with the weight in place.

12. Cool overnight, then unmold and <u>unwrap the towel.</u> Keep the stock for later use. (It can be frozen or used to make aspic.) Cut the headcheese into thin slices and serve with sour pickles, French mustard, a dry white wine or light red wine, and crunchy bread.

Stuffed Pig's Feet

(Pieds de Porc Farcis)

Ordinary pig's feet can be a delicacy whether you stuff them or not. They are excellent just simply boiled and served with a mustardy vinaigrette. They can be used to make aspic because they are very gelatinous in texture. They enhance the flavor and texture of tripe and cold jellied dishes, such as Daube de Boeuf. For our recipe the feet or "trotters" are first soaked in brine for four days. This improves the taste as well as the color. Use the front feet, if possible, because although they are shorter, they are meatier. Prepare the brine as explained in the previous technique.

YIELD: 6 servings

COOKING
6 pig's feet (about 12 ounces/340 grams each)
¼ cup (59 milliliters) white wine vinegar

BRINE, page 417

STUFFING
½ cup (75 grams) finely chopped onions
1 tablespoon (14 grams) unsalted butter
2 cloves garlic, peeled and finely chopped
2 cups (230 grams) finely chopped, loosely packed mushrooms
Dash of fresh thyme leaves
½ teaspoon salt
¼ teaspoon freshly ground black pepper

TO FINISH THE FEET
2 tablespoons strong Dijon-style mustard
2 cups (113 grams) fresh bread crumbs
½ cup (115 grams) unsalted butter, melted

1. Prepare the brine as explained in step 1, page 418. <u>Soak the feet in the brine for 4 days</u>, in a cool place, with a plate on top to keep them immersed in the brine. After 6 days wash in cold water and soak for 30 minutes in clear cold water. Place in a saucepan in one layer with the vinegar and cover with cold water. Cover and bring to a temperature of approximately 170 degrees (77°C). Poach at that temperature for about 3 hours. The water should not boil or the meat will come off the bones.

2. Let the feet cool in the stock. When lukewarm, remove from the cooking liquid <u>and pick off all the bones</u>. Be careful to remove all the small bones in the hoof. Try to keep the meat together in a piece as best you can.

3. Sauté the onions in butter on medium heat for about 1 minute. Add the garlic, mushrooms, and thyme. Cook until most of the liquid released from the mushrooms has evaporated (3 to 4 minutes). Allow the stuffing to cool. <u>Then stuff the feet when they are still at room temperature</u>. If they are allowed to cool off completely, they will harden and will be less easy to work with. Form little packages.

4. Place the stuffed feet, stuffing down, on a tray, one next to another, and <u>place another tray on top with a weight</u>. Refrigerate overnight. The "packages" will harden considerably when cold.

5. <u>Brush the feet with the French mustard</u>, covering the top and sides. The stuffed side should be underneath and the skin side on top.

6. Mix the bread crumbs and melted butter and <u>pat firmly onto each package to coat</u>. Up to this point the feet can be done ahead and kept covered in the refrigerator for a few days. To finish them, preheat the oven to 400 degrees (204°C) and heat on a tray for 20 to 25 minutes or until hot inside. Finish browning under the broiler for a few minutes. Serve immediately with more French mustard and French bread with boiled, mashed, or fried potatoes.

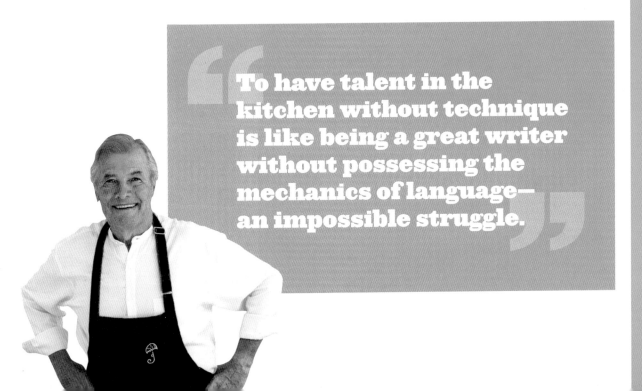

" To have talent in the kitchen without technique is like being a great writer without possessing the mechanics of language— an impossible struggle. "

CARVING

Carving Gravlax

(Découpage du Gavlax)

Once salmon fillets are cured (see page 202), they are ready to be served. They should be used within a few days. Keep them refrigerated until ready to carve; it is much easier to carve the fish when it is very cold.

1. Unwrap the fillets. Place the fillet flat on the table and start carving long, paper-thin slices. <u>Cut on a slant, using a long, thin, and sharp carving knife.</u>

2. This requires some practice. Do not apply too much pressure with your knife, and <u>move the blade back and forth for a uniform slice.</u>

3. <u>Try to cut slices as thin as you possibly can.</u> Spread and arrange about 3 to 4 slices to a plate.

4. Sprinkle 1 teaspoon drained capers on top of each portion.

5. Sprinkle 1 teaspoon of the finest extra virgin walnut or olive oil and ½ teaspoon of lemon juice on each portion. Serve with buttered toast or black bread.

Carving Poached Salmon

(Découpage du Saumon Poché)

A whole poached salmon (see page 205) makes a beautiful presentation carved at the table.

1. Remove the top skin and discard it.

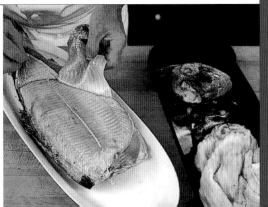

2. <u>Using a knife, extract the back fins</u> (they will slide off the cooked fish when pushed) and discard.

3. <u>Scrape the dark flesh from the top center of the fillet.</u> (It will slide off easily.) This is mostly fat and should be discarded.

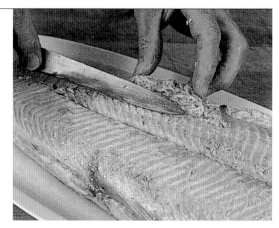

4. <u>Arrange lettuce and parsley around the salmon.</u> Place the head in the appropriate position and decorate the salmon with parsley. Work quickly as the salmon should be served tepid.

5. Run your knife (a thin, sharp blade is best) along the middle line down to the central bone to separate the top fillet into halves. <u>Cut across into chunks about 7 to 10 inches (18 to 25 centimeters) long. Use a fork or spoon to help lift the cut portions off the bones.</u> When the top fillet has been served, gently lift off the central bone and discard it. Cut the bottom fillet into portions, making sure to scrape off the skin and fatty tissue. Arrange on warm plates and serve immediately.

Carving Roast Chicken

(Découpage du Poulet Rôti)

There is nothing as simple and as delicious as a well-cooked roast chicken. The chicken can be trussed or not. Trussing is mostly done for aesthetic reasons. Do not cover a roast chicken with aluminum foil because it makes it steam and taste reheated.

1. Preheat the oven to 400 degrees (204°C). Truss the 3½ to 4 pound (1.6 to 1.8 kilogram) chicken. Season the chicken with salt and pepper inside the cavity and outside. Melt 3 tablespoons (42 grams) butter in a large skillet and roll the chicken all around in the melted butter. Place on its side and bake in the oven for 20 minutes. Turn on the other side and bake another 20 minutes. Place on its back and baste well with drippings.

2. Bake for another 30 to 35 minutes, basting every 10 minutes. To baste, incline the saucepan on one side and scrape out the juices and drippings. Pour over the chicken. This will give moisture to the meat and crustiness to the skin. Remove from the oven and place on a plate. Discard half of the fat in the skillet. Add ⅓ cup (80 milliliters) water or stock to the pan to melt the solidified juices and create a natural gravy.

3. Remove the string. Place the chicken on its side. Insert a fork in the leg and pull lightly while cutting the skin all around.

4. <u>Pull the leg up and separate it from the body</u>. It should come off easily. If you have difficulty, cut the sinews at the joint as you pull.

5. <u>Holding the chicken with the fork, cut through the shoulder joint</u>.

6. <u>Cut along and all the way down to the bone of the breast</u>.

7. <u>Pull the wing and breast off</u>, keeping the chicken from moving by holding the body with the flat side of the knife.

8. Turn the chicken on the other side and <u>lift up the other leg</u>.

9. <u>Cut the shoulder at the joint</u>.

10. <u>Continue cutting down along the breastbone</u>.

11. <u>Lift up the wing and breast piece</u>.

12. The only piece left is the central portion of the breast, the sternum (*bréchet*). <u>Sever at the joint to separate from the backbone</u>.

13. You now have the <u>backbone plus five pieces of chicken</u>.

14. <u>Place the pieces back on the bone</u> in their original position.

15. <u>Chicken carved and reconstituted</u>. Serve with natural gravy.

Carving Turkey

(Découpage de la Dinde)

1. Preheat the oven to 350 degrees (180°C). Truss the turkey. Rub with salt, pepper, and ½ stick (57 grams) soft butter. Place in a roasting pan and bake. A small 10-pound (4.5-kilogram) turkey will take 2¼ hours. Baste every 20 minutes after the first hour. Ten minutes before the baking time is over, add 1 cup (237 milliliters) hot water or stock to the pan to create a natural gravy. Place the turkey on a large serving platter. <u>Insert a kitchen fork into the leg.</u> <u>Cut the skin all around the leg.</u>

2. <u>Pull off the leg</u>, holding the turkey steady with the knife.

3. Place the leg on a plate and <u>separate the thigh from the drumstick at the joint</u>.

4. <u>Slice the thigh around the bone.</u>

5. <u>Slice the drumstick, arranging the dark meat on a hot plate.</u>

6. With a long, thin knife, <u>cut the breast straight down into very thin slices.</u> Hold the turkey with the fork while cutting.

7. <u>Arrange the slices in order on a hot plate.</u>

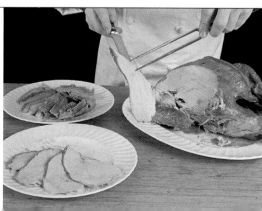

8. <u>Separate the wing at the joint</u>.

9. <u>Dark and white meat from one side of the turkey</u>. Repeat on the other side and serve with the natural gravy.

"To be a great chef you first have to be a technician: great cooking favors the prepared hands."

Carving Rib Roast

(Découpage de la Côte de Boeuf)

A beautiful rib roast (preferably from the loin end, not the shoulder end) makes a lovely presentation carved in the dining room for a special holiday.

1. Trim, tie, and cook the roast. The meat should be rare, about 110°/115° (44°C/46°C) internal temperature, as it will continue to cook for a while after it is out of the oven. If you have cooked your roast with its cover of fat, <u>remove it from the top of the roast</u>. Place the roast under the broiler for 5 to 6 minutes to lightly brown the top. Let the roast "rest" for 20 minutes before carving.

2. "Sit" the roast on its larger side. <u>Using a sharp paring knife, cut straight down a few inches (5 to 8 centimeters), following the ribs.</u> This cut will give a nice clean edge to the slices of meat.

3. <u>Holding the roast in place with the flat side of a fork, carve, holding your knife flat.</u>

4. <u>Cut thin slices</u> and

5. <u>arrange several pieces per person on a warm plate</u>. Serve with the natural gravy. There always are guests who love the roast rib bones, which should be eaten with their fingers.

Carving a Ham

(Découpage du Jambon)

A large ham is always welcome at our house. Sometimes it is just roasted or, other times, with a crust on top. Recooking the ham improves the flavor greatly. During my apprenticeship, ham was sometimes poached with fresh hay to give it an earthy, country flavor. This step is optional.

YIELD: 20 servings

1 store-bought fully cooked ham (16½ pounds/7½ kilograms)
1 large handful fresh hay (optional)

PEACH-MUSTARD GLAZE
⅓ cup (115 grams) peach preserves
½ teaspoon freshly ground black pepper
2 teaspoons dried mustard
Dash ground cloves

1. <u>Place the ham in a large stockpot with the hay</u>. Fill the pot with enough cold water to cover the ham. Bring the water to approximately 180 degrees (82°C). (Do not boil the water or the ham will crack open at the joint.) Cook at that temperature for 3 hours.

2. Lift the ham partially from the water to rest for doneness. Next to the shank bone there is a second smaller bone. <u>With pliers, twist it and pull it out</u>. If it comes out in one piece, the ham is done inside. If not, cook another hour. Let cool overnight in the cooling water.

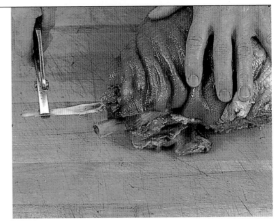

3. Remove the skin. If the ham has been cooked with hay, the skin will be more discolored than it would be otherwise, but it can still be reserved for stews or soups, or for cooking with pea beans (navy beans), black beans, or split peas. <u>Trim the fat and dark surface skin from the underside</u>, leaving only a very thin layer of fat.

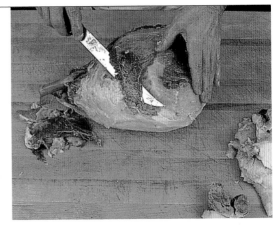

4. Keep trimming the surface of the meat where it is brown and skinlike around the shank bone. To make carving easier later on, <u>remove the pelvis or hip bone by running a knife around it</u>.

5. <u>Remove most of the fat from the top</u>, leaving only a think layer of white fat. The extra white fat can be used in soups, stews, or to enrich casseroles and bean dishes.

6. Run your knife in a criss-cross pattern through the remaining fat on top of the ham, cutting slightly into the surface of the meat. This scoring will help the glaze adhere to the meat while cooking. Preheat the oven to 350 degrees (177°C). Mix together the preserves, pepper, mustard, and cloves. <u>Spread the coating mixture on top of the ham</u>, position it in a roasting pan, and place in the oven for 30 minutes. Reduce the heat to 325 degrees (163°C) and continue cooking for 1 hour and 30 minutes, for a total roasting time of 2 hours. The ham is now ready to be carved.

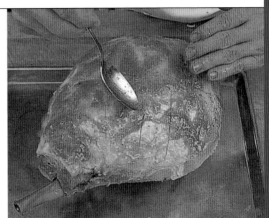

7. To make the carving easier, cut into the ham to approximately 1 inch (2.5 centimeter) above the shank bone. The object is to make a guard that will give a clean bottom edge to the slices and also protect your hand from the knife in case it happens to slide while you are slicing the meat.

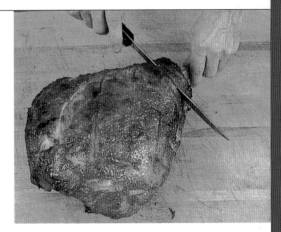

8. Slice the ham on the bias, stopping at the cut edge, and arrange the meat on a platter. Serve as needed.

BREAD & PASTA

Baking Bread

Very simple recipes are often the most deceptive because they are the hardest to make well. What is wine? Simply fermented grape juices. What is salami? Seasoned ground meat dried in a casing. What is French bread? Water, flour and yeast. Yet these ultra-simple recipes demand years of practice to achieve perfection. Once a recipe becomes complicated, the list of ingredients expands and the recipe becomes easier to adjust, change and control. But try to improve a hard-cooked egg! In addition to years of knowledge, professional bakers have the right flour, special equipment, temperature control, humidity control, and especially the brick-lined oven that gives enormous amounts of heat, as well as forced steam, which gives French bread its texture and crust. We have a friend, a professional boulanger, *who makes bread at home once in a while with results that are never as good as the bread he makes at his shop.*

There are a few things to keep in mind when making bread. Use a hard wheat organic flour, high in gluten, which is the protein part of the flour and gives you the elasticity needed for the bread to develop. Keep in mind that the thick, crisp crust is usually caused both by forced steam and dough made only with water. Bread made with milk and with fat will have a softer crust. The smaller the amount of yeast used, the longer the rising time, and the larger the air bubbles in the bread. Some bakers add ascorbic acid (vitamin C) to the dough to make the air bubbles hold better and the bread stronger. Sugar, as well as a warm temperature, helps the enzymes (the yeast) to develop better and faster. If the water or temperature is cold, the bread rises very slowly. Below a certain temperature, the enzymes won't develop any more. Fresh yeast usually comes in .6 ounce (17-gram) packages, and dry yeast comes in 7 gram (¼-ounce) packages. They can be used interchangeably. A *levain* or a dough starter can also be added to the dough to start the fermentation; this gives the dough a slightly nutty, sour taste. It is usually supplemented with yeast. The starter can be made by taking a piece of finished dough and keeping it in a jar with water. Refrigerated, it will keep there for a week to ten days. To measure out the flour, scoop a cup directly from the flour bag. This produces a fairly tightly packed cup (150 grams) and 3 cups will amount to roughly 1 pound (454 grams) of flour. The moisture in the flour varies from season to season. Humidity will be absorbed by the flour in the summer and water should be decreased in the recipe. Vice versa in winter. The following recipe makes a basic dough used to make large country breads as well as thin *baguettes* or small breads.

Country Bread

(Pain de Ménage)

This beautiful, large loaf of country bread can be made, as I have done in this recipe, with the skin of a chicken cooked in the oven into cracklings, or with small pieces of cooked bacon, or you can bake it plain. The decoration on top makes the loaf attractive; pieces of dough (kept in the refrigerator) are placed on top of the loaf just before it goes in the oven.

A freshly baked baguette, the traditional long, crunchy loaf of French bread, is ideal with any meal, from breakfast to dinner. In the recipe here, the top is slashed diagonally on one baguette, another has crosses cut into the top, and the third just a line cut down the center. Two baguettes are sprinkled with flour and one with cornmeal.

YIELD: 1 large loaf and 3 baguettes

DOUGH

2½ cups (593 milliliters) warm water (95 to 100 degrees/35 to 38°C)

2 envelopes active dry yeast

1 teaspoon sugar

starter: 6 ounce (170-gram) piece of dough kneaded, risen, and stored with 1½ cups (355 milliliters) water (if starter is not available, increase the yeast to 2½ envelopes and the water to 3½ cups/828 milliliters)

About 9 cups (1.4 kilograms/3 pounds) organic bread flour

1 tablespoon salt

4 tablespoons cornmeal

Extra flour for the tops

CRACKLING (optional)

Skin from one chicken

⅛ teaspoon salt

1. Combine the water with the 2 envelopes of yeast and sugar, stirring gently just to mix. Set aside to proof for 10 minutes.

2. This starter consists of dough left over from the last time I made French bread and water. It has been in the refrigerator for one week. The water has a slight sour taste, and the dough is very spongy and airy with a sour smell. After the yeast has proofed for 10 minutes, add the starter with its liquid, 7 cups (1 kilogram) of the flour, and the salt.

3. Using the dough hook attachment of an electric mixer, mix the dough on speed 3 (medium) for about 5 minutes. At this point, the dough will be very elastic but still soft. All the flour is not added at the beginning because the mixer is not strong enough to work a very stiff dough and could become damaged. The 7 cups (1 kilogram) of flour produce a soft dough, well-kneaded by the machine and with its gluten well-developed.

Note: Although any of these breads can be kneaded by hand, an electric mixer will make your life easier. But you must use a heavy-duty mixer with a dough hook. I use a KitchenAid, but any comparable appliance will do the job. You will have to adjust your model to the different speeds I recommend for my mixer. It starts off with "stir," then runs from 1 to 10 speeds, which can be translated as slow, medium, and fast.

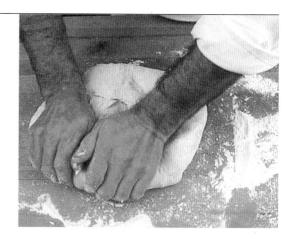

4. With the machine on speed 1, add about 1½ cups (225 grams) flour and mix gently, just enough (approximately 1 minute) to incorporate the flour into the dough. Turn the dough out onto a board with the remaining flour and knead for 5 minutes.

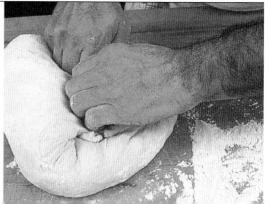

5. Press your hands into the dough, pushing forward, then fold the dough on itself. Press, push, and fold the dough on itself, rotating it each time. Repeat again and again.

6. After about 5 minutes of kneading, the dough will be ready. All of the flour may be used or some may be left, depending on the humidity. The dough should be very smooth but strong. It should resist your fingers when you press them into it, and bounce back when they are lifted.

7. Place the dough in a plastic bowl or other container with a cover (or use plastic wrap), and let rise, covered, in a warm place (70 to 75 degrees/21 to 24°C) for 2 to 2½ hours.

8. Preheat the oven to 400 degrees (204°C). If you decide to make the chicken cracklings, spread the chicken skin on a cookie sheet flesh-side down and sprinkle it with the salt. Place in the oven for 20 to 30 minutes, until well-baked and crisp.

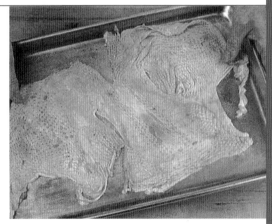

9. When risen, the dough should have doubled in volume. Bring the sides of the dough to the center and knead it again in the bowl to deflate it and make it into a ball.

10. To make a starter for future use, cut a piece (approximately 5 to 6 ounces/142 to 170 grams) from the dough and put it in a plastic container with 1½ cups (355 milliliters) water. Cover and place in the refrigerator. Set aside another 2 ounce (57 gram) piece of dough, covered, in the refrigerator to decorate the loaf after the final rising.

11. Divide the dough: Cut 3 pieces, approximately 12 ounces (340 grams) each, for the baguettes and set aside, covered. With your hands, extend the remaining dough (about 2 to 2¼ pounds/1 kilogram) on a floured work surface to form a rectangle about 16 by 10 inches (40.6 by 25.4 centimeters). Break up the cracklings and arrange the pieces on top of the dough.

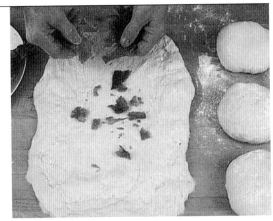

12. Roll the dough tightly on itself with the cracklings inside and form it into a loaf. Press it into an oval shape approximately 11 inches (28 centimeters) long by 6 inches (15.2 centimeters) wide.

13. Sprinkle 2 tablespoons of the cornmeal on a baking sheet and place the loaf on top. Prepare a proof box by inserting a trimmed cardboard box into a large plastic bag. When the bag is closed, you will have a humid hothouse similar to a professional proof box. This provides the perfect environment for the bread to rise properly. Insert the bread on the baking sheet into the proof box, tie it closed, and let rise at room temperature for 1½ hours.

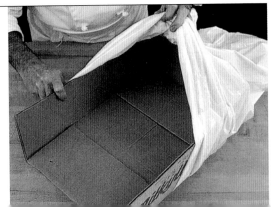

14. Preheat the oven to 425 degrees (218°C). Remove the 2 ounce (57 gram) piece of dough from the refrigerator and make strips by rolling the dough with your hand, making one end thicker than the other.

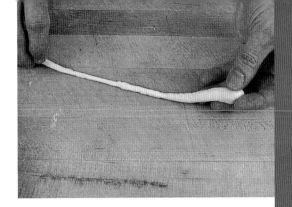

15. Brush the risen loaf with water and arrange the strips of dough on top with the thick part spread out at one end. With scissors, cut into the thick ends of the dough strips to make them resemble wheat stalks.

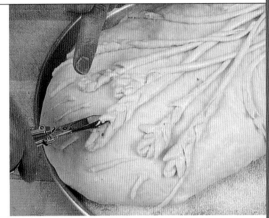

16. Sprinkle the bread with flour from a sieve and, using a razor blade, cut in between and around the "wheat stalks," making slashes that follow the design. Bake in the center of the oven for 50 minutes. During the first 10 minutes of baking, throw water on the bottom of the over to create steam to help the bread develop. At 2- to 3-minute intervals, toss about 2 tablespoons of water onto the floor of the oven and repeat two more times—for a total of three times in the first 10 minutes of baking.

17. Remove the bread from the oven. Note how the steam created by tossing water onto the oven floor has helped the bread form a thick crust on top. Let the bread rest for at least one hour before cutting into it. The dough should be spongy and well-risen inside with pieces of crackling showing. This bread makes a beautiful centerpiece for a buffet. It is good with earthy things, such as pâté, cheese, salami, or a garlicky salad.

18. For the baguettes: <u>Roll the 3 reserved pieces of dough into 18-inch (45.7-centimeter) lengths and place on a cookie sheet coated with the remaining 2 tablespoons cornmeal.</u> Roll one of the baguettes in the cornmeal so it is coated all around.

19. <u>Place the baguettes in the proof box (step 13)</u>, and let rise for 1 hour in a warm kitchen (70 to 75 degrees/21 to 24°C).

20. Preheat the oven to 425 degrees (218°C). Remove the baguettes from the homemade proof box and, if they have dried out a little on top (they should still be sticky), brush with water. <u>Sprinkle the two outside loaves with flour.</u> (The center loaf has been rolled in cornmeal.)

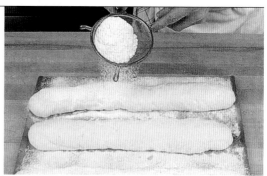

21. With a razor blade or serrated knife, score the surface of 1 floured loaf on the diagonal one way. <u>Repeat on the other floured loaf, cutting a second set of lines across, in the opposite direction, to create a crisscross effect.</u> Cut the surface of the loaf coated with cornmeal lengthwise with one long slit.

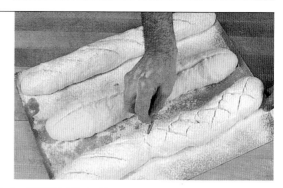

22. Bake in the center of the oven for 30 minutes. After 1 to 2 minutes, throw 2 tablespoons of water in the bottom of the oven to create steam. Repeat 3 to 4 minutes later, and again, a third time, 3 to 4 minutes after that. <u>The loaves should be well-browned and crusty.</u>

Milk Bread

(Petits Pains au Lait)

Dough made with milk and butter will have a more tender crust and a slightly more delicate inside than the regular country bread. This type of dough is often used to make individual rolls. The dough is started in the machine and finished by hand, although it can be made entirely by hand.

YIELD: About 2 dozen (24) 2 ½-ounce (71-gram) rolls

2⅓ cups (552 milliliters) milk at about 90 degrees (32°C)
2 packages dry yeast or 2 packages fresh yeast
1 teaspoon sugar
6 cups (900 grams) all-purpose, unbleached organic flour
½ stick (¼ cup/57 grams) unsalted butter, softened
2 teaspoons salt

1. Mix the milk, yeast, and sugar together in a bowl and let the mixture proof for 20 minutes at room temperature. Meanwhile, place 4 cups (600 grams) of flour in the bowl of the mixer. <u>Add the butter</u> and salt. After about 10 minutes, stir the milk and yeast mixture. Let it proof another 10 minutes, then combine with the flour. Beat on medium speed for about 5 minutes.

2. Add another cup (150 grams) of flour to the bowl and mix to incorporate the flour. <u>The dough should come out of the bowl soft but rubbery</u>.

3. <u>Place the dough on a board and work in more flour by hand.</u> Depending on the humidity and temperature, you may need all the flour or even a few tablespoons more, or you may not need it all.

4. Knead for about 5 minutes, until the dough doesn't stick to your fingers. (<u>It will be slightly softer and stickier than the country bread dough.</u>)

5. <u>Place the dough in a buttered bowl,</u> turning the dough around so it is buttered on top. Cover with a towel and let raise in an 80 degree (25°C) place for 1 hour.

6. To approximate the type of heat in a baker's oven, line a cookie sheet with quarry tiles and place them on the lower shelf of the oven preheated to 425 degrees (218°C). Set a small container of water between the lower shelf and the oven floor to generate humidity and steam. <u>Cut the dough in about 2½-ounce (71-gram) pieces</u> and roll each one into a ball with the palm of your hand, pushing out the air bubbles. Shape the balls into rounds, ovals or any shape you fancy.

7. For the *épi* ("head of wheat"), shape about 1 pound (454 grams) of the dough into a long loaf about 2 inches (5 centimeters) in diameter. Butter a tray lightly, place the dough on it and cut with a pair of scissors. Divide the dough into wedges to simulate a blade of wheat. Alternate from one side of the dough to the other, without cutting completely through. Pull out each "wheat" so it forms a pointed head. Let the breads and *épi* raise for 45 minutes to 1 hour at room temperature in the proof box. Preheat the oven to 425 degrees (218°C). Brush with an egg wash (1 whole egg, beaten) and place in the oven for 25 minutes for the small breads and 30 minutes for the *épi*. Every so often check that there's water in the oven, throwing some in to produce steam during the first 10 to 15 minutes of cooking.

Pullman Bread

(Pain de Mie)

The pullman bread is often hollowed out and filled up with little sandwiches to serve at a buffet. Whereas sandwiches are usually trimmed on four sides, and the trimmings used for bread crumbs, in this technique the whole loaf is trimmed of its crust and the crust becomes a receptacle. After the party it can be transformed into bread crumbs. The dough for the pullman bread is softer than for the petits pains au lait *on page 449.*

YIELD: 1 16-inch (41-centimeter) loaf

2 cups (473 milliliters) milk

1 cup (237 milliliters) hot water

1½ envelopes active dry yeast

1 tablespoon sugar

6 cups all-purpose unbleached organic flour (2 pounds/900 grams)

1 tablespoon salt

1½ sticks (¾ cup/170 grams) unsalted butter, softened

1. Mix the milk and water (the temperature of both should be about 95 degrees/35°C). Mix in the yeast and sugar and stir until dissolved. Place 5 cups (750 grams) of the flour into the bowl of an electric mixer and add the yeast mixture. Using the dough hook, beat on medium speed for 5 to 6 minutes. Then add the rest of the flour, the salt and the butter. Mix again on low speed for 2 minutes. The dough will be sticky when you pull it off the hook, but it will come off clean and spring back as though it were rubber.

2. Butter a large bowl and place the dough in it. Turn the dough in the bowl to coat the top with a film of butter. Place the bowl in a large plastic bag and set it in a warm oven (about 80 degrees/25°C) for 2 hours. The dough, when pushed in with your fingers, should hold the indentation, which is an indication that it has risen enough. Knock the dough down by kneading it a few seconds in the bowl.

3. Place in a buttered 16- by 4- by 4-inch (41- by 10- by 10-centimeter) pullman mold or two smaller molds. Be sure to butter the mold well. The dough should come about one-third of the way up the mold. Let it rise again for 1 to 1½ hours, depending on the humidity, until the dough comes about three-quarters of the way up the mold. Brush with the egg wash (1 whole egg, beaten). Preheat the oven to 425 degrees (218°C).

4. A pullman bread mold has a special lid that slides in to keep the top flat; or you can improvise a cover for the mold. Butter a cookie sheet, place on top of the bread, buttered side down, and place a rock on top to hold it down. Place in the oven for 20 minutes, then remove the cookie sheet or the cover. By then the dough is set and will not rise further. Bake for another 40 minutes until the bread sounds hollow when tapped. If the top browns too much, top with a piece of aluminum foil to prevent further browning. Unmold the bread and cool on a rack.

5. <u>Pictured here is the round country bread, crisscross cut on top, and the long, cooked pullman bread.</u>

6. After cooling, cut off the top of the pullman bread to form a lid. <u>Using a small pointed knife, cut all around the bread, about ¼ inch (6 millimeters) from the edge, to</u> loosen the inside. It is now holding only from the bottom.

7. Place the bread on its side. <u>Insert the knife into the bread about ¼ inch (6 millimeters) from the bottom crust</u> and pivot the blade back and forth to loosen a section of the bottom.

8. The object is to loosen the bottom of the bread without cutting the bottom crust off. <u>Make a few incisions along the base of the loaf, jiggling the knife back and forth at each point of entry to eventually loosen the whole inside.</u>

9. Remove the inside, which should come out easily. <u>Notice that the bottom crust is attached to the sides</u>, except for a few holes along the edge where the knife was inserted.

10. <u>Slice the bread into ¼- to ³⁄₈-inch (6- to 9.5-millimeter) slices.</u> You should have approximately 40 slices. Make different varieties of sandwiches: sliced chicken with fresh herbs and mayonnaise; prosciutto with butter; anchovy fillets and butter; boiled ham and mustard, etc. Avoid fillings that could bleed on other sandwiches. Pack the sandwiches together inside the bread mold, cover with the lid and place on the buffet table. The bread container also can be dried and used as a basket.

Cheese Bread

(Pain au Fromage)

This delicate bread, made with sharp cheddar and dried pears, is lovely to serve with fresh fruit and nuts and is excellent for brunch. Any leftover bread is good cut into slices and toasted, which brings back the taste of the cheese.

YIELD: 1 loaf

1 cup (237 milliliters) milk

I envelope active dry yeast

I teaspoon sugar

3 cups (450 grams) organic bread flour

1 teaspoon salt

¾ stick (6 tablespoons/85 grams) unsalted butter

2 large eggs

2 cups (200 grams) grated sharp cheddar cheese

1 cup (115 grams) diced dried pear

Egg wash made with 1 egg with half the white removed, beaten

1 tablespoon oatmeal (not the instant kind)

1. Heat the milk to about 95 degrees (35°C) and add the envelope of yeast and the sugar. Combine gently and proof for 10 minutes in the bowl of a electric mixer. Add the flour, salt, butter, eggs, and, using the dough hook, beat on medium speed for about 5 minutes. Add the grated cheese and diced pear, and mix about 30 seconds to 1 minute, just long enough to incorporate. This dough doesn't require further kneading. Cover the bowl with plastic wrap and let the dough rise at room temperature for 1½ hours. <u>Fold the dough in on itself from the sides toward the center and press to deflate.</u>

2. Butter a 3-quart (3-liter) charlotte mold and arrange the dough in it. Place in a proof box and let rise for 1 hour. <u>Brush with egg wash.</u> Preheat the oven to 400 degrees (204°C).

3. Sprinkle with the oatmeal and <u>slash two lines with a razor blade across the surface of the loaf.</u> Place in the center of the oven for 15 minutes, then reduce the heat to 350 degrees (177°C) and continue baking for another 20 minutes.

4. Remove from the oven and keep in a warm place for 15 to 20 minutes so the dough doesn't soften and the bread collapse on itself. After an hour, the dough should still be warm and can be cut and served. <u>The center should look buttery</u> and have a yeasty, cheesy smell.

Provence-Style Pizza

(Pissaladière)

The pissaladière *is a French pizza that's usually made from a pizza dough rolled very thin and covered with onions, garlic, anchovies, olives, and olive oil. Other ingredients such as tomatoes, green peppers, tuna, and cheese can be used to vary the filling.*

YIELD: 1 large pizza-style loaf

DOUGH FOR ONE LARGE PISSALADIÈRE

1¼ cups (296 milliliters) water, at about
   80 to 90 degrees (27 to 32°C)

2¼-ounce (7-gram) packages active dry yeast or
   2.6-ounce (17-gram) packages active fresh
   yeast

1 pound (454 grams) all-purpose organic
   flour (3 generous cups)

2 tablespoons virgin olive oil

1 teaspoon salt

FILLING

4 tablespoons virgin olive oil

8 cups (1 kilogram) sliced onions, loosely packed

4 to 5 cloves garlic, peeled, crushed and chopped
   (1 tablespoon)

½ teaspoon salt

½ teaspoon freshly ground black pepper

3 2-ounce (57-gram) cans anchovies in oil

Generous dozen (12-to-13) Spanish or Greek oil-
   cured black olives

1. Mix the water and yeast and let rest at room temperature for 10 minutes. Place 2 cups (300 grams) of flour in the bowl of an electric mixer. Add the water-yeast mixture, olive oil, and salt and beat on medium speed with a dough hook for about 3 minutes. Then add the remaining flour. Mix to incorporate the flour, then turn the dough out on a board and knead by hand for about 2 minutes until the dough is smooth and satiny. Oil a bowl, place the dough in it, and turn over to coat with the oil all around. Cover with a towel and let rise for 1 hour at room temperature, at about 75 to 80 degrees (23 to 27°C). The dough should double in volume. Check by making indentations with your fingers. If the holes remain, the dough has raised enough.

2. Make the filling. Heat 3 tablespoons of the oil in a saucepan and add the onions. Cook on medium to high heat for about 10 minutes, until the onions are cooked and lightly brown. Add the garlic and salt. (It is a small amount of salt because the anchovies are salty.) Add the pepper. <u>Spread the dough out by hand on the table</u> or directly on the cookie sheet.

3. Preheat the oven to 425 degrees (218°C). Oil a 16- by 12-inch (40.6- by 30.5-centimeter) cookie sheet or 2 round pans. <u>Spread out the dough with your hands to enlarge and line the pans.</u> The dough should be about ¼ inch (6 millimeters) thick all around.

4. Arrange the cooked onions on the dough <u>and the anchovies in a crisscross pattern on top.</u> Remove the pits from the olives, cut them in half, and position one in each anchovy diamond. Sprinkle the "pizza" with the remaining tablespoon of olive oil and bake for 30 minutes in the oven.

5. Allow it to cool in the pan for at least 10 to 15 minutes. Brush again with olive oil before serving. <u>It should be served at room temperature.</u>

Croissants and Pain au Chocolat

(Croissants)

Croissants are the essence of the French breakfast. They are never eaten at other meals. The large twisted croissants bought in cafés in the morning are often made with a mixture of shortening and butter. The small straight croissants are usually made with only butter. For pain au chocolat, *strips of dough are rolled up in rectangular pieces (about 3 x 5 inches/7.6 x 13 centimeters) and stuffed with a piece of chocolate. They are baked at the same temperature and for the same amount of time as the straight and crescent-shaped rolls. Croissant dough requires skill to make. It has some of the qualities of puff paste as well as of brioche. It acquires flakiness through the rolling and folding technique of puff paste, but it is also a yeast dough that needs proofing before cooking. We made our croissants with organic all-purpose flour (which is high-gluten, hard-wheat, elastic flour). Small croissants are about 1¼ to 1½ ounces (35 to 42 grams) each; large croissants are about 3 ounces (85 grams) each. See technique for puff paste before starting the croissant dough.*

YIELD: 20 small croissants and 8 *pain au chocolat*

1¼-ounce (7-gram) package active dry yeast or .6-ounce (17-gram) package active fresh yeast

1 tablespoon sugar

1 generous cup (237 milliliters) milk, at approximately 90 to 100 degrees (32 to 38°C)

3 sticks unsalted butter, softened (1½ cups/340 grams)

1 pound (454 grams) organic, all-purpose, unbleached flour (a good 3 cups)

1½ teaspoons salt

2 tablespoons extra flour to mix with the butter

1½ teaspoons salt

1. For croissants: Place the yeast, sugar, and milk in a bowl. Mix well and let it proof for about 5 to 10 minutes at room temperature. <u>Meanwhile, cut 2½ sticks (1¼ cups/283 grams) of the butter into 3 lengthwise slices.</u> Place on a plate and refrigerate. Place the flour with the remaining ¼ cup (57 grams) of butter, salt, and yeast-milk mixture in the bowl of an electric mixer and mix on low speed using the flat beater for about 10 seconds, until it forms a ball.

2. Place on a floured board and roll the dough into a rectangle approximately 20 inches (51 centimeters) long by 12 inches (30 centimeters) wide. Use the extra flour to help in the rolling. <u>Arrange the slices of butter, one next to another, on top two-thirds of the pastry,</u> covering it to within about 1 inch (2.5 centimeters) from the edge.

3. <u>Lift the unbuttered third and fold on the buttered part.</u>

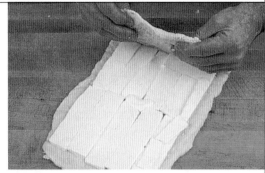

4. <u>Fold the remaining third over</u> and press all around the edges.

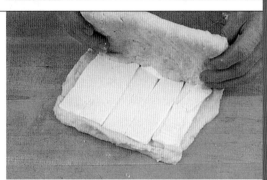

5. On a floured board roll the dough into a 24- by 12-inch (61- by 30-centimeter) rectangle and <u>fold it so that the sides meet in the center.</u>

6. <u>Fold the dough again to create a four-layered piece of dough</u> (this is called a double turn). Let rest refrigerated for at least 30 minutes. Then roll the dough into a 24- by 12-inch (61- by 30-centimeter) rectangle once again and give it another double turn. Refrigerate for another 2 hours, at which point the dough can be rolled into croissants or left refrigerated overnight.

7. After a few hours (or overnight) in the refrigerator, <u>the dough will have risen.</u>

8. Flatten the dough with the palm of your hand. Roll it <u>into a rectangle</u> approximately 12 inches (30 centimeters) wide by 25 inches (63 centimeters) long. Cut the rectangle in half lengthwise to make 2 strips, approximately 6 inches (15 centimeters) wide by 25 inches (63 centimeters) long.

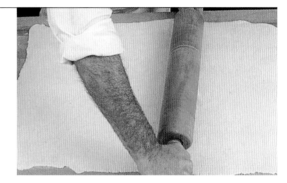

9. <u>Cut into triangles about 5 inches (13 centimeters) at the base.</u> For the small croissants, each triangle will weigh about 2 ounces (57 grams). If the dough gets rubbery at any time, just let it rest again in the refrigerator. Remember that cold temperature and time are allies.

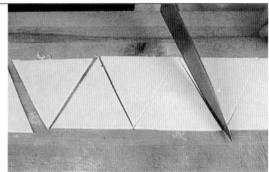

10. Starting at the base of the triangle, <u>use both hands to roll the dough</u>, spreading it out as you roll forward to extend the croissant.

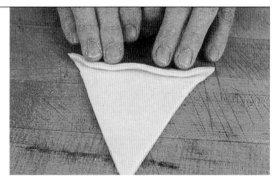

11. Wet the apex of the triangle with water. <u>Keep rolling the dough on itself</u> until you reach the apex where the dough will stick.

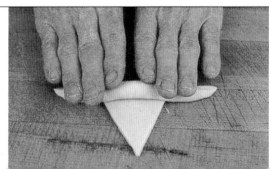

12. Line a cookie sheet with parchment paper and arrange the croissants, <u>bent into a crescent shape</u> or straight, on top. Notice that the points of the croissants are tucked under. Brush the croissants with water to eliminate any flour left on top and to prevent them from drying out.

13. <u>Insert the tray of croissants into a proof box</u> (see page 446) and tie the bag closed. Be sure the plastic doesn't touch the croissants. Let them rise in a warm place at a temperature of 70 to 75 degrees (20-25°C) for about 1½ hours (or less, depending on humidity), until the croissants almost double in size. Preheat the oven to 425 degrees (218°C). Brush with an egg wash. Place in the oven for approximately 15 to 18 minutes. Freeze the remaining unbaked croissants for later use or repeat the rising and cooking procedures.

14. For *pain au chocolat*: You can use pieces of bittersweet chocolate but, if making a great many, it is easier to melt chocolate and spread it in a strip on a piece of parchment or wax paper approximately 3½ inches (9 cm) wide and ⅛ to ¼ inch (⅓ to ⅔ cm) thick. Refrigerate or cool until it begins to set and then cut into sticks approximately ¾ inch (2 centimeters) wide by running your knife through it. Allow the chocolate to harden further and, when completely cold, <u>lift the strips of chocolate from the paper</u>.

15. To make a few *pains au chocolat*, cut pieces of chocolate and arrange them on the dough. Cut the remaining strips of croissant dough crosswise into pieces 3 inches wide (7½ centimeters) and 5 inches (12½ centimeters) long. Dampen with water and place a piece of chocolate on top along one edge. <u>Roll tightly</u> and place, seam-side down, on a cookie sheet lined with parchment paper. Let rise in a proof box for approximately 1 to 1½ hours, depending on the humidity and temperature.

16. Preheat the oven to 400 degrees (204°C). Brush with an egg wash and bake in the oven for 15 to 20 minutes.

Brioche Dough

(Pâte á Brioche)

Brioches are the small, moist and buttery cakes eaten for breakfast throughout France. In parts of the country, like Lyon, this yeast-risen dough is used to encase sausage, goose liver, game, and other pâté. The brioche dough is not as difficult to make as puff paste. It is easiest to use a large mixer rather than beating by hand, but both methods give excellent results. The dough should be very satiny and elastic. A brioche mousseline, which is especially good, is a brioche dough loaded with butter.

YIELD: 18 to 20 small brioches or 1 large brioche

½ teaspoon sugar

¼ cup (59 milliliters) lukewarm water

1 (¼ -ounce/7-gram) package active dry yeast, or ½ cake fresh yeast

2¼ cups (337 grams) all-purpose organic flour

4 large eggs

2 sticks (1 cup/227 grams) unsalted butter, cut into ½ inch (13 millimeter) pieces and at room temperature

½ teaspoon salt

1. In a bowl, mix the sugar, water, and yeast until smooth. Set the mixture aside and let it proof for 5 minutes (the yeast will make it foam or bubble). Place the remaining ingredients in the bowl of an electric mixer. Using the flat beater, start mixing on low, adding the yeast mixture. When all the ingredients hold together, scrape the sides and bottom, picking up any loose pieces. Place on medium speed and beat for 5 minutes. Scrape the sides and bottom twice more during the process so the ingredients are well blended. The dough should be elastic, velvety, and hold in a lump around the beater. It should separate easily from the beater if pulled.

2. If you are making the dough by hand instead of by machine, make a well in the flour, add the yeast mixture, eggs, butter, and salt, and mix until it comes together. Work it for at least 10 minutes. Grab the dough on both sides,

3. lift it from the table and

4. flip it over, slapping it on the table. Repeat for about 8 minutes.

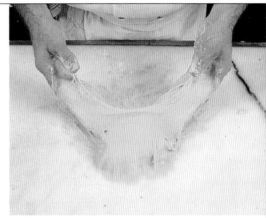

5. The dough should be very satiny. Place the dough in a bowl, cover with a towel, set in a draftless, warm place, and let rise until it has doubled in bulk (about 1½ to 2 hours).

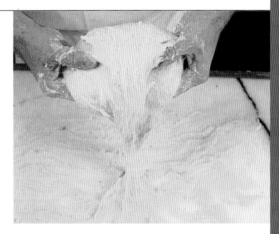

6. Break the dough down by pushing and lifting with your fingers. If you are not going to use the dough immediately, wrap it in a towel and plastic wrap and place it in the refrigerator to prevent the dough from developing too much. It can be made a day ahead.

7. To make small brioches, generously butter individual brioche molds. Divide the dough into balls the size of a small golf ball (about 2½ to 3 ounces/71 to 85 grams) and roll on the table in a circular motion to make the ball round and give body to the brioche. <u>With the side of your hand, "saw" a small piece of the brioche in a back and forward motion.</u> This forms a small lump or "head," which should remain attached to the body of the brioche.

8. <u>Lift the brioche by the "head"</u> and place in the buttered mold.

9. <u>Push the head down into the brioche.</u> Arrange the molds on a cookie sheet and slip into a proofing box (see page 446). Let the brioche rise at room temperature for 2½ hours, until barely doubled in bulk.

10. <u>A large brioche</u> (*brioche parisienne*) is done similarly, but slits are cut all around to give texture to the finished brioche. Let the brioche rise in a proofing box in a warm place for about 3½ hours or until barely doubled in bulk.

11. Preheat the oven to 350 degrees (177°C). Bake the small brioches in the oven for approximately 25 minutes, and the large one for approximately 45 minutes. <u>They should be golden</u>. Let cool completely. Keep in a plastic bag to avoid drying out.

Brie in Brioche Dough

(Brie en Brioche)

The brie in brioche makes a nice presentation to be served at the end of a dinner. Serve the cheese in slices with its own brioche. In the photographs that follow, the decorations were made with regular pie dough. It stands out because it doesn't brown as much as the brioche dough during baking. Of course the decorations can be made with strips of brioche dough. You need a not-too-ripe, 2-pound (908-gram) brie, preferably Brie de Meaux, *and the brioche dough described in the previous technique. This will serve 12 to 14.*

1. Spread out a piece of the brioche dough with your hands or roll it with a rolling pin to about 1 inch (2.5 centimeters) larger than the brie all around and about ¹/₂ inch (12 millimeters) thick. Place on a cookie sheet lined with parchment paper. Place the brie on top. <u>Fold the edges of the dough back onto the brie.</u>

2. Roll out another piece of dough ¹/₂ inch (12 millimeters) thick and 1 to 2 inches (2.5 to 5 centimeters) larger than the brie all around. <u>Brush with egg wash</u> (1 egg plus 1 egg yolk, beaten).

3. Cover the brie, egg-washed side down, and <u>press the dough on the sides</u> so it sticks to the bottom layer. Trim it all around.

4. Brush the dough with egg wash and <u>decorate with little strips of pie dough, puff paste, or brioche dough</u>. Decorate to your fancy with strips to imitate flowers, borders, etc. Brush the decorations with the egg wash and let brie proof for about 20 minutes at room temperature.

5. Preheat the oven to 375 degrees (190°C). Bake for about 30 minutes until golden brown. Let the brie rest at room temperature for a couple of hours, otherwise the cheese will be too runny inside. If done several hours ahead, and the brioche is cold, place in a warm oven for 10 minutes, just to <u>warm up the brioche</u> without heating the cheese. Cut into slices and serve.

Making Cream Puff Dough Cases

(Récipient en Pâte á Choux)

These come in handy to fill with a garnish from poached cucumber for fish to peas for poultry or veal.

¼ cup (59 milliliters) water
2 teaspoon (10 grams) unsalted butter
Dash salt
¼ cup (38 grams) all-purpose organic flour
1 large egg

Put the water with the butter and a dash of salt in a saucepan and bring to a boil. When boiling, add the flour all at once and mix well with a wooden spatula for about 10 to 15 seconds, until the mixture is combined well together. Beat 1 egg in a bowl. Transfer the water-flour mixture to a clean bowl and add 1 tablespoon of the egg mixture at a time, mixing to incorporate. Use the whole egg, making sure the mixture is worked until it is smooth after each addition.

1. Preheat the oven to 350 degrees (177°C). Butter about 9 muffin cups and place the pan in the freezer so the butter gets very hard. Using approximately 2 teaspoons of cream puff mixture in each cup, <u>spread with your finger to coat the bottom and sides of the mold thinly</u>. (Don't worry if the coating is not spread evenly all over.)

2. Place the muffin pans in the oven for 12 to 14 minutes, until nicely cooked and browned. Let cool a few minutes and <u>remove from the pan</u>. Place on a cookie sheet and keep warm in a low oven. Use as needed.

Ratatouille Ravioli

(Ravioli á la Ratatouille)

YIELD: 6 to 8 servings

3 tablespoons olive oil

1 large, coarsely chopped onion
(about 6 ounces/1½ cups/170 grams)

¾ pound (340 grams) unpeeled eggplant
(2 small), coarsely chopped

½ pound (227 grams) green peppers, seeded
and coarsely chopped (1¼ cups)

¾ pound (340 grams) zucchini (2),
coarsely chopped

¾ pounds (340 grams) tomatoes, seeded
and coarsely chopped (2 cups)

3 cloves garlic, crushed and chopped
(2 teaspoons)

1 teaspoon salt

Dash cayenne pepper

RAVIOLI PARSLEY DOUGH

2 cups (300 grams) all-purpose organic
flour

¼ teaspoon salt

½ cup (19 grams) loosely packed Italian
parsley

3 large egg yolks

¼ cup (70 milliliters) water

1 tablespoon olive oil

1. To make the ratatouille mixture: Heat the olive oil in a large saucepan. When hot, add the onion and sauté 2 minutes. Add the eggplant and green peppers and cook for 5 minutes over medium heat, stirring occasionally, until browning begins. Then add the zucchini, tomatoes, garlic, and salt. Mix well, cover, and cook over medium heat for about 20 minutes. Remove the cover and cook over medium heat, stirring occasionally, until most of the liquid has evaporated, 12 to 15 minutes. Add a dash of cayenne, remove to a bowl, and cool. When cool, put the ratatouille in a food processor and pulse a few times to chop coarsely. Or, chop it by hand.

To make the ravioli dough: Process the flour, salt, and parsley in a food processor for about 30 seconds. Add the egg yolks, water, and oil, and process again until the mixture begins to pull away from the sides of the bowl and form into a ball. Press together, wrap in plastic wrap, and refrigerate for at least 1 hour. When ready to roll, divide the dough into 4 segments. Run each segment through the pasta machine on the large setting.

2. Push the dough back through the machine several times, changing the setting, <u>until you reach the level (usually #7) where the dough becomes extremely thin</u> (less than 1/16 inch/1.6 millimeters thick). Each quarter of the dough will give you a rectangle about 24 inches (61 centimeters) long by 5 inches (12.7 centimeters) wide. Cut each rectangle in half crosswise, giving you 2 rectangles, each 12 inches (30.5 centimeters) long by 5 inches (12.7 centimeters) wide. Place one of these rectangles on a piece of waxed paper and brush it with water.

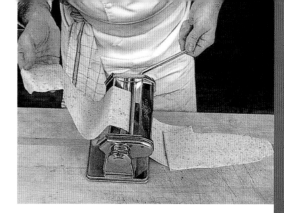

3. Fill a pastry bag fitted with a 1/2-inch (1.3-centimeter) plain tube with the cold ratatouille mixture. <u>Pipe neat mounds (about 1 tablespoon each) of the ratatouille mixture approximately 1 inch (2.5 centimeters) apart in 2 rows the length of the dough.</u>

4. Place the other rectangular piece of dough on top, <u>pressing with your fingers in between the stuffing so the top layer of dough sticks to the wet surface of the bottom layer.</u>

5. Using an inverted shot glass or the dull side of a cookie cutter about the size of the mounds, <u>press around each mound to compact the stuffing into uniform rounds.</u>

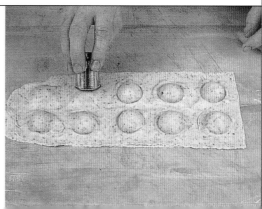

6. Using a larger cutter, <u>cut the ravioli into neat rounds</u>. Repeat with the remaining dough and filling until they are used up. The trimmings can be rerolled for immediate use or cut into pieces and used as a garnish in soup.

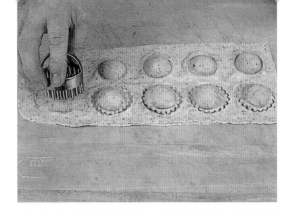

7. <u>Lift up and remove the trimmings of the dough from the waxed paper.</u> Since the ravioli are all arranged on the waxed paper, it is easier to place them with the paper on a tray in the freezer or refrigerator if you are not going to use them right away, or if you are, cook them immediately by sliding them into boiling water to cook gently for 4 to 5 minutes.

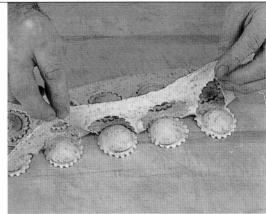

8. To make square ravioli, use the same technique as in steps 3 and 4, pressing with your fingers in between the dough-covered mounds. <u>Then cut between the mounds, making square ravioli.</u>

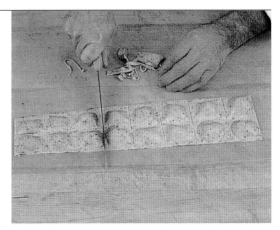

9. To improve the appearance of square ravioli, <u>press around the mounds with a cookie cutter</u> or inverted shot glass so the stuffing is marked and defined neatly inside the squares. When ready to serve, slide into boiling water and cook gently for 4 to 5 minutes. The green ravioli dough will get paler during the cooking. Lift from the water and serve immediately with melted or brown butter.

Fettuccine

(Fettuccine)

YIELD: About 6 servings

2⅓ cups (350 grams) all-purpose organic flour

2 large egg yolks

2 tablespoons oil

⅓ cup (79 milliliters) water

1. Combine all of the ingredients in the bowl of the food processor and process until the mixture forms into a ball (about 15 to 30 seconds). If too dry, add another tablespoon of water. Place the dough on a floured board and roll very thin—mine came out to about a 16-inch (41-centimeter) rough disk. <u>Place directly on the rolling pin to dry for at least 15 to 30 minutes.</u>

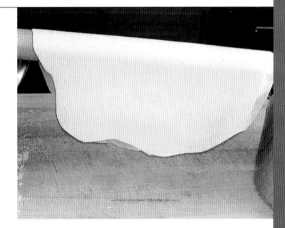

2. Return the dough to the board, fold it in half or fourths, and <u>cut it into strips approximately ⅜ inch (1 centimeter) wide to make fettuccine or tagliatelle.</u> The less it is dried, the faster the fettuccine will cook. Bring 3 to 4 quarts (2.8 to 3.8 liters) of water to a strong boil with ½ teaspoon salt. Add the fettuccine, return to the boil, stir with a fork to separate the strands, and cook for approximately 2 to 3 minutes, depending on the dryness of the pasta, until the fettuccine is cooked al dente (still firm to the bite) or to your taste. Top with butter, Parmesan cheese, salt, and pepper and serve.

Potato-Dill Gnocchi

(Gnocchi aux Pommes de Terre)

There are three types of gnocchi—gnocchi Parisenne, gnocchi Romaine, and potato gnocchi. The Parisian gnocchi is made from cream puff dough seasoned with Parmesan cheese, formed into small dumplings, poached in water, then usually baked in a white sauce and served au gratin all puffed up like little quenelles. The Roman gnocchi is made into a polenta from semolina and milk, cooled, cut into shapes and either fried or baked with butter, cream and cheese. The potato gnocchi is made with cooked potato, flour, and eggs and is poached and served with a sauce.

YIELD: About 6 servings

1 pound (454 grams) potatoes, unpeeled

Dash plus ½ teaspoon salt

1 cup (150 grams) or more organic all-purpose flour

½ cup (135 grams) cottage cheese

¾ cup (75 grams) grated Gouda or cheddar cheese

½ cup (30 grams) finely chopped dill or basil leaves

2 large eggs

TO FINISH

2 tablespoons (28 grams) butter

1. Place the unpeeled potatoes in a saucepan, cover with water, and add a dash of salt. Bring to a boil and cook about 30 minutes, until just tender. Peel the potatoes while still warm and push through a food mill directly onto a wooden board.

2. Add the salt, flour, cottage cheese, grated cheese, and dill or basil, tossing gently to mix. Break in the eggs and mix to make a dough, using a bit more flour if the dough is too sticky, which will depend on the moisture in the potatoes. Mix lightly, wrap the dough in plastic wrap, and refrigerate until cold and firm, at least 1 hour.

3. Flour the board and <u>roll one-third of the dough into a cylinder</u> about 1 inch (2.5 centimeters) thick. Cut into ½-inch (1.25 centimeters) slices. Repeat with the remainder of the dough.

4. Using the tines of a fork dipped in flour, <u>flatten the gnocchi rounds, making a design at the same time.</u>

5. Place half the gnocchi rounds in boiling water. Bring to a boil and simmer for about 5 to 6 minutes, shaking the pan occasionally to prevent them from sticking to the bottom. <u>Remove the gnocchi to ice water</u> and, when cold, drain and set aside until serving time. At serving time, reheat the gnocchi in hot water for 4 to 5 minutes, then drain into a bowl. Add 2 tablespoons butter, a dash of salt and pepper, and toss to coat the gnocchi with butter. Serve immediately.

PASTRY & DESSERT

English Custard Cream

(Crème Anglaise)

Crème anglaise *is a basic and essential cream. It is served with innumerable desserts, flavored in different ways. With the addition of unsalted butter, it can become a fine butter cream* (crème au beurre); *and with the addition of whipped cream and chocolate it becomes a chocolate mousse; frozen it becomes ice cream. It is the base of such desserts as* bavarois, charlotte *and the like.*

YIELD: 1 quart (1 scant liter)

3 cups (710 milliliters) milk
9 large egg yolks
1 cup (225 grams) sugar
1 teaspoon pure vanilla extract
½ cup (118 milliliters) cold heavy cream

1. Bring the milk to a boil. Set aside. Beat the yolks, sugar, and vanilla in a bowl and beat with a wire whisk for about 3 minutes until it forms a "ribbon." The mixture should be pale yellow in color, and when lifted with the whisk, it should fall back into the bowl like a ribbon folded on itself. When the ribbon is "stretched," it should not break. Combine the hot milk and the yolk mixture in a saucepan. Place the cold cream in a bowl with a fine sieve on top. Cook for a few minutes on medium heat, stirring with a wooden spatula, until the mixture coats the spatula.

2. Test by sliding your finger across the cream; the mark should remain for a few seconds. Do not over cook or the eggs will scramble. As soon as it reaches the right consistency and temperature (175 to 185 degrees/79°C to 85°C), strain through the sieve into the cold cream. This will lower the temperature and prevent scrambling. Cool, stirring once and a while. Refrigerate until ready to serve.

Vanilla Pastry Cream

(Crème Pâtissière)

Crème pâtissière *is a versatile and important basic cream. It can be used as a filling for éclairs, cream puffs, cakes and napoléons, or as a base for sweet soufflés. It can be made richer by replacing some of the milk with heavy cream. It can be varied with the addition of whipped cream for* crème chibouche, *or flavored with chocolate, coffee, liqueurs, and the like. With the addition of fresh unsalted butter, it becomes a "lean" butter cream (*crème au beurre*).*

The difference between pastry cream and custard cream is the addition of flour. Because there is flour in pastry cream, when it is brought to a boil to thicken it does not curdle; the flour stabilizes it.

YIELD: about 3 cups

2 cups (473 milliliters) milk

6 large egg yolks

²/₃ cup (150 grams) sugar

1 teaspoon pure vanilla extract

½ cup (75 grams) all-purpose organic flour

1. Bring the milk to a boil. Set aside. Place the yolks, sugar, and vanilla in a bowl and work the mixture with a wire whisk until it forms a "ribbon." This should take about 3 minutes. Add the flour and mix well.

2. Add half of the hot milk to the yolk mixture and mix well. Pour the yolk mixture into the remaining milk, mixing as you go along.

3. Bring to a boil on medium heat, stirring constantly with the whisk. The sauce will thicken as soon as it reaches the boiling point. Reduce heat and cook for 1 to 2 minutes, stirring constantly to avoid scorching.

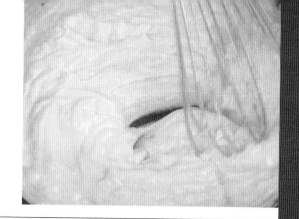

Praline Cream

(Crème Pâtissière)

Crème praline *is crème pâtissière* with the addition of a powdered almond and sugar mixture (nougatine). It is used as a filler for desserts like Paris-Brest.

³/₄ cup (90 grams) confectioners' sugar
³/₄ cup (120 grams) whole almonds

1. To make the nougatine (the cooked almond and sugar mixture), put the confectioners' sugar and almonds in a heavy saucepan. Stir with a wooden spoon. Place the saucepan over medium heat and cook, stirring constantly, until the sugar starts to melt. Since there is no liquid in the mixture, it will take a few minutes before the edges start to melt. Stir the melted and still dry parts together. However, as soon as the sugar melts, it will turn rapidly into caramel. This method produces a very hard and tight caramel.

2. As soon as it turns into caramel, pour the mixture onto an oiled marble surface or an oiled tray. When cooled, break into pieces and crush into powder in a food processor or blender.

3. Fold the mixture into the *crème pâtissière*.

Caramel Snow Eggs

(Oeufs à la Neige)

Snow eggs are the archetypical French dessert, served in starred restaurants as well as at family dinners. Bathed with a custard cream, they are usually coated with caramel. It is important that the temperature of the poaching water does not rise above 180 degrees (82°C) and that the eggs are poached only a few minutes on each side. If they boil in the cooking liquid, they will expand and deflate as they cool and becoming rubbery.

When the caramel is spooned on the eggs in thin threads, it tends to melt faster than when applied in large spoonfuls, which will last for at least 2 to 3 hours. Snow eggs can be poached a few hours ahead of serving and the custard cream can also be made ahead. The dessert should not be assembled more than a couple of hours before serving or the caramel will have melted by serving time.

YIELD: 8 servings

CUSTARD CREAM
½ cup (119 milliliters) heavy cream
1 teaspoon cornstarch
1½ cup (355 milliliters) milk
6 large egg yolks
⅓ cup (62 grams) sugar
1 teaspoon pure vanilla extract

LIGHT MERINGUE MIXTURE
6 large egg whites
¾ cup (169 grams) sugar

CARAMEL
½ cup (93 grams) sugar
2 tablespoons water

TO MAKE THE CUSTARD CREAM: Put the cream in a bowl and set a fine strainer on top. In a saucepan, mix the cornstarch with the milk, and bring to a boil. Meanwhile, with a whisk, mix the 6 egg yolks and sugar together in a bowl, and beat until smooth, about 30 seconds to 1 minute. Pour in the boiling milk, then return the mixture to the saucepan and stir with a wooden spoon over medium heat until it thickens (at about 180 degrees/82°C). The foam created from beating the egg yolks and sugar will disappear when the custard has reached 180 degrees (82°C) and the mixture will thicken. The custard should coat the spoon. Immediately pour it into the cold cream through the fine strainer (to catch any curdled bits); this will lower the temperature of the custard mixture and prevent it from curdling further. Add the vanilla, cover, and cool.

1. TO MAKE THE LIGHT MERINGUE MIXTURE: Place a fairly large saucepan with at least 3 inches (7.5 centimeters) of water in it on the stove, and bring the water to approximately 180 degrees (82°C). For the light meringue mixture: Beat the 6 egg whites by hand with a whisk, or in a mixer, until stiff. When firm, sprinkle the sugar quickly (in 5 to 10 seconds) onto the whites while continuing to beat, and beat for another 10 seconds, just long enough to incorporate the sugar. Using a round ice cream scoop that holds ⅓ to ½ cup, scoop a portion of the meringue, filling the scoop completely, and smooth the top with your fingers to round it.

2. Drop balls of meringue one by one (you should have 6 to 8) into the hot water, rinsing the scoop, if sticky, after each use in a bowl of clean water. The cooking water should not boil when you are poaching the meringues or they will expand and then deflate and get rubbery.

3. Cook the meringue balls for approximately 3 minutes on one side and, sliding a slotted spoon underneath, turn them over and cook them for 3 minutes on the other side. Remove to a paper towel with the slotted spoon. The meringue balls can be made ahead to this point and cooled. To check whether the meringue is cooked, cut one ball in half and press on the cut surface. It should have a spongy texture.

4. TO MAKE THE CARAMEL: Combine the sugar and water in a saucepan. Mix together just enough to moisten the sugar and place over medium heat until the mixture boils. Keep boiling without stirring or shaking the pan until the mixture becomes caramel colored (10 to 12 minutes). Remove the caramel from the heat, resting it for a few minutes so it will thicken a little.

5. For individual servings, spoon approximately 1½ ounces (43 grams) of custard cream on each plate and serve with one of the "eggs." Top with a spoon or two of caramel. For a serving variation, a caramel cage (see page 584) can be made, using a small bowl as a mold, and placed on top of an individual serving of the caramel snow eggs.

> You will discover that there is great satisfaction in conquering dishes that may have frustrated you in the kitchen before becoming a technician.

Almond Floating Islands

(Ile Flottante)

Floating islands are similar to snow eggs but are baked in the oven in a bain marie (double boiler). Here they are demonstrated in individual portions, although the dessert can be made in a large soufflé mold. The recipe uses small glass containers with about a 1½-cup (355 milliliters) capacity as well as small oval ceramic or porcelain dishes with about a 1-cup capacity (237 milliliters).

Floating islands can be cooked a day or so ahead and kept, covered, in the refrigerator so the tops don't get rubbery. Covering also keeps the dessert moist, making it easier to unmold. When left uncovered, the sugar hardens around the edge of the molds and makes the floating islands difficult to unmold.

YIELD: 8 servings

RUM CUSTARD SAUCE
1½ cups (355 milliliters) milk
2 teaspoons cornstarch
⅓ cup (62 grams) sugar
3 large egg yolks
½ cup (119 milliliters) cold heavy cream
1 teaspoon pure vanilla extract
3 tablespoons dark rum

BUTTER CARAMEL
½ cup (93 grams) sugar
4 tablespoons water
2½ tablespoons (38 grams) unsalted butter

LIGHT MERINGUE-NUT MIXTURE
6 large egg whites
½ cup (93 grams) sugar
½ cup (65 grams) toasted slivered almonds, chopped coarsely

DECORATION
Toasted slivered almonds

1. FOR THE RUM CUSTARD SAUCE: In a saucepan, combine the milk, cornstarch, and half the sugar, stirring occasionally. Meanwhile, in a bowl combine the rest of the sugar and the egg yolks, stirring well with a whisk. When the milk-cornstarch-sugar mixture comes to a strong boil, <u>pour it all at once into the yolks and mix thoroughly with a whisk.</u>

2. The quantity of boiling milk as compared to the quantity of egg yolk is such that the egg yolk will be cooked by the hot milk and not require further cooking. <u>Strain the mixture immediately through a fine strainer into a bowl</u> and add the cold cream. When lukewarm, add the vanilla and rum. Set aside until serving time.

3. FOR THE BUTTER CARAMEL: Combine the sugar with 3 tablespoons of the water, just enough to moisten the sugar. Place over medium heat, bring to a boil, and cook, without shaking or moving the pan, until the mixture turns caramel-colored (10 to 12 minutes). When caramelized, remove from the stove, add the butter and remaining tablespoon water, and stir well until combined. <u>Pour 2 tablespoons of the caramel into the bottom of 8 individual molds with a capacity of 1 to 1½ cups (237 to 355 milliliters).</u> Let the caramel cool and harden, then butter lightly around the sides of the molds.

4. FOR THE LIGHT MERINGUE-NUT MIXTURE: Preheat the oven to 350 degrees (177°C). Beat the 6 egg whites until very firm. Sprinkle the sugar quickly (in 5 to 10 seconds) on top while beating at high speed with the whisk, and continue beating for another 10 seconds. <u>Fold in the chopped almonds.</u>

5. Place the meringue mixture in a pastry bag without a tip and <u>squeeze it into the mold on top of the hardened caramel</u>.

6. <u>Tap the molds on a pot holder set on the table</u> so there are no air bubbles in the center of the meringue.

7. Arrange the molds in a pan surrounded by lukewarm water. Place in oven for 25 to 30 minutes, <u>until well set in the center and puffy</u>. Remove from the water and let cool.

8. When cool, the individual desserts can be covered with plastic wrap and refrigerated. They will keep for up to 2 days. At serving time, place about 3 to 4 tablespoons of the rum custard sauce on individual serving plates, unmold the small floating islands on top, letting whatever caramel that comes out drip over them. <u>Decorate with some extra toasted almond slivers</u> and serve immediately.

Meringue

This basic egg white and sugar mixture is employed in different ways to produce innumerable desserts. It can be dried and called meringue; it can be poached and called oeufs à la neige; *it can be piped into a shell and called* vacherin; *it can be mixed with nuts and called a* dacquoise; *it can be used to make cookies such as ladyfingers and as a base for an omelette soufflée. I begin here with simple dried meringue "cookies" and proceed in the next few techniques through the more elaborate meringue confections.*

6 large egg whites
1½ cups (300 grams) superfine sugar, divided
Dash of salt or a few drops of fresh lemon juice
Grated chocolate, cocoa, and sliced almonds for decoration (optional)

1. Whip the whites by hand or electric mixer, adding a small dash of salt or a few drops of lemon juice before you start to whip. Whip on medium to high speed. When the whites are holding a nice shape, gradually add 1 cup (200 grams) of the sugar and keep beating for 1 minute. The mixture should be stiff and shiny. <u>Fold in the remaining ½ cup (100 grams) sugar.</u> Folding in a part of the sugar at the end makes for a tender meringue.

2. Preheat the oven to about 200 degrees (93°C). Coat a cookie sheet with butter and flour. Fill up a pastry bag, and <u>pipe out plain and fluted meringues.</u> Lift the tip of the bag in a quick, swift motion to avoid a long tail.

3. Dip your fingers in cold water and push the tails down. Bake for 1¾ hours. (In restaurants, the meringues are often dried in a plate warmer at about 135 degrees/57°C for 24 hours.) They should be well dried. Though some people insist that meringues should be absolutely white, I fail to see the reason and do not mind if they become slightly beige during baking. Stored dry in a covered container, meringues will keep for months.

4. Meringues can be served on top of ice cream, with chestnut purée, purée of fruits, or plain whipped cream. Spread some whipped cream on the flat side of one fluted meringue and

5. place another meringue against the cream. Place the double meringue on its side and decorate the top with more whipped cream.

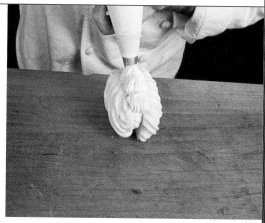

6. Add the grated chocolate.

7. To dress up plain meringues sprinkle them with bitter cocoa and connect two together with <u>whipped cream</u>.

8. Decorate the top with whipped cream and <u>sliced</u> <u>almonds</u>.

Meringue Mushrooms

(Champignons en Meringue)

These little mushrooms are occasionally served by themselves as finger food for cocktail parties or buffets. Most often they are used to decorate a bûche de Noël, yule log. Make the basic meringue mixture following the instructions in the preceding technique. Coat a cookie sheet with butter and flour or line it with a no-stick liner.

YIELD: 12 to 14 mushrooms; amounts vary depending on size

1. Preheat oven to 200 degrees (93°C). Fill a pastry bag with the meringue, using a small plain tube. <u>Squeeze some rounded small meringues and some pointed ones</u> to be used for the stems of the mushrooms. Make them pointed by pulling the meringue mixture up after some of it has been squeezed out of the bag. Reserve some meringue for assembling the mushrooms (step 4).

2. <u>Flatten the tails of the caps using a little cold water on</u> <u>your fingers</u>. Bake in the preheated oven for 75 minutes. Let cool for 15 minutes. (The small vacherin pictured in the background are customarily filled with ice cream, chestnut pureé, flavored whipped cream, and the like.)

3. Holding the cap of the mushroom in one hand, <u>dig a</u> <u>small opening on the flat side with the point of a knife.</u>

4. Using a paper cornet, <u>fill the opening with meringue</u> <u>mixture</u> and

5. <u>stick a stem into place</u>. Bake for 45 minutes.

6. You should have perfect little mushrooms.

7. You can <u>sprinkle them with bitter cocoa</u> before using them for decoration.

> **If you have talent, the techniques are the engine and the means with which to express your talent.**

Large Meringue Shells

(Vacherin)

A large vacherin *makes an impressive dessert for a party. It is not as complicated as it seems, and most of the work can be done ahead of time with little last-minute preparation. You need 1½ times the amount given in the meringue recipe on page 486, which means you'll be working with 9 egg whites instead of 6.*

YIELD: 10 to 12 servings

9 large egg whites

2¼ cups (approximately 506 grams) superfine sugar

A few dashes salt or ¾ teaspoon fresh lemon juice

Ice cream

Strained peaches or apricot halves

Melba or raspberry sauce

Whipped cream

Candied violets for decorating

1. Preheat the oven to 200 degrees (93°C). Prepare the basic meringue mixture on page 486 using the 9 egg whites, sugar, and salt or lemon juice. Coat several large cookie sheets with butter and flour. <u>Make outlines with a flan ring or any round object</u> about 10 to 11 inches (25 to 28 centimeters) in diameter.

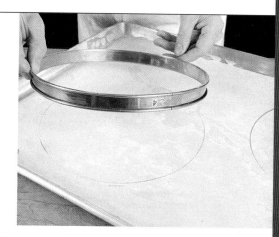

2. Place some meringue mixture in a pastry bag fitted with a plain tube. <u>Fill in one of the outlines to make a solid base.</u>

3. <u>Make plain rings</u> on the other trays

4. <u>or double rings if you want to go a bit faster</u>. You will need 6 single rings or 3 double ones. Bake the base and rings in the preheated oven for 1¾ hours. Let cool in the oven for 15 minutes. Keep in a dry place.

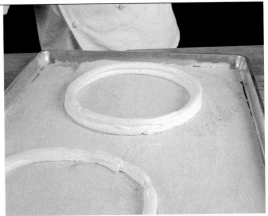

5. Using a paper cornet, <u>place dots of meringue mixture around the outside edge of the baked base.</u>

6. Place a baked ring on top and keep building the vacherin with rings <u>"cemented" with the meringue mixture.</u>

7. Continue until all the rings have been used.

8. Using a metal spatula, <u>coat the outside of the rings with meringue</u>, filling up holes and making it smooth all around.

9. <u>Decorate the top</u> and bottom with a border of meringue.

10. <u>Make strips, or any other motif which suits your fancy</u>, all around the vacherin.

11. <u>Embed small pieces of candied violets in the meringue.</u> Return to the oven and bake for 1 hour. Cool in a dry place.

12. At serving time, fill the vacherin with slightly softened ice cream. Arrange strained peach or apricot halves on top of the ice cream and cover the fruit with a thick melba or raspberry sauce. <u>Decorate with whipped cream and candied violets.</u>

Chocolate Meringue Nut Cake

(Dacquoise au Chocolat)

The dacquoise mixture is akin to meringue but it is made with the addition of nuts and cornstarch, and cooked at a much higher temperature than a meringue. The cake is comprised of two flat disks filled with a chocolate butter cream and a rum-flavored whipped cream. The disks should be dry and brittle like a meringue.

YIELD: 8 to 10 servings

¾ cup (169 grams) granulated sugar
1¼ cups (125 grams) nuts (half almonds, half hazelnuts), toasted in the oven and ground
1 tablespoon cornstarch
6 large egg whites
Dash of salt

CHOCOLATE BUTTER CREAM

1½ cups (355 milliliters) heavy cream
12 ounces (340 grams) bittersweet chocolate
½ stick (2 ounces/56 grams) unsalted butter, softened
1 tablespoon dark rum

1½ cups (355 milliliters) heavy cream
2 tablespoons confectioners' sugar
1 tablespoon dark rum

1. Preheat the oven to 350 degrees (177°C). Coat 2 cookie sheets with butter and flour. <u>Mark the coating with 10-inch (25-centimeter) rings</u>.

2. Mix together the sugar, nuts, and cornstarch. Whip the whites by machine or hand, adding a small dash of salt before you begin. Beat until firm. <u>Fold in the sugar and nut mixture</u>. Work quickly to keep the whites from becoming grainy.

3. Fill a pastry bag fitted with a plain tube with the meringue mixture. <u>Pipe a ring on each tray</u>, following the outline of the 10-inch (25-centimeter) ring.

4. <u>Divide the remaining meringue mixture</u> between the two rings.

5. <u>Spread evenly with a spatula.</u>

6. The disks should be the same thickness all over. Bake in the oven for 20 to 25 minutes, or until nicely browned.

7. Let the disks set for a few minutes, <u>then slide off the tray to a wire rack.</u>

8. After a half hour or so, <u>the meringue should be dry and brittle.</u>

9. <u>Trim the edges to make perfect wheels</u>. Save the trimmings.

10.FOR THE BUTTER CREAM: Chop the chocolate coarsely and combine with the cream in a heavy saucepan. Heat stirring until smooth. Remove from the heat and let cool until thick, but not too hard. Place in a bowl and add the softened butter, in pieces, and the rum. Beat with a whisk for 1 to 2 minutes, which will expand the volume and whiten the cream. The cream should not be overbeaten or it will absorb too much air and become grainy and hard to spread. If this happens, remelt slightly and stir gently until soft enough to use. Place one wheel on a serving platter and, using a pastry bag fitted with a fluted tube, <u>pipe a border all around the wheel</u>.

11. Place a small amount of the butter cream in the middle of the wheel and <u>sprinkle with the trimmings of the cake</u>.

12. Combine the cream, confectioners' sugar, and rum. Whip until firm. <u>Arrange the cream in the middle of the wheel</u>.

13. <u>Place the other wheel, smooth side up, on top</u>.

14. <u>Sprinkle with confectioners' sugar</u>, coating the entire top.

15. <u>Decorate the edges</u> and the middle with the chocolate butter cream.

16. <u>Cake ready to be served</u>. Place in the refrigerator and serve cold, a small wedge per person. Use a serrated knife to cut the cake.

Ladyfingers

(Biscuits à la Cuillère)

In France, ladyfingers are traditionally served as a cookie with champagne. They are also used to line molds, such as for a charlotte, or in an omelette soufflée.

YIELD: 20 ladyfingers

3 large eggs
½ cup (100 grams) superfine sugar
½ teaspoon pure vanilla extract
⅔ cup (100 grams) all-purpose organic flour
Confectioners' sugar

1. Preheat oven to 325 degrees (163°C). Separate the eggs and beat the egg whites by machine or by hand. When beating egg whites, be sure the bowl is clean and that there is no egg yolk mixed with the white. If you are not using a copper bowl, a dash of salt or cream of tartar or a few drops of lemon juice can be added to the whites to help the whipping process.

2. Add the superfine sugar and continue beating for about 1 minute until the whites form firm but creamy peaks. Beat for about 6 seconds longer to incorporate. Using a spatula, fold the vanilla, then the beaten egg yolks into the meringue. Sieve the flour on top of the mixture, folding it in as you go along.

3. Coat 2 cookie sheets with butter and flour. Fit a pastry bag with a plain tube, and fill with the mixture. <u>Hold the tip about 1 inch above the tray and pipe the ladyfingers onto the sheets</u>. They should be approximately 4 inches (10 centimeters) long by 1 inch (2.5 centimeters) wide.

4. <u>Lift up the tip of the bag in a swift stroke</u> against the end of the ladyfinger to avoid a long tail.

5. Sprinkle the ladyfingers heavily with confectioners' sugar. <u>They should be sprinkled twice</u>. Let them absorb the sugar for 1 minute between sprinklings.

6. <u>Turn the filled sheet upside down</u> and give it a little bang with a knife to make the excess sugar fall on the table. This operation should be done rapidly and swiftly. If the mixture is the right consistency, the ladyfingers will not change shape at all.

7. Bake in the preheated oven for 12 to 15 minutes. Let cool for 15 minutes. They should slide easily from the sheet. <u>The color should be light brown.</u> To avoid drying, stick one against the other and store in a covered container.

Soufflé Omelet

(Omelette Soufflé)

The omelette soufflé is closer to a soufflé than an omelet. It is lighter than a regular soufflé because it is not made with a starch base (a béchamel or crème pâtissière). It can be put together quickly and easily but it cannot be prepared in advance, as regular soufflés can. It will also deflate faster than a regular soufflé. To bake an omelette soufflée, you need an ovenproof platter—silver, stainless steel, or porcelain—at least 16 by 12 inches (41 x 30.5 centimeters). The same mixture can be used in a baked Alaska.

YIELD: 10 servings

8 large egg whites

1 cup (200 grams) superfine sugar

6 large egg yolks

8 to 10 ladyfingers, or the same amount of sponge cake (see page 504)

⅓ cup (79 milliliters) Grand Marnier, cognac, or kirsch

1 tablespoon confectioners' sugar, plus additional for garnish (optional)

Coat an ovenproof platter generously with butter and sugar. Beat the egg whites until they hold a soft peak. Reduce the speed and add the sugar in a steady stream. Return to high speed for 1 minute. Beat the yolk lightly with a fork and fold into the whites.

1. Preheat oven to 425 degrees (218°C). <u>Spread about one-fourth of the mixture in the center of the platter.</u>

2. Arrange the ladyfingers or sponge cake on top and <u>moisten with the liqueur or brandy.</u>

3. <u>Cover with more mixture</u>.

4. <u>Smooth with a spatula</u>.

5. <u>Be sure that the ladyfingers are equally covered all over</u>.

6. Fit a pastry bag with a fluted tube and fill with the remaining mixture. <u>Pipe out a decorative border around the edge</u>.

7. <u>Decorate the top and sides to your fancy</u>. At this point, the omelet can be held in the freezer for a couple of hours until ready to bake.

8. <u>Sprinkle with confectioners' sugar</u> and bake in the preheated oven for 10 to 12 minutes, or until well glazed.

9. <u>Baked soufflé omelet</u>. You may sprinkle it with more confectioners' sugar when it comes out of the oven. Serve immediately.

Basic Sponge Cake

(Génoise)

The génoise—a basic sponge cake—is the base of countless cakes. It is also used for croûtes aux fruits, petits fours glaces, and to line molds. The batter can be made with an electric mixer, as shown in the photographs that illustrate this technique, as well as by hand. The recipe makes two 8-inch (20-centimeter) cakes. The flour is sifted into the batter rather than folded in, because if poorly incorporated the cake will be grayish and heavy and will have lumps. The melted butter, added at the end, is heavy and brings the mixture down. To correct this problem, "overwork" the batter slightly. The butter can be omitted or reduced (many cooks use none or only a tiny amount of butter).

YIELD: 2 cakes; 12 to 16 servings

6 large eggs, at room temperature

¾ cup (169 grams) sugar

½ teaspoon pure vanilla extract

1 cup (150 grams) flour (use all-purpose, or ⅔ cup/100 grams all-purpose and ⅓ cup/50 grams cake flour)

½ stick (4 tablespoons/56 grams) unsalted butter, melted

1. Preheat the oven to 350 degrees (177°C). Butter and flour two 8- by 1½-inch (20- by 4-centimeter) cake pans. Place the eggs, sugar, and vanilla in the bowl of an electric mixer. Mix well to combine the ingredients and stir over boiling water, or the burner, for about 30 seconds, so that the mixture is barely lukewarm. Remove from heat and beat on medium to high speed for about 10 minutes. The mixture should make a thick ribbon. It should be pale yellow, and it should have at least tripled in volume.

2. Using a wide spatula, <u>fold the mixture with one hand and sift in the flour with the other.</u>

3. <u>Add the butter, using the same procedure.</u>

4. <u>Fill the prepared cake pans about three-fourths full.</u> Place pans on a cookie sheet and bake in the preheated oven for 22 to 25 minutes.

5. Remove from the oven and, after 5 minutes, turn

6. upside down on racks.

7. The bottom and sides should be pale golden in color. The cakes should be flat (no sagging) and soft and springy to the touch. When cool, they can be served or can be placed in plastic bags to keep them from drying. They will keep, wrapped and refrigerated, for a few days.

Rolled Cake

(Biscuit Roulé)

This batter is for cakes such as jelly rolls and the like. It is essentially the same as the génoise described in the preceding technique with the addition of an egg yolk. The egg yolk makes the cake moist and easier to roll.

YIELD: 1 cake; 8 to 10 servings

3 large eggs, at room temperature
1 large egg yolk
½ cup (112 grams) sugar
¼ teaspoon pure vanilla extract
½ cup (75 grams) all-purpose organic flour
¼ stick (2 tablespoons/28 grams) unsalted butter, melted

Preheat the oven to 350 degrees (177°C). Place the eggs, egg yolk, sugar, and vanilla in a mixing bowl and let the mixture get lukewarm by placing the bowl over boiling water for a few seconds. Remove from the heat and beat on medium to high speed for 6 to 8 minutes. Add the flour, then butter (see steps 2 and 3 in the preceding technique).

1. Butter a 16 by 12 inch (41 by 30 centimeter) rimmed cookie sheet in 2 or 3 spots and line with a piece of parchment or wax paper. (The butter anchors the paper to the cookie sheet.) Butter and flour the paper and then <u>spread the batter evenly in the pan</u>. Bake for 11 to 13 minutes.

2. Remove the cake from the oven and let it set for 5 minutes. Put a piece of wax paper on the table and turn the cake upside down on top of it. Make sure the paper is larger than the cake. <u>Remove the paper adhering to the bottom (now the top) of the cake</u> and then lay it loosely over the cake again.

3. Let the cake cool to barely lukewarm, then <u>roll between the two sheets of paper</u>.

4. <u>Fold both ends to enclose the cake</u> and keep refrigerated or in a plastic bag until you are ready to use.

Christmas Yule Log with Mint Leaves

(Bûche de Noël au Chocolat)

This is a stunning dessert for a Christmas or fall party. It is made up of several procedures that can be used as independent recipes. Cover the cake on the plate well with plastic wrap and refrigerate until serving time because the chocolate tends to absorb tastes from other foods in the refrigerator. After a few moments on the buffet, the chocolate "bark" will soften just enough that it can be cut into pieces with the point of a sharp knife as the cake is sliced. This cake, without the "bark," freezes well, provided it is properly wrapped and not kept frozen for more than a couple of weeks. Defrost under refrigeration.

YIELD: 1 cake; 10 to 12 servings

JELLY ROLL CAKE

8 large eggs, separated

⅔ cup (150 grams) granulated sugar

1 teaspoon pure vanilla extract

⅔ cup (100 grams) all-purpose organic flour

CHOCOLATE PASTRY CREAM FILLING

3 large egg yolks

⅓ cup (50 grams) granulated sugar

2 tablespoons cornstarch

1 teaspoon pure vanilla extract

1½ cups (355 milliliters) milk

5 ounces (142 grams) bittersweet or semisweet chocolate, broken into pieces

RUM-CHOCOLATE GANACHE OR GLAZE

About 4 ounces/113 grams (½ cup/118 milliliters melted) bittersweet or semisweet chocolate

½ cup (118 milliliters) heavy cream

1 tablespoon dark rum

CHOCOLATE BARK WITH LEAVES (optional)

12 ounces (340 grams) bittersweet chocolate

12 to 15 mint leaves plus extra larger leaves for imprinting

DECORATIONS

Confectioners' sugar for dusting cake

Autumn leaves or holly

1. TO MAKE THE JELLY ROLL CAKE: Preheat the oven to 350 degrees (177°C). Beat the egg yolks, sugar, and vanilla together for about 1 minute, until very fluffy and smooth. Then add the flour and mix well with a whisk until smooth. Beat the egg whites by hand or with an electric mixer until firm. Pour the egg yolk mixture on top of the whites.

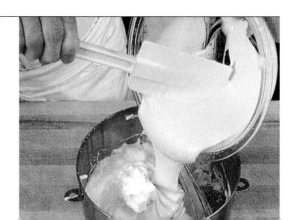

2. <u>Fold the yolks gently into the whites</u> to retain most of the volume.

3. Butter a parchment paper-lined jelly roll pan 12 by 16 inches (30.5 by 40.5 centimeters). <u>Spread the cake batter on the paper</u>, making it of equal thickness all over.

4. Bake in the preheated oven for approximately 13 minutes. <u>The cake will be puffy when removed from the oven</u>. It will deflate and shrink slightly as it cools but will still remain quite soft and pliable.

5. FOR THE CHOCOLATE PASTRY CREAM FILLING:
Beat the egg yolks, sugar, cornstarch, and vanilla together with a whisk. Meanwhile, bring the milk to a boil. Pour the boiling milk into the egg yolk mixture, stirring, then return it to the saucepan. Bring to a boil, stirring with a whisk so the pastry cream doesn't stick and burn on the bottom. Boil for about 10 seconds. Remove from the heat. <u>The mixture will be quite thick.</u>

6. Add the chocolate pieces to the saucepan and <u>stir gently with a whisk</u> to help melt the chocolate. After 5 minutes, stir again.

7. The mixture should be very smooth. <u>Transfer to a bowl</u>, cover, and refrigerate.

8. Slide a spatula under the cooled cake and remove it to a board with the parchment paper underneath still intact. When the chocolate pastry cream is cold, <u>spread it on the top of the cake</u>—the part exposed in the oven—which has visible cracks.

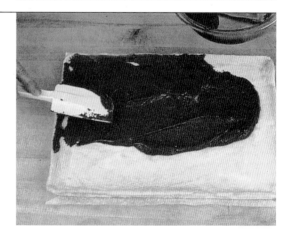

9. Using the paper lining underneath, <u>lift up the cake and begin to roll it on itself</u>, starting at a long end.

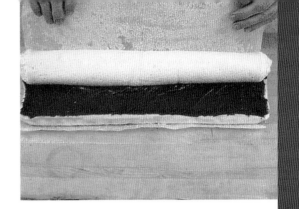

10. <u>Keep rolling, still using the paper</u>, until the cake roll is rolled up tightly.

11. The pastry cream is now completely enclosed in the cake roll. <u>Roll the cake up in the same parchment paper</u> and refrigerate it for up to a day or so.

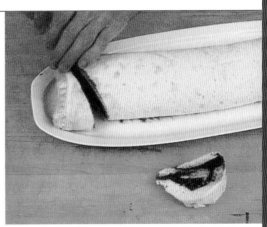

12. To finish the yule log, remove the paper and place the cake on a serving platter. <u>Cut off both ends of the log at an angle</u>. These pieces will be used to simulate stumps on the log.

TO MAKE THE RUM-CHOCOLATE GANACHE: Melt the bittersweet chocolate in a double boiler. Pour the cream and rum into a bowl and, when the chocolate is melted, add it and beat with a whisk for 15 seconds, until the mixture lightens slightly in color and becomes about the consistency of a buttercream. Do not over-whisk because incorporating too much air will whiten the ganache and make it set too hard as it cools. If this should happen, remelt slightly and beat again.

13. Using a spatula, <u>coat the whole cake with a thin layer of the ganache</u>.

14. <u>Place the two end pieces of cake on top</u> to simulate tree stumps.

15. Continue coating the cake and stumps with the ganache. When thoroughly coated, <u>draw the tines of a fork through the soft ganache to create a bark design</u>. Using the point of a knife, make circular designs on top of the stumps and at either end of the log to simulate the design on a tree. At this point, the cake can be refrigerated. When cold, cover loosely with plastic wrap. It is usually served at this point.

16. For a more elaborate serving variation, chocolate bark can be added.

FOR THE CHOCOLATE BARK: Melt the bittersweet chocolate in a double boiler and <u>pour a strip of it about the length of the cake onto parchment or wax paper</u>.

17. With a narrow, flexible spatula, <u>spread the chocolate to a thickness of about ¹/₈ inch (3 millimeters)</u>, smearing the chocolate out at intervals to make a jagged edge along the length on one side to simulate broken pieces of bark.

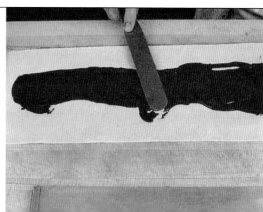

18. While the chocolate is still warm, <u>press the mint leaves and larger leaves into the surface</u>. The mint leaves will be left in the chocolate and the non-edible larger leaves removed at serving time.

19. <u>Press another strip of parchment paper on top</u> of the chocolate and turn the package over onto a tray so the side with the leaves is touching the tray. Refrigerate. Repeat to make a strip of chocolate bark for the other side of the cake.

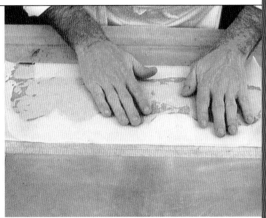

20. When the chocolate bark has hardened, <u>remove the layer of paper from the top</u>. The chocolate should have curled up a little at each end, which at this point will help it fit the contour of the cake.

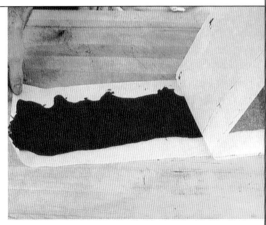

21. <u>Cut through the chocolate and paper along the straighter side</u> to trim it to a clean edge.

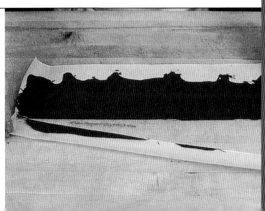

22. Place the chocolate (still attached to the paper), straight-edge down, alongside the cake, <u>pressing it lightly against the cake</u>. If the coating of the cake is still somewhat soft the bark strips will stick to it. (The bark can be made ahead and arranged around the cake before it is refrigerated.) The heat of your hand pressing against the paper may soften the chocolate slightly and make it adhere better to the cake. Peel off the paper.

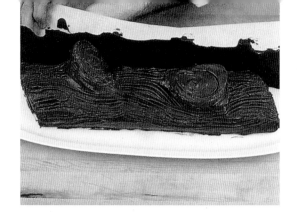

23. <u>Remove the larger leaves from both strips of the chocolate bark</u>; they will have left leaf imprints in the chocolate, which is the desired effect. Leave the mint leaves in place.

24. <u>Sprinkle a very light dusting of confectioners' sugar</u> on the log to simulate snow.

25. <u>Arrange fall leaves or holly around the cake, cut into slices, and serve.</u>

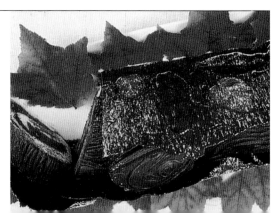

Vanilla-Bourbon Layer Cake

To make this layer cake, bake 2 basic sponge cake layers a few hours in advance or the day before so the cake is set and will not crumble when sliced.

There are many different buttercreams. The traditional mixture is an emulsion of egg yolks and cooked syrup with butter added. It is also made with boiled frosting, meringue, and butter or pastry cream and butter, as well as the fine, delicate version here, which is made of custard cream and butter.

YIELD: 1 layer cake; 8 to 10 servings

1 Basic Sponge Cake, page 504

BOURBON SYRUP

3 tablespoons warm water from the tap

1 teaspoon pure vanilla extract

2 tablespoons sugar

3 tablespoons bourbon

Mix together until smooth and set aside.

VANILLA-BOURBON BUTTERCREAM

1/4 cup (60 milliliters) heavy cream

1 cup (237 milliliters) milk

3 large egg yolks

2 teaspoons pure vanilla extract

2 tablespoons bourbon

2 1/2 sticks (1 1/4 cup/284 grams) unsalted butter, at room temperature

1 small piece (about 1 tablespoon) bitter-sweet chocolate

1/4 teaspoon vegetable oil

1. TO MAKE THE BUTTERCREAM: The delicate part of making a custard is to keep the eggs from scrambling. Pour the cream into a bowl with a fine sieve handy—when cooked, the custard will be strained through the sieve into the cold cream, which will stop further cooking and prevent curdling. Pour the milk into a saucepan and bring to a boil. Put the egg yolks and sugar in a bowl and beat with a whisk for about 1 minute, until fluffy and pale yellow. Combine the boiled milk with the yolk-sugar

mixture. Pour the custard into the saucepan and return it to medium heat, <u>stirring continuously with a spoon until it reaches about 180 degrees (82°C) and thickens</u>. Strain immediately through the sieve into the cold cream and mix well. Add the vanilla.

2. Let cool to tepid. Add the bourbon. The custard should be just thick enough to coat the spoon. <u>A finger run across the coated spoon will leave a mark, as shown.</u>

3. Meanwhile, <u>beat the butter with a whisk until fluffy and soft</u>. Start adding the custard cream to it, ¹⁄₄ cup (60 milliliters) at a time, beating after each addition until smooth and fluffy. Keep adding until all the custard cream is combined with the butter. If it starts to separate, put the bowl over heat for a few seconds; the outside will melt and the mixture will come together when whipped. Hold at room temperature until ready to use.

4. TO BUILD THE CAKE: First measure and cut a piece of cardboard the size of the bottom of the cake pan. Using a long serrated knife, slice the cake into 3 horizontal layers. <u>As you slice, keep the blade level and rotate the cake.</u> The blade should not be removed from the cake until the cutting is complete.

5. If you find the cutting technique difficult to master, use guides such as these spatula handles about ³/₈ to ¹/₂ inch (10 to 13 millimeters) thick. Place the cake between them. <u>The blade of the knife should be long enough to go through the cake and rest on both guides</u>. Start by cutting the first layer from the top of the cake, then placing it on the cardboard upside down. The top of the cake is now the bottom layer of the cake. Brush with bourbon syrup. Spread a thin layer of buttercream on top.

6. <u>Add the second layer</u>. Slice the remaining cake in half the same way.

7. Brush with syrup before coating with buttercream. Place the third layer on top (the bottom of the cake is now the top), brush with remaining syrup, and <u>coat with buttercream on top, spreading it as smoothly as you can with a long, thin metal spatula</u>.

8. Holding the cake up (it will be secure on the cardboard), <u>spread buttercream as smoothly as possible all around the sides</u>.

9. Melt the bittersweet chocolate and add the vegetable oil to it. Make a paper cone (see page 72) and pour the chocolate into it. Cut off the tip and <u>draw a design to your liking on top.</u>

10. Fill a pastry bag fitted with a fluted tip with the remaining buttercream, and pipe a pattern all around the edge of the cake. Refrigerate until serving time. (If the cake is to be kept for several hours, cover it with plastic wrap after the buttercream has set to prevent the cake from absorbing the flavor of other foods in the refrigerator.) <u>Cut into wedges and serve.</u>

Chocolate Cake

(Gâteau au Chocolat)

This recipe makes two 3-layer chocolate cakes. Each cake uses a génoise as the base and is filled with ganache soufflé, topped with ganache, and decorated with glace royale.

The ganache is a delicate, glossy chocolate icing that is made from good bittersweet chocolate and heavy cream melt together. The mixture is poured on the cake while still slightly tepid. If the ganache is allowed to cool, it will become too thick and won't run down the sides of the cake properly. If it is too hot, it will melt the filling and won't stick to the cake.

The ganache soufflé—the filling for the cake—is simply a ganache that has been cooled and then worked with a whisk. It lightens in color, gains in volume, and becomes fluffy due to the addition of air. The glace royale is a simple sugar and egg white icing that is piped onto the chocolate icing in a decorative motif. I have used a different motif for each cake. Begin by baking 2 basic sponge cakes (see page 504). If you want the cakes themselves to be chocolate, you can substitute 1/3 cup (30 grams) bitter cocoa for 1/3 cup (50 grams) of the flour in the basic recipe. Make cardboard bases for the cakes and cut each cake into 3 layers (see page 516, steps 4, 5 and 6).

YIELD: 2 cakes; 12 to 16 servings

2 Basic Sponge Cakes (page 504),
    each cake sliced in 3 layers

WHIPPED CHOCOLATE FILLING
    (*Ganache Soufflé*)
1 cup (237 milliliters) heavy cream
8 ounces (227 grams) chocolate (½ bit-
    ter, ½ semisweet) cut into ½-inch pieces
1 tablespoon dark rum

Put the cream in a saucepan and bring to
a boil. Remove from the heat and add the
chocolate. Wait for 2 to 3 minutes and then
stir to mix. Keep stirring occasionally until
smooth and blended. When cool, place in
the bowl of an electric mixer. Add the rum
and beat on high speed for 3 minutes. It will
lighten in color and approximately double
in volume. Use immediately; it will quickly
become hard and unspreadable.

CHOCOLATE ICING (*Ganache*)
12 ounces (340 grams) (squares) good
    chocolate (½ bitter, ½ semisweet)
1½ cups (355 milliliters) heavy cream
2 to 3 tablespoons water (optional)

Bring the cream to a boil. Remove form the
heat and add the chocolate. Let set for 2 to
3 minutes and then stir until smooth and
blended. Let cool to barely lukewarm. If
too thick or too oily, add 1 to 2 tablespoons
water.

ROYAL ICING (*Glace Royale*)
½ cup (50 grams) confectioners' sugar
About 1½ tablespoons egg white
3 to 4 drops fresh lemon juice

Combine the sugar, egg white and lemon
juice in a bowl. Work the mixture with a
wooden spatula for about 2 minutes until it
is nice and creamy and thick enough to form
a ribbon. If too runny, add a bit of sugar. If
too thick, add a dash of egg white.

1. Place one cake layer, crusty side down, on each cardboard
base and spread the surfaces with some *ganache soufflé*,
using a thin, flexible metal spatula. Place the next layer on,
add more *ganache soufflé*, and then add the last layer of each
cake. Smooth out the coating on top of both cakes, leaving a
little lip of *ganache soufflé* all around.

2. One at a time, hold each cake in one hand and use your spatula to smooth out the sides. <u>Go in a down and forward motion, getting rid of the lip as you go along</u>. Refrigerate the cakes for at least 1 to 2 hours. They should be cold and well set. While the cakes are chilling, prepare the *ganache* and the *glace royale* as explained above.

3. Place each cake in the center of a wire rack set on a piece of wax paper. You will have at least a third too much chocolate icing for both cakes, but you need a great amount to coat the cake correctly. The leftover can be kept for at least 1 month in the refrigerator. Don't be skimpy; <u>pour half of the chocolate icing on top of one cake.</u>

4. <u>Spread rapidly with a long metal spatula.</u>

5. Make sure all the sides are coated and the icing is about ¼-inch (6-millimeters) thick on top and around. If you take too long, the chocolate will cool off and become very thick.

6. <u>Lift up the wire rack and tap it gently on the table</u> to help smooth the sides and the excess chocolate at the bottom. Run your fingers or a spatula under the cake rack to smooth out the drippings of chocolate.

7. The cakes should be decorated with the *glace royale* while the chocolate on top of the cake is still slightly soft. It should not be too set and too hard. Place some icing in a paper cornet. Cut the tip and, for the first cake, <u>pipe out lines about 1 inch (2.5 centimeters) apart.</u>

8. Turn the cake and <u>run a long, thin-bladed knife through the lines</u>. The knife should just barely touch the chocolate. Pull toward you so the white lines are "dragged" through the chocolate.

9. Clean the blade of the knife with a wet rag after each stroke, and <u>repeat about every 1½ inches (4 centimeters)</u>.

10. Turn the cake around and drag the knife between each stroke in the same manner, but <u>pulling the icing in the opposite direction</u>. Refrigerate to have it cold before serving.

11. Using the paper cornet and the *glace royale*, decorate the second <u>cake by drawing a coil</u>. It requires practice to draw it uniformly.

12. <u>Keep going without pausing</u> to avoid breaking the line. You need a steady hand.

13. Using your knife, <u>draw 8 equidistant lines from the center to the outside of the cake.</u>

14. Repeat between each line but this time <u>dragging the knife from the outside to the center</u>. Refrigerate before serving.

Rum Babas with Peaches

Babas and savarin are made with the same dough but babas are cooked in a different size and shape. After baking, both the babas and the savarin can be wrapped and frozen until serving time. Because both babas as well as the savarin have a dry, airy texture they are soaked in syrup, often flavored with rum, before serving. Other alcohol can be substituted for the rum, as well as vanilla extract for a nonalcoholic dessert.

YIELD: 10 to 12 babas

DOUGH

½ envelope active dry yeast

½ cup (119 millilieters) milk, heated to 100 degrees (38˚C)

1 teaspoon granulated sugar

2 cups (300 grams) all-purpose organic flour

3 large eggs

½ teaspoon salt

¼ cup (45 grams) raisins

6 tablespoons (84 grams) unsalted butter, at room temperature

Egg wash made with 1 egg with half of the white removed, beaten

SYRUP FOR BABAS

¾ cup (165 grams) granulated sugar

1½ cups (356 milliliters) warm water

1 teaspoon pure vanilla extract

GLAZE

1 tablespoon dark rum

½ cup (50 grams) confectioners' sugar

GARNISHES

1 cup (237 milliliters) heavy cream

1 tablespoon granulated sugar

12 candied violets

POACHED PEACHES

1½ cups (278 grams) granulated sugar

5 cups (1.2 liters) water

Chopped rind and juice of 1 lemon (2 to 3 tablespoons)

8 peaches (about 5 ounces/142 grams each)

FOR THE PEACHES: Combine the sugar, water, and the rind and juice of the lemon in a saucepan, and bring the mixture to boil. Add the peaches, cover, return to the boil, lower the heat, and continue to cook, covered, over low heat for 6 to 10 minutes, depending on the ripeness of the peaches, until the peaches are tender. Let the peaches cool until lukewarm in the syrup, then remove them and reduce the syrup to approximately 2 cups by boiling down. Skin the peaches and combine them with the syrup.

1. FOR THE BABA DOUGH: Put the yeast with the warm milk and the sugar in the bowl of a mixer. Proof for about 5 minutes, until the mixture bubbles on top.

2. Add the flour, eggs, and salt, and beat approximately 3 minutes with the flat beater on medium speed. <u>The dough should be very elastic.</u> Then, add the raisins and the butter, and beat at the same speed for approximately 1 minute to incorporate. Don't worry if some pieces of the butter are still visible at this point. Cover the dough or batter with a towel or plastic wrap, and let rise at room temperature (about 70 to 75 degrees/21°C to 23°C) for about 1½ hours.

3. Stir the batter gently to push the air out. Butter the baba molds (½- to ¾-cup/119- to 178-milliliter capacity) and <u>fill half full with the batter.</u>

4. For tiny babas, use thimble cups with a capacity of 3 tablespoons. Butter the cups and <u>fill them one-half full with the baba mixture.</u> Set aside in a warm place (70 to 75 degrees/21°C to 23°C) away from any draft, and let the larger babas rise for about 30 to 40 minutes and the smaller ones for approximately 20 minutes. Preheat the oven to 375 degrees (191°C). Brush the top of the risen babas with the egg wash, and bake them on a cookie sheet for about 12 minutes for the tiny babas and about 20 minutes for the larger ones.

5. Let the babas cool for 15 to 20 minutes and then <u>remove them from the molds.</u> At this point, they can be allowed to cool completely, placed in airtight wrapping, and frozen.

6. TO MAKE THE SYRUP: Mix the sugar, warm water, and vanilla together until the sugar is completely dissolved. Place the babas in a gratin dish so they are fairly snug, one against the other, and pour the syrup over them. Let the babas soak in the syrup for 20 minutes or so, turning them occasionally so they can absorb as much syrup as they can. The syrup may not be completely absorbed after this amount of time; push a knife through a baba, and if the center is soft, you can assume that the syrup has penetrated into the middle of the babas. If still hard, soak longer.

7. FOR THE GLAZE: Slice the larger babas in half lengthwise. Combine the dark rum with the confectioners' sugar in a bowl, and mix until smooth. <u>Brush the outside surface of each half baba with the glaze</u> and decorate with a little piece of candied violet.

8. Beat the cream, sweetened with the sugar, to soft peaks. Place two baba halves on each serving plate with the peach halves on either side. Coat each of the peaches with a spoonful of the peach syrup. Mound some of the whipped cream in the center, decorate it with a candied violet, and serve right away.

Bourbon Apricot Savarin

YIELD: 1 savarin; 6 to 8 servings

Rum Babas with Peaches, page 523,
  dough only
Egg wash made with 1 egg, half the white
  removed, beaten

SYRUP FOR SAVARIN
¾ cup (165 grams) granulated sugar
1½ cups (356 milliliters) warm water
1 teaspoon pure vanilla extract
2 tablespoons bourbon
½ cup (165 grams) strained apricot preserves
¼ cup (35 grams) sliced almonds, toasted
Extra raisins for decoration

FRUIT GARNISH
2 tablespoons bourbon
2 ripe peaches, diced
1 cup (150 grams) sliced strawberries
⅓ cup (50 grams) blueberries
⅓ cup (115 grams) apricot preserves

WHIPPED CREAM
1 cup (237 milliliters) heavy cream
1 tablespoon granulated sugar
12 candied violets

1. TO MAKE THE SAVARIN: Butter a savarin mold and
spread the baba dough in it, filling the mold ⅓ to ½ full.
Proof at room temperature (70 to 75 degrees/21°C to 23°C)
away from any drafts for approximately 1½ hours.

2. Preheat the oven to 375 degrees (191°C). Brush the top
of the savarin with the egg wash, place on a cookie sheet,
and bake for approximately 35 minutes.

3. Let cool in the mold for at least 30 minutes and <u>unmold.</u> Place on a round gratin dish slightly larger than the savarin.

4. TO MAKE THE SYRUP: Mix the sugar, warm water, and vanilla together until the sugar is completely dissolved. <u>Pour the syrup over the savarin,</u> and let it soak for about 30 minutes or so, turning it occasionally or basting it with the syrup so most of the syrup is absorbed. Plunge a knife into the cake to make sure that it is moistened in the center. When the syrup as been sufficiently absorbed throughout the savarin, place it on a rack to drain and then on a plate. Brush first with the bourbon and then with the apricot preserves to make it shiny all over.

5. Arrange the toasted almonds in a flower design on top, pushing them into the preserves so they adhere to the cake. <u>Use raisins as the flower centers.</u>

6. FOR THE SAVARIN FRUIT GARNISH: Combine the bourbon with the peaches, strawberries, blueberries, and apricot preserves, and mix well. Whip the cream and sugar until stiff. Arrange the savarin on a large platter with the fruit garnish around it and inside the hollow center. Pile the whipped cream on top of the fruit in the center, piping it from a pastry bag fitted with a star tip. Decorate the cream in the center with a few pieces of fruit and serve immediately.

Proust's Small Coffee Cakes

(Madeleines de Commercy)

Here are the famous small cakes so dear to Marcel Proust in A La Recherche du Temps, Perdu, *Remembrance of Things Past. They originated in the small town of Commercy. The madeleines can be made in a special tray or in small individual brioche molds.*

YIELD: 16 to 18 madeleines

1 stick (½ cup/113 grams) unsalted butter, softened
½ cup (112 grams) sugar
½ teaspoon baking powder
½ teaspoon pure vanilla extract
½ teaspoon grated orange rind
2 large eggs
1 cup (150 grams) all-purpose organic flour

1. Preheat the oven to 400 degrees (204°C). Place the butter and sugar in the bowl of an electric mixer and mix on medium to fast speed until light and fluffy, about 1 minute. Add the baking powder, vanilla, orange rind, and 1 egg. Beat on low speed for about 1 minute, until smooth and light. Add the other egg and mix another minute at the same speed. Finally, stir in the flour with a whisk until the mixture is smooth. Do not overwhisk. Butter a madeleine tray well and divide the dough among 16 to 18 molds. Hit the tray on the table to flatten the dough in the molds or push it down with the tips of your fingers. <u>Bake in the preheated oven for about 20 minutes.</u>

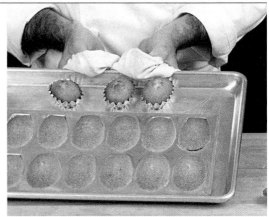

2. Let the madeleines rest or set 10 minutes before unmolding. Unmold, <u>cool on a wire rack</u> and, when cool, place in a plastic bag or a tightly lidded tin box to prevent drying. Use as needed. They are the ideal coffee cake but are also served as garnish for ice cream, or with berries and whipped cream as a type of shortcake.

Fresh Raspberry Linzer Torte

(Tarte à la Confiture)

The linzer torte is a specialty of Austria. The dough is extremely rich and delicate. The torte is easy to make and is well suited to buffets or whenever desserts have to hold for a few hours.

YIELD: 1 torte, 8 to 10 servings

FILLING
12 ounces (340 grams) fresh seedless raspberries or a 12-ounce (340-gram package unsweetened frozen raspberries
²/₃ cup (160 grams) raspberry preserves

LINZER DOUGH
1½ cups (180 grams) all-purpose organic flour
¾ cup (75 grams) ground almonds

¼ cup (36 grams) granulated sugar
¼ teaspoon mace powder
¼ teaspoon ground cinnamon
1 teaspoon pure vanilla extract
1½ sticks (¾ cup/175 grams) unsalted butter, cut into pieces
3 large egg yolks
Confectioners' sugar for dusting the cake

1. FOR THE FILLING: Push the fresh or defrosted unsweetened frozen raspberries along with the raspberry preserves through the fine screen of a food mill.

2. To be sure there are no seeds left, strain the purée through a sieve, banging the rim of the sieve with a spatula or your hand to make the seeds bounce and allow the clear liquid to go through. Then, press the seeds to extract any remaining liquid. The yield should be about 1¹/₃ cups (340 grams).

3. FOR THE LINZER DOUGH: Put the flour, almonds, sugar, cinnamon, and vanilla in the bowl of a food processor and process until the almonds are as finely ground as the flour. Add the butter and egg yolks, and pulse the motor of the processor about 10 times, until the mixture just begins to hold together. Turn the dough out onto the table and smear it with your hands, pressing it forward in the technique of the *fraisage* (see page 562), until the dough is thoroughly mixed. Place two-thirds of the dough on a large cookie sheet, cover with a piece of plastic wrap, and, with a rolling pin, roll it out to a thickness of ¼ inch.

4. Preheat the oven to 375 degrees (191°C). Using a 10- to 11-inch (25- to 28- centimeter) flan ring, press through the plastic to cut a circle on the dough.

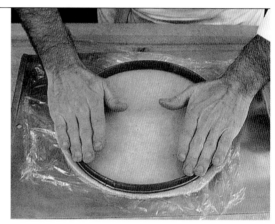

5. Remove the plastic wrap and the trimmings around the rim.

6. Fit the flan ring around the disk of dough. Make some of the extra dough into rolls about ¾ inches (19 millimeters) thick and place them all around the inside of the ring to create a border.

7. Press on the border of dough, sealing it to the disk of dough beneath and extending it slightly above the rim of the ring.

8. Pour the raspberry mixture into the shell. Using a little extra flour, roll the remaining dough into ropes about the thickness of a pencil. Place one of the ropes across the center of the torte and arrange four additional ropes parallel to it.

9. Then, arrange five ropes going in the other direction across the top of the torte.

10. Fold the extended border of dough back on top of the ropes and filling.

11. Bake in the center of the oven for approximately 45 minutes. Remove from the oven and immediately sprinkle some confectioners' sugar on top. If the sugar is added while the jam is still bubbling, any that touches the filling will melt and only the sugar on the dough will remain.

12. Serve the linzer torte at room temperature, cut into wedges.

English Trifle

(Trifle Anglais)

The English trifle is simple to assemble. It can be done a few hours ahead because in this case the cake should get soft. It can be made with sponge or pound cake, with or without fruit, with pastry cream or only whipped cream. Keep refrigerated until ready to serve.

YIELD: 8 to 10 servings

2 Basic Sponge Cakes (see page 504) or
   1 large pound cake

PASTRY CREAM
2 cups (473 milliliters) milk
¼ cup (56 grams) sugar
4 large egg yolks
½ teaspoon pure vanilla extract
2 tablespoons all-purpose organic flour

POACHED PEARS
½ cup (112 grams) sugar
1½ cups (355 milliliters) water
Rind of ½ lemon
2 cored Bartlett pears

FILLING
½ cup (118 milliliters) good seedless raspberry jam
¼ cup (59 milliliters) good, dry sherry
1½ cups (355 milliliters) heavy cream
2 tablespoons sugar

1. FOR THE PASTRY CREAM: Bring the milk to a boil. Place the sugar, egg yolks, and vanilla in a bowl and whisk until the mixture is pale yellow and thick, about a minute. Mix in the flour, then pour in the boiling milk. Mix well. Place the mixture back in the saucepan and bring to a boil, stirring with a whisk. Let it boil for a few seconds, then transfer to a clean bowl, cover with plastic wrap and allow to cool. Cut the cakes into 3 layers each and spread one layer with half of the raspberry jam. <u>Cut into 6 triangles.</u>

2. TO POACH THE PEARS: Boil the sugar, water, and lemon rind for 2 minutes. Peel the pears and cut each one into 6 wedges. Place in the boiling syrup and simmer for 2 to 3 minutes or until the pears are tender. Let them cool in syrup, and then drain. <u>Line the bottom of a glass or crystal bowl with the cake triangles, jam-side against the glass.</u>

3. Place a layer of plain cake in the middle of the bowl and sprinkle with 1 tablespoon of sherry. Pour the cooled custard on top. Break slices of cake into pieces and <u>embed in the custard to cover.</u> You may not need all of the cake. Sprinkle with 2 tablespoons of sherry.

4. Combine the cream with the sugar and 1 tablespoon of the sherry and beat until firm. Place a generous cup (approximately 240 milliliters) of the whipped cream into a pastry bag fitted with a tube tip, and <u>spread the rest on top of the custard and cake.</u>

5. Spread the whipped cream with a spatula so that the top is smooth. Spread another layer of cake with the remaining jam, cut into triangles. <u>Place on top of the whipped cream.</u>

6. <u>Arrange the wedges of pear between the triangles of coated cake.</u>

7. <u>Decorate the edges</u> and the center with the whipped cream.

8. <u>The jam-coated cake shows through the bowl as well as being visible on top.</u> Refrigerate until serving time. Serve with a spoon.

Poached Peaches with Raspberry Sauce

(Péches Pochés à la Purée de Framboises)

Poached fruit is easy to make, light and elegant, and particularly well suited as a finale to an elaborate meal. Poach fruit in the summer when peaches are ripe and tasty. If you cannot find good peaches, you can substitute pears, apricots, or even apples.

YIELD: 8 servings

SAUCE

1 cup (170 grams) fresh raspberries

1 package (283 grams/10 ounces) unsweetened frozen raspberries

½ cup (118 milliliters) good seedless raspberry preserves

1 tablespoon raspberry brandy, cognac, or kirsch

Bring all the sauce ingredients except the brandy to a boil and simmer for 2 to 3 minutes. Strain through a fine strainer or a food mill, cover with plastic wrap, and let cool. When the sauce is cool, stir in the brandy

POACHING

2 cups (450 grams) sugar

6 cups (1.4 liters) water

Juice and rind of 1 lemon

8 ripe peaches (about 2¾ pounds/1.25 kilograms), at room temperature

TO FINISH THE DISH

1 pound cake cut into 8½-inch (21.5-centimeter) slices, each slice cut into a disk with a cookie cutter (use the trimmings to make a pudding)

1 sprig fresh mint, cut into sprigs, one for each peach

1. TO POACH PEACHES: Mix the sugar, water, and lemon in a saucepan, bring to a boil and boil for 5 minutes. Add the peaches. Place a piece of paper towel on top of the peaches and push them down into the syrup so the paper towel gets wet with the syrup. If the peaches are in contact with air, they will discolor. Cover with a lid and simmer for 3 to 5 minutes, or until the peaches are tender. Let the peaches cool in the syrup. When the peaches are cool, remove from the syrup <u>and peel the skin off</u>. (Reserve the syrup to poach other fruit.)

Spread approximately 2 tablespoons of raspberry sauce on each individual plate and place a disk of pound cake in the center. Place a peach on the cake and decorate with a sprig of fresh mint. For an alternate method, coat the peaches with the raspberry sauce, then arrange on the pound cake and decorate with the mint.

Angel Hair

(Cheveux d' Ange)

Angel hair is very decorative and, though making it is a messy business, it can turn an ordinary dessert into a glorious affair. Although it can be made with sugar and water, we use corn syrup instead of the water because it prevents the sugar from crystallizing during and after cooking, making it more "flexible" and easier to use.

1 cup (225 grams) sugar
¾ cup (178 milliliters) corn syrup
2 teaspoons pure beeswax candle (optional)

1. Combine sugar and corn syrup in a saucepan. Mix well and place on medium heat. Do not stir the mixture anymore. After it boils, cook 12 to 14 minutes on medium to low heat until the sugar turns a very light ivory color (about 318 degrees/159°C on a candy thermometer). If there is any crystallized sugar on the sides of the pan, cover the saucepan for 30 seconds to 1 minute during the cooking. The steam produced will melt the sugar crystals.

2. Remove the sugar from the heat and <u>grate the pure beeswax candle into the saucepan</u> (optional). The pieces will melt right away and mix with the sugar. Angel hair has a tendency to stick together, especially during hot summer days. The wax will coat the sugar threads, making them "dry," smooth, and easier to store and use. Pure beeswax is from the honeycomb and is a natural, edible product.

3. Let the syrup cool for a few minutes. You may place the saucepan in a bowl of cold water to accelerate the process. <u>Using 2 forks side by side</u>, lift some of the syrup. It should be thick.

4. Cover the floor with newspaper. Place a wooden spatula on the table so it extends over the edge of the table. Dip both forks into the syrup and <u>wave them over the spatula, high enough and broadly enough so that the threads are long, thin,</u> and have time to solidify in the air. You may have to use a step stool to get higher.

5. <u>Slide the angel hair away from the wooden spatula</u> and use or store in a tightly covered container. Use as needed.

Glazed Strawberries

(Glaçage des Fraises)

When strawberries are in season, fresh and abundant, they always are welcomed desserts, either plain with brown sugar and sour cream, or simply topped with a dusting of sugar. For a buffet or elegant dinner they can be glazed and passed to the guests at the end of the meal. Here are two different ways to glaze strawberries. One is a currant jelly glaze and the other—the most sophisticated and delicate—is a cooked sugar syrup.

YIELD: 1 dozen jelly-glazed and 1 dozen sugar-glazed strawberries

CURRANT JELLY GLAZE

1 jar (12 ounces/355 milliliters) currant jelly

1 dozen (12) medium-size strawberries, cold, with long stems

SUGAR-SYRUP GLAZE

1 cup (225 grams) sugar

¼ cup (59 milliliters) water

½ teaspoon cream of tartar diluted with 1 teaspoon water

1 dozen (12) medium-size strawberries, with long stems

1. CURRANT-GLAZED STRAWBERRIES: Place the currant jelly in a saucepan on the stove and bring to a boil. Mix with a spoon until smooth. If the mixture is not smooth, strain it. Cool to lukewarm.

2. Holding the cold strawberry by the stem, dip in the mixture, <u>twist to coat, and allow excess jam to fall off</u>. Place on a very cold plate; refrigerate. The coating will harden as it cools. At serving time, transfer to a clean plate.

3. SUGAR-SYRUP-GLAZED STRAWBERRIES: Place the sugar and water in a heavy saucepan and stir just enough to wet the sugar. Bring to a boil but do not stir the mixture or the sugar may crystallize. Boil for 4 to 5 minutes, then add the cream of tartar. Boil for another minute, at which point it should be at the hard-crack stage (about 310 degrees/155°C), which is the stage before it turns into caramel. Dip a teaspoon in the mixture, lift it, and dip in cold water right away. If the mixture sets hard on the spoon, it is at the hard-crack stage. Incline the pan so the syrup gathers in one corner. Dip the strawberries one by one in the hot sugar syrup. Twist the berry and rub gently against the sides of the saucepan so the excess syrup drips off. The coating should be thin.

4. Place on an oiled metal tray until hard. The hot syrup will begin to cook the berry and the berry will release juices, which, in about ½ hour, will start melting the sugar coating. The berries should be eaten just before the sugar coating starts to melt as, at that moment, the coating is the thinnest.

St. Valentine Custard Cake

("Gâteau" de Semoule St. Valentin)

This unusual creation is not a cake in the traditional sense of the word but rather a molded custard served with poached fruit. It is made with farina, though rice or semolina could be used instead. Serve with any fruit in season—pear, peach, apricot, or apple—or serve plain, without fruit, like a rice pudding.

YIELD: 1 heart-shaped cake, 3 to 4 servings

8 medium-sized pears (William, Comice or Bartlett)

1 vanilla bean

Peel of 1 lemon and 1 orange

1½ cups (337 grams) granulated sugar

Grated rind of 1 orange

5 large egg yolks

1 teaspoon pure vanilla extract

1½ envelopes unflavored gelatin

2 cups (473 milliliters) milk

¼ cup (56 grams) farina

2 cups (473 milliliters) heavy cream

3 tablespoons confectioners' sugar

Almond or peanut oil to coat mold

1 (296-milliliter/10-ounce) jar apricot jam, strained

Food coloring

1 ounce (28 grams) chocolate (½ ounce/14 grams bitter, ½ ounce/14 grams semisweet)

2 tablespoons lukewarm water

Pear brandy

1. Peel the pears and remove the cores, leaving the stem attached, and place in a large casserole. Add the vanilla bean, lemon and orange peel, 1 cup (225 grams) of the sugar, and enough cold water to cover the pears. Bring to a boil. Place a piece of paper towel over the casserole, so that the tops of the pears are kept moist and do not discolor. Cover and simmer slowly for 5 minutes if the pears are well-ripened, and up to 35 minutes if they are green and hard. They should be tender to the point of a knife. Let cool slowly in the liquid overnight.

2. <u>Remove the paper.</u>

3. <u>Drain the pears on paper towels.</u>

4. Mix together the grated orange rind, egg yolks, the remaining ½ cup (112 grams) sugar, the vanilla extract, and gelatin. <u>Whisk until the mixture forms a ribbon.</u>

5. Bring the milk to a boil and <u>add the farina.</u> Boil, stirring, for 2 minutes until thick.

6. <u>Add the egg yolk mixture</u> and bring to a boil again. Remove from the heat, transfer to a clean bowl and cool to lukewarm, stirring occasionally to avoid a skin forming on top.

7. Mix the heavy cream with the confectioners' sugar. <u>Whip to a soft peak</u>. Do not overwhip or the custard will taste of butter, rather than of sweet cream.

8. When the farina mixture reaches room temperature, <u>fold in the whipped cream</u>.

9. Rub a 6-cup/1.4-liter mold very lightly with almond or peanut oil. Pour the mixture in, <u>cover with plastic wrap</u>, and refrigerate overnight.

10. <u>Run a knife around the "gateau."</u>

11. Invert on a large platter and <u>cover for a few seconds with a towel</u> wrung in hot water to help the unmolding.

12. <u>Unmold</u>.

13. If the sides or top are a little rough or coarse from the unmolding, <u>smooth out with a spatula or knife</u>.

14. <u>Place 1 tablespoon of the apricot jam in each of the 3 cups.</u> Add a couple of drops of red, green, and yellow food coloring to have three different colored jams. If you object to food coloring, you may use mint jelly (for green), currant jelly (for red), and apple jelly (for yellow). Prepare 4 small paper cornets.

15. Melt the chocolate in a small bowl or microwave oven. Add 1½ teaspoons lukewarm water and mix. It will curdle; add more water (up to 2 tablespoons) a little at a time, and stir well until the mixture is smooth and shiny. Fill a paper cornet with chocolate and cut the tip off. <u>Draw letters, flowers, leaves,</u> and the like according to your fancy.

16. Fill the 3 cornets with the different colored jams, and <u>squeeze inside the chocolate outlines.</u>

17. Place the pears around and <u>coat with cool apricot glaze diluted with pear brandy.</u> (Strain the remaining apricot jam through a fine sieve and dilute with the pear brandy.) Serve with extra apricot glaze.

Crêpes Suzettes

Though crêpes are best when they are fresh out of the pan, they can be refrigerated (stacked and covered) and kept for a few days. The basic crêpe can be used both for desserts and entrees. The best-known dessert crêpe is the crêpe suzette, flavored with orange and flamed at serving time with cognac and orange liqueur. You will need a large well-seasoned or no-stick skillet and a powerful gas or electric burner.

YIELD: 2 dozen crêpes

CREPE BATTER

1½ cups (225 grams) all-purpose organic flour

3 large eggs

1 teaspoon sugar

¾ teaspoon salt

1½ cups (355 milliliters) milk

⅔ stick (76 grams) unsalted butter, melted

½ cup (118 milliliters) cold water

THE SAUCE

2 sticks (1 cup/227 grams) unsalted butter, softened

8 tablespoons sugar

Grated rind of 2 oranges or 4 tangerines

Juice of 1 orange or 2 tangerines

Cognac and Grand Marnier

1. FOR THE CREPES: To make a smooth batter, put the flour, eggs, sugar, and salt with half of the milk in a bowl, and mix with a whisk. You will notice that the batter is still thick and lumpy.

2. Keep working the batter without adding more liquid. Because the mixture is thick, the threads of the whisk will break down any lumps in the flour and make the batter smooth. When smooth, thoroughly mix in the remaining milk and water, then add the melted butter and whisk until smooth. The batter should have the consistency of heavy cream; if it is too thick, add up to 1 tablespoon more water. It does not have to rest.

3. TO MAKE THE CRÊPES: Heat a 6-inch (15-centimeter) crêpe pan, or no-stick skillet. When hot, <u>spoon about 3 tablespoons of the batter into the near side of the inclined pan.</u> Shake the pan so the batter runs down the bottom of the pan and spreads over most of its surface.

4. The thinness of the crêpe is determined by the speed with which the batter is spread. As the batter touches the hot pan surface, it solidifies. If it is not spread quickly, it will solidify thickly, so it is imperative that the batter be moved quickly. It is better to have too little than too much batter in the pan. If there are holes in the crêpe, they can be filled in with a little more batter. <u>Add a few drops of batter to fill any holes in the crêpe.</u>

5. <u>The edge of the crêpe is very thin and full of tiny holes.</u> It is called a crêpe *dentelle*, which means "lace" in French. If the batter is liquid enough and it is spread quickly, the edge of the crêpe will look lacy.

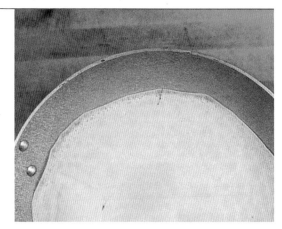

6. Cook the first side of the crêpe for approximately 1 minute. Then, <u>flip it over.</u> An alternative method of turning the crêpe is to use a fork. Lift up the cooked crêpe along the edge with the fork, then grab the crêpe between your thumb and finger and turn it over.

7. <u>Cook the crêpe for approximately 30 seconds on the other side</u>. Then remove the crêpe to a plate so the side browned first is underneath. When the crêpe is stuffed and rolled, you want to have this side showing because it looks best.

8. <u>Note that the crêpe is very thin but elastic</u> so it can hold a stuffing inside. If the crêpe were rich in cream or egg yolk, it might be thin but it would have a tendency to break. Stack the crêpes up on a plate, cover with plastic wrap, and set aside until the dessert is assembled. They will stay very moist and pliable and will separate easily when needed.

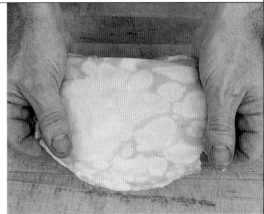

9. To make the sauce, place the butter, sugar, grated orange rind, and juice in a food processor and process until smooth. <u>Transfer to a bowl</u>.

10. At serving time, <u>melt 4 to 6 tablespoons of the sauce in the skillet</u> (about 1 tablespoon per crêpe).

11. When sizzling hot, place 4 to 6 crêpes flat in the sauce. <u>Using a fork and a spoon, turn the crêpes in the sauce.</u> When coated, fold each one into fourths (the nice side showing) and arrange in the skillet as you go along.

12. <u>Pour 1½ to 2 tablespoons of both cognac and Grand Marnier</u> on top of the crêpes.

13. Ignite with a match and, keeping your head back, <u>stir the crêpes in the flaming sauce</u>.

14. <u>Serve the crêpes on warm plates, 2 or 3 per person, with some sauce.</u> Repeat to make all the crêpes in several batches. Add more cognac and Grand Marnier to each batch.

Chocolate Cigarettes

I like bittersweet chocolate containing 70% cocoa (chocolate liquor). Take your time when you melt chocolate. Chocolate burns easily, stiffening and becoming granular and bitter when burned. The best method is to place the chocolate in a glass or stainless-steel container and leave it overnight in a regular oven with the pilot light on. Stir to get it smooth. The microwave oven is also an excellent place to melt it. Microwave the chocolate in 1 minute intervals, leaving 2 or 3 minutes between each one to prevent burning. If microwaved for 3 minutes straight, the chocolate might scorch.

Chocolate cigarettes, as well as chocolate strips and flowers, are often used in decoration. They require a bit of practice to make, but the chocolate can be melted again and reused as many times as necessary until the technique is perfected.

6 ounces (177 milliliters) melted good quality bittersweet chocolate, preferably 70% cocoa

1. You need to work on a flat, hard surface such as marble, stainless steel, or glass. <u>Pour the melted chocolate on the marble surface.</u>

2. <u>Spread with a long, narrow spatula</u>, going back and forth until the top of the chocolate becomes cloudy. It should be thin, but not too thin, at least ⅛ inch (3 millimeters) thick.

3. Take a large, strong knife. <u>Holding it on an angle, start cutting into the chocolate</u>, applying pressure down and forward on the blade of the knife. The pressure should be strong enough to bend the blade slightly.

4. <u>The chocolate rolls onto itself as you move the knife down</u>. The consistency is very important. Chocolate which is too soft will gather in a mush; chocolate which is too hard will flake and crumble under the blade. If this happens, scrape it from the marble, melt it again, and try until it works.

Fruit Salad Ambrosia

(Salade de Fruits)

This flavorful fruit salad is made with fresh as well as dried fruits that have been macerated in a sweet-sour sauce made from honey, lemon juice, rind of citrus fruit, apricot preserves, and Kirshwasser. The acid in the lemon juice keeps the fruit from discoloring. The sauce can be made ahead and the dried fruit prepared and combined with the sauce and kept in the refrigerator, ready to be added to the fresh fruit an hour or so before serving. The sauce and dried fruit mixture will keep several weeks in the refrigerator. The mixture of fruit used should be changed according to what's available in the market and your own personal taste. Look for different flavors in the fruit as well as different textures and colors. Remember that even though pineapples, apples, pears, and bananas may look different before they are peeled, their flesh is basically the same color.

YIELD: 6 to 8 servings

FRUIT MACERATING SAUCE
3 strips lemon rind

3 strips lime rind

3 strips orange rind

⅓ cup (80 milliliters) honey

⅓ cup (80 milliliters) fresh lemon juice

¼ cup (59 milliliters) apricot preserves

2 tablespoons Kirshwasser

DRY FRUIT MIXTURE
¼ cup (37 grams) dark raisins

⅓ cup (50 grams) dried apricot halves

8 pitted prunes, cut into ½-inch (1.3-centimeter) slices

2 dried peach halves, cut into ½-inch (1.3-centimeter) strips

FRESH FRUIT MIXTURE
1 pineapple (to make 1½ cups/240 grams pineapple pieces)

1½ cups sliced mixture of papaya and mango

1 banana, sliced

1 cup (100 grams) pitted cherries

1 cup (100 grams) seedless grapes

½ persimmon, peeled and cut into wedges

1. FOR THE FRUIT MACERATING SAUCE: Stack 3 strips each of lemon, lime, and orange rind (peeled with a vegetable peeler) and cut into a fine julienne. You should have approximately 2 tablespoons of the combined julienned rinds.

2. In a bowl, combine the rind with honey, lemon juice, apricot preserves, and Kirschwasser. This makes a nice base for the fruit mixture.

3. Add the dried fruit mixture to the macerating sauce. This mixture can be made ahead and stored in a jar in the refrigerator for several weeks.

4. FOR THE FRESH FRUIT: Cut the pineapple into halves and then wedges. Cut off the top of each wedge—the central woody core of the fruit—and then <u>cut the flesh to separate it from the rind</u>.

5. With the pineapple wedges still on the rind, <u>cut into little slices about ½ inch (1.3 centimeters) thick</u> and add to the mixture in the bowl.

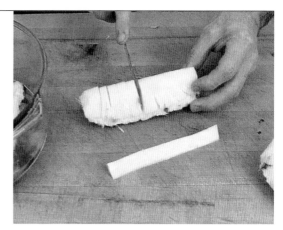

6. Add the balance of the fresh fruit mixture and <u>mix well</u>. Spoon into dessert dishes and serve.

Strawberry Sherbet

(Sorbet aux Fraises)

There are lots of different types of "iced desserts"—ices, sorbet, spum, marquise, granité. All are conventionally made from fruits or fruit juices, although different cooks may interpret them differently. Fruit sherbets or sorbets have a truer taste when made only with water, sugar, and a fruit purée. With the addition of cream the fruit tends to lose its identity. Very juicy fruits like lemon or pineapple, or berries such as black currants, raspberries, or strawberries, make the best sherbets. Commercial sherbets are made in ice cream machines. We prefer to use the machine for regular ice cream only, because it tends to emulsify the sherbert mixture too much. Beating air into a mixture of milk, cream, and eggs makes it light and smooth. However, in sherberts too much air changes the color and taste of the fruit. It makes it too light and too foamy and changes the texture, as well as diluting the fruit taste. The less distinctive the taste of the fruit, the less it should be emulsified.

YIELD: 6 servings

1½ pounds (681 grams) fresh strawberries or raspberries, ripe, hulled

¾ cup (169 grams) sugar (or more or less depending on the sweetness and ripeness of the fruit)

Juice of ½ large lemon (¼ cup/59 milliliters)

2 tablespoons corn syrup

RASPBERRY SAUCE

1 cup (170 grams) fresh raspberries

1 10-ounce/283-gram package frozen unsweetened raspberries, defrosted

⅔ cup (158 milliliters) seedless rasberry preserves

1 tablespoon raspberry brandy, kirsch, or cognac

Strain combined sauce ingredients through a fine strainer or food mill.

1. FOR THE SHERBET: Place the ingredients for the sherbet in a food processor and process for about 1 minute. Strain to remove seeds. <u>Place the mixture in a stainless steel bowl</u> in the freezer for 2 hours. Stir it once in a while.

2. When the mixture is partially frozen and grainy, place it back in the food processor for about 30 seconds to emulsify. It will liquefy and get softer, whiter, and much smoother. <u>Place back in a bowl</u>, cover with plastic wrap, and freeze to harden for a few hours before serving. At this point, the mixture is usually spooned with an ice cream scoop and served with the raspberry sauce.

3. TO MAKE INDIVIDUAL BOMBES: Line small containers with plastic wrap, fill with the sherbert and freeze. When the mixture is hard, <u>hollow the center with a spoon</u>, place a piece of plastic wrap into the cavity and keep it in the freezer until needed.

4. Before serving time, <u>fill the center of the mold with fresh berries</u>, top with a plate and invert. Serve with raspberry sauce around.

Vanilla Ice Cream in Netty Cups with Spicy Cherries in Wine

This rich vanilla ice cream made with fresh vanilla beans is distinctive in taste and has a luscious texture. Although it can be served by itself, the crunchy texture and nutty taste of the cookie cup is quite complementary.

The quantity of dough needed for each cup is approximately 1½ tablespoons. If the cups are made ahead, be sure to store them carefully in a tightly sealed container to keep them for getting soggy.

The cherries are cooked in red wine and spices, with port wine and cognac added. They make an excellent dessert by themselves with a little sour cream and a slice of pound cake. The cherries will keep in a jar, refrigerated, for weeks.

YIELD: 8 servings

VANILLA ICE CREAM
2 to 3 vanilla beans, depending on size
2 cups (474 milliliters) milk
2 cups (474 milliliters) heavy cream
4 large egg yolks
1 large egg
1 tablespoon pure vanilla extract
1 cup (225 grams) sugar

SPICY CHERRIES IN WINE
3 pounds (1.4 kilograms) Bing or sweet cherries, pitted
¾ cup (169 grams) sugar
½ teaspoon ground cinnamon
⅛ teaspoon ground allspice
⅛ teaspoon ground nutmeg
⅛ teaspoon ground cloves
Dash cayenne pepper
1 tablespoon pure vanilla extract
1½ cups (355 milliliters) dry red wine

1½ teaspoons cornstarch dissolved in 1 tablespoon water
¼ cup (60 milliliters) sweet port wine
2 tablespoons cognac

NETTY CUP DOUGH
¾ cup (115 grams) blanched almonds
2 tablespoons all-purpose organic flour
⅔ stick (2.5 ounces/76 grams) butter
1 tablespoon milk
¾ cup (169 grams) sugar

FOR THE DOUGH: Grind the almonds in the food processor with the flour until very fine. (The flour will absorb any oil released by the almonds and will produce a finer mixture). Add the butter, cut into pieces, and the milk and sugar. Process for 8 to 10 seconds, just long enough for the mixture to form into a ball.

1. FOR THE VANILLA ICE CREAM: Break the vanilla beans, <u>place them in a small coffee or spice grinder or mini food processor, and pulverize them into a powder.</u> If the vanilla-bean mixture is still a bit soft and gooey, add some of the sugar from the recipe to the grinder so that it grinds into a fine powder.

2. Pour the milk and 1 cup (237 milliliters) of the cream into a saucepan and bring to a boil. Pour the remaining cold cream into a large bowl. Mix the egg yolks, egg, vanilla extract, sugar, and powdered vanilla with a whisk. Combine with the boiling milk and cream, and place the mixture back over the heat just long enough for it to thicken, which will occur when it reaches approximately 180 degrees (82°C). Do not overcook the mixture or it will tend to curdle. As soon as the mixture thickens, <u>pour it into the cold cream, which will cool it and prevent it from cooking further and curdling.</u> <u>Combine well.</u>

3. Place the mixture in an ice cream maker and make according to the manufacturer's instructions (it should take from 30 to 45 minutes). <u>Then tightly pack the ice cream in a bowl or other container,</u> and place it in the freezer, covered, until serving time.

4. FOR THE SPICY CHERRIES IN WINE: <u>Place the cherries, sugar, cinnamon, allspice, nutmeg, cloves, cayenne, vanilla, and dry red wine in a large saucepan, preferably stainless steel.</u> Bring the mixture to a boil and cook for 2 to 3 minutes, covered. Let cool, still covered, until lukewarm. Strain off the juice (approximately 2 to 3 cups/ 474 to 711 milliliters), and reduce it to 1¼ cups (296 milliliters). Add the cornstarch dissolved in water to the juice and bring to a boil. Pour over the cherries. When the cherries are lukewarm, add the port wine and cognac and mix well. At this point, the mixture can be poured into a jar and refrigerated.

5. FOR THE NETTY CUPS: Preheat the oven to 350 degrees (177°C). Line a cookie sheet with a piece of parchment paper (cut the paper into fourths) oiled very lightly on both sides and pressed flat on the cookie sheet. Place about 1½ tablespoons of the dough on each of the 4 pieces of paper. Wet your fingers or a spoon and press the dough into disks about 2½ inches (6 centimeters) across, making them as round as possible.

6. Bake for approximately 12 minutes. The dough should spread and be nicely browned all around. Lift up each piece of paper, turn it over, and peel the paper off. Reserve the paper (it does not need to be oiled again) for the next cookies.

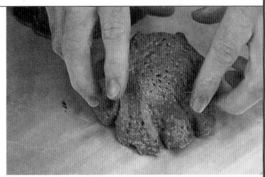

7. Press the hot cookies (top side out) around half-cup molds (little Pyrex cups are ideal), pushing gently all around so they conform to the shape of the molds. Allow to harden before removing. Work quickly. If the cookies get too cool, they will break. If they are too hot, they will separate on the molds. If they harden too much to shape them, return to the oven for 1 minute to soften.

8. The cherries in wine should be served very cold. Place 2 to 3 tablespoons of the cherry and juice mixture on each serving plate.

9. Place the netty cup in the center of each plate and fill with a ball of the vanilla ice cream. Top with a cherry, spoon a little juice over the ice cream, and serve immediately.

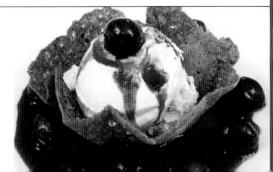

Pie Dough and Pie Shell

(Pâte Brisée et Croûte)

Pie dough, pâte brisée, is certainly the most useful all-purpose dough in French cooking. Though the dough is easier to make with a combination of butter and shortening, an all-butter dough is finer. However, for quiche, tourte (meat pies), and the like, the difference is difficult to detect. The reasons are that the quiche is served hot or lukewarm, and the filling (bacon, mushrooms, onions, and the like) has a strong taste of its own. The difference would be quite apparent in a shell for a raspberry tart because it is served cold and the filling is very delicate.

When working with dough, remember that the more you knead and the more water you use, the more elasticity and shrinkage you get. The less water and the more fat you use, the more crumbly and lax the dough will be. At one end of the spectrum you have the bread dough (flour and water) which is elastic, springy and unrollable. At the other end of the spectrum, the cookie dough (mainly flour and fat) is soft, crumbly, and hard to roll. The pie dough is in the middle and will lean toward one side or the other, depending on your ingredients and method.

YIELD: 1 pie shell

2 cups (300 grams) all-purpose organic flour
1½ sticks (6 ounces/168 grams) unsalted butter, very cold and cut into ¼-inch cubes
¼ teaspoon salt
½ teaspoon sugar
⅓ cup cold water, approximately

1. Place the flour, butter, salt and sugar in a large bowl. Mix the ingredients enough so that <u>all the butter pieces are coated with flour.</u>

2. Add water and <u>start kneading the ingredients to gather the dough into a ball.</u> Do not worry if there are little pieces of plain butter here and there. This will give flakiness to the dough, making it slightly similar to a puff paste. The dough should be malleable and usable right away. If overworked, it will become elastic, in which case you should let it rest in the refrigerator for 1 hour before using.

3. Place the dough on a floured board and <u>roll uniformly, turning the dough a quarter of a turn as you are rolling</u> so that it forms a nice "wheel." Be sure the board is well floured underneath. The dough should be approximately ⅛-inch (3-millimeters) thick, although many cooks like it thicker.

4. <u>Roll the dough back</u>

5. <u>on the rolling pin.</u>

6. Lift up and

7. unroll on a flan ring or other mold.

8. With the tips of your fingers, push in the corners so that the dough does not get stretched, which would cause it to shrink during the baking.

9. Squeeze a lip all around the inside of the flan ring, working the dough between your thumb and forefinger.

10. Use a knife, or <u>roll your pin on top of the ring to trim the excess dough.</u>

11. <u>Remove the trimmings.</u> (The excess dough can be stored in the refrigerator for a few days, or frozen.) Re-form the edge between your thumb and forefinger.

12. <u>Mark the edges with a dough crimper</u> or the tines of a fork, or by squeezing it between your fingers. Re-form the edges between thumb and forefinger.

13. <u>Shell, ready to be used.</u> If your recipe calls for a precooked shell, line the shell with wax paper and weight it down with beans or the like to prevent the dough from shrinking during the first 15 minutes of baking. Then remove the beans and paper and continue cooking.

Sweet Pie Dough and Pastry Shell

(Pâte Sucrée et Croûte)

The sweet pie dough, pâte sucrée, is quite different from the pâte brisée described in the preceding technique. The texture is not flaky or tender, but rather is close to that of a cookie dough. The dough is not at all elastic or springy. It rolls easily but is a little difficult to pick up. It makes an excellent shell for runny ingredients because it does not get soggy as easily as regular pie dough. This recipe makes enough dough for two 9-inch (23-centimeter) pies.

YIELD: 2 pastry shells

3 cups (450 grams) all-purpose organic flour

2½ sticks (1¼ cup/283 grams) unsalted butter, cut into pieces, softened

½ cup (112 grams) sugar

¼ teaspoon salt

1 large egg and 1 large egg yolk, beaten lightly with a fork, for egg wash

1. Preheat the oven to 400 degrees (204°C). Place the flour in the middle of the work table. Make a well in the center and add the remaining ingredients. Gather the dough, with a pastry scraper or your fingers, into a compact mass.

2. Place the dough close to you and, with the heel of your hand, take a mass about the size of a golf ball and "smear" it about 10 inches (25 centimeters) forward. Keep your fingers pointed upwards. Repeat, smearing more and more of the dough forward, until it has all been processed. Gather the dough into a ball and repeat the operation once more. The two smearings (*fraisage* in French) help homogenize the ingredients, making a well-blended dough.

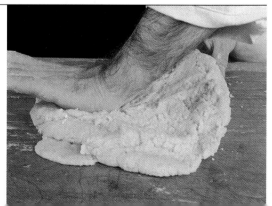

3. Roll the dough and fit it into a mold as described in steps 3 to 7 of the preceding technique. You can use a flan ring or a tart mold with a removable bottom, as pictured here.

4. Cut a round disk of wax paper, fold into triangle, and fringe the edge with a pair of scissors.

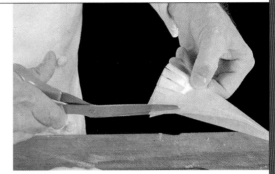

5. Line the dough with the paper. Fill the shell with dry beans, rice, pebbles, or any heavy, dry ingredient, to hold the dough in place during the baking.

6. Place on a cookie sheet and bake for approximately 45 minutes. Remove the paper and beans and keep for later use.

7. Brush the inside of the shell with an egg wash. Return to the oven for 10 minutes.

8. <u>Remove from mold</u>. The egg coating forms a waterproof layer and prevents the dough from getting soggy when filled with cream or juicy fruits. The same technique is used with *pâte brisée* on those occasions when you precook a shell for quiche or custard.

9. The dough should always be well cooked and crunchy (better overcooked than underdone). If, by a stroke of bad luck, the dough burns underneath, turn upside down when cool, and <u>rub with a grater to remove the blackened part</u>.

Cream Cheese Dough

(Pâte au "Cream Cheese")

1 cup (120 grams) all-purpose organic flour (about 5½ ounces)
½ stick butter (¼ cup/57 grams)
4 ounces (114 grams) cream cheese, at room temperature

Preheat the oven to 375 degrees (191°C). Place the flour and butter, cut in pieces, into the bowl of a food processor, and process for about 10 to 15 seconds. Then add the cream cheese in pieces and process approximately 10 seconds more, until the mixture forms a ball. The dough can be made ahead and refrigerated or used immediately. To roll, <u>flour a board lightly and roll the dough out very thin (¹/₈ inch/3 millimeters thick) into a circle</u>. Roll it back onto the rolling pin and place in a mold and weight as per the previous technique. Bake for 20 minutes.

Apple Tart
(Tarte aux Pommes)

Open-faced tarts are as distinctly French as apple pie is American. The dough can be arranged in a flan ring as shown below, or in a removable bottom mold, or in a regular pie plate. It can also be cooked free form on a cookie sheet with the edges rolled to hold in the filling. I like the dough rolled very thin and the shell well-cooked. Any apple can be used, keeping in mind that some are more tart than others, and some hold their shape better than others while cooking.

Prepared Pie Dough, page 562
4 to 5 apples
3 tablespoons sugar
2 tablespoons (28 grams) unsalted butter
Apricot or apple jam (optional)
Calvados, cognac, or kirsch (optional)

1. Preheat the oven to 400 degrees (204°C). Make your pie dough and fit it into a 9-inch (23-centimeter) ring or mold. Trim both the stem and flower ends of 4 to 5 good-sized apples. Holding a paring knife by the blade, use only the point of the knife and your thumb as a pivot to cut the stem off. (This technique can also be used for pears, tomatoes, and the like.)

2. Using a vegetable peeler or a sharp paring knife, peel the apples. Cut into halves through the stem and remove the seeds with the point of the knife, using the method described in step 1.

3. <u>Cut into about ¼-inch (6-millimeter) slices</u>. Chop the end slices coarsely, reserving the uniform center slices.

4. <u>Arrange the chopped apples on the bottom of the pie shell</u>.

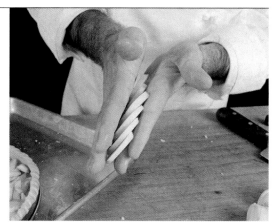

5. <u>Fan out the center slices as you would a deck of cards</u> and

6. <u>arrange on top of the chopped apples</u>. (You may arrange the slices one by one if you feel it is easier.)

7. <u>Arrange apple slices in the center of the shell</u>

8. <u>to simulate the petals of a rose</u>.

9. <u>Sprinkle with sugar and butter cut into pieces</u>.

10. Bake for approximately 75 minutes. It should be well browned and the crust golden. <u>Remove the flan ring</u>. The pie shrinks slightly during baking, making the ring easy to remove.

11. Using a large metal spatula, remove the pie from the cookie sheet and glaze (optional) with an apricot or apple jam. (Strain apricot jam through a fine sieve and dilute slightly with calvados, cognac, kirsch, or even water, if you object to alcohol.) Serve at room temperature; refrigeration is not recommended.

Tarte Tatin

Tarte tatin is the famous upside-down, caramelized apple tart created many years ago by two sisters called the Demoiselles Tatin. It is an example of a dish that originated in the home kitchen, became a regional specialty, and eventually made its way into most of the great restaurants.

There are many variations on the original concoction. In my version, I cook the apples with the skins on to give a crustier, chewier texture. Dried currants (although regular dried raisins could be substituted), slivered almonds, and dried apricots help fill the holes between the large segments of apple and give taste as well as texture to the tart. Additional apples on top of the large apple segments make the dish thicker and create a flat surface for the pastry to sit on, which results in a nicer shape when unmolded.

The extra caramel added at the end can be omitted for a tarter dish. The tart should be served at room temperature or slightly warm.

YIELD: 8 to 10 servings

PATE BRISEE

1 cup (150 grams) all-purpose organic flour (about 5½ ounces)

¾ stick (6 tablespoons/85 grams) unsalted butter

⅛ teaspoon salt

½ teaspoon sugar

3 tablespoons ice cold water

FILLING

¼ cup (56 grams) sugar

5 tablespoons (72 grams) unsalted butter

1 tablespoon fresh lemon juice

4 pounds (1.8 kilograms) Golden Delicious apples (about 10)

¼ cup (25 grams) slivered almonds

½ cup (75 grams) sliced dried apricots

⅓ cup (50 grams) dried currants

¾ cup (178 milliliters) water

2 tablespoons (28 grams) unsalted butter

TO GLAZE THE DOUGH

2 teaspoons sugar

CARAMEL GLAZE (OPTIONAL)

3 tablespoons sugar

1 tablespoon water

1 teaspoon (5 grams) unsalted butter

GARNISH

1 cup (237 milliliters) heavy cream

1. FOR THE DOUGH: Preheat the oven to 400 degrees (204°C). Although the dough can be made by hand, a mixer with the flat beater attachment does the job well and easily. In the summer, it is a good idea to keep the flour in the freezer and the butter refrigerated until ready to add since it is important in a *pâte brisée* to mix all the ingredients together quickly to keep the gluten from developing too much. The butter should remain visible in the dough—not blended into it. The butter will melt during the baking and develop some of the flakiness you find in a puff paste. Put the flour in the mixer bowl and cut the butter into ¼-inch (6-millimeter)-thick slivers, letting them fall into the flour.

2. Add the salt and sugar and, using the flat beater, mix on low speed of an electric mixer for about 45 seconds. At that point, pieces of butter should still be visible in the dough. Add the cold water and mix on low speed for about 20 seconds, just until the mixture starts gathering together. Note the texture of the dough as you turn it out onto a large piece of plastic wrap.

3. Cover the dough with another piece of wrap the same size. Roll the dough out between the plastic sheets. (If you were to roll it out on the table at this point, the softness of the butter would make it necessary to use a great amount of flour to prevent the butter from sticking, and this would tend to make the dough tough.) The pieces of butter are still visible in the dough through the plastic. Place in the refrigerator for 10 to 15 minutes while preparing the apples. The dough is only partially rolled out—it is still too thick to use.

4. Remove the cores from the apples at the stem end and at the opposite end, using your thumb as a pivot and rotating the tip of a sharp paring knife as you cut into the apple. Split the apples in half, and remove the cores from the centers with the same circular cutting motion. Then, cut again into quarters.

5. FOR THE FILLING: Heat the sugar, butter, and lemon juice in a 12-inch (30-centimeter) skillet, and cook until it becomes caramel—3 to 4 minutes. Add the slivered almonds and cook for 10 to 15 seconds. Remove from the heat.

6. Arrange the apple quarters on top of the caramel, placing them skin-side down in one layer, making two concentric rows with a piece of apple in the center. You will use 6 to 7 of the apples, 20 to 25 pieces.

7. Sprinkle the apricots and currants on top. Slice the remainder of the apples thin and add to the skillet to fill it completely.

8. Add the water, bring the mixture to a boil, cover, and boil gently for 5 to 6 minutes. The object here is to soften the apples so they sink down and form a flat surface. Remove the lid and continue cooking on top of the stove over medium heat for about 7 to 8 minutes, <u>until there is no visible liquid when you incline the pan slightly</u>. This indicates that most of the moisture has been boiled away and what remains is the sugar and butter, which is beginning to caramelize.

9. Remove the dough from the plastic wrap and place it on the board. Sprinkle with a little flour and <u>roll very thin</u> (no more than ⅛ inch/3 millimeters).

10. Trim the edge and <u>fold it in on itself</u> to form an edge that is a little thicker all around.

11. Dot the top of the tart with the butter, broken into pieces, and <u>place the circle of dough on top</u>. Press it down with your hand so it lies completely flat. Pierce with a fork all over and sprinkle with the sugar, which will caramelize on the dough during cooking.

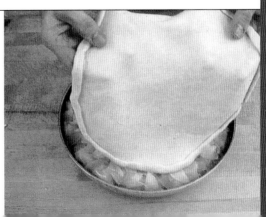

12. If the handle of your skillet is plastic, wrap it with several layers of aluminum foil to protect it, and bake for 45 minutes. To see if the juices are caramelized, incline the pan. If any visible juices remain, place the skillet back on the heat for 3 to 4 minutes, until you see that the boiling juices have turned into caramel throughout and the top is a solid mass when the tart is moved.

13. At serving time, heat the tart to make sure it is loose, and invert the apples onto a serving platter.

14. To make a caramel glaze (which is optional), heat the sugar, water, and butter in a skillet until the mixture turns a light caramel color. Immediately, using a brush or spoon, coat the surface of the apples. This coating of caramel will last for a few hours but will eventually melt down.

15. Beat the heavy cream until firm but not too stiff to use as a garnish. No sugar is needed since the apples are sweet. Cut the tart into wedges and serve immediately with a good tablespoon of whipped cream per serving.

Galette of Rhubarb

(Galette de Rhubarbe)

For this large country-style galette, the dough is rolled very thin, from ¹⁄₁₆ to ⅛ inch (1 to 3 millimeters). Any type of fruit can be placed in the center, then the edge of the dough is folded over the fruit, and the resulting galette is baked in a hot oven. For any fruits that tends to produce a lot of liquid when cooked—such as plums, rhubarb, grapes, and the like—spread a mixture of ground almonds, flour, and sugar on the dough before adding the fruit to absorb the liquid.

YIELD: 8 to 10 servings

PROCESSOR PATE BRISEE
1½ cups (180 grams) all-purpose organic flour
¼ teaspoon salt
1½ sticks (¾ cup/170 grams) cold unsalted butter, cut into pieces
⅓ cup ice cold water

FILLING
2½ pounds (1.1 kilograms) rhubarb
⅓ cup (62 grams) sugar
3 tablespoons (42 grams) unsalted butter

BOTTOM MIXTURE
3 tablespoons ground almonds
3 tablespoons all-purpose organic flour
¼ cup (60 grams) sugar

GLAZE
Mixture of ¾ cup (250 grams) apricot and raspberry or plum preserves, strained together

1. Preheat the oven to 400 degrees (204°C). To make the dough in a food processor, the butter should be very cold and cut into small pieces. Place the flour, salt, and butter in the food processor and process for about 5 seconds. The butter should still be in pieces. Add the cold water and process about 5 seconds more, just enough for the dough to start gathering together. The little pieces of butter should still be visible in the dough. Remove the dough from the processor and gather it into a ball. Refrigerate or use immediately.

2. <u>Roll the dough out into a large oval no more than ⅛ inch (3 millimeters) thick.</u> It will be approximately 18 to 19 inches (46 to 48 centimeters) long by 16 inches (41 centimeters) wide. Tiny pieces of butter should still be visible in the dough at this point. Transfer the dough to a cookie sheet, rolling it up on the rolling pin and unrolling it onto the sheet, and refrigerate it while you prepare the bottom mixture and filling.

3. <u>Cut the rhubarb into 2- to 2½-inch (5- to 6½-centimeter) pieces</u> and, if the ribs are large, split them in half the long way. Discard the leaves.

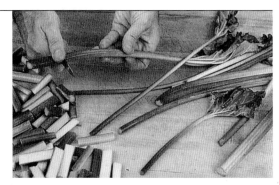

4. Combine the ground almonds, flour, and sugar, and <u>spread the mixture out on the dough</u> to within approximately 2 inches (5 centimeters) of the edge.

5. Place the rhubarb pieces casually in the center of the dough. Fold the edges of the dough up over the fruit to create a border of about 2 inches (5 centimeters), and <u>sprinkle with the sugar and butter.</u> Some of the sugar should be sprinkled on the border of the dough.

6. Bake the galette for 1 hour. <u>The dough should be very crunchy, well-cooked, and brown, and the fruit in the center very soft.</u> If any of the juices have leaked through the dough onto the tray, be sure to slide a knife underneath and move the pie slightly while it is still hot because the juices will harden and the pie will stick to the tray as it cools.

7. Spoon the glaze over the top of the *galette* and spread it with a spoon or brush. Spread some of the glaze on the dough border. <u>Cut into wedges and serve at room temperature</u> as is or with a little whipped cream.

Galette of Lemon

(Galette au Citron)

A galette is an open-faced tart, very thin and crunchy, usually made in a round shape and cut into large, pizza-type slices. Although it is usually a country dessert, it can become very elegant with the addition of a sauce. The lemon galette is made with a pâte sucrée (sweet dough) and the apple galette, with a pâte brisée (pie dough). It is a good dessert for a large party. It's easy to make and serve, and keeps quite well for hours.

YIELD: 10 to 12 servings

PATE SUCREE
- 3 cups (450 grams) all-purpose organic flour
- 2½ sticks (1¼ cup/283 grams) unsalted butter, softened
- ½ cup (112 grams) granulated sugar
- ¼ teaspoon salt
- 1 large egg and 1 large egg yolk, beaten

To make the dough, combine the pâté sucrée ingredients in a bowl and work until it holds together. Place on the table. Crush or smear the mixture with the palm of your hand a few times until the mixture is well blended. Or place in a food processor and process until it gathers together. Divide into two pieces. Roll the first piece into a 14-inch (35.5-centimeter) round, about ¼ inch (6 millimeters) thick.

LEMON FILLING
- 10 large egg yolks
- ¾ cup (169 grams) granulated sugar
- 1 tablespoon, plus 1 teaspoon, cornstarch
- Grated rind of 2 lemons (approximately 1 tablespoon)
- Juice of 3 lemons (approximately ⅔ cup/158 milliliters)
- 1 lemon, peeled and cut into very thin slices

SAUCE
- 3 large egg yolks
- ½ cup (50 grams) confectioners' sugar
- 3 tablespoons Grand Marnier
- 2 cups (473 milliliters) sour cream

1. Preheat the oven to 400 degrees (204°C). Roll 1 piece of the dough on your rolling pin and unroll onto a cookie sheet. It is a delicate dough to roll as it tends to break. Remembering that the *pâte sucrée* cannot be rolled as thin as a *pâte brisée* or a puff paste or it will burn. Trim the edge of the dough and <u>fold it back onto itself all around</u>.

2. Fold the dough over once again to make a border approximately ½ inch (13 millimeters) high. Press the border with your fingers to bring it to a point on top. <u>The base will be wide and the top pointed like a triangle (see arrow)</u>. This keeps the border from collapsing during cooking.

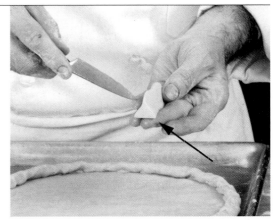

3. <u>Use your fingers to pinch and press a decorative border all around</u>.

4. Roll the rest of the dough and trim it into a rectangular or square shape. Make the border.

5. Bake both shells for 12 to 15 minutes to pre-cook lightly. They will be baked again later with their fillings. If there are any holes in the crust, underline patch with a bit of extra dough or water mixed with flour. The lemon galette batter is liquid and if there are any holes it will seep through during cooking.

6. Reduce the oven to 375 degrees (191°C). To prepare the lemon filling, mix the yolks and sugar together and whip with a whisk for 2 to 3 minutes, until it reaches the ribbon stage. Add the cornstarch and lemon rind, mix well, then add the lemon juice. underline Divide the mixture between the two pre-cooked shells.

7. underline Arrange the slices of lemon on top and immediately place in the oven. The oven rack and the cookie sheet must be very flat or the batter will run on one side or spill over. Bake for 18 to 20 minutes.

8. As the dough cooks, underline the batter will pleat and pull around the slices of lemon and form a design by itself. Let cool and cut into wedges. For the sauce, mix the egg yolks and sugar together and work with a whisk for 1 to 2 minutes. Stir in the Grand Marnier and sour cream. Serve 2 tablespoons next to each slice.

Cream Puff Dough

(Pâte à Choux)

Along with pâte brisée, *and* feuilletage, pâte à choux *is one of the mother doughs of French pastry making. It is used to make countless desserts such as éclairs and* choux, *gâteau St. Honoré and Paris-Brest, as well as such dishes as pommes dauphine and even quenelles. It is always made with what is called a* panade—*a combination of water, butter, and flour—to which eggs are added.*

YIELD: Dough for 14 to 16 *choux* or éclairs

1 cup (237 milliliters) water
½ stick (4 tablespoons/57 grams) unsalted butter
¼ teaspoon salt
1 cup (150 grams) all-purpose organic flour
4 large eggs

1. Combine the water, butter (cut into pieces), and salt in a heavy saucepan. Bring to a boil. <u>When the butter is completely melted, remove from the heat and add the flour all at once.</u>

2. <u>Mix rapidly with a wooden spatula until the dough gathers together and begins to form a ball.</u>

3. Place the mixture on top of a low flame and "dry" for 1 to 2 minutes, mixing with the wooden spatula. <u>The dough should be soft</u> and should not stick to your fingers when pinched. This mixture is called the *panade*.

4. You will notice that <u>the bottom of the pan is covered with a thin crust</u> (an indication that the dough has been sufficiently dried). The eggs are mixed into the *panade* in the bowl because if they were added in the pan, the white crust at the bottom would break into dried little pieces that would stick in the dough.

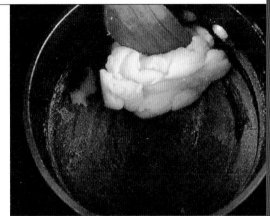

5. Transfer the *panade* to a clean bowl. Let the dough cool for at least 5 minutes. Add the eggs one at a time, <u>beating carefully after each addition</u> so that the mixture is smooth before the next egg is added. As you add the eggs, it will seem as though they will not blend. Keep mixing; the dough will come together and smooth out. It can also be mixed in a food processor.

6. <u>The dough should be smooth, shiny, and as thick and as heavy as mayonnaise</u>. This makes enough dough for 14 to 16 *choux* or éclairs, which are described in the following technique.

Cream Puffs

(Choux et Eclairs)

The only difference between a choux *and an* éclair *is that the former is round and the latter is long. Both can be filled with flavored whipped cream, pastry cream, ice cream, jam, and the like. The smallest* choux *are known as* profiteroles *and are often filled with vanilla ice cream and served with a lukewarm chocolate sauce. (The* ganache *used for the icing in the* gâteau au chocolat *can be diluted with water and used as a chocolate sauce.)*

1. Preheat the oven to 375 degrees (191°C). Prepare the *pâte à choux* following the recipe in the preceding technique. Fill a pastry bag with the dough and coat a large cookie sheet with butter and flour. <u>Squeeze out puffs about the size of small golf balls</u> or elongated éclairs.

2. <u>Brush the tops with an egg wash</u> (1 whole egg, with half of the white removed, beaten), pushing down the "tails." The *choux* can also be formed by dropping spoonfuls of dough on the cookie sheet.

3. Drag the tines of a fork to make a design on top of the éclairs. Let the *choux* and éclairs dry for at least 20 minutes before cooking. (The egg wash gives a shiny glaze, providing it is allowed to dry for a while before baking.)

4. Bake for 35 minutes, or until well puffed and golden. Shut off the heat, open the oven door halfway (to get rid of any steam) and let the puffs cool slowly and dry for 30 minutes inside the oven. *Pâte à choux* will soften and collapse if cooled too fast. Cut into halves to fill or, if you want to, keep them whole. Using the tip of a knife, make a hole in the bottom of each *choux*. Fill a pastry bag with your filling of choice and insert the tube through the opening and squeeze the filling inside.

Cream Puff Swans

(Cygnes en Pâte à Choux)

YIELD: 12 swans

Cream Puff Dough, page 578

RASPBERRY SAUCE
12 ounces (340 grams) raspberries or 1 twelve-
  ounce (340-gram) package frozen unsweetened
  raspberries, thawed
1 cup (320 grams) seedless raspberry preserves

1 tablespoon raspberry brandy or framboise

CARAMEL FOR CAGE
1 cup (220 grams) granulated sugar
3 tablespoons water

Confectioners' sugar for dusting the swans

1. Preheat the oven to 375 degrees (191°C). Prepare the *pâte à choux* (page 578). Fill a pastry bag with the dough and coat a large cookie sheet with butter and flour. Squeeze large teardrops of dough onto the cookie sheet. The technique is to press some dough on the cookie sheet, stop pressing and pull the pastry bag back to create a tail.

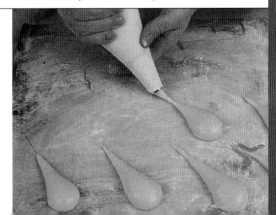

2. Make a paper cornet, fill with dough, and <u>squeeze out small necks shaped like question marks</u>.

3. <u>Make a pointed beak by pulling the cornet up.</u>

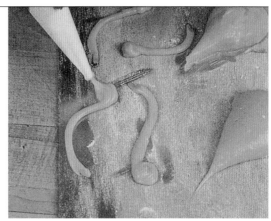

4. Brush the piped pastry shapes with an egg wash (1 whole egg, beaten). Bake for 10 to 12 minutes. Remove the small question marks and return the cream puffs to the oven for another 25 minutes, a total baking time for the cream puffs of 35 to 40 minutes. Shut off the heat and open the oven door halfway, allowing the steam to escape. Let cool in the oven and dry for 30 minutes.

5. Holding the *choux* on the side, <u>slice off the top</u> on a diagonal with a sharp, long-bladed knife. These are the swan bodies.

6. <u>Cut the removed lids in half lengthwise.</u> They will be used as wings on the swan bodies.

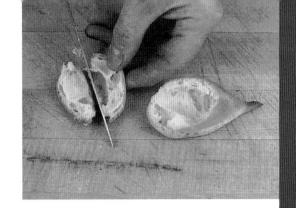

7. <u>Fill the swan bodies with sweetened whipped cream.</u>

8. Place both pieces of the lid on the cream to simulate wings. The cream will hold them in place. <u>Stick the neck into the cream between the point of the wings.</u> Sprinkle with confectioners' sugar. (Variation: Place 1 tablespoon of raspberry jam in the bottom of the opened swan. Top with a small scoop of vanilla ice cream and decorate with whipped cream. Place the wings and the necks into place.) Just before serving, pour diluted raspberry jam or raspberry sauce into a large platter. Arrange the swans so they appear to be swimming in the sauce. Surround with angel hair (see page 536).

TO MAKE THE RASPBERRY SAUCE: Place the raspberries with the preserves in the food processor and process until smooth. Pour through a fairly coarse strainer. At first, do not press on the seeds with a spatula while straining the sauce as this tends to plug the holes of the strainer. <u>Instead, bang on the rim of the strainer with a wooden spoon or spatula to make the mixture jump</u>, thus keeping the little seeds from clogging the holes of the strainer and allowing most of the liquid to go through.

Finally, to extract any remaining liquid, press on the seeds. Add 1 tablespoon of raspberry brandy to the strained sauce.

9. Place about 3 tablespoons of raspberry sauce on a serving plate and position a swan in the center. Serve immediately.

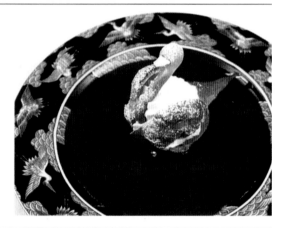

10. An alternative way of serving is to place about 1 cup of the raspberry sauce on a large platter and <u>arrange the swans on top so they face one another.</u>

11. To make the serving platter even fancier, a caramel cage can be placed on top of the swans.

FOR THE CARAMEL CAGE: Combine the granulated sugar and water in a saucepan, and cook on top of the stove until the mixture turns a caramel color. Then remove the pot and place in cold water for 10 to 15 seconds, stirring it to cool the mixture and thicken the caramel (it should be fairly thick for making the cage).

To make the cage, oil an inverted copper or stainless steel bowl. (The copper bowl is nice because it has a rounded bottom rather than a flat base.) To make a caramel cage successfully, follow the principles of good construction: i.e., don't splatter the caramel indiscriminately all around the mold but first go from one side to the other to create supporting "beams" across. <u>Drizzle a few rings around the bottom, rotating the bowl to form a base for the cage and to hold the beams together.</u>

12. <u>Swirl some interconnecting caramel lines into the open spaces between the crossed lines on top. Make several circles in the center on top</u> to strengthen the construction, and continue spooning the caramel to create a design and hold the lines together.

13. After it cools and sets on the mold for at least 10 to 15 minutes, <u>lift off the cage</u> by pushing it up in a couple of places on one side. The pushing will be registered on the other side and the entire cage can be easily removed from the oiled mold.

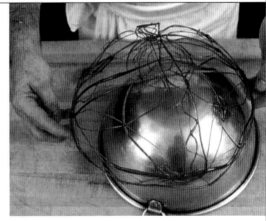

14. Place the cage on top of the swans. Add a few fresh flowers, inserting them into the "iron work" of the cage for a more striking effect, and serve.

Cream Puff Ring

(Paris-Brest)

The Paris-Brest *is made from a ring of* pâte à choux *that is baked and filled with praline cream and whipped cream, then topped with sliced almonds and confectioners' sugar.*

YIELD: 12 to 18 servings

Cream Puff Dough, page 578

PRALINE
½ cup (110 grams) sugar
¾ cup (120 grams) whole almonds
1 tablespoon sliced almonds
Slightly sweetened whipped cream

1. Preheat the oven to 400 degrees (204°C). Coat a cookie sheet with butter and flour. Using a flan ring, or any circular mold, mark an outline about 10 inches (25 centimeters) in diameter. Prepare the *pâte à choux*. Fill a pastry bag with the dough. Squeeze out a ring of *pâté à choux* about 1 inch (2.5 centimeters) wide, following the outline. Squeeze another ring inside or outside the first, depending on how large you want the cake to be. Squeeze 1 ring on top of the others, a total of 3 rings of dough.

2. Brush with an egg wash (1 whole egg, beaten). Dip a fork in the wash and run it around to create lines simulating the bark of a tree.

3. Sprinkle 1 tablespoon sliced almonds on top.

4. Let the cake dry for about 20 minutes. Bake for 45 minutes. Shut off the heat, open the oven door halfway to let the steam escape, and leave the cake in the oven for 1 hour so it cools and dries.

5. Using a long-bladed knife, cut a lid off the cake.

6. TO MAKE THE PRALINE: Place the sugar in a saucepan, preferably a stainless steel or unlined copper pan. Cook over medium to high heat, stirring occasionally. This will be a dry sugar caramel (no liquid added), which makes a very hard caramel. Stir the sugar as it melts. As the melting sugar is stirred into the dry sugar, the mixture often crystallizes, making it hard to stir. Keep cooking the sugar until most of the pieces of crystallized sugar melt.

7. <u>When the mixture is a light amber color (with some crystallized sugar still visible in it), add the almonds.</u> Keep cooking on top of the stove. Don't worry if the mixture sets into large lumps. Continue cooking; the sugar pieces will eventually melt and the almonds will separate from the sugar, which will turn a rich caramel color.

8. <u>At that point, pour the mixture onto an oiled tray,</u> spreading it slightly to help it cool.

9. When cool, you can lift the almond sugar from the oiled tray in one block. <u>Break into pieces, place them in a mortar,</u> then pound with a pestle to form a crumbly consistency.

10. Sprinkle crushed praline onto the bottom half of the cake. <u>Then decorate with slightly sweetened whipped cream.</u>

11. <u>Cut the lid of the *Paris-Brest* into as many portions as you want to serve</u> (from 12 to 18).

12. <u>Place the lid back on top of the cake.</u>

13. Thrust a knife through the lid at the separations, then cut down through the cake to <u>divide it into servings</u>. Serve.

Three Ways to Make Puff Paste

(Feuilletage)

Puff paste, or feuilletage, is the hardest dough to make, and it has its pitfalls even for professionals. The dough will be easier to make and will rise well if you use shortening, which melts at a higher temperature than butter. However, nothing can replace the taste or the fragrance of butter. The difference is evident.

Puff paste is made with flour and butter in equal proportions. The flour is bound with a liquid, usually water, into an elastic and shiny dough (détrempe). The butter is encased in the dough, and both elements are rolled together. By folding, rolling, and folding the dough, a multilayered effect is achieved, with layers of elastic dough and layers of butter. The butter melts during cooking and develops steam which tries to escape, pushing the layers up into the "thousand-leaf" effect. All-purpose flour is high in gluten (the protein part of the flour that makes the dough elastic). Use all-purpose flour or a mixture of pastry and all-purpose flour.

The butter and the detrempe should be the same temperature and consistency. If the butter is too cold, it will break and crumble and push through the dough during the rolling. If it is too soft, it will be "squished" and will run between the layers. Beware of hot and humid days; the ingredients are limp and have a tendency to blend together.

Puff paste tends to darken and become quite elastic when stored in the refrigerator. However, well wrapped, it freezes beautifully.

CLASSIC PUFF PASTE DETREMPE

YIELD: approximately 2½ pounds

1 pound (454 grams) all-purpose organic flour, very cold (put a bag of flour in the freezer overnight)

2 tablespoons (28 grams) unsalted butter, at room temperature

½ teaspoon salt

About 1 cup (237 milliliters) cold water (depending on humidity)

BUTTER MIXTURE

1 pound (454 grams) unsalted butter, at room temperature

¼ cup (35 grams) all-purpose organic flour

PUFF PASTE #2 (FAST PUFF)

YIELD: approximately 2½ pounds

1 pound (454 grams) all-purpose organic flour, very cold (put a bag of flour in the freezer overnight)

½ teaspoon salt

About 1 cup (237 milliliters) cold water (depending on humidity)

1 pound (454 grams) unsalted butter

PUFF PASTE #3 (INSTANT PUFF)

YIELD: approximately 2¼ pounds

1 pound (454 grams) all-purpose organic flour, very cold (put a bag of flour in the freezer overnight)

3 sticks (12 ounces/375 grams) unsalted butter

½ teaspoon salt

¼ teaspoon lemon juice

About 1 cup (237 milliliters) cold water (depending on humidity)

1. TO MAKE THE CLASSIC PUFF PASTE (FOR DETREMPE): Place the flour, butter, salt, and water in the bowl of an electric mixer. Using the flat beater, mix on medium low for about 45 seconds, until well combined. Gather the dough together, wrap it in plastic wrap, and place in the refrigerator.

2. Place the pound of butter with the ¼ cup flour in the bowl of an electric mixer and, using the whisk attachment, mix until the ingredients are well-homogenized, about 15 to 20 seconds. Using plastic wrap, pat the butter mixture into a 5- to 6-inch (13- to 15-centimeter) square about 1 inch (2.5 centimeters) thick on another piece of plastic wrap. Refrigerate for at least 30 minutes along with the flour dough.

Roll out the *détrempe*, using as little flour as possible, into a square about 12 by 12 inches (30 by 30 centimeters).

Place the butter mixture at an angle in the center of the dough, positioning it so the corners of the butter face the sides of the *détrempe*.

3. Bring the corners of dough over the butter, overlapping them slightly to encase the butter completely.

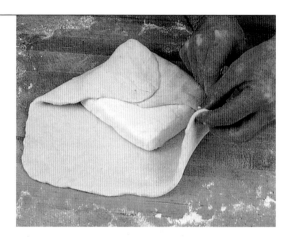

4. Pound the dough gently with a rolling pin to extend it. Flour the surface of the dough and roll it into a rectangle 20 inches (50 centimeters) long by 10 inches (25 centimeters) wide by $^3/_8$ inches (10 millimeters) thick.

5. Brush the dough to remove any flour from the surface and fold one-third of the dough back onto the rectangle.

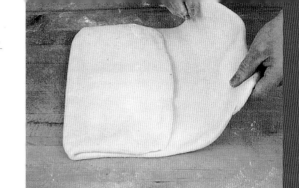

6. <u>Bring the remaining single thickness of dough back over the double thickness</u> so the rectangle is folded into thirds like a letter. Brush off any flour as you fold. This is the first "turn." Wrap the dough in plastic wrap or place in a plastic bag in the refrigerator for 30 minutes to let it rest before giving it another turn.

Place the rectangle on the table with the folded side facing you and roll it out again into a rectangle 20 inches (50 centimeters) long by 10 inches (25 centimeters) wide by ³/₈ inches (10 millimeters) thick. Fold again into thirds. This is the second turn. Re-wrap and refrigerate again for 30 minutes. Roll again into a 10- by 20-inch rectangle and fold into thirds, again brushing any flour from the center as you fold. If you feel that the dough is well-rested and not elastic at that point, give the dough another turn immediately, which will be two turns in a row, making a total of four turns. Let the dough rest again for 30 minutes or longer.

Eventually, give a fifth and sixth turn, allowing the dough to rest in the refrigerator 30 minutes between each turn. The finished dough will have six turns. After the dough has rested, it can be rolled into long, thin rectangles and stacked on a tray with plastic wrap between the rectangles.

After it rests, the dough won't shrink when cut out for *vol-au-vents* or other shapes. The dough can be frozen whole or rolled, cut into shapes, and frozen. To use, defrost the large pieces to roll. The frozen shaped pieces should be placed in the oven frozen for best results.

7. TO MAKE THE FAST PUFF PASTE #2: Use cold flour (from the freezer). Since the dough will be worked out very quickly with several turns in a row, the cold flour will absorb the heat generated through manipulation and rolling. Place the flour, salt, and water in the bowl of an electric mixer, and mix with the flat beater for about 15 seconds, just enough for the dough to be well-homogenized and hold together.

Place the dough on the table. <u>Cut each of the 4 sticks of unsalted butter into 3 lengthwise slices.</u>

8. Roll out the *détrempe* into a rectangle approximately 18 inches (46 centimeters) long by 9 inches (23 centimeters) wide by ¼ inches (6 millimeters) thick. <u>Arrange the butter slices over two-thirds of the dough to within ¾ of an inch (19 millimeters) of the outside edges.</u>

9. <u>Bring the lower third of the dough (not covered by butter) on top of half of the butter.</u>

10. <u>Bring the remaining third of the buttered dough over the top</u>, creating a sandwich with five alternating layers of dough and butter. Press along the sides to ensure that the dough is sealed together.

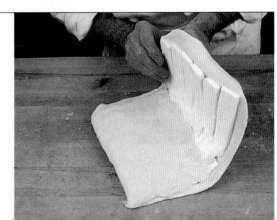

11. <u>Pound the dough gently with a rolling pin to start extending it.</u> Then, flour (minimally) the dough and roll it into a rectangle about 9 to 10 inches wide by 20 inches long by ¼ to ³/₈ inches (6 to 9 millimeters) thick.

12. <u>Bring each end of the rectangle toward the center so it joins,</u> and roll gently to seal.

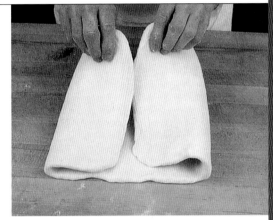

13. <u>Fold the dough in half again, creating a four-layer dough</u> rather than the three layers of the classic puff paste. This is what is called a double turn. Roll again into a rectangle and give the dough another double turn. Wrap and refrigerate the dough for at least 30 minutes.

   Flour the board and roll the dough again into a 10 by 20-inch rectangle, fold into the center and then in half again (another double turn). At that point, if the dough is not too elastic, give it a fourth double turn. Wrap and refrigerate. After it has rested, the dough will be ready to use.

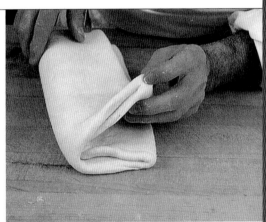

14. TO MAKE PUFF PASTE #3 (INSTANT PUFF):
(Notice that the proportion of butter is less and the flour is very cold.) Place the pound of cold flour in a bowl and <u>slice the 12 ounces of butter in ¹/₈ -inch slivers on top of it.</u>

15. Add the ½ teaspoon salt, ¼ teaspoon lemon juice, and 8 to 9 ounces ice cold water, and <u>mix with a spoon until most of the flour is moist</u> and most of the mixture holds together. Do not overmix.

16. Place on a work surface, preferably cold, and press the dough with the heel of your hand without smearing it forward into a coarse rectangle approximately 9 by 12 inches.

17. If the dough sticks to the work surface, <u>use a dough scraper to lift it up and fold it into thirds</u>, as indicated in steps 5 and 6.

18. Flour the dough, pound it, as shown in photographs 4 and 11, to start extending it, and <u>roll the dough again into a rectangle about 9 by 20 inches</u>. You can see that the pieces of butter are still quite visible.

19. Fold the dough into a double turn, making sure to brush the flour from the center. Again, extend the dough to make a rectangle about 8 by 20 inches and give it another double turn. Let it rest refrigerated for at least 30 minutes.

20. Roll the dough out for the third time into a rectangle about 8 by 20 inches. Notice that the butter is still visible but less and less so. Fold the dough again into a double turn, a total of 3 double turns. At that point, the dough will be quite elastic. Wrap in plastic wrap and place in the refrigerator for at least 1 hour before using. If, after you've let the dough rest in the refrigerator, you want it more flaky, give it another single or double turn before using.

Puff paste is used in several of the dishes that follow and any of the puff paste recipes here can be used, depending on availability.

Large Patty Shell
(Vol-au-Vent à l'Ancienne)

Vol-au-vent *are customarily filled with sweetbreads, chicken, quenelles, and mushrooms, lobster meat, and the like, usually bound with a sauce. They are one of the most delicate pastries to make and must be made with perfect puff paste dough. Begin by making the classic puff paste dough. One pound (454 grams) of flour will make enough dough for two vol-au-vent.*

1. Preheat the oven to 400 degrees (204°C). Roll the dough ⅜ inch (10 millimeters) thick. Using a round object as a guide (in this case a cake pan), <u>cut two disks 8 inches (20 centimeters) in diameter</u>. Be sure to cut the dough with a sharp knife. If the dough is cut with a dull blade, the layers will squish together and will not rise properly.

2. Using a smaller round object, <u>cut a disk from one of the wheels to make a ring</u>. The ring should be at least 1¼ inches (3 centimeters) across.

3. Place the solid disk on a cookie sheet lined with parchment paper. <u>Brush the surface with water.</u>

4. <u>Place the ring of dough carefully on top</u> and press all around so that it adheres well to the bottom layer. The dough is now ¾-inch (19 millimeters) thick at the edge.

5. <u>Brush the ring with egg wash</u>. It is important that the wash does not run down the sides of the shell. If this happens, the layers will be "glued" together by the wash and will have difficulty rising.

6. Using the dull side of the blade, <u>mark the edge all around</u>.

7. <u>Cut about ⅛-inch (3 millimeters) deep into the bottom layer following the curve of the ring to create the "lid."</u> Carve a trellis in the center of the lid. Let the *vol-au-vent* rest in a cool place for 1 hour. Bake for 45 to 55 minutes. If, after 10 minutes, the shell is rising unevenly, cut the high side at the lid incision to let steam escape and allow the other side to level off. When baked, cut off and remove the lid, fill, cover with the lid, and serve.

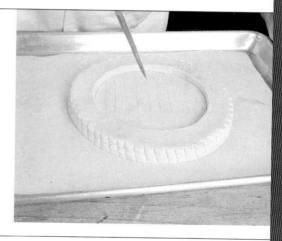

Large Patty Shell

(Vol-au-Vent à la Moderne)

This is an easier and more dramatic way of making a large patty shell. Fast puff paste as well as puff paste trimmings are adequate, and it can also be done with a pâte brisée, although it is not as spectacular as when made with puff paste. To begin, make the puff paste.

1. Roll the puff paste dough into a rectangle about 10 inches (25 centimeters) wide and 20 inches (50 centimeters) long. Cut into 2 squares. Place 1 square on a damp, or parchment-lined, cookie sheet. Place a ball of aluminum foil, about 3½ inches (9 centimeters) in diameter, in the middle of the square. Brush the dough all around the ball with water. <u>Put the second square on top of the foil.</u>

2. Use a 9-inch (23-centimeter) flan ring to mark a circle. Be sure that the dough is stretched uniformly around the foil ball. <u>Trim the dough so it is even with the bottom.</u> Cut with a sharp knife.

3. Brush the dough with an egg wash (1 whole egg, beaten). Do not let the wash run down the sides. <u>Cut long, thin strips of dough from scraps and decorate the shell to your fancy.</u> Cut lozenges from scraps of dough to simulate leaves and finish decorating the shell.

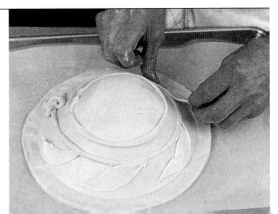

4. <u>Cut out little triangles from the edges.</u> Brush again with egg wash. Do not let it run down the sides.

5. Make a hole at the top to let the steam escape during baking. Let the shell rest in a cool place for 1 hour. Preheat the oven to 400 degrees (204°C). Bake for 40 to 45 minutes.

6. Let the shell cool for 10 to 15 minutes and <u>cut the lid off,</u> following the outline of the decoration.

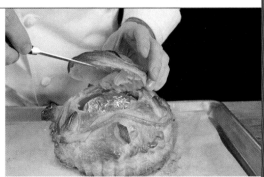

7. Being careful not to damage the shell, <u>slide your thumb and index finger on both sides of the aluminum foil</u> and squeeze to reduce the size of the ball.

8. Pull the foil out. <u>The shell is now ready to be garnished or filled.</u>

Individual Patty Shells

(Bouchées)

Make the classic puff paste dough on page 591. For individual patty shells, as well as for fleurons, cheese straws, and other puff paste garnishes described in the following technique, it is preferable to roll the dough in long sheets (about ³⁄₁₆ inch/5 millimeters thick) a few hours ahead of time, allowing it to rest, or relax, in the refrigerator. This prevents the dough from shrinking when it is cut.

1. Preheat the oven to 400 degrees (204°C). <u>Cut rounds about 3 inches (7.6 centimeters) in diameter with a plain or fluted-edge cutter.</u> Be sure that the cutter is sharp. If the edge is dull, the layers will get squeezed together and will not rise properly.

2. Using a smaller cutter, <u>cut a piece from the center of half of the rounds.</u> The outside rings are used to form the walls of the patty shells. They should be ½ inch (13 millimeters) wide.

3. Rub your finger underneath the cutting edge of the cutter to be sure that the outside ring of the dough is free.

4. Place the rounds on a cookie sheet lined with parchment paper. Brush the tops with water. Position the ring (still attached to the cutter) over the round and push it into place. Remove the cutter. Reserve the piece of dough inside the cutter for decorating tart or pie shells.

5. Brush the ring with egg wash. Do not let it run down the sides. To make the shells rise evenly, place a wire rack on top.

6. The shells should rise five to six times their original thickness. Hence, the wire rack should not be more than 2 inches (5 centimeters) high at the most. If the shells rise crookedly, the high side will be stopped when it touches the rack, and the other side will equalize itself. Bake for about 30 minutes. Fill to your liking.

Puff Paste Cheese Straws

(Paillettes, Diablotins, Fleurons)

Paillettes and diablotins are cheese straws; the first are flat strips and the other twisted. You can serve them with consommé for a very elegant first course, or with cheese or drinks. Fleurons (crescents) are classically used to garnish whole fish or fish fillets served with a sauce and glazed, such as sole Bercy. Both can be made with classic, fast, or instant puff paste, page 591.

YIELD: About 4 dozen straws

Puff Paste (page 591)
1 large egg, beaten, for egg wash
⅔ cup (67 grams) freshly grated Parmesan cheese
2 tablespoons Spanish paprika

1. Preheat the oven to 400 degrees (204°C). For the cheese straws, roll the dough ⅛ inch (3 millimeters) thick. Brush the surface of the dough with egg wash. Mix together the Parmesan cheese and paprika. <u>Sprinkle half of the mixture on top</u> and rub so that the whole surface is covered.

2. Turn the dough upside down and coat the other side with the mixture. Both sides of the dough are now covered with the cheese and paprika mixture. Fold in half. <u>Cut strips about ⅜ inch (10 millimeters) wide.</u>

3. Unfold the strips. To make twisted cheese straws, place one hand at each end of the strip. In a swift movement, roll the strip forward with one hand and, at the same time, roll backward with the other.

4. The strip will be twisted into a corkscrew-like spiral.

5. Place the strips, whether they are twisted or flat, on a parchment-lined cookie sheet. To prevent the strips from shrinking during baking, smear the ends onto the cookie sheet so they stick and hold the dough stretched.

6. Bake for about 12 minutes, or until nicely browned and crisp.

7. Trim the ends off and cut into 4-inch (10-centimeter) sticks.

Anchovy Sticks and Fish

(Allumettes aux Anchois)

Anchovies wrapped in puff paste make attractive finger food for buffets or to serve as an hors d'oeuvre with drinks. They are customarily shaped into sticks (Method 1), but can also be made to look like little fish (Method 2). Make the puff paste.

YIELD: Makes about 12 sticks and 12 fish

Puff Paste, page 591

FILLING FOR STICKS

1 large egg, beaten

1 can anchovy fillets in oil

3 tablespoons chopped parsley

2 large hard-cooked eggs, coarsely chopped

FILLING FOR FISH

2 large hard-cooked eggs

1 can anchovy fillets in oil (2 ounces /57 grams)

3 tablespoons minced chives

¼ teaspoon freshly ground black pepper

METHOD 1

1. Preheat the oven to 400 degrees (204°C). Roll the dough into 4-inch (10-centimeter)-wide strips, about ⅛ inch (3 millimeters) thick. <u>Brush with water.</u>

2. Arrange anchovy fillets about 2 inches (5 centimeters) apart on the dough. Sprinkle the anchovies with chopped hard-cooked egg and chopped parsley. <u>Place another layer of dough on top.</u>

3. <u>Press the side of your hand between each anchovy</u> so that the top layer of dough adheres well to the bottom.

4. Brush with an egg wash and <u>cut into individual pieces</u>.

5. <u>Decorate the top of each piece with the point of a knife.</u> Let rest for 1 hour in the refrigerator before baking. Bake for about 30 minutes.

METHOD 2

1. Put the eggs and anchovy fillets in a food mill or mini food processor and process to a paste. Mix with the chives and pepper. Roll the pastry to a rectangle about 14 to 15 inches (36 to 38 centimeters) long by about 10 to 12 inches (25 to 30 centimeters) wide with a thickness of approximately 1 inch (2.5 centimeters). Cut the rectangle lengthwise into 2 strips. <u>Spread the anchovy paste on top of one of the strips</u>, leaving 1 inch (2.5 centimeters) of pastry around the filling on all sides.

2. Brush the exposed edges of pastry with cold water and <u>place the other strip of pastry on top</u>, pressing all around the edges to seal. Brush with the egg wash. Place the "sandwich" of anchovies in the freezer for about 10 minutes to firm up the dough.

3. Cut continuous fish shapes the width of the pastry, the <u>head of one fish forming the tail of another</u> as the pastry is cut.

4. Trim the tail of the fish. <u>With the point of a knife or a pastry tip, draw the scales, gills, and eyes of a fish.</u> Let the dough rest for a good hour.

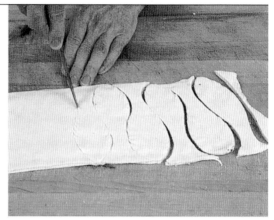

5. Preheat the oven to 400 degrees (204°C). Bake forabout 30 minutes.

6. <u>Arrange the fish on a tray and serve at room temperature.</u>

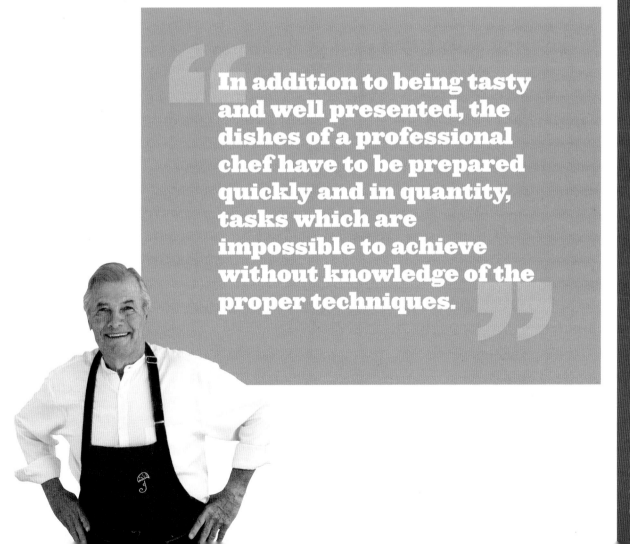

> **In addition to being tasty and well presented, the dishes of a professional chef have to be prepared quickly and in quantity, tasks which are impossible to achieve without knowledge of the proper techniques.**

Puff Paste Almond Cake

(Pithiviers)

This famous puff paste almond cake is named after the small town of Pithiviers, between Paris and Orléans. Here is the classic cake, with the spiral design on top made with a knife, and the top brushed with corn syrup to create a beautiful shine and glaze when baked.

The cake is best eaten when just lukewarm. If there are pieces left over, they should be reheated slightly in the oven before serving. The cake is also excellent served with ice cream.

YIELD: 8 servings

About 2½ pounds (1.1 kilograms) Puff Paste, page 591

ALMOND FILLING
¾ cup (120 grams) whole unskinned almonds
½ cup (75 grams) confectioners' sugar
½ teaspoon cornstarch
½ stick (4 tablespoons/56 grams) unsalted butter, softened
1 large egg
1 tablespoon dark rum
½ teaspoon pure vanilla extract

GLAZE
Egg wash made with 1 large egg with half the white removed, beaten
1 tablespoon corn syrup

FOR THE ALMOND FILLING: Preheat the over to 400 degrees (204°C). Place the almonds on a cookie sheet and brown in the oven for about 12 minutes. Put the toasted almonds, confectioners' sugar, and cornstarch in the bowl of a food processor and process until the mixture is finely ground. Add the butter, egg, rum, and vanilla, and process again until smooth. Place in a bowl and, if not using right away, refrigerate. The mixture tends to thicken as it cools in the refrigerator.

1. Roll the puff paste dough into a large rectangle approximately ¼ inch (6 millimeters) thick. Using a 10-inch (25-centimeters) flan ring, mark two circles in the dough.

2. With a sharp knife, cut out the circles. (Don't use the flan ring to cut the dough since it would crush rather than cut the dough, preventing it from rising properly.) Place one of the circles on a cookie sheet lined with parchment paper. Arrange the almond filling on top, spreading it with a spatula to within 1 inch of the edge of the circle.

3. Moisten the exposed edge of the filled dough with water and place the remaining circle of dough on top. Press around the edge to seal the two dough rounds together. Place the cake in the freezer for 5 to 10 minutes so the dough hardens a little.

4. Press around the edge with your thumb while notching with a spoon handle to create a design. Press firmly with your thumb to make firm indentations.

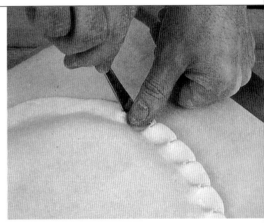

5. Brush the top of the cake with the egg wash and, using a knife, mark concentric lines from the outer edge to the center of the cake and make a hole through the dough in the center with the point of a knife.

6. Bake in the preheated oven for approximately 30 minutes. Reduce the heat to 375 degrees (191°C). Brush the corn syrup on the cake. Continue cooking for approximately 15 minutes. <u>By that time, the surface should be beautiful glazed</u>. If not, place under the broiler for a few minutes to finish glazing.

7. After cooling for 20 to 30 minutes, <u>cut into wedges</u> and serve lukewarm.

Pears in Caramel on Puff Paste

(Feuilleté de Poires au Caramel)

Rolled pieces of sugared puff paste, cut into ovals and baked, are called carolines. *They are large puff paste cookies and can be served with fruit or whipped cream, or with poached pears and a caramel cream sauce, as we do below.*

YIELD: 6 servings

1 pound (454 grams) puff paste (page 591)

1 cup (225 grams) sugar

3 medium-sized ripe pears, peeled and cut into halves

½ cup (112 grams) sugar

¼ cup (59 milliliters) water

1 cup (237 milliliters) heavy cream

1. Spread the 1 cup sugar on the table. Using the sugar as if it was flour to prevent the dough from sticking, roll the dough approximately ¼ inch (6 millimeters) thick. Sprinkle with some of the sugar and fold into thirds like a letter. Roll out the dough again into a rectangle about ⅜ inch (10 millimeters) thick. Using a large oval cookie cutter (about 5½ inches/14 centimeters long by 3 inches/7.6 centimeters wide), cut 6 *carolines*. Place them on a cookie sheet lined with parchment paper and set in the refrigerator or freezer for 30 minutes.

2. Preheat the oven to 400 degrees (204°C). Bake the *carolines* for 25 minutes until nice and brown. Remove from the paper as soon as possible or the sugar which has melted around the dough will harden and make the dough stick. Let cool on a wire rack.

3. Peel the pears, cut them in half, and core. Mix ½ cup of sugar and ¼ cup of water together in a large saucepan and place on high heat. Cook until it turns into a caramel, then add the pears, cover, and cook on low heat about 5 minutes, depending on the ripeness of the fruit. Do not let the pears fall apart. When tender to the point of a knife, add the cream, bring to a boil and simmer for a couple of minutes, uncovered. Set aside until cool. Remove the pears from the caramel, slice each half and arrange on top of a *caroline*. Pour some of the sauce over and around the puff paste and serve immediately.

Small Fruit Tarts

(Tartelettes de Fruits)

Small fruit tarts are an ideal summer dessert. The pâte sucrée (page 562) shells are precooked, filled with a purée of fruit or pastry cream (page 478), topped with fruit, and glazed. For raspberries, strawberries, or blueberries, use a glaze of currant jelly or raspberry preserves. If a jelly is used, heat to liquefy, and brush on while still warm. Any preserve which is not jelled need only be sieved and flavored with alcohol. For fruits such as banana, pear, pineapple, oranges, and the like, use an apricot or peach preserve, strained and seasoned with a bit of Kirschwasser or cognac.

1. Preheat the oven to 375 degrees (191°C). Roll out the *pâte sucrée* to ¼ inch (6 millimeters) thick. It should not be too thin. If too thin, *pâte sucrée* tends to burn. Line up your tartelette molds. (They line up better if they are all the same size—like ours.) Roll the dough back onto the rolling pin and unroll on top of the molds.

2. Take a lump of dough, dip it in flour so it doesn't stick, and use it to push and stretch the dough into each mold.

3. Trim the dough by rolling the pin on top of the molds. The weight of the pin will cut through the dough. Finish by pressing with your fingers.

4. Place another mold on top of the dough and press it down, to keep the dough from puffing during baking. Alternatively, line with wax paper and weight with rice or beans. Bake for 5 to 8 minutes. Remove the upper molds and return to the oven for 10 more minutes or until lightly browned.

5. Fill with about 2 tablespoons pastry cream per shell, then arrange the fruit on top. Glaze with the appropriate preserve and serve as soon as possible.

Fruit Tart Strips

(Bandes pour Tartes aux Fruits)

This rectangular fruit tart is excellent for large gatherings because it is easy to serve. You just carve across at the end of each piece of fruit. The tart is made from a base of sweet dough bordered with strips of puff pastry. The dough is baked, spread with a layer of pastry cream (page 478), and topped with fruit.

1. Roll the pâte sucrée ¼ inch (6 millimeters) thick. Cut in a strip the length of your cookie sheet and about 5 inches (13 centimeters) wide. <u>Cut two strips of puff pastry about ½ inch (13 millimeters) wide for the border.</u> Dampen about 1 inch (2.5 centimeters) on each side of the base with water and position the strips in place, pressing to make sure they adhere.

2. Using the dull side of the blade, <u>decorate the edges of the tart with a knife</u>. Brush the border with an egg wash (1 whole egg, beaten).

3. <u>Prick the center with a fork</u> (you don't want the dough to develop too much in the center). Let the dough rest for at least 30 minutes.

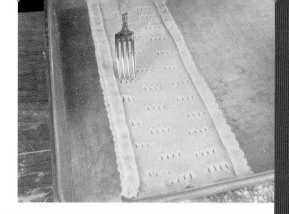

4. Preheat the oven to 400 degrees (204°C). Bake for about 30 minutes. Place a ¼- to ½-inch (6- to 13-millimeter) layer of pastry cream on the bottom and <u>arrange poached apricot or peach halves on top</u>. (Be sure the fruits are well drained to prevent the cream from thinning.) You may use any kind of berries also.

5. Brush the fruits with an apricot glaze and <u>sprinkle confectioners' sugar on the border</u>. Serve as needed.

Square Fruit Tart

(Tarte Carrée)

Make some puff paste, either classic, fast or instant, page 591.

1. Preheat oven to 400 degrees (204°C). Roll the dough ⅛ inch (3 millimeters) thick and into a 10- to 12-inch (25-centimeter to 30-centimeter) square. <u>Let it rest for at least 1 hour.</u>

2. <u>Fold the dough in half diagonally</u> and trim it to have a folded square. You now have a right-angle triangle.

3. <u>Cut a border on both square sides of the triangle,</u> about ¾ inch (19 millimeters) wide.

4. <u>Be sure that the borders are still attached in the right-angle corner</u>.

5. Unfold the dough and <u>dampen the edges with water</u>.

6. <u>Bring half the border over</u> and place on the damp edge of the dough.

7. <u>Then bring over the other half</u>. Press to make sure the border adheres.

8. <u>Trim the corners</u> where the dough overlaps. The square can also be left untrimmed.

9. <u>Prick the center with a fork</u>. Bake for 30 to 35 minutes. If the dough rises in the center during baking, just press it down with a fork.

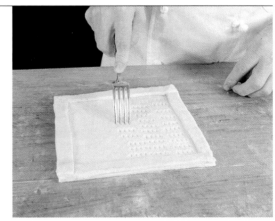

10. Mix ½ cup (112 grams) sugar and ¼ cup (59 milliliters) water together in a large saucepan and place on high heat. Cook until it turns into a caramel and <u>pour inside the shell, covering the whole bottom with a thin layer.</u> The caramel gives crunchiness to the tart and keeps the cream from making the dough soggy.

11. <u>Cover with pastry cream</u> (page 478).

12. Fill with orange sections, banana slices, berries, or the like. <u>Glaze the top with an apricot or peach glaze.</u> Serve as soon as possible.

Palm Cookies

(Palmiers)

These are classic "pig's ear" cookies made from sugared puff paste.

1. Sprinkle the board and dough generously with sugar. Roll the dough in the sugar, using it as if it was flour. <u>Roll to about ⅛ inch (3 millimeters) thick.</u>

2. <u>Fold both ends of the dough so that they meet in the middle.</u>

3. <u>Roll the pin lightly on top to make the dough flat</u>.

4. <u>Fold again so that the ends meet again in the middle</u>. Roll lightly with the pin.

5. <u>Fold both sides together to make a simple loaf</u>. Let the dough rest in the refrigerator or freezer for 30 minutes.

6. Preheat the oven to 400 degrees (204°C). <u>Slice into cookies about ³/₈ inch (10 millimeters) thick</u>.

7. <u>Arrange the cookies flat on a cookie sheet</u>. Turn the edges outward slightly to give them a nicer shape. Bake for approximately 30 minutes. After 20 minutes, turn the cookies on the other side so that both sides are uniformly glazed with the sugar.

Glazed Puff Paste

(Allumettes Glacées)

The allumettes glacées *are often served with ice cream or plain as coffee cake.*

YIELD: 12

About 1 pound (454 grams) puff paste (see page 591)

GLAZE

1 cup (100 grams) confectioners' sugar

1 large egg white

2 tablespoons cornstarch

1. Roll the puff paste into a rectangle about 14 inches (35.5 centimeters) long by 6 inches (15 centimeters) wide and ¼ inch (6 millimeters) thick. Combine the sugar and egg white in a bowl and work for about 2 minutes until creamy. Add the cornstarch and work for another minute. <u>Pour on top of the puff paste right away</u>. If the glaze is kept it should be covered with a wet towel or a crust will rapidly form on top.

2. <u>Use a spatula to spread the mixture as evenly as you can</u> on top of the puff paste. Refrigerate for at least 1 hour so the glaze stiffens and forms a crust.

3. Preheat the oven to 375 degrees (191°C). Trim the outside of the puff paste and <u>cut into strips about 1½ inches (4 centimeters) wide</u>.

4. Bake for 30 minutes. The icing should be beige in color, shiny, and brittle. Let cool before eating.

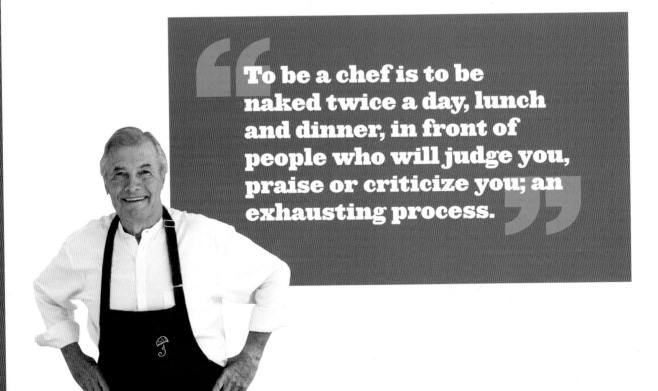

> **To be a chef is to be naked twice a day, lunch and dinner, in front of people who will judge you, praise or criticize you; an exhausting process.**

Apple Charlotte

(Charlotte de Pommes)

There are two kinds of desserts called charlotte. The first and the oldest is the lukewarm apple charlotte. The other, made with cream and lined with ladyfingers or génoise cake, is served cold. The apple charlotte is the subject of this technique, and a cream-filled charlotte is described in the next.

YIELD: 8 to 10 servings

8 to 10 apples, depending on size

¾ stick (6 tablespoons/85 grams) unsalted butter

Grated rind of 1 lemon

Juice of 1 lemon

2 to 3 tablespoons sugar (depending on sweetness of apples)

3 tablespoons apricot jam

10 to 12 slices firm white bread, crusts trimmed

Pare and core the apples and cut into ¼-inch (6-millimeter) slices. Pick apples that will hold their shape during cooking (Calville, Rennet, Granny Smith or the all-purpose green or Golden Delicious). Melt 4 tablespoons (56 grams) of the butter in a large skillet. Add the apple slices and sauté until all the juices are released and they start to boil. Add the lemon rind, juice, and sugar. Cook on medium heat until most of the liquid has

evaporated. Take off the heat and stir in the apricot jam. It is important that the apple mixture be thick; otherwise, the charlotte will collapse when it is unmolded. Set aside. Butter a 1-quart (1 scant liter) charlotte mold generously with the remaining 2 tablespoons (28 grams) butter.

APRICOT SAUCE

1 cup (237 milliliters) apricot jam

1 tablespoon sugar

3 tablespoons water

3 tablespoons Armagnac, cognac, or kirsch

Place jam, sugar, and water in a saucepan. Bring to a boil and boil for 2 to 3 minutes. Strain through a fine sieve. Cool, stirring occasionally. When lukewarm, add the alcohol.

1. Preheat the oven to 400 degrees (204°C). Cut 4 of the bread slices in half diagonally and trim into triangles.

2. <u>Arrange the triangles tightly together in the bottom of the mold.</u>

3. Cut the remaining bread slices into halves lengthwise. <u>Arrange, overlapping, around the side of the mold.</u>

4. <u>Fill the prepared mold with the apple mixture.</u>

5. <u>Pack it as much as you can in the center because the charlotte sinks as it cools.</u> Cover with a round piece of wax paper. Bake for approximately 35 minutes.

6. Remove from oven. Press down with a spoon to pack the apple mixture tightly. <u>Trim the pieces of bread which are exposed above the apple mixture</u> and place on top. Cover with wax paper and return to the oven for another 10 minutes. Let cool until lukewarm.

7. <u>Run a knife around the charlotte.</u>

8. Place a platter on top of the charlotte, then <u>turn upside down</u>.

9. <u>Remove the mold.</u> Serve with the apricot sauce.

Chocolate Charlotte

(Charlotte au Chocolat)

YIELD: 8 to 10 servings

Ladyfingers (page 499)

4 large egg yolks

½ cup (50 grams) confectioners' sugar

1 tablespoon dark rum plus ¼ cup (59 milliliters) dark rum or cognac

8 ounces (227 grams) chocolate (4 ounces/113.5 grams sweet, 4 ounces/113.5 grams bitter)

2 sticks (1 cup/227 grams) unsalted butter, softened

1 tablespoon warm water (optional)

8 large egg whites

Whipped cream

Candied violets

Crème anglaise (page 477)

1. Prepare both long and tear-shaped ladyfingers. <u>Trim the tear-shaped ones slightly.</u>

2. Place a round piece of wax paper in the bottom of a 1-quart (1-liter) charlotte mold. <u>Arrange the tear-shaped ladyfingers upside down in a petal effect on the bottom of the mold.</u>

3. Place a fringed strip of wax paper around the inside of the mold. <u>Trim one end of the long ladyfingers and the sides so that they are slightly narrower on one end</u>. Arrange the trimmed ladyfingers, cut ends down, with the rounded side touching the wax-paper-lined mold.

4. <u>Be sure they fit tightly</u>, one against the other.

5. Combine the egg yolks, sugar, and 1 tablespoon rum in a bowl. Beat with a whisk for 4 to 5 minutes until fluffy. Melt the chocolate. <u>Combine the chocolate and softened butter</u> and whip for 1 minute. Combine with the egg yolk mixture. If it curdles, add 1 tablespoon warm water and whisk until it smoothes out. Keep the mixture lukewarm.

6. Whip the egg whites until stiff. Whisk about one-third of the whites into the chocolate mixture. <u>Fold in remaining whites</u>. The mixture will lose volume. Try to go as fast as you can to prevent the whites from getting grainy.

7. Fill the mold alternating the chocolate mixture with a layer of ladyfinger trimmings sprinkled with rum or cognac until all ingredients have been used. End with the chocolate mixture.

8. With a pair of scissors, trim the ladyfingers at the level of the filling and place on the chocolate to cover the top. Cover and refrigerate for at least 4 hours.

9. Unmold and remove the wax paper. Decorate with whipped cream and candied violets, and serve with *crème anglaise* (page 477).

Raspberry Soufflé

(Soufflé aux Framboises)

Even for the professional, making a soufflé always involves an element of suspense. A soufflé is usually made of a base into which egg whites are folded. As the soufflé bakes, the air beaten into the egg whites, in the form of little bubbles, swells and pushes the soufflé up. Although regularly made in a special soufflé mold, soufflés can be made in any oven-proof container. Soufflés are also served unmolded or lukewarm and rolled. The ice-cold soufflé is a made-up soufflé—an unbaked mousse mixture shaped in the form of a soufflé.

There are two basic types of soufflés. The most common is made with a cream sauce base (*béchamel*) flavored with spinach, cheese, etc., into which egg yolks and beaten egg whites are added. The second type uses a purée of the main ingredient as a base, to which egg yolks and the beaten egg whites are added. It can be a purée of cauliflower or mushrooms, or, in our case, raspberries. The flourless soufflé cooks faster and is lighter in texture.

Most soufflés can be prepared ahead, placed in a mold, and kept refrigerated for a couple of hours before cooking. Remember that the smaller the soufflé, the easier and better it works. Large soufflés are harder to make and an 8- to 10-cup soufflé is about the maximum. It is important that large soufflés be cooked in the center of the oven so there's equal heat all around.

Remember that the equipment used to beat the whites must be immaculately clean. The egg whites should have no egg yolk in them. If they do, the egg whites will not expand to the right volume during beating. Beat the whites in an unlined copper bowl cleaned with vinegar and salt for the most volume. (Or add a dash of salt or lemon juice or cream of tartar for the same effect.) Do not beat the whites in aluminum or they will discolor. Have the base ready before you beat the whites. When you start beating, do not stop. If you stop, the whites become grainy. As soon as they are ready, combine with the base as quickly as possible. At that point the mixture can be placed in the mold and kept for a while. The base should be lukewarm when the whites are added. Whisk about a third of the egg whites into the base mixture to lighten it, then fold the rest of the whites in with a spatula. If all the whites are beaten into the base instead of being folded in, the mixture will lose volume and become too dense. The size of the mold is important and the mixture should fill it to the rim. A half-full soufflé mold will not look right after baking, even if the mixture has risen properly. The soufflé should go from the oven directly to the table, so seat your guests in advance.

Be sure when separating the eggs that all the white is removed from the shell. If a bit is left it will amount to a whole egg white for every five or six eggs. If the eggs are small, add one or two egg whites. It is better to have too much egg white than not enough.

For the recipe that follows you will need a 5- to 6-cup (1.2- to 1.4-liter) soufflé mold. Butter the mold, coat with sugar, and set aside.

SOUFFLE

6 large egg whites

Pinch of salt

¾ cup (169 grams) sugar

2 cups (340 grams) very ripe raspberries

SAUCE

1 cup (170 grams) fresh raspberries

1 10-ounce/283-gram package frozen raspberries, defrosted

⅔ cup (158 milliliters) seedless raspberry preserves

1 tablespoon raspberry brandy, kirsch, or cognac

Confectioners' sugar for sprinkling

Strain combined sauce ingredients through a fine strainer or food mill.

1. Preheat the oven to 375 degrees (191°C). Place the egg whites and a pinch of salt in the bowl of an electric mixer and beat on medium to high speed until they form a peak. Add sugar gradually while continuing to beat, keep beating on high speed for about 30 seconds. With a fork, crush ½ cup (85 grams) of raspberries coarsely and <u>fold along with the whole ones into the egg whites</u>. Fill the mold with the soufflé mixture. Smooth the top with a metal spatula and make ridges with the spatula to decorate, place the soufflé on a cookie sheet in the preheated oven for 20 minutes. If, after 10 to 15 minutes of cooking, the soufflé appears to be browning too fast, place a loose piece of aluminum foil over it and continue to bake.

2. Remove from the oven and sprinkle confectioners' sugar on top. <u>Serve immediately with raspberry sauce</u>.

Caramel Lime Soufflé with Lime Sauce

(Soufflé au Citron et Caramel)

This soufflé is made at least five hours before serving and preferably the day before. It is then unmolded and served cold with the lime sauce. It can also be served hot (step 7) with the same sauce.

The soufflé mold is first lined with caramel and the soufflé is cooked in a double boiler. Soufflés cooked in this manner tend to rise evenly without cracking and hold their height for 15 to 20 minutes after they come out of the oven. But unless the mold is lined with caramel, as is done in this recipe, a soufflé baked in a water bath will be wet and white around the sides. It will not have the golden exterior of a regular soufflé that is cooked dry in the oven.

The cold caramel lime soufflé makes a delicate, light, cold dessert that is delicious with the lime sauce.

YIELD: 8 to 10 servings

CARAMEL
2 cups (450 grams) sugar
½ cup (118 milliliters) water

LIME SAUCE
⅓ cup (80 milliliters) fresh lime juice
1 tablespoon water
Half the caramel recipe from above
2 tablespoons Grand Marnier

SOUFFLE MIXTURE
5 large egg yolks
¼ cup (56 grams) sugar
2 tablespoons cornstarch
1 teaspoon pure vanilla extract
Grated peel of 1 lime (1½ teaspoon)
1¼ cup (296 milliliters) milk
6 large egg whites

1. TO MAKE THE CARAMEL: Combine the sugar and water in a saucepan and stir gently, just enough to moisten the sugar. Bring to a boil and cook over high heat without stirring or shaking the pan, until the mixture turns a golden caramel color, approximately 10 to 12 minutes. <u>Pour about half the caramel into a 6-cup (1.4 liter) soufflé mold.</u>

2. Incline the mold on its side, holding it over a cookie sheet to catch any caramel drippings and, <u>using a bristle brush (not nylon), turn the mold and brush the caramel onto the sides as it flows,</u> until the sides of the mold are completely coated. Work quickly so you can finish coating the mold before the caramel hardens.

TO MAKE THE LIME SAUCE: Add the lime juice and water to the remaining caramel and bring the mixture to a boil, stirring. Set aside to cool.

3. FOR THE SOUFFLE: Preheat the oven to 350 degrees (177°C). Place the egg yolks in a bowl with the sugar, cornstarch, vanilla, and grated lime peel, and mix well with a whisk. Bring the milk to a boil and combine with the egg yolk mixture. Pour into a saucepan and bring to a boil, stirring with the whisk, especially around the bottom edge of the saucepan to prevent the mixture from scorching. As soon as it comes to a boil (it should be thick and smooth), remove from the heat. Beat the egg whites until firm and add one-third to one-fourth of them to the egg yolk mixture, <u>mixing them in well with the whisk to lighten the mixture.</u>

4. Add the soufflé base, now lightened by the addition of the egg whites, to the rest of the beaten egg whites and <u>fold in with a spatula.</u> Work quickly to prevent the mixture from getting grainy. It should not take more than 20 to 30 seconds.

5. <u>Pour the mixture into the caramel-lined mold.</u> It should fill the mold.

6. Place the mold in a pan and <u>surround it with lukewarm water.</u> Place in the oven for 1 hour 10 minutes.

7. When it emerges from the oven, <u>the soufflé should have risen at least a couple of inches above the mold and be brown on top.</u> It will hold its shape for about 15 to 20 minutes and can be served hot with the lime sauce.

8. To serve the soufflé cold, allow it to cool overnight or at least 5 to 6 hours in the refrigerator, covered (so the edge of the soufflé mold doesn't dry out and get sticky from the sugar, thus causing the soufflé to stick to the sides; if covered, the soufflé will develop moisture and the outside will stay moist). The soufflé will sink down but should not sink below its original volume before baking. <u>Pull the sides of the soufflé toward its center to loosen it all around.</u>

9. Stir the Grand Marnier into the lime sauce. The sauce should be <u>about the thickness of heavy syrup</u>.

10. Unmold the soufflé; it will slide out easily onto a serving platter. <u>Coat with some of the sauce.</u>

11. Cut the soufflé into wedges and serve with additional sauce.

Chocolate Soufflé with Rum Sauce

(Soufflé au Chocolat Sauce au Rhum)

This soufflé does not need flour because the chocolate has enough body to hold the egg whites. More than any other soufflé, the chocolate soufflé should not be overcooked but slightly wet in the center. Serve hot right out of the oven with the sauce or let it cool, unmold and serve in wedges like a cake with or without a sauce.

YIELD: 6 to 8 servings

RUM SAUCE

1½ cups (355 milliliters) milk

2 teaspoons cornstarch

1 teaspoon pure vanilla extract

3 large egg yolks (reserve the whites for the soufflé)

¼ cup (56 grams) sugar

2 tablespoons good dark rum

Place the milk, cornstarch, and vanilla in a saucepan. Mix with the whisk and bring to a boil. Meanwhile, combine the egg yolks and sugar in a bowl and whisk for 1 to 2 minutes until the mixture is light, fluffy, and pale yellow. Pour the boiling milk all at once directly on top of the yolks, whisking to combine well. The hot milk will cook the egg yolks. Cover with plastic wrap and let cool. When cold, add the rum.

SOUFFLÉ

4 ounces (113 grams) bittersweet chocolate (or 3 ounces/85 grams sweet and 1 ounce/28 grams bitter)

½ cup (118 grams) milk

4 large eggs at room temperature, separated, plus the 3 egg whites reserved from the sauce

3 tablespoons sugar

Confectioners' sugar for sprinkling

1. Preheat the oven to 375 degrees (191°C). Butter and sugar a 6-cup (1.4-liter) soufflé mold and refrigerate until ready to use. Place the chocolate in a saucepan with the milk and melt on top of the stove. Stir until it comes to a simmer. Remove from the heat and whisk the yolks in. Beat the 7 egg whites until they reach soft peaks and add the sugar. Keep beating for about 1 minute until stiff.

2. <u>Whisk about one-third of the egg whites into the chocolate</u>. Pour the chocolate mixture back onto the beaten egg whites.

3. Carefully fold the chocolate mixture into the egg whites, <u>then pour into the soufflé mold</u>. It should reach the rim of the mold. At this point, the soufflé can be kept for a up to an hour, refrigerated or at room temperature.

4. Place on a cookie sheet in the oven and cook for 18 to 20 minutes. <u>The baked soufflé</u> should be moist in the center. Sprinkle with confectioners' sugar and serve immediately with the rum sauce around it.

5. You can leave the soufflé to deflate and cool overnight <u>and then unmold it</u>, cut into wedges and serve with sweetened whipped cream or with the rum sauce. It will have the consistency of a very light cake.

Chocolate Leaves

(Feuilles en Chocolat)

The best and easiest way to make chocolate leaves is to coat real leaves with chocolate. Natural leaves come in all shapes and sizes and make beautiful designs. Use dark chocolate, milk chocolate (which has a lighter color), or white chocolate.

1. Select your leaves. Try to pick leaves all the same size. Decide whether you are going to coat the top or the underside of the leaves. The design on the underside is usually in more relief and will give more texture to the chocolate. Melt the chocolate in the microwave oven or over hot water.

2. Dip a side of the leaf in the chocolate, making sure that it is coated all over. Or, spread chocolate on the leaf with a spatula.

3. Place the leaves, chocolate side up, flat on a piece of parchment or wax paper.

4. White chocolate is usually thicker. <u>Use a spatula or a knife to spread it well</u>. Place the coated leaves flat on the paper.

5. When the chocolate is almost set but still soft, <u>place leaves in a curved pan to mold</u>. If the chocolate is still too soft it will run toward the center of the leaves; if it is too hard it will break when bent. Set the pan in the refrigerator until the leaves are set.

6. <u>Pull each leaf from the chocolate</u>. They should come off easily.

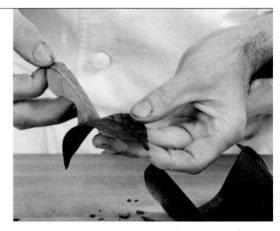

7. <u>A white chocolate leaf</u>. Arrange all your leaves on a platter or use to decorate a cake or a cold soufflé.

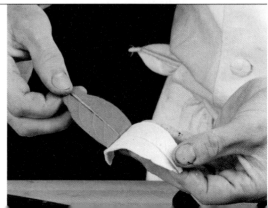

Chocolate Truffettes

(Truffettes en Chocolat)

These small chocolate truffles, or truffettes, freeze quite well and can be made ahead of time. Many of the chocolate truffles on the market have a soft and creamy interior and it is impossible to keep them for more than a few days, but these have a firm consistency that lasts.

The basic mixture can be flavored differently. I have used three flavor combinations: orange and Grand Marnier, coffee and rum, and cognac and almond.

Each variety has a different coating, which makes the flavors easy to identify. One is dusted with bitter cocoa powder, another is rolled in roasted sliced almonds, and the third is coated with melted chocolate.

Chocolate truffles can also be flavored with a praline paste, which is a mixture of caramelized sugar and almonds, or vanilla, as well as cinnamon or bourbon. Other coatings—from white chocolate to shaved chocolate—can be used.

YIELD: About 60 to 70 truffettes about the size of large cherries.

BASE MIXTURE
½ pound (8 ounces/227 grams) 70% cocoa chocolate, bittersweet or semisweet
½ stick (¼ cup/58 grams) butter
2 large egg yolks

ORANGE TRUFFLES
1 teaspoon grated orange rind
1 tablespoon Grand Marnier
Bitter cocoa powder for dusting

COFFEE-RUM TRUFFLES
2 teaspoons coffee extract
2 teaspoons rum
3 to 4 ounces (85 to 144 grams) bittersweet chocolate, for coating

COGNAC-ALMOND TRUFFLES
1 tablespoon cognac
¾ cup (95 grams) sliced almonds

1. FOR THE BASE MIXTURE: Put the bittersweet chocolate in a saucepan and melt over hot water, or melt in a microwave oven. <u>Add the butter and stir with a whisk</u> until smooth and glossy.

2. <u>Add the egg yolks and whisk.</u> The mixture will thicken and lose some of its shine.

3. FOR THE THREE FLAVORS: Divide the mixture among three different bowls. To one of the bowls, <u>add the 1 teaspoon orange rind and 1 tablespoon Grand Marnier</u>, and mix well. To a second bowl, add the 2 teaspoons each coffee extract and rum, and stir to mix thoroughly. To the chocolate mixture in the remaining bowl, add the 1 tablespoon cognac and mix well. After the addition of liquid to each of the bowls, the chocolate may become shiny again or it may remain dull; either way is fine. Refrigerate the bowls until the chocolate mixture hardens.

4. When the chocolate mixtures are hard, make truffettes, one batch at a time, by <u>scooping out teaspoonfuls and placing them on a cookie sheet lined with wax or parchment paper.</u>

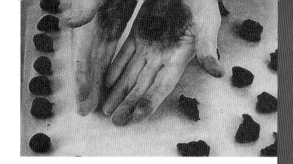

5. Take each of the little chocolate balls and <u>roll between the palms of your hands</u> to round them, making them look like a real truffle that might be found underground.

6. FOR THE ORANGE TRUFFLES: Place the orange-flavored truffles on a plate dusted generously with bitter cocoa powder and <u>shake the plate so they roll in the powder and are coated on all sides</u>. Set aside.

7. FOR THE COFFEE-RUM TRUFFLES: Melt the 3 to 4 ounces chocolate in a double boiler and, when cool enough to handle, pour about 2 tablespoons of it into the palm of one hand. <u>Roll the coffee-rum truffles one by one in the chocolate in your hand</u> until well-coated and place them on a cookie sheet lined with wax paper. Refrigerate until the outside chocolate has hardened.

8. FOR THE COGNAC-ALMOND TRUFFLES: Preheat the oven to 400 degrees (204°C). Spread the almonds on a cookie sheet and place in the oven to brown for 8 to 10 minutes. When the almonds are cool, <u>press the balls of cognac-flavored truffles into them, crushing the nuts slightly and embedding them into the truffles to coat them on the outside</u>.

9. <u>The assortment of truffles are ready to be arranged for serving</u>.

Chocolate Goblets

(Petits Bols en Chocolat)

These make attractive receptacles for fruit, cream, or other desserts.

YIELD: 4 goblets

12 ounces (340 grams) bittersweet chocolate
2 ounces (57 grams) white chocolate

1. Melt the bittersweet and white chocolate separately in double boilers, making certain that no water gets into the chocolate as this will thicken it and make it lose its shine. If the chocolate is too thick, add a little corn or cottonseed oil. Cool both the chocolates to tepid (about 100 degrees/38°C). Blow up the balloons until they are 4 to 4¼ inches (10 to 11 centimeters) wide, then close them at the neck with plastic-coated wire twisters. Dip each balloon directly into the melted bittersweet chocolate, inclining it slightly to form a roundish shape on one side.

2. Twist the balloon and dip it in the chocolate again to create another large roundish shape around the base, lift it out and dip it again—3 or 4 times in all—then place on a parchment-lined tray. Some of the chocolate will run down the balloon and accumulate at the base to form a thicker and more stable pedestal. Refrigerate until set or, if you want to add a white chocolate design, proceed with the instructions below.

3. For a different look, pour about 2 tablespoons of the melted white chocolate into a paper cornet, fold the cornet, and cut the tip off.

4. <u>Pipe lines of white chocolate around the still-soft chocolate on the dipped balloon</u>. The white chocolate will run slightly into the dark chocolate and create a marbled effect.

5. Or if you prefer to have the inside of the goblet marked with the white chocolate, <u>pipe lines directly on the outside of a balloon</u>.

6. <u>Then dip the base of the balloon into the bittersweet chocolate</u>, as described in step 2. Place on a tray and refrigerate until hard.

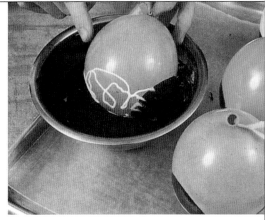

7. After the chocolate has set hard, <u>open the balloon and release the air inside</u>. Although the sides of the balloon will separate from the chocolate around it, the goblet base may adhere more stubbornly to the balloon.

8. <u>Pry up the balloon at the base with your fingers.</u> If it takes too long, and the chocolate begins to soften, return to the refrigerator or freezer to harden slightly before finishing the removal of the deflated balloons.

9. <u>The goblets, some smooth inside and some with white chocolate marbling, are ready to be filled.</u> At this point, they can be stored in a container in the refrigerator or carefully wrapped in plastic wrap and frozen.

How to Peel and Glaze Chestnuts

(Epluchage et Marrons Confits)

When buying chestnuts, select carefully, checking for small holes which indicate that the chestnut is wormy. Choose them plump and shiny. Fresh chestnuts are delicious just plain roasted in the oven, over charcoal, or in the fireplace. However, after roasting and peeling they can be braised and served whole or boiled and puréed. Although dehydrated chestnuts are readily available, they do not compare to fresh ones. Before braising chestnuts with a roast pork or turkey, both the outer shell and inside skin have to be removed.

For a purée, usually served with a red wine venison stew or other game, cover the peeled chestnuts with water (or water and chicken stock), add a dash of salt and a rib of celery and simmer, covered, for about 40 to 45 minutes until tender. Then purée through the fine blade of a food mill and finish with butter, salt, pepper, and a bit of heavy cream.

For a dessert purée, such as the Mont-Blanc (a concoction of meringue, whipped cream, and purée of chestnuts), peel the chestnuts, then cook in milk with a dash of sugar and vanilla. Purée in the food mill and sweeten with a sugar syrup.

For a stuffing, peel the chestnuts, cook in water for about 30 minutes, then mix with the other stuffing ingredients. If the chestnuts are not cooked in water first, they will be tough in the stuffing.

Regardless of how they are served, the chestnuts must be peeled first.

YIELD: About ¾ pound (340 grams) glazed chestnuts

TO GLAZE CHESTNUTS
1 pound (454 grams) chestnuts (about 20 large)
12 cups (3 scant liters) water
2 cups (450 grams) sugar
1 teaspoon pure vanilla extract
2 tablespoons rum or cognac

1. Preheat the oven to 400 degrees (204°C). <u>Make a slice against the grain on both sides of the chestnuts.</u> Be careful to slice only the outer and inside skins without going to much into the flesh.

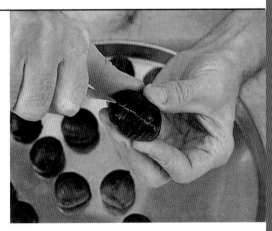

2. Place on a cookie sheet and roast for approximately 15 to 20 minutes in the oven. <u>Press the chestnuts to crack them open.</u>

3. <u>The chestnut should come out in one piece</u>. Put the ones that don't peel easily back into the oven for a few minutes. Don't roast too many at one time unless you have helpers to peel them with you while they are hot. As they cool, they become hard to peel.

4. <u>To glaze the chestnuts, place the chestnuts, water, sugar and vanilla in a large shallow saucepan</u>, bring to a boil and boil for 1 minute. Reduce the water to a bare simmer and cook gently, covered, for about 3 hours at a 180-degree (82°C) temperature. Uncover and cook slowly for another hour, or until a heavy syrup has formed and all the chestnuts are coated with it.

5. <u>Half of the chestnuts may be broken</u>. Fortunately, most recipes call for pieces of candied chestnuts. Let the chestnuts cool and then place in a jar. Add 2 tablespoons of rum or cognac to the syrup. Cover with the syrup. Keep refrigerated and use when needed.

Chestnut Chocolate Cake

(Turinois)

This is a rich cake, made with melted chocolate, purée of chestnuts, and butter. It should be served very cold, cut in thin slices, plain or with a chocolate sauce or a custard cream. Leave plain or decorate with confectioners' sugar, and glazed or almond chestnuts. If you decorate the top with confectioners' sugar, do it at the last moment; otherwise the sugar will dissolve within 20 to 25 minutes because of the moistness of the cake.

YIELD: 18 to 20 servings

2 pounds (908 grams) peeled chestnuts (about 2¾ pounds unpeeled), page 646
2 sticks (1 cup/227 grams) unsalted butter
¾ cup (169 grams) sugar
1 pound (454 grams) bittersweet chocolate, melted
2 tablespoons dark rum
½ cup (170 grams) pieces of candied chestnuts (optional)
Confectioners' sugar

1. Place the peeled chestnuts in a kettle and cover with water. Bring to a boil and simmer gently for 40 to 45 minutes until tender. The 2 pounds of chestnuts will absorb moisture during cooking, which will bring their weight up to about 3 pounds (1.4 kilograms) when cooked. Drain the chestnuts (most will have broken) and <u>pass through the fine blade of a food mill while still hot</u>.

2. Mix the butter and sugar together and work with a whisk until smooth. <u>Add the chocolate</u>, the purée of chestnuts, and the dark rum and mix well until the mixture is smooth. Then add the pieces of candied chestnuts (optional).

3. Line a loaf pan with a large strip of parchment paper. Place the mixture in the mold.

4. Refrigerate for at least 4 hours or overnight before unmolding. Run a knife all around the cake, unmold, then remove the paper.

5. To decorate, make a rectangular stencil with a piece of wax paper and place on top of the cake. Sprinkle confectioners' sugar over the stencil, then remove.

6. Decorate the top with almonds or candied chestnuts. Serve plain or with a custard sauce flavored with rum.

Almond Shells

(Nougatine)

A nougatine is made from caramelized sugar and sliced almonds and can be either used as a garnish on cakes (cut into different shapes—from triangles to strips) or pressed into molds, as done below, to create small receptacles to hold different types of fillings. The nougatine can also be crushed into pieces and added to ice cream, custard cream, or pastry cream.

Nougatine is hard to cut, particularly when it is too thick. To make it thinner (the thinner the better), cut out rough round or rectangular shapes to fit the molds you have selected, and then place them back in the oven to soften the nougatine until it is pliable enough to be pressed thinner.

Nougatine is better prepared on a dry day; it is difficult to keep it in areas that have a lot of humidity and moisture. Store in a cookie jar or plastic container with a tight-fitting lid so it doesn't get soggy and sticky.

Be extra careful when making the caramel so as not to burn yourself. Pour it out onto an oiled marble surface or metal tray; don't use wood—it will stick. Be sure to oil the dough scraper lightly as well as your metal rolling pin (I have used a piece of cast-iron tube about 1¾ inch/4 centimeters in diameter, which can be obtained from a local hardware or plumbing supply store) to keep the pieces of nougatine from sticking. (A metal rolling pin is also excellent for rolling out dough, since it is heavy, smooth, and stays cool.)

The caramel is made from dry sugar, although it can also be made from sugar and water. Dry caramel, however, produces a more brittle, harder nougatine that is less prone to stick.

YIELD: 8 servings

NOUGATINE SHELL
1 pound (454 grams) granulated sugar
2 cups (250 grams) sliced almonds

CHANTILLY FILLING
Cointreau, Grand Marnier, and/or rum (½
   teaspoon per portion to soak the cake)
3 to 4 sliced strawberries for garnish

1 cup (237 milliliters) heavy cream
½ cup (50 grams) confectioners' sugar

OTHER OPTIONAL GARNISHES
Pound Cake
Chocolate Mousse
Candied Violets

1. Put the sugar in a saucepan and cook over medium to high heat, stirring occasionally with a wooden spatula (every 5 to 10 seconds). As some of the sugar around the outside edges of the pan starts to melt, stir it back into the dry sugar.

2. After 4 to 5 minutes, the sugar will begin to get liquid. Keep stirring. Lumps of crystallized sugar will be mixed with the melted sugar. Eventually, the lumps will melt as the temperature of the sugar goes higher.

3. After about 7 to 8 minutes, the sugar will liquefy further and turn a caramel color, although there will still be some lumps in it. Lower the heat and continue cooking and stirring until the lumps have completely melted. The caramel will be slightly cloudy and a rich brown color. The total cooking time will be approximately 10 minutes, although it can take longer, depending on the size, the type of metal, and the shape of your pan, as well as the intensity of the heat.

4. Add the almonds and stir gently to incorporate into the melted sugar. Keep cooking for 1 to 2 minutes, until the mixture liquefies again and becomes smooth.

5. Oil a marble slab or metal tray lightly with a tasteless oil (such as cottonseed or corn oil) and <u>pour the nougatine onto it, using a wooden spoon to help scrape it out of the pan.</u>

6. Lightly oil a dough scraper and <u>spread the nougatine, being careful the hot mixture doesn't touch your fingers.</u>

7. <u>Using an oiled metal rolling pin, press down and roll out the nougatine further to make it smooth.</u> It won't expand too much at this point but should form an irregular circle with a diameter of about 12 to 14 inches (30 to 36 centimeters). If you feel the nougatine is thin enough—no more than ¼ inch (6 millimeters) thick—and soft enough to handle at this point, begin cutting it into shapes using a big, sharp knife or cookie cutter.

8. If the nougatine is too hard to cut at this point, <u>lift it up off the slab or tray, place it on a cookie sheet,</u> and put it in a preheated 200 to 250 degree (93° to 121°C) oven, checking it every couple of minutes, until it has softened again.

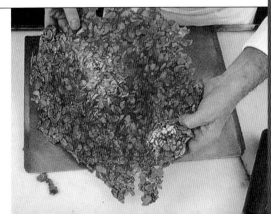

9. Remove the nougatine from the oven and <u>roll it out again directly on the cookie sheet into a thinner layer</u>. It should not be more than ¼ inch (6 millimeters) thick.

10. <u>Press cookie cutters firmly into the soft nougatine.</u> You may have to hammer the top of the cutters down with your metal rolling pin to cut through the nougatine.

11. Using a large, heavy knife, cut out rectangles from the nougatine and place them directly on top of molds of about the same size. They should be a little too small to fit the molds at this point. Put the nougatine cutouts in their molds into the oven to soften further. <u>Push the nougatine trimmings together roughly</u> and return them to the oven to soften. When soft enough, roll them out again into a smooth, single piece.

12. For a larger version of the nougatine receptacle, <u>press a large piece of softened nougatine all around on a lightly oiled inverted pie plate</u>. It will conform to the plate to form a large receptacle. Trim the edges with scissors.

13. When the nougatine in the small molds begins to soften, remove the molds from the oven and, <u>holding them with a towel, press the nougatine with the back of an oiled spoon to thin and extend it further up the sides of the molds.</u> If the edges of the nougatine are jagged at this point, trim them with scissors to make them even. (The trimmings can be pulverized and stored, refrigerated, in a jar for use as a flavoring in ice cream, pastry cream, etc.) Set the molds aside.

14. After 10 to 15 minutes, the nougatine will have hardened in the molds. <u>Using the point of a knife, pry the shells out of the molds.</u> They should release easily.

15. <u>To make a variety of desserts:</u> Cut the pound cake into ½-inch slices <u>and then into round or rectangular shapes to fit the molds.</u> Place the pieces in the appropriate molds and sprinkle either with rum (if you are using chocolate mousse as a filling), or Cointreau or Grand Marnier (if using the Chantilly filling).

16. FOR THE CHANTILLY FILLING: Whip the cream with the confectioners' sugar until stiff. Spoon into a pastry bag fitted with a fluted tip and <u>pipe a mound of cream on top of the Cointreau or Grand Marnier-soaked cake in the molds.</u> Decorate the top with sliced strawberries or other fruit.

17. Using an ice cream scoop, <u>place a scoop of chocolate mousse on top of the rum-soaked cake.</u>

18. Decorate the chocolate filling with a little rosette of whipped cream and a piece of candied violet and serve immediately. (These desserts should not be assembled more than 30 minutes before serving as the liqueur-soaked cake and fillings will make the nougatine shell sticky if filled too far ahead.)

Almond Paste Flowers

(Fleurs en Pâte d'Amandes)

Almond paste is used to flavor cream or ice cream, to coat a cake, to stuff dried fruit or, as in this technique, to make little objects like animals, vegetables, or flowers. Although almond paste can be made from scratch, the commercial product on the market is quite good and easy to use. Keep it in a plastic bag or a well-sealed container since it dries out very fast. If it gets too dry, work it with a tiny bit of egg white until it gets smooth and malleable. If the paste is too soft, work it with confectioners' sugar to harden to the right consistency. Use confectioners' sugar instead of flour to roll out the almond paste. The flowers will be soft as they are shaped but after a while they will dry out and harden. They can be kept for a few days on a cake and a few weeks in a closed tin box.

1. If the almond paste is too soft, <u>mix with confectioners' sugar to make it harder</u>. If slightly dry, add a dash of egg white and work until smooth and soft.

2. Divide the paste and <u>work a few drops of red, yellow, and green food coloring into each batch</u>. (The green is kept for the stems and leaves. Make flowers with the other colors or with plain white paste.)

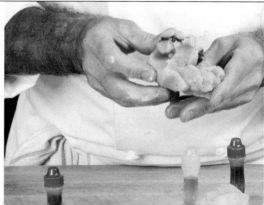

3. To make a rose, <u>shape a piece of paste into a cone</u>. This will be the heart of the rose.

4. <u>Flatten a piece of almond paste with the tip of your finger</u> or a metal spatula, to make it very thin on one edge.

5. Lift the flat piece with a spatula and <u>roll it around the center cone</u>.

6. Roll another piece flat and place around the flower bud. <u>Continue the process, adding more petals</u>. Turn the petal edge outward.

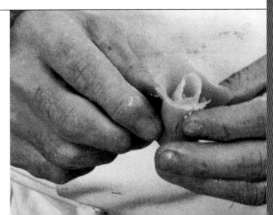

7. To make a carnation, use pink almond paste. Roll in a long cylinder about ¼ inch (6 millimeters) thick and <u>flatten with a spatula, pressing forward so that one edge of the strip is ultra thin.</u> Use confectioners' sugar to prevent sticking.

8. Using a fork, <u>make ridges on the thin side of the strip.</u> The tines of the fork must go all the way through the almond paste.

9. <u>Slide a flexible metal spatula under the strip to loosen it.</u>

10. <u>Fold the strip left to right on top of itself into wave-like pleats.</u>

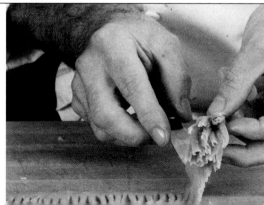

11. <u>Roll the end of the strip around the flower to encase.</u>

12. <u>Press the bottom together gently between your fingers.</u>

13. <u>Squeeze and the carnation will open to form a beautiful flower.</u> Make small and large carnations. Let rest and dry out for at least 1 hour.

14. To make stems for the flowers, roll out a strip of green almond paste and, with the point of a knife, <u>cut little indentations on each side to simulate thorns, nodes, etc.</u>

15. Form lozenge- or triangle-shaped leaves and use your knife to sketch veins in the leaves. Fold into different shapes and let dry. Decorate a cake with the flowers, leaves, and stem.

Cake Glazed with Fondant

(Gâteau Fondant)

Cakes, especially wedding cakes, are beautiful glazed with a shiny fondant (sugar icing). To glaze a cake, layer a genoise with a butter cream or ganache, then cover with a layer of almond paste so the top is absolutely smooth for the fondant.

YIELD: 8 to 10 servings

1 8- to 10-inch (20- to 25-centimeter) diameter cake
  about 3 inches (8 centimeters) high
About 1 pound (454 grams) almond paste

FAST FONDANT
3 cups (300 grams) confectioners' sugar
¼ cup (60 milliliters) hot water
1 tablespoon light corn syrup

1. Place the cake on a cardboard round. Roll the almond paste to about ⅛ inch (3 millimeters) thick. Use confectioners' sugar instead of flour to help in the rolling.

2. <u>Roll the almond paste back onto the rolling pin</u>, lift it up and place it on the cake.

3. Press the paste all around the cake so it adheres well. Trim the base. If there are any cracks, patch closed. <u>Brush the cake</u>. It should be smooth all around and on top.

4. To make the fondant, mix together the confectioners' sugar, water, and corn syrup. Work it for about 1 minute with a whisk. <u>The mixture should be glossy and smooth</u>. Use right away or cover with a wet towel or else it will crust on top very rapidly.

5. Place the cake on a wire rack and <u>pour the fondant on top</u>.

6. <u>Spread with a spatula so the fondant runs all around</u>. Work as quickly as possible.

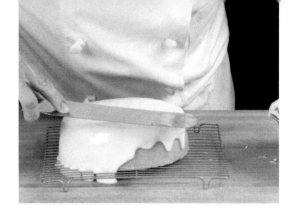

7. Lift the cake and <u>bang the wire rack on the table a few times to encourage excess to drip off</u>.

8. Lift the cake and <u>run your fingers around the bottom edge to make it smooth</u>. The cake can now be refrigerated or served.

Candied Lime and Grapefruit Peels

(Pelures de Citron Vert et Pamplemousse Confites)

Candied lime and grapefruit peels are easy to make and they can be used in so many ways: chopped and mixed into pastry cream, cut into a julienne to decorate cakes and soufflés, as well as diced and combined with other dried fruit (such as raisins and apricots) to be soaked in rum and cognac, and then added to a fruitcake.

YIELD: 24 pieces

1 to 2 large, very green limes

1 large, bright-skinned grapefruit

3 cups (711 milliliters) cold water

FOR THE PEELS OF EACH FRUIT

1 cup (185 grams) sugar

1½ cup (356 milliliters) water

2 cups (370 grams) sugar, to roll the peels in

About 2 ounces (57 grams) bittersweet chocolate, melted, for dipping

About 2 ounces (57 grams) white chocolate, melted, for dipping

1. Using a vegetable peeler, cut about 12 strips of peel from each large lime and grapefruit. (Strips cut with a peeler will be thin and thus cook quite quickly.) Place the strips in a pan with the cold water. Bring to a strong boil over high heat, boil for 30 seconds, then drain and wash under cold water. Repeat to blanch once more. Put the lime and grapefruit peels in separate pans, and add ½ cup sugar and ¾ cup water to each pan. (They should not be cooked together, as their flavors tend to blend.) Bring the liquid in each pan to a boil, and cook over medium to high heat. Cook the lime peel for about 6 minutes, until the syrup gets thicker and the lime skin begins to get transparent.

2. Using a fork, lift out the strips of lime peel and place them on a cookie sheet coated with the sugar. Turn the peels, pressing down on them so the sugar adheres to both sides, and then arrange them on a plate.

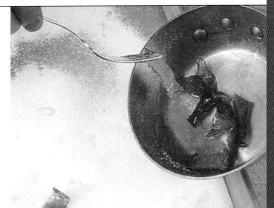

3. The grapefruit peels will take a little longer to cook, about 8 to 10 minutes total. <u>When transparent, lift them out of the syrup with a fork and place in the sugar.</u>

4. <u>Turn the peels in the sugar, pressing them so they are well-coated on both sides with the sugar.</u> Arrange on the plate with the lime peels and set aside for 30 minutes. If they are not to be used right away, place them in a plastic container with a tight-fitting lid so they don't dry out. They can be stored like this in the refrigerator for weeks.

5. Chocolate peels: <u>Dip the tip of each grapefruit peel into the melted bittersweet chocolate,</u> and arrange on a cookie sheet lined with parchment paper.

6. <u>Dip the lime peels into the melted white chocolate,</u> and arrange them on the cookie sheet with the grapefruit peels. Refrigerate until the chocolate hardens.

Cheesecake

(Gâteau au Fromage)

Although cheesecake should be made the day before serving so it has time to rest and set, it should not be served ice cold from the refrigerator. If it is refrigerated, it should be brought back to room temperature for serving because it is moister and more flavorful this way. If baked in a cake pan with a removable bottom, as done here, the cake can remain on the pan base and be placed as such on the serving platter. This prevents damage to the platter when the cake is cut.

YIELD: 10 to 12 servings

CHEESECAKE DOUGH
About 12 graham crackers (7 ounces/198 grams)

¾ stick (3 ounces/85 grams) unsalted butter

1 teaspoon ground cinnamon

1 tablespoon fresh lemon juice

1 teaspoon grated lemon rind

FILLING
1¾ pounds (795 grams) cream cheese, at room temperature

1 cup (225 grams) sugar

1 cup (237 milliliters) sour cream

2 tablespoons fresh lemon juice

1 tablespoon grated lemon rind

2 teaspoons pure vanilla extract

4 large eggs

1. Preheat the oven to 350 degrees (177°C).

TO MAKE THE DOUGH: Break the graham crackers and place them in a food processor with the butter, cinnamon, lemon juice, and grated lemon rind. Process for a few seconds, until the dough comes together. Remove from the food processor and line the removable bottom of a 9-inch (23-centimeter) cake pan that is 3 inches (7.6 centimeters) deep.

2. Reserve approximately half the dough for the sides of the pan. Press a piece of plastic wrap on top of the remaining dough on the pan base and <u>roll to spread it</u>. It should be very thin, approximately ⅛ inch (3 millimeters) thick.

3. <u>Trim the dough around the edge of the pan's removable bottom with your fingers</u>. Reassemble the pan and press the remainder of the dough up around the inside of the pan so it comes up about 1 to 2 inches (2.5 to 5 centimeters). This border of dough on the sides doesn't have to be exactly the same height all around; it can vary a little to lend an interesting design to the side of the cake.

4. FOR THE FILLING: In a food processer, put the cream cheese, sugar, sour cream, lemon juice, lemon rind, vanilla and the eggs, and process until smooth. <u>Pour into the pan and place on a cookie sheet.</u>

5. Bake for 1 hour. Turn the oven off and allow the cake to continue resting in the remaining heat in the oven for 1 hour longer. <u>The cake should be lightly browned on top</u>. <u>Let cool for a couple of hours before unmolding.</u>

Crème Brulée with Verbena

Crème Brulée is a rich custard and, for this reason, I cook it in small molds, approximately ½ cup (118 milliliters) each. Sometimes the dessert is made even richer by using only heavy cream, but I find it rich enough with milk and cream in equal proportions.

It is important that the crème brulée be baked slowly in a water bath in the oven. Use tepid water from the tap. The water should not come to a boil as the custard cooks. If the crème brulée is cooked too fast, the albumen will develop and start expanding and little holes will form all around the sides of the custard making it look like a sponge when it should be very smooth and silky in texture.

YIELD: 8 servings

CREME MIXTURE
1 cup (237 milliliters) milk
½ cup (36 grams) loose verbena leaves or 2 verbena tea bags
2 teaspoons grated lemon rind
4 large egg yolks and 1 whole large egg
3 tablespoons sugar
1 cup (237 milliliters) heavy cream

TOPPING
5 tablespoons light brown sugar (about 2 teaspoons per serving)

1. Preheat the oven to 350 degrees (177°C).

FOR THE CREME: Put the milk, verbena leaves or 2 teabags, and lemon rind in a saucepan, and bring to a boil. As soon as it boils, cover, remove from the heat, and let steep for 5 minutes.

2. Beat the 4 egg yolks and 1 whole egg with the granulated sugar and add the cream. <u>Combine the steeped verbena mixture with the egg yolk mixture, stirring well to mix thoroughly.</u>

3. <u>Strain the mixture through a fine strainer.</u>

4. Preheat the oven to 350 degrees (177°C). Arrange 8 small molds (the ones used here have a capacity of about ½ cup/118 milliliters) in a roasting pan and <u>fill with the crème mixture.</u> Add enough tepid tap water to the pan to come three-fourths of the way up the outsides of the molds. Bake the molds for approximately 25 to 30 minutes, until set. The water around the molds should not boil. Should the water begin to boil, add a few ice cubes.

5. Remove from the oven and let cool. When cool, cover and refrigerate.

FOR THE TOPPING: At serving time or not more than 1 to 1½ hours beforehand, <u>spread 2 teaspoons of light brown sugar over the top of each crème.</u>

6. Place the molds under the broiler and broil (watching them closely) until the sugar bubbles and turns uniformly brown, approximately 3 minutes or, alternatively, use a blowtorch. Let cool for at least 10 minutes, until the sugar surface hardens, and serve. To eat, crack the sugar shell with the back of a spoon and eat with a nice pound cake as an accompaniment.

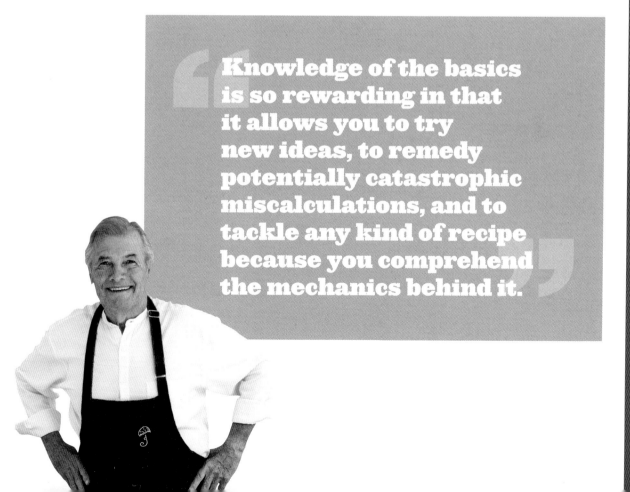

"Knowledge of the basics is so rewarding in that it allows you to try new ideas, to remedy potentially catastrophic miscalculations, and to tackle any kind of recipe because you comprehend the mechanics behind it."

PRESENT

ATION

Butter Flowers

(Décoration en Beurre)

The butter flower brings elegance to your table. Fill a container with cold water and place the "roses" in it. Keep the roses in water in the refrigerator before using. Butter, uncovered, will pick up tastes from for the fridge.

1. BUTTER ROSES: The temperature and quality of the butter are important here. If the butter is too soft, the knife will make it mushy and if it is too cold, it will flake on top and you will not be able to create the flowers. Unsalted, high-quality butter tends to have less water, is more pliable, and is the best. Using the point plus about 1 inch (2.5 centimeters) of the blade of a small paring knife held vertically, <u>scrape across the butter from one end of the stick to the other.</u>

2. <u>Scrape the top of the butter several times from one end to the other to collect a long strip of butter</u> on top of the blade. The repeated scraping will create a thin strip of butter striated on the top side.

3. <u>Curl the strip of butter around the tip of the blade,</u> making sure that the surface with the jagged look is inside the "flower." Form the strip into one large corolla or cup.

4. <u>Place the butter corolla stem-side down on a plate</u>.

5. Make another long strip of butter and, this time, <u>curl it more tightly on the point of a knife</u>. (You are making the center of a flower.)

6. <u>Slide the center of the flower off the tip of the knife blade and</u>

7. <u>place it in the center of the corolla</u>.

8. <u>Drop the butter roses into ice cold water</u> and refrigerate. Immersed in water, the flowers won't pick up tastes in the refrigerator. In addition, they will get very hard, making them easier to handle.

9. For another effect, lift one of the ice-cold flowers from the water, impale it with the point of a knife through the base, and, holding it upside down, <u>lower it so the very outer edges of the petals touch the paprika spread in a dish.</u>

10. <u>Two flowers, one with the paprika, one without.</u> The flowers, with and without paprika, are presented on a plate or arranged on individual dinner plates.

Potato Rose

(Rose en Pomme de Terre)

Often restaurants garnish with flowers sculpted from potatoes, carrots or white turnips. To avoid discoloration, the potatoes, after being carved, should be blanched in boiling water for 1 minute and cooled off under cold water. Then they can be soaked in a mixture of red food coloring and water to obtain a nice pink color. Carve a whole "bouquet" of these flowers and stand each one on a toothpick in a carved orange or grapefruit basket. Surround with curly parsley.

1. Using a small sharp knife, cut a pointed shape from a peeled potato. Trim the shape to make it look like a child's toy top.

2. Make slits all around the base to simulate petals.

3. Using the tip of the knife, <u>trim the edge all around above the petals</u>.

4. <u>Pull out the strip of potato, exposing the bottom layer of petals</u>.

5. Keep cutting layers of slits, <u>alternating the petals to get the right effect</u>.

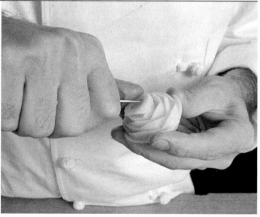

6. <u>Cut the top of the rose</u>, which will be too pointed, and blanch.

Tomato Receptacles

(Récipient en Tomate)

1. Cut a tomato in eighths, <u>going approximately two-thirds to three-fourths of the way through</u> from the top to the bottom.

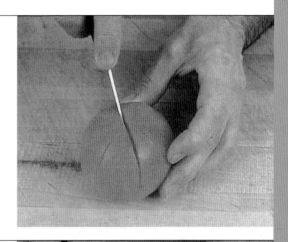

2. <u>Remove each alternating section of the tomato.</u> Then, using a spoon, remove the inside pulp of the tomato and press the juice out to create a receptacle. The inside pulp can now be sorted out, setting aside the juice, seeds, and skin for use later in a stock.

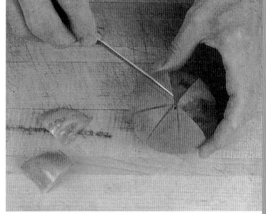

3. To give a more elegant effect to the receptacle, one by one lay each of the cut points flat on the table and, using a knife held flat, <u>separate the skin from some of the flesh.</u>

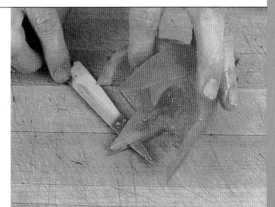

4. The tomato is a hollow shell, ready to be filled, <u>and each of the four points has been split into skin and flesh.</u>

Tomato Roses and Other Vegetable Flowers

(Roses en Tomate et Autres Fleurs en Légumes)

You do not have to be a professional to excel in decoration. The spectrum of colors that you can choose from is large: truffles, black or green olives, tomatoes, scallions, leeks, carrots and so on. Only edibles should be used and they should be "tasteless." Raw orange or lemon peel on top of a mousse or a poached fish might impart some bitterness to the dish.

1. To make a tomato rose, <u>start by cutting a "base" from a tomato.</u> Do not sever it from the tomato.

2. Continue cutting a narrow strip about ¾ inch (19 millimeters) wide, tapering it into a point. <u>Use your knife in a jigsaw, up and down motion to give a natural edge to the petals of the flower.</u> The strip should not be too thick.

3. <u>Cut another straight strip</u> as long as the first one.

4. <u>Curl the first strip of skin onto its base</u> with the flesh side on the inside of the flower.

5. <u>Roll the second strip into a tight scroll and</u>

6. <u>place it in the middle to make the heart of the rose.</u>

7. To make stems and leaves, blanch the green part of a leek or scallion by plunging it into boiling water for about 30 seconds and cooling it immediately under cold water. The boiling water makes it greener and pliable, and the cold water stops the cooking and keeps it green. Dry and lay the green flat and, on the table, cut long strips following the grain of the leek. <u>To make leaves, cut a wider strip with a pointed end.</u>

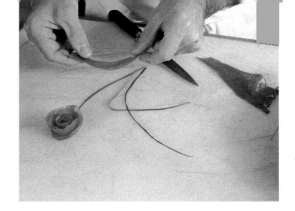

8. <u>Cut lozenges of green and arrange around the stems to make small leaves.</u> Use pieces of black from olives, the red of a tomato, and

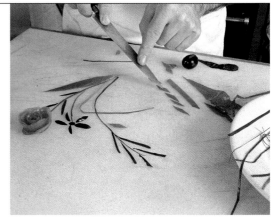

9. <u>the yellow of a hard-cooked egg.</u> Let your imagination help your fingers.

10. <u>Create a nice bouquet</u> to decorate a salad, a cold fish, a ham, or a chicken.

Mushroom Fish

(Champignon Sculpté en Poissons)

You can sculpt one fish on top of a mushroom or, as below, three.

1. Start with a large mushroom that's very firm and very white. Cut the top of the cap off the mushroom. The newly formed surface will become the background for the fish. Starting at the center of the mushroom, <u>make 3 curved cuts at spaced intervals</u>. These will be one side of the fish.

2. Then, starting at the edge of the mushroom, <u>make 3 corresponding cuts to form 3 ovals</u>. Each oval represents the body of a fish, minus the tail.

3. Pretending that the fish are interwoven, "draw" a <u>forked tail at the end of each body</u>.

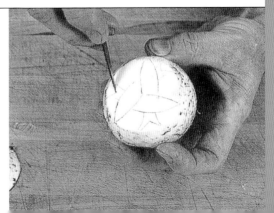

4. To set the fish in relief—to make them raised—you have to remove a thin layer (⅛-inch/3 millimeters or less deep) of mushroom all around them. <u>Slide your knife into the mushroom, in between each cut, and gently lift out the pieces of mushroom.</u> Work all around the mushroom until the fish are in relief.

5. If you want to make a more elaborate carving, cut a small triangle between each fish and remove the piece of mushroom. Within that triangle, cut another triangle and remove the piece of mushroom. Then, within the second triangle, make a third one and so forth, making a sort of triangular steps which form designs in all the free spaces around the fish. With the point of a knife make the eyes, the gills, and the scales, <u>then trim the mushroom around.</u> Slice the decorated part off the cap, coat with lemon juice to keep it white or poach in a mixture of lemon juice and water for a few seconds, and use to garnish the top of a fish dish or a cold salad.

> **Any good cook knows that good cooking and good health are inseparable.**

Fluted Mushrooms

(Champignons Tournés)

To "turn" or flute a mushroom means, in cooking vocabulary, to cut strips from the mushroom cap in an elegant, spiral pattern. It is a difficult technique to master, and may cost you a few hours of frustration before you get any results. You need a small, sharply pointed paring knife. Use firm, white, fresh mushroom caps.

1. Hold the blade of the knife loosely in your fingers on a bias, cutting edge out. <u>Place the side of your thumb behind the blade, on top of the mushroom.</u>

2. <u>Starting at the center of the cap and using your thumb as a pivot, push the blade forward and down in a smooth motion by twisting your wrist.</u> The slanted cutting edge should carve a strip out of the mushroom cap. The rotation should be smooth and regular.

3. If the center is not perfectly formed, <u>make a star by pushing with the point of the knife into the center of the cap.</u> Separate the carved cap from the stem with the knife.

4. Making a relief from a mushroom cap is much easier than fluting. Slice off the crown of the mushroom. "Draw," in this case a little fish, with the point of your knife. Cut about ¼ inch (6 millimeters) deep into the flesh.

5. Cut the flesh around the outline so that the little fish comes out in relief. Mark the head, eyes, and scales with the point of the knife.

6. Trim the cap around the fish and

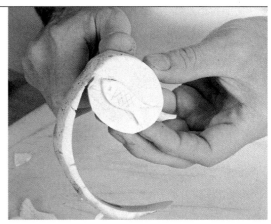

7. slice underneath to make a nice "coin" shape with the relief on top.

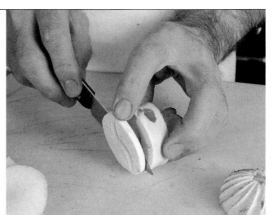

8. Different carved shapes. To stay white, the fluted and carved mushrooms should be poached in water with a few drops of lemon juice, salt, and butter. One minute is sufficient to cook them. Mushrooms cooked in this manner are usually used to decorate fish dishes and cold dishes, such as salads.

Vegetable Flowers

(Fleurs en Légumes)

To dress up a buffet, there is nothing as colorful and festive as a bunch of flowers made of vegetables. They are fun to make and rewarding—follow the instructions below, but extend the idea and create on your own. Use your imagination since the possibilities of shape and color are practically endless.

1. Peel a carrot. With this carrot, we will first make several flowers similar to a daisy. With the point of a knife, cut petals from the tip of the carrot. Cut into the carrot on an angle but don't cut through as you want the petals attached. Rotate the carrot as you carve so the tip of the carrot comes to a point as you cut. Be sure not to separate each petal.

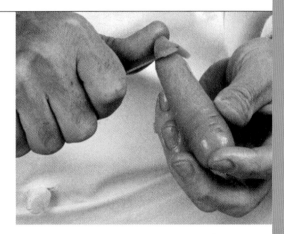

2. Rock the "flower" back and forth to gently separate it from the carrot in one piece.

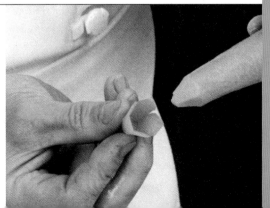

3. Place the flowers as they are cut in a bowl of ice water to keep them crisp and bright until ready to use. <u>Then finish with a little piece of black olive in the center of one flower</u>, a caper in the center of another one, and a piece of pimiento in the center of a third.

4. Proceed the same way with radishes. Choose oval radishes, if possible, <u>and start cutting the petals.</u>

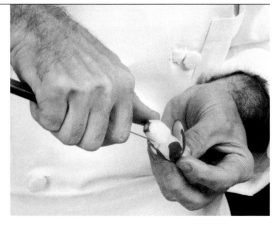

5. <u>Place half of a small olive upside down in the center of the radish</u>. (A piece of red tomato or pimiento or green pepper can replace the olive for a different flower.)

6. <u>Slice a piece of peeled carrot very thinly, without separating the slices.</u> Turn the carrot so that all the slices are stacked one on top of the other. Cut into thin strips, which are still held by the core.

7. <u>The carrot is now cut into thin strips held together at one end.</u> Place in ice water for a few hours or overnight—the strips of carrot will curl and the "flower" will open up. Proceed as shown in the picture.

8. Peel a white onion but leave the root on. <u>Start cutting it into slices held together by the root end.</u>

9. <u>Slice the onion across so all the slices are cut into strips held together by the root.</u> Place in ice water.

10. <u>On the right you have an onion that's completely cut and ready for immersion in ice water. On the left is an onion which has been soaked in ice water for a few hours.</u>

11. Here is a variety of flowers made with radishes. <u>The one being worked on is made the same way as the carrot and the onion in steps 6 to 9.</u>

12. Taking a green or black olive with the pit in it, insert your knife through the skin and <u>cut around the pit to loosen</u>. Remove the pit so you have a hollow receptacle.

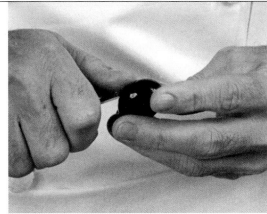

13. Cut the root of a scallion. Trim away the green. <u>Insert your knife three quarters of the way down through the stem of the scallion and split it open.</u> Turn it around. Keep pushing your knife through and pulling it up to split the scallion into fine strips.

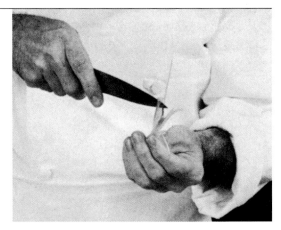

14. <u>Scallions after having been crisped in ice water for a few hours.</u>

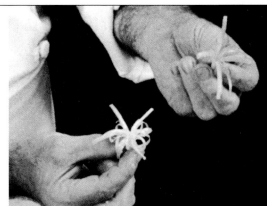

15. <u>Place the crisped scallion into the cavity of an olive</u> to make another flower.

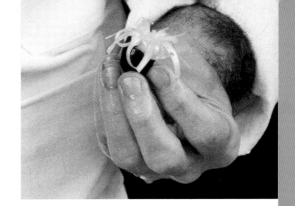

16. Slice a yellow turnip into very thin strips; <u>roll a slice and fold it in half.</u>

17. Hold the folded slice of turnip with a toothpick and <u>insert a piece of feathered red pimiento, carrot, or radish in the two holes.</u> This forms another flower.

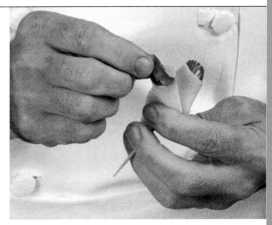

18. Using a vegetable peeler, make thin carrot slices. <u>Stack them together and shred both ends.</u>

19. Overlap several slices to form a large, shaggy, open flower. <u>Stick half a radish, a piece of cherry tomato, or a piece of olive in the center.</u>

20. To form stems for your flowers, use thin pieces of wood such as long matches or pieces of wire cut from coat hangers. <u>Use the green of scallions to shield and dress the wires. Insert the wire in the hollow of the scallion.</u>

21. Once the wire is dressed, stick a cut radish on top or another flower. <u>The green of the scallion should be longer than the metal stem so it can be turned under and around the bottom of the flower to form the chalice.</u> Remember that these are only a few examples of the flowers that can be made with vegetables. Use your imagination to create new flowers—try working with lemon peel, pimiento, leeks, asparagus, etc. It is important that the flowers be kept in ice water for a few hours so they crisp into the right shape.

Carrot Butterflies

(Papillon en Carotte)

1. Cover 1 large peeled carrot with water. Bring to a boil and boil for about 10 minutes. Cool off under cold water. The carrot should be tender enough to be pierced with a knife but still firm and slightly undercooked. Cut a large chunk of carrot about 2 to 2½ inches (5 to 6 centimeters) long and carve, cutting to create a design resembling the wing of a butterfly. To create the antennae of the "butterfly," slice a very thin strip at the large rounded end of the carrot chunk, but do not cut through completely.

2. Next, using a vegetable peeler or a sharp knife, cut a very thin crosswise strip of carrot, again being careful not to cut completely through so one end is still attached to the carrot. This slice represents one wing, and the place where it is attached is the body of the "butterfly." Then cut another strip, but this time cut through the carrot to create the second wing. You can use the vegetable peeler just to start the slice and continue cutting with a knife.

3. Place the "butterfly" flat on the table and cut through the middle a bit farther, until the wings just hold together at the body.

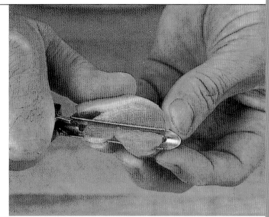

4. The "butterfly" is completely carved.

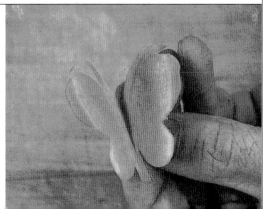

Olive Rabbits

(Lapins en Olive)

An amusing way to transform olives into a decoration is to make little rabbits out of them. Choose extra large black or green olives with the pits in.

1. Cut a slice lengthwise from one side of the olive. Carve a small triangle from the slice.

2. Place the olive cut-side down. With a small knife, make an incision halfway down, close to the pointed side of the olive.

3. Twist the blade to open the cut. Insert the slice so that the pointed ears stand in the air.

4. Three little rabbits.

Apple Swans

(Cygnes en Pommes)

Apple swans are easy to make and lovely for decorating a buffet or a cold aspic dish. They make a simple centerpiece when several are arranged in the center of a table.

1. Take a large apple (Greening, Red Delicious, etc.) and cut about a ½-inch (13-millimeter) slice off one side of the apple.

2. Place the slice flat side down and, using a small pointed knife, "draw" a head and neck in one piece the full length of the apple slice. Carve it out and set it aside.

3. <u>The head piece can be done in a multitude of ways, with the head looking down or up</u>. Use your imagination and try to make the most out of the shape and thickness of the apple slice.

4. With the point of a knife, "drill" a small hole on one side of the apple to hold the neck in place. <u>Insert the neck and adjust until the neck fits snugly</u>. Then set the neck aside, so it does not get in the way while you work on the wings and tail.

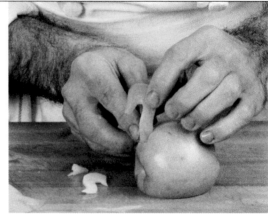

5. On one side of the apple cut wedges <u>by first holding the knife vertically and slicing down</u> and then holding it horizontally and slicing across.

6. You should remove approximately 5 wedges for each wing, keeping them as thin as possible (as the wedges get larger they become more difficult to cut out). <u>Repeat the same procedure on the other side of the apple to make the other wing.</u>

7. After the two sides have been carved for the wings, <u>cut the back of the "swan" to make the tail</u>. Four wedges are enough for the tail.

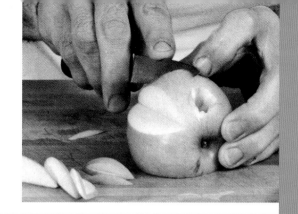

8. Now that all the cutting is done, the wedges are put back together to simulate the tail and the wings. <u>Stagger the wedges at spaced intervals so they fan out</u>. You will notice that the wedges stick to one another nicely.

9. <u>Repeat the process with both wings and place the head on the swan</u>. Sprinkle the whole apple with lemon juice to keep it from discoloring.

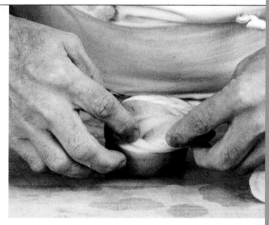

10. <u>The "swans" are delicate and make an elegant decoration</u>. Alternate green, yellow, and red apples.

Orange Baskets

(Paniers d'Oranges)

Orange baskets make a delightful garnish for compatible cold dishes, or for classic dishes such as duck à l'orange. Baskets can be made with whole large navel oranges, or with halves. For large baskets, it is essential to have a stripper tool to strip the peel off the orange.

WHOLE ORANGE BASKET

1. Cut a thin slice off the blossom end to make a flat sitting surface. Using a stripper, start at the top and cut strips all around the orange, almost down to the flat surface. The strips should fly free but remain attached to the orange.

2. Cut away wedges on both sides so you are left with a "handle" in the middle of the basket.

3. Carefully cut away the flesh from the handle.

4. Fold the strips over and onto themselves to make loops all around the orange. Fill the area underneath the handle with watercress or parsley to simulate a basket.

HALF ORANGE BASKET

1. Cut a thin slice off both ends of the orange to make a flat sitting surface. Using a round object as a guide, outline half-moons with a knife all around the orange. Cut with a knife, following the outline. Be sure to penetrate deep enough to the center of the orange. Pull apart and you will have two different orange baskets.

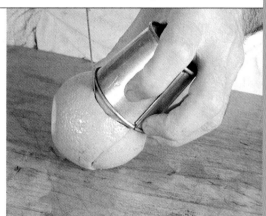

2. Cut a strip of skin just below, following the outline of the curve. Empty by scraping the inside of the basket with a spoon.

3. Fill up with orange sections or parsley.

Orange Rind Grated

(Pelures d'Oranged Râpé)

1. When a recipe calls for grated orange or lemon rind, be sure to <u>grate only the bright orange or yellow part of the skin</u>. The white part underneath is bitter and should not be used. Remove the grated rind from the grater by banging the grater on the table, or use a dry brush to pry out the rind.

Candied Orange Rind

(Pelures d'Oranges Confites)

The thin outer layer of the orange skin contains most of the fruit's essential oil and flavor and is very potent in cold Grand Marnier soufflés, orange butter creams, orange génoise, and the like.

1. <u>Use a vegetable peeler to remove only the orange part of the rind</u>. The white skin between the peel and the flesh is bitter.

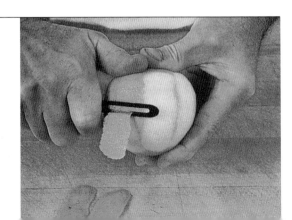

2. Blanch in boiling water for a minute. Drain, place back in the pan with water, and bring to a boil again. Drain, rinse the rind under cold water, and and place the peels back in the pan with 1 cup (237 milliliters) water and ⅓ cup (75 grams) sugar. Bring to a boil and cook for approximately 20 minutes at a gentle boil, <u>until the peels are translucent and the syrup is thick</u>.

3. Lift the peels out with a fork and place them on a tray covered with about ½ cup (110 grams) sugar. Turn the peels in the sugar, <u>pressing and patting them until they are saturated with sugar on both sides</u>. Set aside for 30 to 40 minutes. The crystallized orange peels can be placed in a jar and kept in the refrigerator almost indefinitely.

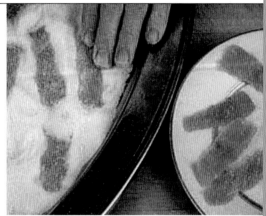

Orange Peel Julienne

(Julienne de Peau d'Oranges)

Any vegetable, meat or fruit cut into thin, strawlike strips is called a julienne. The julienne of lemon or orange peel decorates dishes such as duck à l'orange and galantine. The julienne can also be cooked in sugar and the candied strips used in cakes, cold soufflés, or as a garnish for fruit desserts.

1. Remove orange rind with a vegetable peeler as explained in the last technique. <u>Stack a few peels together; fold the stack in half and cut into very thin strips</u>. Whether used as a garnish or candied, the julienne should be blanched at least twice to remove the bitterness. Plunge the julienne in boiling water. Return to a boil and let cook for 1 to 2 minutes. Pour into a strainer and rinse under cold water. Repeat this process once more. Keep in cold water until ready to use.

Lemon

(Citron)

There are innumerable ways of cutting a lemon, from the simple lemon wedge or slice to one of the more sophisticated ways shown below. Lemon is served with fish, shellfish, oysters, meat (veal or chicken), vegetables (such as asparagus, string beans), dessert (fruit salad), to name a few.

LEMON PIG

1. Choose a lemon with a nice pointed "nose." With the point of a knife, make one hole on each side of the nose and <u>fill each with a black peppercorn</u> or a piece of parsley or olive.

2. Cut a little wedge in the middle of the nose, without separating the piece from the lemon, to imitate the tongue. <u>Cut "ears" on each side of the lemon.</u> Curl up a little piece of parsley to imitate the tail and place toothpicks underneath for the legs.

OTHER DECORATIONS

1. Cut a thin slice off both ends of the lemon to make a flat sitting surface. Cut the lemon into halves. <u>Cut two strips of peel of equal size from the sharp edge of the half lemon.</u>

2. <u>Fold each strip around and make a knot to secure.</u> Be careful not to break the strips.

3. Alternatively, cut one long strip of peel from the edge of the half lemon <u>and make a knot with a loop</u>. Place a piece of parsley in the loop.

4. For another treatment, cut both ends of the lemon. With a sharp-pointed paring knife <u>cut "lion teeth" all around the lemon</u>. Cut deep enough to go to the core of the lemon.

5. For a slightly different look, repeat the same technique as described in step 4, <u>but cut the teeth on a bias.</u>

6. <u>Decorate the different lemons with curly parsley.</u>

LEMON SLICES FOR FISH

1. Trim the lemon, removing the yellow and most of the white skin underneath. <u>Slice into ¼-inch (6-millimeter) slices, removing the seeds as you go along.</u>

2. <u>Fold each slice and dip into chopped parsley.</u> By folding the slice, only the center gets covered with parsley. You can cover whole slices, half slices, and so on to vary your decoration.

Carving Watermelon

(Décoration d'une Pastéque)

A simple dessert, such as fruit salad, can become glorious when served in a carved watermelon. Choose a watermelon as dark green as possible and without too many variations of color so that the markings stand out.

METHOD 1

1. Fold a piece of wax paper in half.

2. Fold it in half again and cut with scissors to make a pattern for the handle of the basket.

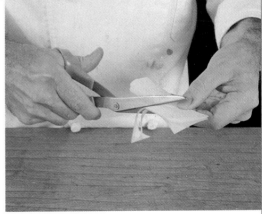

3. Pattern for the handle of the basket.

4. <u>Place the pattern on top of the watermelon and outline it with the point of a knife</u>. Sketch the shape of a lid on both sides of the handle with the knife.

5. <u>Cut a decorative strip under the outline of each lid</u>.

6. <u>Remove the strip to expose the flesh of the melon</u>.

7. <u>Carve little petals with the point of a sharp paring knife</u>.

8. <u>Cut out stems for flowers and leaves</u> on the top and all around the melon.

9. Carve a butterfly, or any other object you fancy, on top of the lid. <u>Following the outline of the lid, cut through the top of the melon with the paring knife.</u>

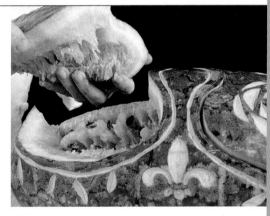

10. <u>Remove both lids</u> and clean the insides with a spoon and a small knife.

11. <u>Cut the flesh away from the skin all around.</u>

12. With a spoon, <u>scoop the flesh out and pour into a bowl.</u>

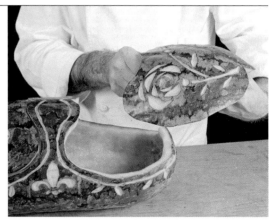

13. <u>Replace the carved lids on top of the melon.</u>

14. <u>Watermelon ready to be filled with fruit salad.</u>

METHOD 2

1. Trim the melon on both ends. <u>Trace waves around the melon using a glass or a small bowl as a guide.</u>

2. <u>Following the contour, separate the melon into halves</u>. Carve a freehand decoration around the melon. You can use small objects (round, square, triangular) as guides to outline a geometric design. Once the pattern is outlined, cut out strips of skin to delineate the design.

3. <u>Scoop out the inside flesh</u>. You may use some of it in the fruit salad.

4. <u>Carved and uncarved halves of melon</u>. Once the melon is carved, cover well with plastic wrap to keep the sculpture relief fresh and vivid looking. It will keep at least one week in the refrigerator. When you are ready to use your masterpiece, empty the melon of any liquid and fill up with fruit salad, using different colored fruits to give an artistic effect. It may also be used to serve a cold punch or ice cream.

Cornucopia Molds
(Cornets)

Cornets are pastries, ham or salmon slices, or other foods shaped in the form of a horn. A tinned cornucopia mold is used to shape the food. The cornets can be stuffed with a variety of fillings. The stuffed cornets can be served on a vegetable salad, the recipe for which appears below.

HAM CORNETS (CORNETS DE JAMBON)

1. Roll a square slice of ham so that one end is pointed. Roll as you would a paper cornet.

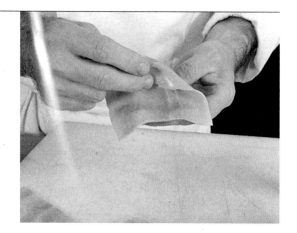

2. Slip into a cornucopia mold. Prepare your favorite stuffing or the one that follows. For 4 horns: 1½ tablespoons (21 grams) butter; ¾ cup (83 grams) chopped, cooked spinach; 1 hard-cooked egg, coarsely chopped; ⅓ cup (75 grams) chopped ham; salt, freshly ground black pepper, and nutmeg. Melt the butter in a skillet until dark and foaming. Add the spinach and cook, stirring for 1 minute. Remove from heat and add remaining ingredients. Let cool.

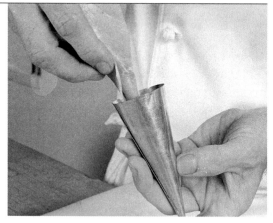

3. When cool, stuff the mixture into the ham cornet.

4. <u>Trim the ham at the level of the stuffing</u>.

5. Remove from the mold; the cornet should slide out easily. <u>Trim the ham for a neat, pointed cornucopia</u>.

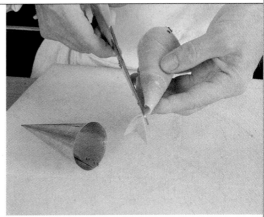

SALMON CORNETS (CORNETS DE SAUMON)

1. Using slices of smoked salmon or gravlax <u>twist the slices and fit them into the mold</u>.

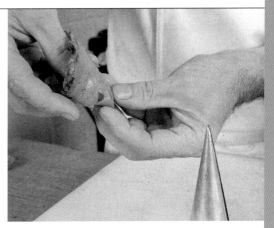

2. <u>You may have to overlap slices to have the mold well lined</u>. Stuff with a mixture of finely chopped hard-cooked eggs mixed with softened butter or mayonnaise and seasoned with salt and pepper.

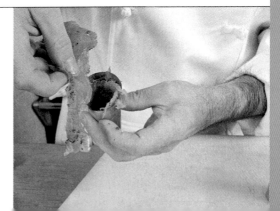

VEGETABLE SALAD (MACÉDOINE DE LÉGUMES)

YIELD: 4 to 6 servings

½ **cup (62 grams) cooked peas**
½ **cup (113 grams) diced cooked carrots (¼-inch/6-millimeter cubes)**
2 **cups (500 grams) diced cooked potatoes (½-inch/13-millimeter cubes)**
3 **tablespoons finely chopped onion**
½ **cup (118 milliliters) mayonnaise (preferably freshly made)**
½ **tablespoon wine vinegar**
¼ **teaspoon salt**
¼ **teaspoon freshly ground black pepper to taste**

Mix together all the ingredients and arrange on a platter with the ham or salmon cornets on top and a tomato rose in the middle.

DESSERT CORNETS (CORNETS À LA CRÈME)

1. Preheat the oven to 400 degrees (204°C). Dessert cornets are shaped on the outside of the mold. Cut strips of puff paste ⅛ inch (3 millimeters) thick by about 1 inch (2.5 centimeters) wide and 18 inches (45.7 meters) long. Moisten the strips with cold water on one side.

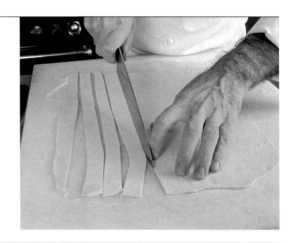

2. Squeeze the dough at the tip of the mold to secure it.

3. <u>Wrap the strip around the mold</u>, overlapping slightly, with the wet side of the dough touching the mold.

4. Trim the extra dough on the edge of the base of the mold. Holding the horn with your fingers inside, <u>brush beaten egg over the dough</u>.

5. <u>Place standing up on a cookie sheet and bake in the oven for 15 to 18 minutes.</u> Let cool slightly before unmolding. Run a knife between the dough and the mold to loosen the pastry and make it easier to slide off.

6. Fill with sweetened whipped cream.

Round, Square, and Heart-Shaped Croutons

(Croûtons Ronds, Carrés, et en Coeur)

When bread is cut into a variety of shapes and fried, it is called a crouton. Round croutons are used as a base for filet, steak, poached eggs, and other dishes. Small croutons cubes are used as a garnish for hot and cold soups and in stuffings and meat loaf. They may be fried or toasted in the oven. Heart-shaped croutons are served as a decorative garnish for coq au vin, purée of spinach, and beef or veal stews. Trimmings are used to make bread crumbs.

1. Cut slices approximately ¾ inch (19 millimeters) thick.

2. For round croutons, use a glass or round crouton cutter to cut out circles. Fry in a skillet in a mixture of butter and oil.

3. For square croutons, stack 2 or 3 slices of bread together and trim the edges. <u>Cut into strips</u>.

4. <u>Cut the strips across to make cubes</u>. Fry in butter and oil or sprinkle with olive and peanut oil and brown in a 400 degree (204°C) oven for about 10 minutes.

5. For heart-shaped croutons, <u>cut slices of bread into halves diagonally</u>.

6. <u>Trim each half</u> to obtain a more pointed triangle.

7. Trim each piece into the shape of a heart.

8. Fry in a mixture of butter and oil. Dip the tip of each crouton in the sauce of the dish it is to be served with and then into a small bowl of chopped parsley. The parsley, which adheres to the bread because of the wet tip, forms a decorative point.

Melba Toast

(Toasts Melba)

Escoffier created this super-thin toast for the cantatrice Melba. Though melba toast can be bought ready-made, it is easy to make and quite good.

1. Toast regular slices of bread in the toaster. Trim on four sides.

2. Keeping the slice flat, and using a thin knife, <u>cut through the soft middle to split the slice into halves</u>. It is relatively easy because both sides are crusty and will separate easily.

3. Serve it as is or place the slice, <u>soft side up</u>, under the broiler until dry and brown.

4. <u>Slice the thin toast into halves.</u>

Canapés

(Canapés)

Canapés are small appetizers made from plain and toasted bread, spread or covered with meat, cheese, caviar, anchovies, and the like. They can be shaped and varied almost indefinitely, according to your own taste.

1. <u>Make an incision straight down</u>, close to the crust, on one side of a loaf of bread. This becomes a "guard" to protect your hands from the knife.

2. <u>Cut wide slices horizontally about ⅓ inch (9 millimeters) thick.</u>

3. You can use plain white bread as it is or you can toast it. Egg salad, tomato and the like, being moist, are better off on toast than on fresh bread which has a tendency to become soggy. <u>Spread a thin layer of butter on the slices.</u>

4. <u>Cover the slices with ham</u>, salami, prosciutto, and so on.

5. To make lozenges, <u>trim the slice all around</u> and cut in half lengthwise.

6. Position the two strips side by side <u>but stagger them slightly</u>.

7. <u>Cut into lozenges</u>.

8. Cover another slice of buttered bread with smoked salmon, trim all around and <u>cut into neat triangles</u>.

9. Fill a paper cornet with soft butter. Cut a straight opening and pipe out a <u>"G clef" on each of the salmon canapés</u>. Decorate the prosciutto canapés with another butter design.

10. Cover square pieces of toasted and buttered bread with caviar. Cut the tip of the cornet on both sides to make open pointed lips. <u>Pipe out small leaves or petals, three per canapé.</u>

11. With the point of a knife, <u>deposit a little dash of red paprika</u> in the middle of the butter to simulate the pistil of the flower.

12. Arrange your canapés attractively on a platter and decorate with small pieces of curly parsley.

Folding Napkins

(Pliage des Serviettes)

There are an infinite number of ways to fold napkins, whether they are used as a liner for food, or placed next to the dinner plate for a guest. The napkins should be large, square, of good quality linen, ironed, and preferably lightly starched. When the napkins are used as liners in the kitchen or dining room they can be folded very fancifully. Next to my plate, I like a napkin which has not been "handled" too much. It is fine simply folded in half or quarters.

1. Using a napkin already folded into a square, fold the opened corner three-quarters of the way up toward the pointed side.

2. Grab the opposite corners with both hands and fold underneath. The napkin can be used just the way it is.

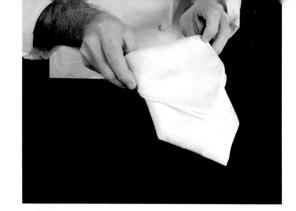

3. Or the opened corners can be folded back onto themselves.

Flower, Artichoke, and Gondola Napkins

(Serviettes en Tulipe, Artichaut, et Gondole)

FLOWER

1. This is the most commonly used napkin fold in food presentation. Start with a napkin that is perfectly square. Bring both corners of the same side toward the center.

2. <u>Then bring the two opposite corners to the center.</u>

3. Holding the four corners in place, <u>turn the napkin on the other side</u>. Repeat the above operation by bringing the four corners toward the center.

4. <u>Turn the napkin on the other side and "unfold" the four centered corners onto themselves.</u>

5. <u>Folded napkin ready to use.</u> It is usually filled with fried foods such as potatoes or fish. Be sure to hold one hand underneath when transferring the napkin to a platter, or it will unfold.

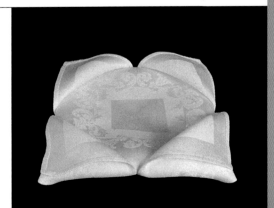

6. To make an eight-petaled flower, fold another napkin in the same manner, but give it one more turn and place it on top of the first one.

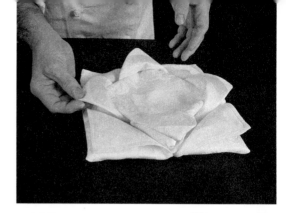

ARTICHOKE

1. To make a napkin into an artichoke, place a square piece of foil in the center of the opened square napkin. Bring the four corners toward the center.

2. Bring the four new corners toward the center.

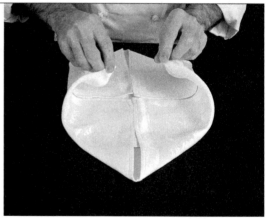

3. Repeat once more bringing the 4 corners together (a total of three times).

PRESENTATION

4. Turn the napkin on the other side and fold the four corners toward the center.

5. Holding the four corners on the center, <u>turn the napkin over a tall glass</u> and press the napkin on the glass to round it slightly.

6. <u>Pull the pointed pieces out</u>, as if you were pulling off leaves of an artichoke.

7. Keep pulling the leaves until the last layer, <u>where the aluminum foil is, is exposed</u>.

8. <u>Turn the artichoke down on the middle of a folded flower napkin</u>. Fill with pommes soufflés or gaufrettes.

GONDOLA

1. To make a gondola, place a square piece of aluminum foil in the center of a square napkin (see step 1, artichoke). Fold in half to obtain a long rectangle. <u>Fold one side into the center of the rectangle,</u>

2. <u>then the other side to form a triangular "hat."</u>

3. Fold in the same manner, <u>making the triangle thinner.</u>

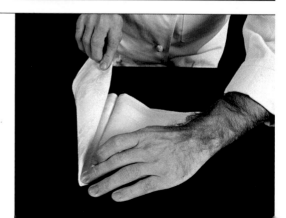

4. <u>Fold a third time</u>, making a long, narrow, and sharply pointed triangle.

5. <u>Then bring both sides together at the last fold.</u>

6. Keeping the napkin in place with one hand, <u>fold the point inward so it resembles the curved tip of a gondola.</u> Fold a second napkin in the same manner.

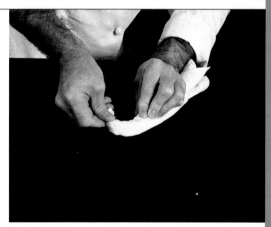

7. Open each gondola and arrange on a platter so that the curved side is on the outside of the platter. <u>Cover the center with a square napkin</u>. Use to present *coulibiac* of salmon, hot pâté in crust, cold fish, or even asparagus or artichokes.